Contemporary Perspectives on Adult Development and Aging

Contemporary Perspectives on Adult Development and Aging

Alicia Skinner Cook
Colorado State University

Macmillan Publishing Co., Inc.
New York

Collier Macmillan Publishers
London

Macmillan Publishing Co., Inc.
866 Third Avenue, New York, New York 10022

Collier Macmillan Canada, Inc.

Library of Congress Cataloging in Publication Data

Cook, Alicia Skinner.
Contemporary perspectives on adult development and
aging.

Includes index.
1. Adulthood.   2. Adult Development.   3. Aged.   4. Aging.
I. Title.
HQ799.95.C66   305.2'4   82-15312
ISBN 0-02-324600-6   AACR2

Printing: 1 2 3 4 5 6 7 8   Year: 3 4 5 6 7 8 9 0

ISBN   0-02-324600-6

Dedicated to

Edna Earle Skinner, who through her own work and expressive nature taught me that writing can be a natural extension of oneself;

and

Robert Brown Skinner, whose patient perseverance and stamina I was fortunate to know and learn from for many years.

Preface

I approached the task of writing this book convinced that learning should be rewarding, enjoyable and challenging. I was determined to write a textbook that would be all of these things for students—enjoyable to read, intellectually stimulating, and applicable to their own lives. My first editor at Macmillan, John Beck, had told me that writing a book is more appropriately viewed as a process rather than a task. Indeed, his experience and insight into the art of writing a textbook proved correct. Although my objectives remained the same, I considerably altered my initial ideas as I clarified my own thinking and gained fresh insights as the work progressed. While I previously thought that I had a fairly broad perspective from which to approach the field of adult development and aging, the process of writing this book enabled me to further synthesize and integrate the material. I hope that this book reflects the quality of the process I experienced.

The text is organized topically because I consider this a useful vantage point from which to approach the subject matter. Within each of the topics presented, the developmental stages of early, middle, and late adulthood and their corresponding characteristics are each considered as they affect and are affected by societal and cultural factors.

A strong international flavor has also been given to the book. In my view, students attending institutions of higher learning deserve wider exposure to cultural variables. A global perspective is essential for any real understanding of the aging process, and cultural awareness is becoming more and more critical as our concerns extend beyond the geographical boundaries of our home countries.

Even within our own cultures, we often fail to recognize the significance of cultural factors. With the ethnic diversity that exists in the United States, we can no longer restrict our textbooks, and consequently our learning, to the mainstream of society. In addition to studying white, middle-class adults, the broader society and its variations must be considered. A major strength of this text is its inclusion of a chapter on adult development and aging within specific ethnic groups in the United States.

The following individuals have enhanced the quality of this work and deserve recognition: Nancy Houser, who several years ago significantly affected my thinking and increased my sensitivity to ethnic and cultural variables; Meg DeWeese for her directness, sound judgment and accessibility, and for providing me with feedback on what superior students value in a textbook; Bob Harvey for his excellent professional consultation and assistance with the photographs used in the text, which I feel convey their own messages to the reader; and Mary Grace Coming, my typist, whose interest in the content of the book and commitment to reach the publisher's deadlines did a great deal to help maintain my enthusiasm during the many months of intense work.

Finally, the suggestions of my reviewers were extremely valuable in giving me a different perspective on my work and in refining the final product. These individuals, who provided feedback at various points in the writing of the text, are as follows: George A. Hughston (Northern Illinois University), Peter J. Stein (The William Paterson College of New Jersey), L. Eugene Thomas (University of Connecticut), and Sally Van Zandt (University of Nebraska-Lincoln).

Alicia Skinner Cook

Contents

Part V.   Epilogue   345

Chapter 11   Enhancing the Adult Years   347

Author Index   361
Subject Index   371

Contemporary Perspectives on Adult Development and Aging

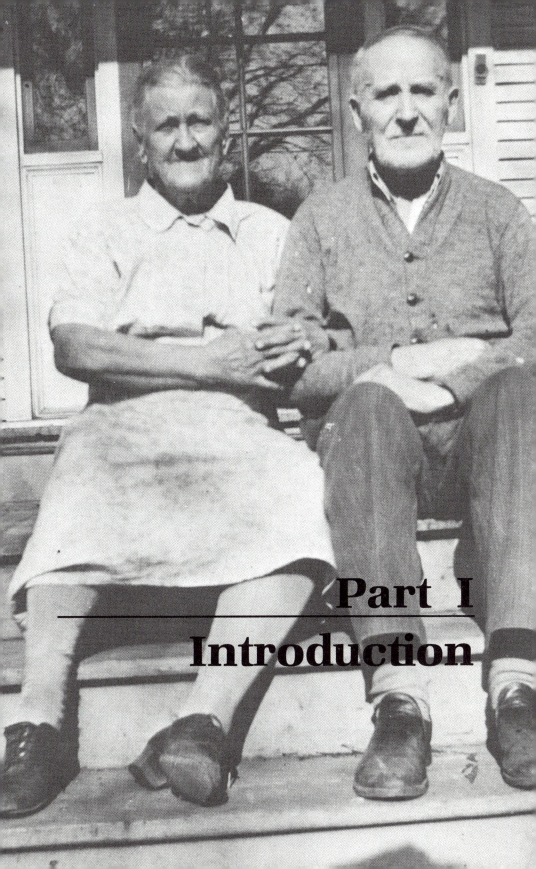

Part I
Introduction

Chapter 1

Introduction

Why do you want to learn about adult development? Perhaps you have an aged grandmother or middle-aged parents and you want to better understand what they are experiencing, or perhaps you want to gain more insight into your own present stage of development and find out what you can expect as you advance in years. You might be planning a career working with adults or the elderly and therefore view this course as part of your professional preparation. On the other hand, you may not really think you have an interest in the topic and are taking a course in adulthood and aging because it is a requirement or the only course you could fit into your schedule.

Regardless of the reason you now find yourself reading this textbook, you are about to be introduced to the field of adult development and aging. As the author of this textbook, I have attempted to present the material in both an intellectually stimulating and personally-relevant manner. It is an exciting area to learn about—*enjoy the process.*

Why Study Adult Development and Aging?

Development: the processes whereby the individual goes from a less differentiated to a more differentiated state, from a less complex to a more complex organism, from a lower or early stage to a higher or later stage of an ability, skill, or trait (Birren & Woodruff, 1973, p. 307).

It is commonly assumed that development ends after adolescence, thus leaving the remainder of life—the adult years—to be lived in a rather steady, stable state. Emerging empirical evidence on adult life, however, has forced us to question this assumption. Indeed, available data support the notion that development and change occur throughout the human life span.

Lack of knowledge of these predictable changes in adult life can be detrimental. The belief that one enters into adulthood and adopts a stable life pattern that lasts more or less indefinitely is "a cruel illusion since it leads people in early adulthood to believe that they are, or should be, fully adult and settled, and that there are no major crises or developmental changes ahead" (Levinson, Darrow, Klein, Levinson & McKee, 1976, p. 23). When these transitions are encountered without adequate preparation, individuals often feel as though they have done something

Adulthood is not just the state of being an adult; it is a process—a process that is both dynamic and developmental. Changes occur in both the individual and the roles he or she will assume at different stages of the lifespan. (Dave Schutz, photographer)

wrong. They are often operating under the assumption that upon making major life decisions in early adulthood, everything should be "set" for them for the rest of their lives.

As we shall see throughout the pages of this text, life does not progress that way. Adulthood is not just the state of being an adult; it is a process—a process that is both dynamic and developmental. Changes occur in both the individual and the roles he or she will assume at different phases of the adult lifespan. The interplay between the two has been explained by Neugarten (1976) in this way:

> The end of formal schooling, leaving the parents' home, marriage, parenthood, occupational achievement, one's own children growing up and leaving, menopause, grandparenthood, retirement—in our society, these are normal turning points, the markers or the punctuation marks along the life cycle. They call forth changes in self-concept and in sense of identity, they mark the incorporation of new social roles, and accordingly, they are the precipitants of new adaptations (p. 18).

Learning about transition periods of adulthood can facilitate the process of adaptation. Anticipatory socialization leads to role rehearsal which can prepare individuals for these turning points in life. However, the transitions are not always smooth. At times people get stuck at some point and have difficulty proceeding with their "developmental work."

Professionals working with adults (for example, counselors, educators) need a background in human development. They specifically need to be knowledgeable about the primary developmental issues faced by individuals in different periods of adult life since they are likely to be consulted by individuals during these times.

Another reason for the increased interest in the study of adulthood and aging is the changing demography of our nation. Figure 1-1 shows the rising numbers of elderly among our population. Current figures show that persons over 65 constitute approximately 11.2 percent of the total population, up from 4.1 percent in 1900, and the number of older people in our society (at 25.5 million in 1980) is expected to almost double by the year 2020 (U.S. Bureau of the Census, 1979, 1981).

Several factors have influenced the "aging" of our population. In part, the shift in demography resulted from the high fertility rates around the turn of the century. Individuals born at that time comprise an extremely large cohort group now beyond age 65. Increased longevity is a second factor contributing to the increase in the elderly population. More and more people today are living to experience their 70s, 80s and 90s. Thirdly, the immigration of large numbers of young adults to the United States prior to World War I has impacted on the current size of the elderly segment of our society (Bouvier, Atlee & McVeigh, 1975).

Change

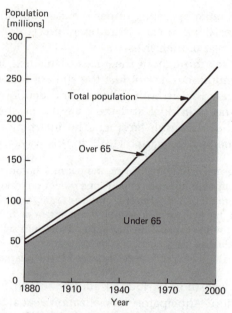

Population
[millions]

300

250

Total population

200

Over 65

150

100

Under 65

50

0

1880   1910   1940   1970   2000
Year

Figure 1–1. Population growth in the United States for groups over and under age 65: 1880 through 1970 and projected to 2000. (Source: The Commission on Population Growth and the American Future, *Demographic and Social Aspects of Population Growth.* Washington, D.C.: U.S. Government Printing Office, 1972.)

The increase in both the proportion and absolute number of older individuals in our society has created a need for more professionals trained in the field of *gerontology*, the study of adult development and aging. The past decade has produced a variety of human service occupations aimed at providing services to the over-65 age group. Training in the social, psychological, biological and developmental aspects of aging is essential for those who plan to work in this field. Also, recent research suggests a need for understanding these processes from the beginning of adulthood, since the adjustment and adaptation to aging has its foundation in the choices, behavior patterns and lifestyles established earlier in life.

Developmental Theory

Erik Erikson is a developmental theorist who believes that early stages of development have a definite effect on later life. He has proposed a theory based on critical psycho-social crises that individuals encounter at each stage of development. These crises crystallize particular life

Table 1–1. Erikson's Eight Stages of Development.

Life Stage	Psycho-Social Crisis
Stage 1: Infancy	Basic trust versus mistrust
Stage 2: Toddlerhood	Autonomy versus shame and doubt
Stage 3: Preschool	Initiative versus guilt
Stage 4: School-age	Industry versus inferiority
Stage 5: Adolescence	Identity versus role confusion
Stage 6: Early Adulthood	Intimacy versus isolation
Stage 7: Middle Adulthood	Generativity versus stagnation
Stage 8: Late Adulthood	Integrity versus despair

Source: Adapted from E. H. Erikson, Identity and the Life Cycle: Selected Papers, *Psychological Issues*, Monograph No. 1, 1959.

themes that integrate past activities and provide a foundation for further development. Erikson has divided the life span into eight stages, with each stage having a central theme (see Table 1–1). For optimum development at successive stages, the psycho-social issues at earlier stages must be positively resolved.

The central issues of adulthood are: intimacy versus isolation, generativity versus stagnation, and integrity versus despair. The major developmental theme of early adulthood involves achieving a mutually satisfying and intimate relationship. Resolution of this crisis in a positive direction is possible only when one has the capacity for mutual trust with another and the willingness to share one's life. Failure to develop intimate relationships leads to preoccupation with self and superficial interactions with others. In middle age, individuals face the issue of generativity versus stagnation. Do they feel they are making significant contributions to the next generation? Do they feel they are being productive and creative members of society? When failing to achieve this sense of generativity, individuals often experience feelings of stagnation and personal impoverishment. Erikson has stated that the final stage of life, late adulthood, holds the task of growing old and facing death with integrity. However, if one feels he or she has lived a life void of meaning, death will come too quickly. When a person feels it is too late to make up for a life that does not measure up to one's final assessment, life will end in despair, bitterness and depression (Erikson, 1964).

Erikson places much emphasis on the building-block nature of these issues as an individual progresses through life. One is incapable of en-

Life will end in integrity when trust, competency, and a sense of who one is as a person have been experienced. (Sibyl Stork, photographer)

gaging in true intimacy and sharing with another unless one is sure of one's own identity, an issue that is the prevailing theme of adolescence. Going back further into one's life, unsuccessful resolution of the basic trust-versus-mistrust issue will also influence one's ability to form close interpersonal relationships. In middle age, achievement of a sense of generativity is facilitated if stages 2 and 4 have been resolved in the direction of autonomy and industry. And finally when one reaches the end of one's time, life will be judged as meaningful and thus end in integrity when the individual has experienced trust, competency and a sense of who one is as a person.

Another developmental stage theorist, Robert Havighurst, has emphasized the importance of developmental tasks. According to Havighurst (1953):

A developmental task is a task which arises at or about a certain period of the life of the individual, successful achievement of which leads to happiness and success with later tasks, while failure leads to

8

unhappiness in the individual, disapproval by the society, and difficulty with later tasks (p. 2)

Table 1–2 lists the developmental tasks which Havighurst has identified for young, middle and late adulthood. Young adulthood is viewed as a critical time for decision making. The decisions made during this stage will have a major influence on the remainder of one's adult life.

Table 1–2. Developmental Tasks of Early, Middle, and Late Adulthood.

Early Adulthood:
1. Selecting a mate
2. Learning to live with a marriage partner
3. Starting a family
4. Rearing children
5. Managing a home
6. Getting started in an occupation
7. Taking on civic responsibility
8. Finding a congenial social group

Middle Adulthood:
1. Achieving adult civic and social responsibility
2. Establishing and maintaining an economic standard of living
3. Assisting teen-age children to become responsible adults
4. Developing adult leisure time activities
5. Relating oneself to one's spouse as a person
6. Accepting the physiological changes of middle age

Late Adulthood:
1. Adjusting to decreased physical strength and health
2. Adjustment to retirement and reduced income
3. Adjusting to death of spouse
4. Establishing an explicit affiliation with one's age group
5. Meeting social and civic obligations
6. Establishing satisfactory physical living arrangements

Source: R. J. Havighurst, *Human Development and Education* (New York: Longmans, Green, 1953).

Middle age is a period of peak productivity and influence in society. It is also the time when the greatest demands are placed on individuals. The final stage of life brings additional tasks which have to be completed for healthy development to occur. Several of the tasks associated with this stage involve adjusting to loss: loss of spouse, loss of job and loss or reduction of certain abilities.

An examination of Havighurst's developmental tasks over the life span shows a major difference between those of childhood and those of adulthood. While developmental tasks of children are largely biologically determined (for example, learning to walk), the tasks of adulthood are more determined by social norms (such as adjusting to retirement).

Age Norms and Expectations

Adult development occurs in a societal context. Many of the associations that have been found between age and behavior result from societal norms and are not an inherent part of individual development.

The effect of social factors on development can readily be seen in the area of age norms and expectations. Societies generally have rules and customs regarding appropriate behaviors for different age groups. Also, as Neugarten (1977) has pointed out, socially prescribed timetables exist for the ordering of major life events such as marriage, parenthood and retirement. An age range is typically delineated in which certain behaviors and events are considered acceptable and encouraged while others are thought to be unacceptable. This age range will vary for specific behaviors. For example, a study in the United States found that at least four out of five respondents thought that people should go to work between 20 and 22 and retire between 60 and 65 (Neugarten, Moore & Lowe, 1965). Harbert and Ginsberg (1979) view these age norms and expectations operating "as probes and brakes to behavior, in some instances hastening and in others delaying it" (p. 15). The following commonly-heard statements show how age norms affect our perceptions of events and behaviors:

> "He married late."
> "He is too young to marry."
> "He's too old to be working so hard."
> "She's too young to wear that style of clothes."
> "That's a strange thing for a man his age to say."

As individuals proceed through life, they learn what is expected in terms of behavior patterns and activities, and they tend to engage in behaviors and adopt roles consistent with these expectations. In fact, strong pressure exists to do so. Noncompliance with norms can mean contending with negative reactions. The reprimand, "Act your age!" is familiar to many. As a consequence, being out of step with societal norms can result in personal devaluation and doubt.

In addition, this type of age bias can restrict development, as in the case of older individuals who decide against going back to school or marrying in their 60s because these actions are not in keeping with the so-called "social clock." It can also produce stereotyped beliefs about aging that are inaccurate and result in generalized negative attitudes toward particular age groups (Troll & Nowak, 1976). In the opinion of gerontologist Alex Comfort (1976), 75 percent of "aging" is imposed on older people and has no physical basis, a phenomenon he calls *sociogenic aging*. The term *ageism* is used frequently by social gerontologists to refer to discrimination against older individuals simply on the basis of their age. Bulter (1969) has contended that this bias against older persons can be compared with racism and sexism—it is yet another form of bigotry. We need to understand how age norms operate in our society and in our own lives.

Box 1–1

Assessing Your Age Bias

Below are a few questions which have been taken from the Age Norms Inquiry, an instrument designed by Schlossberg, Troll and Leibowitz (1978) to assist individuals in recognizing their age-related biases:

All other things being equal, a man:

1. Should be self-supporting from _____ years to _____ years old.
2. Is attractive from _____ years to _____ years old.
3. Can go to college from _____ years to _____ years old.
4. Can have his last child from _____ years to _____ years old.
5. Can remarry from _____ years to _____ years old.

All other things being equal, a woman:

1. Should begin her career from _____ years to _____ years old.
2. Can change her career as bus driver to a career as sociologist from _____ years to _____ years old.

3. Is attractive from _____ years to _____ years old.
4. Should be self-supporting from _____ years to _____ years old.
5. Can date from _____ years to _____ years old.

Source: N. K. Schlossberg, L. E. Troll, Z. Leibowitz, *Perspectives on Counseling Adults: Issues and Skills* (Monterey, Ca.: Brooks/Cole, 1978).

Research Considerations

Whatever exists must exist in some quantity, and therefore can be measured.

R. L. Thorndike

When empirical data are not available, ideas and views toward adulthood and aging tend to come from personal impressions. For example, perceptions of aging may be based solely on observations of an elderly person who lives next door. Also in the absence of scientific information, folklore shapes our thoughts about aging. Much recent research has demonstrated that many of the common assumptions that people hold about the aging process are simply not true and are based on misconceptions.

While the early years of life have been an area of academic and scientific interest for some time, the study of adult development and aging is relatively new. Despite its infancy, an abundance of empirical research has been conducted in this area over the past few decades. Also, the growth in gerontology programs has been dramatic. A generation ago, few if any courses were available in gerontology; today there are literally thousands of these courses offered at universities, colleges and junior colleges across the nation (Sprouse, 1976). In addition, gerontological centers which offer specialized training have been established, and several professional journals seek to further our knowledge by publishing current research findings on the aging process (Palmore, 1980).

Some Methods of Studying Adult Development

A central focus in developmental research is change in a particular variable over time. For example, a researcher might be interested in ego strength and how it changes (if at all) as one progresses from young adulthood to the later years of life. An effective method of studying this aspect of development would be to design and implement a longitudinal investigation. In this type of study, a group of subjects would be selected and then assessed using ego-strength measures. As these individuals moved through adulthood, periodic measurements of ego strength would continue to be taken using the same instruments at each testing interval. Any differences found could be referred to as *age changes* and would represent intra-individual variations over time.

While there are obvious benefits to obtaining information through longitudinal research, some distinct disadvantages also exist. First of all, the time factor poses some difficulties. To follow a group of adults over several stages of adulthood could consume most of the experimenter's career. A second problem relates to techniques used in the study. A measurement technique appropriate at the beginning of the study may be seen as simplistic and unrefined twenty years later when the study is nearing completion. While more sophisticated techniques may be available at that time, the same or equivalent measurement devices must be used at each testing period to enable the researcher to make appropriate and meaningful comparisons. One must be careful, however, to avoid obtaining "practice effects" through subject familiarity with the instruments over time. A third potential problem is related to the high drop-out rate that occurs with this type of study. Some persons in the sample move and cannot be located, while others do not live long enough to complete the study. The problem stems not from the attrition rate *per se* (given that it is kept at reasonable levels), but the possibility that the variable being studied (for example, personality style) is highly correlated with the reason for attrition. If this is the case, the final results of the study will be distorted and not accurately reflect developmental trends. A final disadvantage of longitudinal designs is the confounding of age with year of measurement. For example, if a measure of cigarette smoking was taken at the same time that new evidence on the high correlation between smoking and lung cancer was publicized, changes might be observed that are related more to time of measurement than developmental trends. Despite the time factor and potential problems in interpreting findings, longitudinal research does offer valuable developmental data.

Another basic research design is the cross-sectional paradigm. With this approach, measurements on subjects from several age groups are obtained at a single point in time. The differences obtained in this type of study are referred to as *age differences*. While more time-efficient than longitudinal studies, cross-sectional studies present other difficulties. Differences between groups of age cohorts (individuals born at a particular time in history), rather than intra-individual changes, are measured with cross-sectional designs. Different age cohorts have different social and cultural experiences, but cultural-historical factors cannot be separated from age differences in cross-sectional data. Therefore, any observed differences can be at least partially explained by the different experiences of the cohort groups. For example, cross-sectional studies of intellectual functioning have found patterns of I.Q. decline (Botwinick, 1967; Jones, 1959). In contrast, longitudinal studies have reported stability in intellectual functioning with age and even gains in some instances (Baley, 1968; Baley & Oden, 1955; Nesselroade, Schaie & Baltes, 1972). The findings of the cross-sectional studies no doubt reflected differences in educational attainment among the generations sampled.

Schaie (1965, 1968) has proposed a model which combines the two approaches: a short-term longitudinal study of age change for several cohort groups. Subjects are compared across age groups at a single point in time and within age groups at two or more points in time. This approach avoids some of the problems encountered when cross-sectional or longitudinal designs are used alone, yet takes advantage of the strengths of both methods.

As should be evident, obtaining valid developmental data is not an easy task. In spite of methodological limitations, a considerable quantity of information is now available on developmental change. Hopefully, you will become acquainted with much of this information as you begin your study of adult development and aging.

Learning About Adults: The Author's Approach

Each writer has his or her own unique way of selecting and organizing information to be presented in a textbook. The decisions on style and content are based on the author's orientation to the subject matter. It is important for the reader to know from the outset the author's particular perspective. How does the book proceed in terms of logical progression? What framework helps integrate the material in the text?

Based on ideas put forth by Troll (1975), I view the developing adult as part of three interacting systems: the self system, the family system and the larger social system. These systems all operate within a particular cultural and historical context. Development of the individual cannot be discussed in a vacuum. All systems must be taken into account when studying the adult development and aging process.

Figure 1−2 illustrates the relationship among these three systems. As individuals develop, they move from young adulthood through mid-

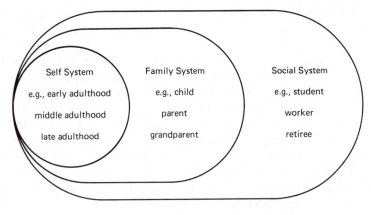

Cultural Milieu
in a Particular Historical Period

Figure 1–2. Development of the individual within the self, family, and social systems.

dle age to late adulthood. While ages assigned to these stages vary with theorists, the generally accepted ages corresponding to each of the three stages are 18–40, 40–60 and 60 and above. The stage of late adulthood has recently been further differentiated into the categories of young-old and old-old.

Development also occurs in the family system. Families move from a beginning stage with no children through the childbearing years to the launching stage, which is followed by the post-parental and aging family stages. Correspondingly, the roles of adults are altered as they move through this system. At times new roles are assumed (for example, parent role), some are maintained and expanded (parent role expanding into grandparent role), and others are lost (husband or wife role upon death of spouse).

The roles of adults also extend into the larger social system. For example, the work role is a major role for most adults. Other societal roles include those associated with civic responsibilities and religious duties. Additional structures of the society in which adults may have membership include social class and ethnic groups. Over the life span, the roles one assumes in the community are altered. For example, individuals typically move from the role of student to worker to retiree.

On a broader scale, development is occuring on a societal level as countries move from being underdeveloped into modern, industrialized nations. These societal developments, while occurring over a much greater span of time than individual or family development, greatly influence the self, family and social systems they encompass. As examples, a prolonged period of education, the concept of retirement, and increased longevity are associated with modern societies, whereas early age at marriage and a short period of adolescence are associated with less modernized countries.

With this model in mind, let us look at this text's organization. Following this introduction, a unit on family relationships and work is presented. Many of the major transitions in adulthood relate to family and work roles (that is, parenthood, marriage, retirement, widowhood). Decision making in these areas is an important part of adult life. Next, individual change and development in intelligence and creativity, sexuality, personality, and mental and physical health over the adult years are discussed. Included in these discussions are the implications of change in these areas for role enactment and task performance within the family and social systems. A unit on culture and aging follows. Rather than merely discussing differences among various cultural and subcultural groups, the reader is helped to conceptualize some of the major causative factors related to variations found among the aged and their families. The book concludes with a brief look at enhancing adult life through preparation for life transitions and education for predictable life events.

The end of each chapter contains exercises and activities designed to help you apply the information from the text to your local communities and your own life. In addition to gaining knowledge of the current theories and empirical findings in the field of adult development and aging, the information presented in this book will hopefully better prepare you for the remainder of your journey through adult life.

Suggested Activities and Exercises

1. Examine your responses to the Age Norms Inquiry. What factors influenced your answers to each question?
2. In what ways do you see *ageism* operating in society? Give examples of statements you have heard lately that reflect age bias.
3. What problems would be encountered if one attempted to study changes in muscular strength using a cross-sectional design? How could the study be redesigned to obtain more valid data on developmental change?

References

Bayley, N. Cognition and aging. In K. W. Schaie (Ed.), *Current topics in the psychology of aging: Perception, learning and cognition, and personality.* Morgantown: West Virginia University Library, 1968.

Bayley, N., & Oden, M. The maintenance of intellectual ability in gifted adults. *Journal of Gerontology*, 1955, *10*, 91–107.

Birren, J. E., & Woodruff, D. S. Human development over the life span through education. In P. B. Baltes & K. W. Schaie (Eds.), *Life span developmental psychology: Personality and socialization.* New York: Academic, 1973.

Botwinick, J. *Cognitive processes in maturity and old age.* New York: Springer, 1967.

Bouvier, L., Atlee, E., & McVeigh, F. The elderly in America. *Population Bulletin* (Vol. 30, No. 3). Washington, D.C.: Population Reference Bureau, 1975.

Butler, R. N. Age-ism: Another form of bigotry. *The Gerontologist*, 1969, *9*, 243–46.

Comfort, A. Age prejudice in America. *Social Policy*, 1976, *7*, 3–8.

Erikson, E. H. *Childhood and society.* (2nd ed.) New York: Norton, 1964.

Erikson, E. H. Identity and the life cycle: Selected papers. *Psychological Issues*, Monograph No. 1, 1959.

Harbert, A. S., & Ginsberg, L. H. *Human services for older adults: Concepts and skills.* Belmont, Ca.: Wadsworth, 1979.

Havighurst, R. J. *Human development and education.* New York: Longmans, Green, 1953.

Jones, H. E. Intelligence and problem solving. In J. E. Birren (Ed.), *Handbook of aging and the individual.* Chicago: University of Chicago Press, 1959.

Levinson, D. J., Darrow, C. M., Klein, E. B., Levinson, M. H., & McKee, B. Periods in the adult development of men: Ages 18 to 45. *Counseling Psychologist*, 1976, *6*, 21–25.

Nesselroade, J. R., Schaie, K. W., & Baltes, P. B. Ontogenetic and generational components of structural and quantitative change in adult cognitive behavior. *Journal of Gerontology*, 1972, *27*, 222–28.

Neugarten, B. L. Adaptation and the life cycle. *Counseling Psychologist*, 1976, *6*, 16–20.

Neugarten, B. L. Adaptation and the life cycle. In N. K. Schlossberg & A. D. Entine (Eds.), *Counseling adults.* Monterey, Ca.: Brooks/Cole, 1977.

Neugarten, B. L., Moore, J. W., & Lowe, J. C. Age norms, age constraints, and adult socialization. *American Journal of Sociology*, 1965, *70* 710–17.

Palmore, E. United States of America. In E. Palmore (Ed.), *International handbook on aging.* Westport, Ct.: Greenwood Press, 1980.

Schaie, K. W. A general model for the study of developmental problems. *Psychological Bulletin*, 1965, *64*, 92–107.

Schaie, K. W. Age changes and age differences. In B. Neugarten (Ed.), *Middle age and aging.* Chicago: University of Chicago Press, 1968.

Schlossberg, N. K., Troll, L. E., & Leibowitz, Z. *Perspectives on counseling adults: Issues and skills.* Monterey, Ca.: Brooks/Cole, 1978.

Sprouse, B. (Ed.) *National directory of educational programs in gerontology.* Washington, D.C.: Administration on Aging, Department of Health, Education and Welfare, 1976.

The Commission on Population Growth and the American Future. *Demographic and social aspects of population growth.* Washington, D.C.: U.S. Government Printing Office, 1972.

Troll, L. E. *Early and middle adulthood.* Monterey, Ca.: Brooks/Cole, 1975.

Troll, L. E., & Nowak, C. "How old are you?" The question of age bias in the counseling of adults. *Counseling Psychologist,* 1976, 6, 41–43.

U.S. Bureau of the Census. *Population profile of United States: 1980.* (Current Population Reports, Series P-20, No. 363). Washington, D.C.: U.S. Government Printing Office, 1981.

U.S. Bureau of the Census. *Prospective trends in the size and structure of the elderly population, impact of mortality trends, and some implications.* (Current Population Reports, Series P-23, No. 78). Washington, D. C.: U. S. Government Printing Office, 1979.

Part II
Primary Roles of Adulthood: Family and Work

Chapter 2

Primary Relationships of Adulthood

In his presidential address to the American Psychological Organization in 1958, Harry F. Harlow stated, "So far as love or affection is concerned, psychologists have failed in their mission. The little we know about love does not transcend simple observation, and the little we write about it has been written better by poets and novelists."

A decade and a half later Ashley Montagu (1975), well-known anthropologist and social biologist, continued to comment on the absence of attention social and behavioral scientists have paid to the topic of love. While many have viewed this topic unworthy of scientific investigation, the problem stems partly from the lack of an acceptable definition of love. As Montagu states, "we live in a time in which there is much talk of love and much confusion concerning its meaning." Certainly it is a difficult subject to be quantified, measured objectively and treated as a variable in a scientific study. Yet because it is such a potent force and influence on adult relationships, it deserves more attention from professionals in the area of adult development. The need to be loved and express our love for others is an essential aspect of the human experience.

In this chapter, we will explore the personal relationships of adult life. These relationships vary in nature, intensity and duration, yet all contain the common element of meaningfulness and allow us to express the humanness in ourselves. Following a discussion of the development of intimacy, the following topics will be presented: the marital relationship, alternatives to the heterosexual marriage (cohabitation, singlehood and homosexual relationships), the parenting decision and parent-child relationships throughout the life span, grandparent-grandchild and adult sibling relationships, and adult friendships.

The Development of Intimacy

The Role of Self-Disclosure

Levinger (1977) offers a definition of interpersonal closeness which includes a combination of social, physical and psychological nearness. He views intimacy as requiring frequent interaction between individuals in close, physical proximity who share significant common goals, engage in mutual self-disclosure, and care deeply about each other.

Several writers have emphasized the importance of self-disclosure in the development of intimacy and have presented disclosure reciprocity as the critical process by which relationships are formed and strengthened (Cozby, 1972; Jourard & Friedman, 1970; Worthy, Gary & Kahn, 1969). Derlega and Chaikin (1975) in their book *Sharing Intimacy* provide an excellent description of the disclosure reciprocity process:

> Friendship begins when one person risks ridicule or rejection by disclosing some personal information about himself to the other. The second person reciprocates by sharing something equally intimate about himself. The first person then responds, either at the same time or at a later meeting, by revealing something intimate about himself. In turn, this elicits a comparable disclosure from the other person. Little by little, in a spiraling fashion, this reciprocal exchange builds and strengthens bonds of intimacy, understanding, and trust between the two persons.

Of course, this process can be disrupted whenever one member of the pair decides not to reciprocate, often due to fear that his or her disclosure will result in rejection by the other person. Disclosure of self assumes a certain level of acceptance and trust. Individuals move slowly in revealing themselves until through testing out the other person, the discloser feels comfortable and expects his or her disclosure to be received in an accepting, nonthreatening way.

During initial and superficial encounters persons tend to engage in role-defined behaviors or present only those attributes of themselves they perceive to be positive. When trust and intimacy are established between two persons, the need to hide behind roles and present a preferred image to gain acceptance dissipates. With an increase in intimacy, communication is facilitated and messages are transmitted and received more openly and honestly.

Individuals may not always feel comfortable revealing information of a highly emotional and personal nature even to close friends. Certainly individuals have part of their lives they prefer to keep private. However, a large degree of self-disclosure is necessary for the development of emotional closeness. If we hide most of the feelings, thoughts and experiences that make us unique as persons, we are not allowing others to fully know and understand us and, therefore, we will be unable to fulfill one of the fundamental tasks of adulthood—the establishment of intimate, mature relationships. Jourard (1964) has posed the question, "How can I love a person whom I do not know?"

Intimacy in Modern Society

In reviewing the history of close personal relationships between opposite-sex adults in the United States, Gadlin (1977) argues that intimate relationships as we know them today emerged during the early decades of the nineteenth century. This period in American history was characterized by rapid urbanization and industrial development which separated the world of work from the home environment. According to Gadlin's thesis, this separation of the public from the private led to a great expansion of personal consciousness for individuals and the emergence of contemporary forms of interpersonal intimacy. He adds that a recent trend in the twentieth century is to more realistically assess the potentiality of relationships rather than expecting all of our personal and emotional needs to be met through a bond with another person. Commenting on the future direction in relationships, Gadlin warns against the transformation of persons into commodities where they are appreciated in terms of their ability to satisfy the needs of others and cites computer matching and mate swapping as examples of this process.

The increased mobility in American society tends to increase the number of superficial and casual encounters we have and interferes with the development of intimacy in social relationships (Derlega & Chaikin, 1975). Toffler (1970) adds that temporariness increasingly characterizes human relations in the age of super-industrialism—"for just as things and places flow through our lives at a faster clip, so, too, do people." One of our greatest challenges of the future may be the development and maintenace of stable, intimate relationships in our lives.

The Marital Relationship

Most young adults express an interest in an intimate relationship in a marital context. In a study conducted at Brown University in 1974 (Williamson, Putman & Wurthmann, 1976), undergraduate students were asked to write "future autobiographies" describing their lives from high school graduation to age 80. Eighty-eight percent of both women and men expected marriage to be part of their futures. Eighty-one percent of the men assumed that the marriage would remain intact until age 80 compared with 76 percent of the women. The possibility of divorce was rarely mentioned; most of the students anticipated more than 50 years of marriage with the same person. The researchers concluded that "unless the current mortality rates of men drastically decline and these students experience no higher rates of divorce than their parents, their marital realities will probably be quite different from what they anticipate."

An Examination of Romantic Love

"When two people are under the influence of the most violent, most insane, most delusive, and most transient of passions, they are required to swear that they will remain in that excited, abnormal, and exhausting condition continuously until death do them part."

George Bernard Shaw

The expectations of a long, enduring relationship expressed by subjects in the Williamson et al. (1976) study reflect the romantic love ideal—that for every male and female, a perfect match exists waiting to be met and loved, and ready to begin the journey toward the "happily everafter." This powerful myth has shaped the lives of many young adults.

Many modern sociologists have commented on the importance of romantic love in mate selection in America and its lesser importance in other societies (Murstein, 1974; Udry, 1974). Romantic love has been characterized by Stephens (1973) as having the following components: strong attachment and attraction to a single person, extremes of mood (elation and depression), and idealization and possessiveness of the loved one. The antithesis of romantic love is conjugal love—the love between a settled, domestic pair.

Both European and American cultures have been greatly influenced by the twelfth century ideas of courtly love as well as the sexual restrictiveness of Christianity. In contrast, Elliott (1970) states that "Scandinavian countries have been very little touched by the traditions of romantic love that have influenced the West for over a thousand years." In fact, no vocabulary for courtship has developed in these countries. While Scandinavians appear low on romance, they are also probably the most sexually permissive (Christensen, 1970; Luckey & Nass, 1969). After examining data from 24 diverse cultures, Wilkinson (1978) concluded that romantic love in marriages will be maximized in societies that (1) promote a long courtship period of free association but with sexual restrictions, (2) restrict sexual relations and romantic involvement outside of marriage, and (3) socialize its members in the belief that romantic love, marriage and sexual relations go together.

In applying the above criteria to the United States, Wilkinson (1978) found that all three conditions have traditionally been met. However, he calls attention to changing trends in the United States—primarily the greater acceptance of permissiveness during courtship and the increase in extramarital relationships. He predicts that if these trends continue, the emphasis on romantic love as a basis for marriage in this country will decline.

Arranged Marriages: An Alternative to Love Marriages

Based on Hindu scriptures, the system of arranged marriage in India was well established during the Vedic period (4000–1000 B.C.) and has been closely adhered to by the vast majority of the population since that period. Marriage is seen as an indispensable event in the life of a Hindu and the unmarried person is viewed as incomplete and ineligible for participation in certain social and religious activities (Rao & Rao, 1977).

The practice of arranged marriage cuts across all caste lines, regional boundaries and language barriers in India. Marriage is treated as an alliance between two families rather than two individuals. In the common joint family arrangement where several generations are living together, the prospective bride is evaluated on her suitability as part of the entire family environment rather than only as a wife to her husband. Love is not viewed as an important element in mate selection nor is courtship thought to be necessary for testing the relationship. In fact, romantic love is regarded as an uncontrollable and explosive emotion which interferes with the use of reason and logic in decision making. Love is thought to be a disruptive element since it implies a transference of loyalty from the family of orientation to another individual. Thus, mate selection by self-choice is seen as endangering the stability of the entire joint family since it could lead to the selection of a mate of unsuitable temperament or background. Gupta (1976) has estimated that Indian marriages based on love occur among less than one percent of the population. Critical life decisions, such as choosing a mate, are generally determined by responsible members of the family or kin group, thus reflecting the cultural emphasis on familism as opposed to freedom of the individual and persuance of personal goals. However, it is anticipated that close ties and feelings of affection will develop between the couple following marriage (Gupta, 1976; Rao & Rao, 1977; Ross, 1961).

Most marriages in India are arranged and are considered an alliance between two families rather than two individuals. (Sue Ellen Charlton, photographer)

In urban areas of India, newspaper ads have become a convenient and acceptable method of finding a suitable spouse. In 1960 Cormack noted that the practice of using matrimonial advertisements was growing in most metropolitan Indian cities. Eleven years later, Kurian (1971) obserbed that it had become an established "go between" for arranging marriages. These advertisements typically list the characteristics of the young men and women that are considered desirable. Studies by Kurian (1974) and Ross (1961) show strong sex differences in preferred qualities for males and females. In the Indian culture, a male is highly valued for the social and economic status of his family, his educational level and potential earning power. Personal qualities such as appearance and personality are not considered very important. In women the following qualities are emphasized: moral character, beauty, ability to cook well and manage a home, and education.

Primary Roles of Adulthood: Family and Work

Matrimonials for Grooms	Matrimonials for Brides
Wanted Suitable Match Army officer, engineer or government officer drawing about Rs. 1,000/per month for smart, beautiful and impressive Sikh girl. M.A. 162 cms, height, belonging to respectable Gursikh family, father in responsible advisory position in Central government, eldest son civil engineer, having own flat & other properties.	Wanted Really Beautiful Slim, tall Convent educated bride match 20–22 years for Science Graduate very smart, tall, 175 cms., very well settled at Dhanbad. Father Central Govt. officer. Family of respectable Punjabi Aroras. Girl's merits main consideration.
Well Established Bengali Brahmin (Rahri) non-Chatterjee groom for fair-looking graduate. 155 cms., 20 years girl for decent marriage.	Well Qualified Good-looking bride for engineer. Company executive 39, also for brother 34, Ph.D. well placed. Send horoscope & details.
Matches for Two Sisters 26 and 22 years both are fair, slim, with outstanding academic careers, elder is 160 cms and had professional training in U.K. in arts. Younger is 170 cms and is in university. Family Ahluwalia Clean Shaven Sikhs, father Director in well reputed foreign firm, prefer boys who are well settled in own business or profession, caste no bar.	U.S. Resident Jain Computer engineer Ph.D. 28 yrs. 168 cms. earning $32,000 yearly invites correspondence from parents of educated, attractive, fair complexioned, Hindi speaking Digambar Jain girl. No dowry, visiting India in December.
Match for Smart, Fair, M.A. (English). Lecturer, studying M. Phil. 25, 165 cms well versed in household affairs. Daughter of senior Class I Officer.	M.Sc., govt. employee in Delhi, salary Rs. 1,200/–, fair, religious, wants an exceptionally and extremely beautiful, fair complexioned, educated, homely, religious, modest and gentle girl of respectable family.

Source: The Times of India, December, 1979.

Most research on modern family life in India suggests that there has been little change in the views of Indians toward marriage. However in their 1976 study of college students, Rao and Rao found that an increasing number of young adults in India wish to have more choice in the selection of their future mate, although they still prefer their parents to arrange their marriages. Cormack (1961) also states that the custom of prohibiting a prospective couple from seeing each other until their wedding day is becoming obsolete in most urban areas and among college-educated youth.

Marital Satisfaction

While a comparison by Rollins and Cannon (1974) of marital satisfaction over the family life cycle revealed no great variation, some fluctuation has been consistently shown by researchers. Pineo (1961) has suggested that some degree of disenchantment may be a natural consequence of the idealistic attitude toward marriage of most Americans. Most researchers have reported a slight decrease in marital satisfaction during the middle years. Middle age usually includes the experience of having adolescent children. While children appear to be an important source of satisfaction for adults, they can also have adverse affects on marital relationships (Hayes & Stinnett, 1971). Middle age is also a period of questioning the meaning of one's life which includes marital relationships.

Marital satisfaction has been found to increase during the empty-nest period when all the children have left home (Troll, 1971). For many couples, freedom from the responsibilities of raising children allows them to refocus on their relationship with each other and strengthen their emotional bonds (Stinnett, Carter & Montgomery, 1972). Sometimes, however, couples find that the only common element in their lives have been their children and decide to terminate their marriages. Statistics on divorce rates during this period are affected by the previous tendency of adults in an unsatisfactory relationship to wait until their children were reared to get a divorce. "Staying together for the sake of the children" has been a commonly cited reason for continuation of unhappy marriages (Atchley, 1977).

The majority of older couples in a Stinnett et al. (1972) study reported that their later years were their happiest years of marriage and their marriage had improved with time. While the evidence shows that most marriages of older persons have relatively high levels of marital satisfaction, Stevens-Long (1979) points out that most of the data is from cross-sectional rather than longitudinal studies. She then raises the question, "Is it possible that marital satisfaction is higher among older persons because all the unhappy couples have finally gotten divorced?"

Types of Marriages

One of the problems with the literature on marital satisfaction is the lack of concensus on what constitutes a "good" marriage. Enduring marriages are not necessarily happy marriages. Cuber and Harroff (1968) have developed a typology of marital relationships that demonstrates how different couples adopt diverse marital styles. This classification system is based on interviews with a large sample of men and women whose marriages had lasted ten years or longer and who stated that

Many older couples report that they are happy and that their relationship has improved with time. (Sibyl Stork, photographer)

they had never seriously considered divorce or separation. The five types of relationships that emerged from this study were as follows: (1) conflict-habituated, (2) devitalized, (3) passive-congenial, (4) vital, and (5) total.

The conflict-habituated relationship. This relationship is characterized by the presence of tension and conflict ranging from active quarreling and nagging to more subtle intermittent conflict. Cuber and Harroff describe this situation as one in which both spouses privately acknowledge their incompatibility and most of their interactions can be viewed as psychological battles. The following statement by a fifty-year-old physician who had been married for twenty-five years to the same woman shows the pervasiveness of conflict in their relationship:

> You know, it's funny; we have fought from the time we were in high
> school together. As I look at it, I can't remember specific quarrels; it's
> more like a running guerrilla fight with intermediate periods, some-
> times quite long, of pretty good fun and some damn good sex. In fact,
> if it hadn't been for the sex, we wouldn't have married so quickly.
> Well, anyway, this has been going on ever since. It's hard to know
> what we fight about most of the time. You name it and we'll fight
> about it.

The devitalized relationship. The devitalized relationship shows a lost zeal and vitalness of the early years of marriage. While there is typically little overt tension or conflict, these couples appear lifeless, apathetic and emotionally numb. The little time the members of the pair spend together is usually "duty time"—sharing activities with the children, entertaining friends and participating in community activities. They have sex less often and find it less enjoyable than they did in the early years of marriage, when the couples had extremely close, loving relationships. Disappointment and disillusionment often stem from this discrepancy between "what was" and "what is." Cuber and Harroff found this type of relationship common among the couples they interviewed and often observed that persons in these relationships reassured themselves by making comparisons with other married couples with similar relationships. An attitude of acceptance of this type of relationship was voiced by one housewife in her late forties:

> Judging from the way it was when we were first married—say the first
> five years or so—things are pretty matter-of-fact now—even dull. . . .
> Now, I don't say this to complain, not in the least. There's a cycle to
> life. There are things you do in high school. And different things you
> do in college. Then you're a young adult. And then you're middle-
> aged. That's where we are now."

Other persons in a devitalized relationship showed less of a willingness to give up their previous expectations of marriage:

I know I'm fighting it. I ought to accept that it has to be like this, but I don't like it, and I'd do almost anything to bring back the exciting way of life we had at first . . .

The passive-congenial relationship. The passive-congenial relationship resembles the devitalized but the interaction pattern is present from the very beginning of the relationship. These couples appear to have never expected anything much different from their present marital style. The term "comfortably adequate" is used by Cuber and Harroff to describe this association. Persons are usually engaged in this mode of marital interaction for one of two reasons: (1) a passive relationship sufficiently expresses their existing bond which lacks depth, or (2) this arrangement is desired so as to free the members of the pair and allow more investment of their interests and creative energies into careers, raising of children, or community activities instead of having so much of themselves invested in the marital relationship. Cuber and Harroff point out that this style of marriage is very functional for the career-oriented person who wants a minimum of distractions from his or her work. This view was expressed by a dedicated physician:

> I don't know why everyone seems to make so much about men and women and marriage. Of course, I'm married and if anything happened to my wife, I'd get married again. I think it's the proper way to live. It's convenient, orderly, and solves a lot of problems. But there are other things in life. I spent nearly ten years preparing for the practice of my profession. The biggest thing to me is the practice of that profession, to be of assistance to my patients and their families. I spend twelve hours a day at it. And I'll bet if you talked with my wife, you wouldn't get any of that 'trapped housewife' stuff from her either. Now that the children are grown, she finds a lot of useful and necessary work to do in this community. She works as hard as I do.

The vital relationship. Persons involved in vital relationships have a close psychological bond. The relationship itself is of primary importance and sacrifices are readily made to enhance the quality of the relationship. These couples have a genuine sharing of life which offers mutual satisfactions yet allows each person to maintain a separate identity. The focus of their lives is the relationship; all else is seen as subordinate and secondary. One member of a vital marriage in the Cuber and Harroff study made the following statement regarding her relationship with her husband: "We've been married for over twenty years and the most enjoyable thing either of us does—well, outside of intimate things—is to sit and talk by the hour." Conflict is avoided in vital rela-

31   Primary Relationships of Adulthood

tionships, but it tends to be settled quickly when it does occur and it usually involves important rather than trivial issues.

The total relationship.   The total relationship resembles the vital relationship with the addition of a broader, more multifaceted style of interaction in which all important aspects of life are enthusiastically shared by the couple. Few areas of tension exist; serious difficulties of opinion have usually been settled in the early stages of the relationship. When disagreements do arise, however, they are faced with little pretense. Cuber and Harroff stress that this type of relationship is rare. When it does exist, it is extremely reinforcing to the individuals involved as is apparent in the following example:

> It seems to me that Bert exaggerates my help. It's not so much that I only want to help him; it's more that I want to do those things anyway. We do them together, even though we may not be in each other's presence at the time. I don't really know what I do for him and what I do for me.

Cuber and Harroff stress that the typology which they describe represents relationships, not personalities. A person may be in a devitalized relationship and express his or her vitality in a career or in a relationship outside of the marriage. Nor should the five types be interpreted as representing degrees of adjustment. The case examples presented show that different types of adjustment are contained in each type of marriage. Most persons in all five types of marital relationships expressed contentment which further emphasizes the different personal meanings people expect and receive from their marital experiences.

While shifts in marital types can occur as a result of a change in life circumstance, perspectives or attitudes, established patterns of marital interaction tend to persist. Intervention by a marriage counselor can often be effective provided that both members of the couple are dissatisfied with the relationship and have a sincere desire to change the nature of their interactions. A change through termination of the relationship is also a possibility. Cuber and Harroff state that divorce and separation can occur in any of the five types of relationships.

Marital Roles

Traditionally, sex roles in marriage have been very specialized with the husband as sole provider and the wife functioning as housekeeper and childrearer. Increasingly, traditional marital roles are being challenged. Mousseau (1975) has observed that women are assuming additional functions in the family and serving as "economic associates" in their marriages. Weitzman (1975) has questioned the fairness of giving males the total responsibility of financial support of the family and assigning women the exclusive responsibility for performing household chores and caring for children. He suggests that such divisions of labor "derive from sexual steroetypes and produce both an unnecessary rigidity and specificity." Rapoport and Rapoport (1975) add that it is indeed difficult to "disentangle one's sex stereotypes from an assessment of what one's actual capabilities are."

Several studies have revealed sex differences in preference for marriage types. Males have been found to generally prefer more traditional marriages than females. Williamson, Putnam and Wurthmann (1976) found that female undergraduates were thinking about how to combine careers, marriage and children, whereas men did not seem similarly concerned. Russo and Stadter (1971) have written of a "cultural lag" with regard to egalitarianism among male students in the United States, especially white males. An increasing number of women are desiring egalitarian relationships with opportunities for the fullest development of their capabilities. This disparity suggests that when men and women in the United States refer to marriage, they are conceptualizing quite different institutions.

Developmental Changes in the Conception of Marriage

Changes in views of marriage are indeed occurring as people challenge traditional structures and experiment with relationships in and out of marital contexts. While the potential influence of social forces, such as the women's movement, on the institution of marriage has long been recognized, only recently has it been proposed that adult conceptions of marriage could be linked to a specific developmental sequence.

Tamashiro (1978) has postulated the existence of developmental stages in the conception of marriage and discusses the implications for marriage counselors. He states that "marriage is rarely recognized as a mental concept, much less treated seriously as a concept that evolves in an individual's lifetime." According to his theory, the stages are consecutive and in the following order: Magical, Idealized Convention, Individualistic, and Affirmational.

The first stage (Magical) involves a magical way of viewing marriages as illustrated in many fairy tales which end "and they lived happily ever after." The simplistic belief of "marry into a rich family and you'll be happy" is encompassed in this stage. Concrete criteria such as money, sex or children are used to evaluate the quality of marriage.

In stage two, Idealized Convention, marriage is viewed in terms of strict, conventional rules. These rules are uncritically accepted and used to determine the "right" way and the "wrong" way to maintain a marital relationship. The basis for judging the relationship is determined by the social reference group of the person and may include personal appearance, friendliness, health, reputation and social acceptance. "Getting along together" is perceived as the cornerstone of building a secure, successful relationship.

In advancing from stage two to the Individualistic Stage (stage three), the individual becomes increasingly aware of inner feelings and emotions. The person discovers that simply following rules does not make the marriage emotionally satisfying and fulfilling. During this stage, socially accepted standards are replaced by self-chosen standards influenced strongly by personal preferences and desires. Emotional well-being, developing a sense of self, and psychological growth stemming from the relationship are used to assess the quality of the marriage. Marriage is seen as worthwhile only if it supports personal goals and allows individuals to live in a manner consistent with their values and beliefs. The enhancing of one's personhood is the dominant concern during this stage.

The Affirmational stage is the fourth and final stage which Tamashiro proposes. In this stage, persons face their inner dilemmas and acknowledge their vulnerability in an uncertain and confusing world. At this stage, marriage is conceptualized as multi-faceted and a deepened regard is expressed for oneself and others. Because individuals are not overly attached to social rules or a rigid set of personal standards, conversations tend to be more open and affirming.

The implications of couples marrying with different conceptions of marriage or members of the pair progressing through the sequence at different rates are obvious. Professionals working in the area of marriage and family counseling should initially explore with couples their ideas about marriage and the basis on which they are judging their relationship. However, Tamashiro points out that while these stages represent "a continuum of increasing cognitive complexity, deepening emotional awareness and greater interpersonal sensitivities, each stage has its own inherent difficulties. Problems developed in previous stages are not necessarily resolved as one moves upward through the stages." Empirical research needs to be conducted to determine the validity of Tamashiro's proposed stages. If they prove to be valid, questions such as, "What factors affect the rate at which one moves from one stage to another?" and "How are the stages related to one's sex and age?" will need to be addressed.

Termination of Marriages

Koch and Koch (1976) have commented on the current prevalence of traditional problems of marriage such as lack of communication, problems with children, money, infidelity, in-laws, alcoholism and physical abuse. Tsoi-Hoshmand (1976) adds that marriage relationships can also be strained because one partner has outgrown the other. This situation most often occurs when women neglect the development of their own potential to support a husband in his education or profession; however, in some cases the wife may feel she has outgrown the husband. It is common for both members of a couple contemplating divorce to feel that they have gradually grown apart from each other during the course of the relationship.

Increasingly couples are seeking professional assistance when trying to resolve their marital difficulties. Approaches of marriage counselors and therapists can vary considerably as can their levels of competence. Regardless of the skill of the therapist, he or she cannot be effective unless the couple is genuinely willing to deal with their problems openly and honestly (Koch & Koch, 1976). Therapists can facilitate communication between the couple and provide insight into their problems, but they cannot be expected to supply the pair with quick, simple solutions to complex areas of interpersonal relations. Reconstructing a damaged relationship requires considerable effort and determination on the part of both partners.

A recent shift in the philosophy of many marriage and family counselors is reflected in the view of divorce as a positive outcome of therapy in some instances. This approach necessitates letting go of the concept of divorce as failure. Tsoi-Hoshmand (1976) has expressed the belief that a marriage that is destructive to either partner and interferes with personal growth may not be worth maintaining.

An increasing number of persons are opting for termination of their marital relationships. Between 1970 and 1980, the ratio of number of currently divorced persons per 1,000 persons in intact marriages rose by 113 percent. By 1980, there were 100 divorced men and women for every 1,000 individuals living with their spouse (U.S. Bureau of the Census, 1981b).

Persons experiencing divorce report significant emotional trauma as well as practical problems, especially during the first year following divorce. The degree of difficulty experienced is related to such factors as length of the marriage, age of the person, and number and ages of children involved (Hethington, Cox & Cox, 1977; Stinnett & Walters, 1977). Most divorced persons, however, are interested in and capable of establishing another marital relationship. In fact, 5 out of 6 divorced men and 3 out of 4 divorced women eventually remarry (U.S. Bureau of the Census, 1981a).

Several suggestions have been offered to reduce conflict in marriage and combat the rising divorce rate. Kelly (1975) has suggested the use of a personal contract negotiated prior to marriage. The contract would contain agreements in areas of the most concern to the couple such as division of household labor, financial arrangements and plans for children. Of course, the contents of individual contracts would vary considerably and would probably require some revision at various intervals in the relationship. This process would provide a formal structure whereby opinions regarding important issues of adult relationships could be explicitly stated and agreed upon. All too frequently, couples wait until after the actual marriage to discuss such issues and find that they have made inaccurate assumptions and important areas of disagreement exist.

Another innovative approach to marriage is the concept of the renewable trial marriage in which persons contract for a union for a specified period of time (usually three to five years) at which point the relationship is reevaluated. Both parties are free at that time to decide against renewal of the contract. This procedure eliminates the cost and emotional strain of present divorce procedures.

Box 2.1

Trial-Run Marriages Proposed
in Alaska

JUNEAU, Alaska (AP)—Alaska would be the first state to permit renewable trial marriages under a bill introduced Tuesday in the Legislature.

The measure, sponsored by Rep. Mike Beirne, R-Anchorage, would allow people to get married for a specific period agreed on by the man and woman in advance.

The "marriage contract" would automatically expire when the period is up unless both agree to renew the pact.

If married people don't want to renew their vows, then they shouldn't be married," said Beirne.

Beirne said he introduced the measure in recognition of the many unmarried Alaskans who are living together because they feel traditional marriage does not meet their needs.

Before tying the knot, couples would be required to write an agreement outlining the disposition of assets acquired before or during marriage and custody arrangements for any children who might be born during the marriage.

"This compels the parties to think realistically and practically about what they're doing," Beirne said. "Today, people are jumping into a marriage contract very easily without any serious deliberations or concern for the consequences.

The bill would allow a couple married under current law to file before a state court to have a time limit put on the marriage.

Beirne said legislative researchers checked with all other states, but did not find any similar legislation on the books.

Source: Rocky Mountain News, February 6, 1980.

Alternatives to Marriage

Cohabitation

Although the phenomenon of men and women living together unmarried is not new (Berger, 1871; Rodman, 1966), it has only been in the past decade that nonmarital cohabitation has been openly practiced by a large number of middle-class Americans. The first professional article on cohabitation was published in 1972 (Lyness, Lipetz & Davis, 1972; Macklin, 1972). Since that time, a considerable number of studies have been conducted on this topic, providing us with increased information on the prevalence and experience of cohabitation.

Prevalence. Most of the estimates on the incidence of cohabitation have been derived from college-student populations. Because of the large variations among campuses, overall prevalence has been difficult to determine. Macklin (1978), after reviewing the current literature on cohabitation, concluded that approximately one-quarter of the present undergraduate student population of the United States has had a cohabitation experience. In addition, it appears that an additional 50 percent would consider cohabitating if they were involved in a close relationship with someone and were not in a situation prohibiting cohabitation.

Studies show a sharp contrast between views of student and parent generations regarding cohabitation. In responding to the question, "What has caused young people today to accept a behavior which was unthinkable a generation ago?", Macklin (1978) cites several interacting factors such as changes in the sexual values and behaviors, the challenge of the double standard resulting in increased freedom for women, availability of effective contraception, and a change in housing regulations for students. She also adds that the human growth movement in the United States has questioned the traditional courtship process and an early commitment to marriage, resulting in many individuals desiring living arrangements that allow for intimacy as well as freedom for change.

Primary Relationships of Adulthood

Currently cohabitation is viewed more as a part of courtship rather than a replacement for the institution of marriage. While some cohabiters may choose nonmarital cohabitation as a permanent lifestyle, Macklin (1978) has predicted that the role of cohabitation will not change significantly in the United States because of the strong societal sanctions and interest in marriage. However, the percentage of couples engaging in cohabitation prior to marriage could increase dramatically as it has done in Sweden. Currently, approximately 99 percent of all Swedes who marry have cohabitated premaritally (Trost, 1977).

Comparisons of cohabitaters and noncohabitaters. Researchers comparing cohabitating students with those without a cohabitation experience have found more similarities than differences. Contrary to popular opinion, students who cohabit are *not* more likely to come from unhappy or divorced homes, do not have lower academic averages, and are not significantly less likely to want to marry eventually. They do appear to hold more liberal attitudes, have more friends who have cohabitated, have lower rates of church attendance, and perceive themselves as being more liberated from traditional sex roles than noncohabitants. Macklin (1976) views cohabitation as more of a result of opportunity rather than being linked to a specific set of demographic characteristics. However, she does add that cohabiters will likely possess personal and religious values that are compatible with this lifestyle as well as sufficient interpersonal skills to initiate such a relationship.

Although engaging in a nontraditional relationship, cohabitating couples show strong similarities to married couples regarding division of labor and sexual activity. Cohabitating couples were found no more egalitarian in their relationships than married couples (Bower, 1975; Stafford, Backman & di Bona, 1977). Despite their expression of liberal attitudes, division of labor between cohabitating pairs appears consistent with traditional sex-role norms. Also, Montgomery (1973) found that most cohabitating couples voluntarily restricted their sexual activity as evidence of their commitment to the relationship even though they believed in sexual freedom. Little is known about how societal discrimination and parental disapproval affect the nature of the cohabitating relationship. However, few differences in overall satisfaction have been found between married and cohabitating couples (Budd, 1976; Stevens, 1975).

Findings from studies on commitment suggest that commitment between engaged pairs may be based more upon qualitative measures, such as length of the relationship, whereas degree of commitment for cohabitating couples may depend more upon the quality of the relationship. Perhaps engaged couples tend to believe "things will be different after we are married and living together" while couples already living together have a more realistic basis by which to assess their potential success as a married couple. Overall, unmarried cohabitants as a group tend to show as much commitment to their relationships as do engaged couples but are less attached to the concept of marriage (Lewis, Spanier, Storm & Lettecka, 1975).

Legal right of cohabitaters. With an increase in cohabitation, the legal rights of individuals involved in cohabitating relationships has become a matter of concern. Because cohabitation is not recognized as an "official" status, these relationships offer little legal protection. In fact, as late as July 1976 cohabitation was considered a crime (although rarely enforced) in 20 states (Lavori, 1976). While laws exist to determine distribution of property following the dissolution of a marriage, unmarried couples terminating a relationship have to rely on judicial decisions if there is a dispute over property or a violation of a personal agreement. Job and housing discrimination constitutes an additional area of concern for cohabitating couples. Macklin (1978) has asserted that "legal statutes and practices need to be adapted to reflect the changing societal realities."

Singlehood

In speaking of the cultural imperative to marry in most societies, Stein (1981) poses the following questions to the reader: Are you expected to marry? If so, what are your earliest recollections of messages about marriage? Who conveyed the messages to you and how were they conveyed? Why do you think you are expected to marry?

Unfortunately in our society, persons who have chosen to remain single have been subjected to a variety of negative labels, a familiar one of which is "old maid." Being single has implied being less socially desirable and incomplete as a person. Recently, traditional stereotypes of singles have been replaced by more contemporary, but equally damaging, terms. Single persons, especially young ones, are typically portrayed in the media as "swingers." The exploitation of this image has resulted in a $40-million-a-year industry which includes singles bars, singles resorts and singles housing complexes (Jacoby, 1974). According to Peter Stein (1978), "single" is a word used to categorize an extremely diverse group of individuals whose common characteristic is simply that they are not married. An examination of the typology of singlehood in Table 2–1 reveals the variety of reasons why a person may not currently be in a marital relationship. Some individuals are in temporary states of singleness, while others may have made the conscious choice of an alternative lifestyle. In total, never-married persons represent 29 percent of the male and 22 percent of the female population over 15 in the United

Table 2–1. Typology of Singlehood.

	Voluntary	Involuntary
Temporary	Younger never-marrieds postponing marriage for a few years	The divorced, widowed, and deserted seeking re-marriage
	Recently divorced persons who are "single again" but seeking mates	Single parents seeking mates
	Never-marrieds who were not interested in marriage for a number of years but are now actively seeking a mate	Younger never-marrieds actively seeking mates
	Cohabitators who now want to marry	
Stable	Men and women choosing to be single	Older widowed, divorced, and never-marrieds who wanted to marry or re-marry, have not found a mate, and have accepted the idea of singlehood as a probable life state
	Single parents not seeking spouses	
	Religionaries	
	Cohabitators not intending to marry	Never-marrieds who are impaired physically or mentally in some way and not able to succeed in the marriage market
	Formerly marrieds not seeking to remarry	

Source: P. J. Stein, "The Lifestyle and Life Chances of the Never-married," *Marriage and Family Review*, 1978, *1*, 1—11.

States; however, these percentages decrease to 5.9 and 5.1, respectively, for the 40 and above age group (U.S. Bureau of the Census, 1981a).

The pushes and pulls of marriage and singlehood. Stein (1978) has discussed the complex factors that enter into the decision to remain single, to marry or to become single at some point after marriage. He presents these factors in terms of "pushes" (negative factors in a situation) and "pulls" (attractions to a potential situation). In his research, he found that the strength of various pushes and pulls are affected by several factors such as age, sexual identification, extent of involvement with parents and family, availability of friends and peers, and perception of choice.

For some persons, a push to early marriage will result from societal and parental pressures. Other individuals may be attracted to early marriage because of emotional attachment to another person and the security marriage offers. Later in their lives, these persons may be pulled toward a single lifestyle because of the freedom it affords for career development and social autonomy, or they may be pushed away from marriage into single status because of an unsatisfactory marital relationship and perceived obstacles to personal development.

Individuals who have remained single during young adulthood may perceive the pulls and pushes of singlehood and marriage differently as they age. Darling (1976) found that late marriages of bachelors were associated with major turning points in their careers including promotions, career changes and geographical moves. Darling concluded that these men felt particularly vulnerable at these times and turned to marital relationships for emotional support. With age individuals may also become more aware of and affected by social and institutional policies that favor married persons.

Box 2.2

Comments From Adults Who Have Not Married

I have some married friends who have been coupled almost since they left their parents' homes. And they say they wish they could have their own space to do what they want without compromise. They wish they could buy things without having to justify them. They feel that their husbands and their children come first. My self-indulgence is very appealing to them. I mean, I only have me to take care of. They eat their hearts out looking at my life, especially when they have an aggravation at home. They drop in at my house and it looks wonderful to them.

They really have an unreal view of my life. They don't realize that I have to do it all. I have to take the garbage out *every* time. I have to wash the sink *every* time. I have to change *every* lightbulb, I have to pay *every* bill, I have to pick up *every* single thing that I mess up. I have to do every dish. I clean the refrigerator every time. I do it all. I hate doing it all. My married friends see my life as the ultimate freedom. And it is. But it's also the ultimate responsibility, and they forget that part.

Sara C., age 31

When I was younger I had a chance to look at the lives of my friends who had gotten married. It wasn't a life style that I envied. They all had babies within the first year or two. I will admit that I was never terribly attracted to the idea of having a lot of little kids in diapers. I was never very patient with kids and I could sense I wouldn't have been a very good mother of small children. And then, too, they were struggling financially for the most part and living in cramped quarters. So I didn't see things that made me want to get married.

Lynn H., age 45

It may be the way I was brought up or society. Who the hell knows? But I've always had the feeling that I am going to get married and live happily ever after. I think it's a fantasy that most other single people still believe—that we're going to meet that right person.

Tom E., age 30

It's an incredible feeling of self-indulgence, of liberty, of freedom to move, of being able to do what I want. I make the decisions. I can fit everything I own into my car. I can say goodbye to a job and take off for some new life. The possibilities that that presents to my mind are overwhelming. That awes me. Sometimes I become totally amazed by the incredible potential.

George P., age 25

I know there are problems in being married but they don't frighten me. The kinds of problems I have right now are not very real. Going out with women, getting a date, sleeping with somebody. It's all so transitory. After you do that, what have you got anyway? When you have a permanent relationship you have something that's really worth working for. Like if you have kids you're dealing with how their lives will come out. That's a very important thing. I'm not doing anything important right now.

I always thought I'd get married, but now that I'm not I wonder what people think about me. Here I am, 34 and not married. Will they feel sorry for me? I don't feel sorry for myself. I'm not talking about people who know me because my friends know that not being married is part of the way I live, part of my ideology. But people who look at my résumé or something. They just see the statistics of my life. And they'll think, "Oh God, poor guy. He's not married. Wonder what's wrong with him."

Jesse F., age 34

Raised as a Catholic, I had a very difficult time relating to sex. Raised as a snob, I had a difficult time accepting anyone who was not "good enough." Constant moves during my teens and college made long-term relationships difficult to establish. I did have a number of proposals but turned them down because I probably never really wanted to get married. It was never a conscious choice. It just happened.

Ruth G., age 45

Source: Bradley et al., *Single: Living Your Own Way* (Reading, Mass.: Addison-Wesley, 1977).

A small but growing number of individuals are choosing singlehood on a permanent basis. Stein (1978) notes that the increasing divorce rate has made many question the appeal of marriage and family life. While a single lifestyle is apparently more accepted than in the past, Adams (1976) emphasizes that singles must learn to cope with the prevalent societal view of singlehood as a pathological state. Although Adams writes about the advantages of being single, she indicates that in order to make singleness a viable lifestyle one needs economic independence, social and psychological autonomy, and a clear intent to remain single by preference.

Persons who desire marriage but are single because they have been unable to find a suitable marriage partner or because they lack the interpersonal skills necessary to attract a mate comprise another significant group of singles. For whatever reasons, these individuals are single involuntarily and oftentimes engage in activities (cruises for singles) or join organizations (Lonely Hearts Clubs) that will increase the possibility of meeting a potential spouse. Schwartz (1976) has found that in some cases these experiences can result in a decline of self-esteem and reinforcement of a negative self-image.

And what about the small percentage of older persons (approximately 4 percent of men and 6 percent of women) living today who have remained single all of their lives? Being single was reported by Gubrium (1975) as an advantage in old age because it avoids the negative effects of bereavement following the death of a spouse. Summarizing the small amount of information available on the elderly never-married, Gubrium stated that these individuals tend to be lifelong isolates and did not appear to be especially lonely during late adulthood. In fact, their evaluation of everyday life was similar to the married elderly, and both evaluations were more positive than those of divorced or widowed aged persons.

The book *Single: Living Your Own Way* (Bradley, Berman, Suid & Suid, 1977) provides insight into the experience of being single in a couple-oriented society. Containing case studies of a wide array of individuals currently living single lifestyles, this book discusses common problems and advantages associated with singlehood and suggests resources that facilitate living as a nonmarried person.

Sex differences. The experience of singlehood appears to be quite different for men and women. Campbell (1975) has observed that "single women of all ages are happier and more satisfied with their lives than single men." Reviewing mental health studies, Gove (1972) found that never-married men have significantly more mental health problems than single women. Other characteristics of single men and women vary considerably. In general, men who remain unmarried have lower incomes, less education and jobs with lower status than married men. Conversely, unmarried women are higher achievers than married women (Bernard, 1972). In 1970, one in every five women around the age of forty with graduate-school education or an income of $20,000 or more was single compared to only one in every 20 women with no college education (Glick, 1975). Obviously assessment of the singlehood experience for males and females is complicated by initial differences between the samples.

Stein (1978) has suggested that a significant factor contributing to the higher rates of mental illness among single men is the absence of adequate support networks. Knupfer, Clark and Room (1966) found that older single men in their study had fewer friends and were more isolated than older women. However, more recent research indicates a shift in the direction of greater participation of older single men in friendship networks and social organizations (Farrel, 1974; Pleck, 1975; Pleck & Sawyer, 1974).

Homosexual Couples

While homosexuality is no longer considered a mental illness by most psychologists and psychiatrists, homosexual couples are still subjected to strong social pressures to give up their lifestyles and conform to heterosexual norms. Despite continued discrimination in employment and other areas, homosexuality is becoming more visible.

Very few gay couples have had homosexual parents to model a gay love relationship for them. In addition, marriage manuals and positive models in television and film have not been available for gay couples and, therefore, they have had to "wing it when it comes to pulling together workable love and life partnerships" (Berzon, 1979). Acknowledging the difficulties in establishing and maintaining all intimate relationships, Berzon (1979) has stressed that same-sex coupling presents a special challenge in the absence of sanctions and supports from societal institutions.

However, Toder (1979) thinks that having few models for lesbian relationships may be an advantage. By not being confined by traditional models, lesbian couples can be free to create more positive relationships. The following quote explains Toder's view:

> The fact that we are in a same-sex relationship means that the predetermination of roles by gender, so destructive a force in heterosexual relationships, is not relevant to our lives. Each member of the same-sex couple is free to act from individual interests, predilections, and skills, rather than having to choose between conforming and rebelling against the cultural norm. . . . In many ways we have an easier time of creating a truly egalitarian, mutual and mature relationship.

It is difficult to obtain samples of older gay individuals because most do not identify with gay organizations and many have never openly acknowledged their homosexuality. Therefore, a paucity of research exists on the characteristics and lifestyles of aging homosexual men and women. Kimmel (1979) points out that if the estimates of homosexuality in the adult population apply to persons over the age of 65, the percentage of elderly homosexuals is twice as high as the percentage of older people living in nursing homes (which is around five percent).

In a report of their preliminary findings on the adaptations of homosexual men and women 60 years of age and older, Minnigerode and Adelman (1978) found that gays of both sexes reported that gaining self-acceptance and self-esteem had been a major struggle in their lives. Numerous gay relationships have lasted for years but have never been publicly acknowledged. Martin and Lyon (1979) quote a letter received from a couple in Utah:

> We are in our fifties, have been together for eighteen years, but have never declared our love for each other in front of a third party. When we shut our door at night we shut the world out . . .

This self-imposed secrecy about one's lifestyle can interfere with the physical and emotional support that is important during the later years of life.

Martin and Lyon (1979) have discussed the pain gay individuals experience with the break-up of a relationship or upon the death of a partner. If couples have not been open about their love relationship, friends and relatives will be unable to understand the grief reaction when the relationship is terminated and can offer little support. Even if the couple has acknowledged the nature of their relationship, often relatives will refuse to accept it. Lack of respect and acceptance of the relationship is demonstrated when relatives distribute a gay individual's belongings upon death without concern for the partner's wishes or the sentimental value of the possessions. Lack of property rights is one of many examples of the economic disadvantages of gay relationships. Rogers (1979) has identified several prerogatives of heterosexual couples denied to gays, such as filing joint income tax returns, and receiving certain disability, unemployment, social security and pension benefits.

In addition to legal restrictions on the rights of gay couples, the more subtle signs of nonrecognition and nonacceptance can be even more disturbing to a person involved in a gay relationship. For example, if a person is hospitalized and in intensive care, hospital rules instantly limit visitation to the immediate family. Because these relationships are not recognized and legitimized by society, gay individuals will be denied access for the support and care of their partners during this particularly vulnerable time.

Parent-Child Relationships

The decision of whether or not to parent is usually made during young adulthood. This decision has a permanent, irreversible effect on the lives of adults.

Desire for Children

Desire for children has been repeatedly shown to be an important factor in mate selection for both males and females (Goldsen, Rosenberg, Williams & Suchman, 1969; Hill, 1945; Hudson & Henze, 1969; McGinnis, 1958). In the Cornell Value Study conducted by Rockford and Ford in 1945, the most important requirement the Cornell student had for a future mate, next to love, was an interest in having a family. Studies in the 1950s and 1960s continued to find a strong commitment to parenthood.

The majority of women in a Stolka and Barnett study (1969) felt it was a woman's main responsibility in life and her social duty to have children, leading the investigators to hypothesize that changing the emphasis on the woman's role in society could result in an increase in the percentage of women who remain childless by choice and reduce the incidence of women having three or more children. The 1970s have witnessed a proliferation of women's consciousness raising groups, support groups for nonparents, and other social and political groups with the aim of increasing women's awareness of their options. What impact have these social forces had on the desire for children? Studies conducted during the 1970s provide some light on this question. These studies have found a decrease in the number of children desired when compared to earlier studies, yet over three-fourths of the samples indicated parenthood as part of their future plans (Cook, West & Hamner, 1982; Williamson, Putnam & Wurthmann, 1976). Assessing changes in sex-role perceptions among college women between 1969 and 1973, Praelius (1974) found that while the 1973 sample was less likely than the 1969 group to view motherhood as the most important role for a woman, few respondents were willing to sacrifice marriage and motherhood for occupational success. These students continued to perceive parenthood as an integral part of their lives even when showing other signs of sex-role change. While a strong desire to become parents is still prevalent among young people in American society, recent studies show some changes in attitudes toward childbearing. Blake (1974) reported that from 1961 to 1971 the proportion of college women preferring childlessness increased from 1% to 9%. In comparing responses from female students attending a large southern university in 1972 and 1979, Cook et al. (1982) found that women in the latter half of the decade were more willing to consider nonparenting as an option than they were in 1972. Nearly one-fifth of the 1979 sample expressed no desire for children. In both groups, however, the majority of students preferred two or three children. These data are presented in Table 2-2.

Hoffman and Hoffman (1973) suggest nine basic values related to having children. This set of values, presented in Table 2-3, was derived

Table 2–2. Number of Children Desired: Comparison of 1972 and 1979 Samples.

| | *Desired Number of Children* | | | | |
Groups	**None**	**One**	**Two**	**Three**	**Four or more**
1972 Sample (N = 368)	8.0%	5.0%	42.0%	31.0%	14.0%
1979 Sample (N = 356)	19.0%	3.0%	36.0%	24.0%	18.0%

Source: A. S. Cook, J. B. West, and T. J. Hamner, "Changes in Attitudes Toward Parenting Among College Women: 1972 and 1979 Samples," *Family Relations,* 1982, *31,* 109—113.

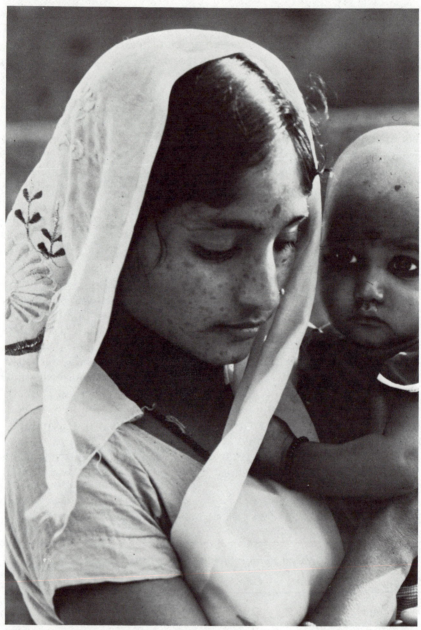

Considerable cultural variation exists in values pertaining to parenting. In less developed countries of the world in which the population is primarily rural, large numbers of children are often necessary for the economic survival of the family. (Alicia Cook, Photographer)

Table 2–3. Values Related to Childbearing.

1. **Adult Status and Social Identity**—parenthood contributes to definition of self and confers adult status

2. **Expansion of the Self**—continuance of family name (which places emphasis on having male children); way of reproducing oneself, having one's characteristics reflected in another who will live longer thus attaining a kind of immortality; having and rearing children evokes new and untapped dimensions of personality; expands self-concept to include parental role in context of family and larger society

3. **Morality**—religious views which view children as "a sign of God's blessing;" individual altruism related to sacrifices required by parenthood; group altruism whereby one chooses to have children to perpetuate one's identification group (ethnic, religious, etc.) or chooses not to have children because of concern for overpopulation; norms regarding sexuality and virtue which reflect the view that "motherhood" and "good women" are synonymous and that women who have children are more virtuous and less sexually impulsive; negative stereotypes associated with adults who chose not to have children

4. **Primary Group Ties, Affiliation**—establishment of primary group to offer companionship and source of affection and to protect against loneliness and isolation; belief that children contribute to marital stability and strengthen the bond between husband and wife (empirical data does not support this assumption)

5. **Stimulation, Novelty, and Fun**—children valued for elements of spontaneity, excitement and pleasure they add to a family

6. **Creativity, Accomplishment, Competence**—physically producing and rearing a child can meet adult needs for creative achievements and feelings of competence

7. **Power, Influence, Efficacy**—illustrated by the control of material and emotional needs of the child as well as the opportunity to guide, teach, control, and have tremendous influence over another human being; motherhood provides women with official status within family group

8. **Social Comparison, Competition**—having children as a symbol of potency and to prove femininity/masculinity; children valued for their achievement potential

9. **Economic Utility**—children viewed as economically useful in terms of government benefits, work performed, and old-age security which they provide for their parents

Based on: L. W. Hoffman and M. L. Hoffman, "The Value of Children to Parents," in J. T. Fawcett (Ed.), *Psychological Perspectives on Population* (New York: Basic Books, 1973).

from a comprehensive examination of empirical data and theoretical literature on the topic of childbearing. Hoffman and Hoffman emphasize that the strongest values for any individual or couple will be influenced by particular psychological needs and the social structure. In addition, considerable cultural variation exists in values pertaining to parenting. For example, economic utility of children is strongly associated with level of development within a country. In less developed countries with primarily rural populations, large numbers of children are often necessary for the economic survival of the family. Caldwell (1976) reported that children's value in Nigeria is primarily determined by the work and service they provide for their families. Increased industrialization and urbanization in the United States have resulted in an increase in the cost of raising children and in turn decreased the economic benefits. This trend has been observed by researchers in developing countries as well (Caldwell, 1967; Mueller, 1970; Rainwater, 1965; Siddiqui, 1967; Whelpton, Campbell & Patterson, 1966).

Fertility levels in the United States are at a historic low and have shown a continuous decline since the 1950s (Rindfuss & Sweet, 1975). Several family researchers have linked the decline in fertility to the development and availability of effective birth control technology (Westoff, 1978; Wrigley & Stokes, 1977). Wrigley and Stokes (1977) suggest that improved contraceptive methods offer women freedom to choose combinations of work, school, marriage and childbirth that are compatible with their view of the female role and their individual preferences. Other trends identified by Glick (1975) as contributing to the decline in birth rate are an increase in the number of women in college and the labor force, the influence of the women's movement, and an increase in singleness.

While Westoff (1978) suggests that a subsidization of reproduction may be necessary if fertility rates continue to decline, the current evidence on attitudes toward future parenting does not provide a basis for concern over replacement fertility. Family demographer Paul Glick (1977) does indicate, however, that women entering marriage in the 1970s compared to those married during the first decade of the century are expected to have between one to two fewer children, to end childbearing three years earlier, and to have eleven more years of married life after the last child leaves home.

The One-Child Family

A significant number of adults, approximately 10%, choose to have only one child (General Social Science Survey, 1975). Stereotypes of only children and their parents have been well documented and most people are familiar with comments such as "It's not fair to the child to not have brothers and sisters" or "It takes at least *two* children to make a real family." Hawke and Knox (1977, 1978) point out that the findings from research on one-child families are in sharp contrast to commonly-held beliefs about only children and their parents. While the lifestyle of the one-child family is significantly different from that of the multi-child family, most members of one-child families view the differences in positive terms.

Advantages for parents include having more time for themselves and their spouses. As one parent in the Hawke and Knox (1978) study expressed it: "I can experience the joys and frustrations of being a parent without getting tied down to parenting responsibilities so that I haven't time to pursue my own interests." With each additional child, adjustment becomes more difficult (Rossi, 1972) and marital adjustment declines (Feldman, 1971; Knox & Wilson, 1978). While parents of only children report having more time, money and energy for their child, they often refer to the difficulty in determining between healthy attention and overindulgence. Other disadvantages cited were fear of the child dying and being left childless and having only one chance to succeed as a parent.

And how do the children fare? Ninety-eight percent of the 105 only children surveyed by Hawke and Knox (1978) believed that being an only child had its advantages such as more privacy, lack of comparison with siblings (even though some reported extra pressure from parents to succeed), and greater affluence. From elementary school to college, the performance of only children is equal to or superior to children with siblings (Lee & Stewart, 1957; Bayer, 1966), and from preschool to adulthood, only children demonstrate more self-reliance and self-confidence than their peers with siblings (Guilford & Worchester, 1930; Dyer, 1949; Rosenberg, 1965). Less is known about only children as adults but they appear to be at no disadvantage when the personal and professional aspects of their lives are examined (Cutts & Moseley, 1954).

Hawke and Knox (1978) stress consideration of the one-child family alternative by adults who are planning to have a second child *only* to satisfy grandparent's wishes, to attempt to have a child of the opposite sex than the first, or to conform to the two-child model portrayed as the ideal by the media.

Voluntary Childlessness

Almost all cultures historically have been characterized by pronatalistic attitudes and values. *Pronatalism* refers to a general cultural orientation that places a high value on procreation and parental roles (Veevers, 1979). Veevers (1979) has discussed the prevalence of this emphasis in Canada and the United States and the social policies in these countries encouraging fertility. Other authors have written of the strong cultural expectations regarding procreation. Russo (1976) labeled this moral imperative for women to bear children as the "motherhood mandate." Veevers (1973) has pointed out that the parenthood mystique includes the notion that having children is necessary for self-actualization in adults.

Because of strong societal dictates for childbearing, voluntary childlessness is usually viewed in negative terms among the general public (Griffith, 1973; Polit, 1978; Blake, 1979). Voluntarily childless couples consistently report disapproval by others, in varying degrees, of their decision not to parent (Ory, 1976; Cooper, Cumber & Hartner, 1978). Indeed, Polit (1973) found that voluntarily childless couples were perceived as less socially desirable, less well adjusted, less nurturant, less autonomous, and more socially distant than individuals of other fertility statuses. Voluntarily childless wives were perceived more negatively than were husbands who preferred a child-free lifestyle. Some variation was apparent in family size attitudes among the sample: younger respondents and those with higher education displayed more positive views toward voluntary childlessness when compared with older respondents and those of lower educational levels. The data from this study, however, clearly show that fertility decisions are factors by which social desirability and adjustment are judged. While evidence exists for more tolerance of nontraditional lifestyles in contemporary society, couples deciding not to have children must still contend with negative stereotypes associated with their decision.

In the United States in 1979, 13 percent of married women between the ages of 30 and 34 were childless (U.S. Bureau of the Census, 1981b). It is important to note, however, that census records do not differentiate between voluntary and involuntary childlessness. Veevers (1979) in his recent review of the literature on voluntary childlessness concluded that approximately 5 percent of all couples in the United States—one in twenty—make the decision in favor of life-long childlessness. Detailed studies of the incidence of childlessness confirm that it has increased since 1960, especially among young wives (De Jong & Sell, 1977; Poston & Gotard, 1977). During the 1960s alternatives to parenting became more visible (Veevers, 1979), evidenced by the increase of articles on voluntary childlessness in popular magazines. A review of the magazine articles written during this period reveal titles such as "A Vote Against Motherhood" (Greene, 1963) and "Motherhood: Who Needs It?" (Rollins, 1970). The National Organization for Nonparents (now the National Alliance for Optional Parenthood) was organized in 1972 to combat pronatalistic sentiment in the United States and to promote the right of individuals to chose a child-free lifestyle. This nonprofit organization stresses examination and clarification of values and motives for parenthood. During the 1970s, workshops on voluntary childlessness were conducted across the country and support groups for childless couples were formed (Russell, Hey, Thoem & Walz, 1978; Houseknecht, 1977).

Does Having and Raising a Child Fit the Lifestyle I Want?

1. What do I want out of life for myself? What do I think is important?
2. Could I handle a child and a job at the same time? Would I have time and energy for both?
3. Would I be ready to give up the freedom to do what I want to do, when I want to do it?
4. Would I be willing to cut back my social life and spend more time at home? Would I miss my free time and privacy?
5. Can I afford to support a child? Do I know how much it takes to raise a child?
6. Do I want to raise a child in the neighborhood where I live now? Would I be willing and able to move?
7. How would a child interfere with *my* growth and development?
8. Would a child change my educational plans? Do I have the energy to go to school and raise a child at the same time?
9. Am I willing to give a great part of my life—AT LEAST 18 YEARS—to being responsible for a child? And to spend a large portion of my life being concerned about my child's well being?

Source: "Am I Parent Material?" Pamphlet available from the National Alliance for Optional Parenthood, 2010 Massachusetts Avenue, NW, Washington D.C. 20036.

Although there have always been some individuals who have questioned and sometimes rejected the dominant norms of wanting and having children, voluntary childlessness by a sizable segment of the married population has become a viable alternative only since the availability of reliable birth control techniques. Family specialists generally agree that low fertility is here to stay and many predict an increase in voluntary childlessness. Grindstaff (1975) has estimated that by the year 2001, 20 percent of the married women in Canada between the age of

Primary Relationships of Adulthood

30–34 will be childless. As career and educational opportunities expand for women, an increasing number may indeed elect to forego the responsibility of children and thereby have more time and energy to devote to their work.

Veevers (1979) lists three major goals to consider in terms of social policy and parenting: (1) the development of a valid "parent test" which will provide guidance to individuals and couples when making the decision whether to parent or not, (2) creation of an atmosphere of choice in which parenting is an increasingly conscious decision and persons are not forced into parenting by social pressures, and (3) support of childlessness as an alternative lifestyle rather than merely being tolerant of persons who do not wish to parent.

The Experience of Parenting

During the first few months following marriage, most couples are temporarily childless. Only approximately 8 percent of women have a child before their first marriage and another 16 percent become parents before they have been married seven months. For the remainder of couples, childbearing typically occurs within the first few years following marriage. In the United States, the median interval from marriage to the birth of the first child is less than 20 months, and 90 percent of all first births occur within the first five years of marriage (U.S. Bureau of the Census, 1976).

Most young adults have unrealistic notions about what parenting entails and the time, energy and financial resources required to successfully raise a child in American society. Considering that parenting is a major role for most adults, it is ironic that in a country wherein education is so highly valued we fail to educate adults in one of the most important and challenging jobs they will encounter—raising children. As Sidney Callahan (1973) points out ". . . we must pass a test and show skill to receive a license to drive an automobile but nothing is required of future parents." Rogers (1979) has also commented on the neglect in teaching parenting skills and stresses that parents should continue to update and refine their parenting skills as their children grow up.

Changes in the ages of children do require changes in the parental role. As one parent expressed it: "I never realized that each age in development brings its own joys and rewards as well as challenges in parenting . . . as one hurdle is conquered there are always new ones on the horizon." The majority of literature on parent-child relations has focused on infancy and adolescence, giving the impression that these two stages are the most difficult for parents.

While several researchers have reported the birth of the first child

Entrance of the first child into a family requires considerable adjustment, but most parents indicate high levels of gratification from this experience. (Bob Harvey, Photographer)

as a major crisis (Dyer, 1963; Le Masters, 1957; Wainwright, 1966), more recent research has found considerably less difficulty for couples having their first child (Hobbs, 1965, 1968; Hobbs & Cole, 1976). Certainly the introduction of a third member, especially a dependent one, into a family requires some adjustment, but it is important to note that parents in general indicate a high level of gratification from this experience (Hobbs & Patterson, 1980; Russell, 1974).

As a child grows and develops, a major parenting task is to promote increasing independence on the part of the child. The dependence/ independence issue often becomes a source of conflict during adolescence. Adolescents are struggling for adult status yet they remain the legal responsibility of their parents. Many authors view adolescence as a tumultuous time and pinpoint this period of childrearing when referring to pressures created for parents by our rapidly changing society. Many of the contemporary issues facing adolescents were experienced very differently by the parents' generation, such as drugs, sexuality, and even the development of coping skills for the future (Campbell, 1969; Thornburg, 1977). Gould (1975) also notes that parents in their forties (which usually coincides with having adolescent children) begin to feel regrets for past mistakes they perceive in their parenting practices. When parents feel they have not measured up to their ideals, their feelings of adequacy can be negatively affected.

The final phase of parenting is usually the "empty-nest" stage after all the children have left home. However, an additional stage—the "refilled nest"—is becoming more prevalent as economic hardships result in a large number of mature children returning to their parental home to live after completing college. This situation can create new tensions as adult children accustomed to independent living return to a situation in which patterns of parental dominance have usually been established ("The American family: Bent but not broken," 1980).

Fathering. The traditional responsibility of fathers for the economic support of their families has limited the extent of interaction with their children. With the advent of the Industrial Revolution, work was removed from the context of the home and men were separated from their children during most of the day. Research on fathering conducted during the past decade suggests that there are considerable rewards for both the father and the child, as well as other members of the family, when the father invests more time in child care (Broderick, 1977). Indeed, many fathers have discovered the satisfaction of becoming more actively involved with childrearing. In a recent issue of *U.S. News & World Report* ("The American family: Bent but not broken," 1980), a feature article on the changing roles in American families included the following quote from a 42-year-old "househusband" who cares for his two-year-old twin daughters while his wife works:

> I'm at the point in life that labels don't mean much. . . . There's a lot to be said for doing what you enjoy most, regardless of what other people say. Most traditional fathers have no idea what I experience. There are daily triumphs and little victories that until recently only mothers had known.

While some males are beginning to more fully realize the pleasures of raising a child, many men still view child care primarily as a "feminine activity." However, research has shown that primary caretaker fathers can be extremely responsive to the needs of their infants, and that differences in responses to infants are based more on degree of familiarity with the infant than on the sex of the parent (Parke & O'Leary, 1975).

In view of the current research findings on fathering, it is necessary to reassess traditional beliefs regarding maternal and paternal differences and to offer more societal acceptance and support to males who opt to assume primary or shared responsibility for child care in their families. Robey (1975) notes that social institutions must also change to allow fathers to have more involvement with their children. The following section from an article appearing in the *Wall Street Journal* shows how Sweden's policies are changing to accommodate the demands of fathers:

> *Stockholm*—Jonny Bjarskog heats a jar of baby food on the gas stove, peels a banana and mashes it with a fork, squeezes three drops of vitamins into a spoon and starts to feed Lena, his wailing baby daughter.
>
> Thus, the blond-haired young Swede passes another morning at his newest job: being a father. Full-time. Paid.
>
> Jonny Bjarskog, who has just turned 30, is taking advantage of one of Sweden's newest responses to the push for sexual equality: paternity leave. And in many regards, what he is doing may well be the way of the future.
>
> Since last August, Jonny has stayed home with the baby, who was born last March 29. That enabled her mother, Jonny's girlfriend Karin Marcus with whom he has lived for almost four years, to return at the start of the fall school term to her job as a music teacher.
>
> Jonny gets the same benefits that Karin would get, were she staying home—including 90% of his salary, drawn from a state insurance program financed 85% from a social-security tax on employers and 15% from the national budget. His employer, a Swedish record distributor, is required by law to hold his job open until he returns, as he expects to do soon.

According to Sweden's Ministry for Social Affairs, about 10 to 12 per cent of eligible fathers—or approximately 6,000 a year—take paternity leave, and the average leave for a father lasts about 42 days. Introduced in 1974, paternity leave is only one part of this country's effort to involve fathers more actively in the rearing of their children. Other aspects of the program include allowing parents of preschoolers to work fewer hours per week with little reduction in pay and providing time off to care for sick children (Morgenthaler, 1979).

Aging parent and adult child relationships.   As children reach adulthood, parents begin to establish adult-adult relationships with them. Rhodes (1977) contends that parents and adult children who rediscover each other have a sense of continuity and wholeness. Unless this rediscovery process occurs, parents are likely to experience feelings of despair and loss. Rediscovery on the part of the parents entails accepting the ability and right of adult children to live their own lives without interference by parents. A task of adult children is to acknowledge and appreciate their parents as individuals.

As both parents and adult children age, they tend to maintain regular contact through visiting or by telephone and mail if they live at a distance from each other. Special family occasions such as holidays are usually celebrated together (Troll, 1975). In addition to frequent inter- action, parents and adult children typically develop mutually satisfying support networks. Older parents usually have low expectations in terms of receiving assistance, especially money, from their children. While only 7 percent of persons over 65 receive regular financial help from relatives, 12 percent of older parents give financial or other types of assistance to their children despite their own limited resources (Watson & Kivett, 1976). In fact, parents provide a wide variety of services for their adult children. Table 2–4 illustrates the types of services adult children say they receive from older parents or grandparents (Harris, 1975).

Physical decline that accompanies advanced age may result in par-

Table 2–4. Ways in Which Public 18 to 64 Say They Receive Help From Parents or Grandparents Over 65 (by Age) (Base: Have parents or grandparents over 65).

	Total Public %	Public 18–24 %	Public 25–39 %	Public 40–54 %	Public 55–64 %
Give you gifts	85	94	85	80	73
Give general advice on how to deal with some of life's problems	58	62	61	57	34
Help out when someone is ill	57	74	57	49	28
Take care of small children	42	53	46	35	16
Give advice on running a home	42	50	41	40	25
Give advice on bringing up children	40	45	40	39	23
Help out with money	35	52	34	24	20
Give advice on job or business matters	31	44	33	19	17
Shop or run errands	30	42	31	22	17
Fix things around your house or keep house for you	22	31	20	18	9
Take grandchildren, nieces or nephews into their home to live with them	21	25	23	15	10

Source: *The Myth and Reality of Aging in America*, 1975, a study prepared for The National Council on the Aging, Inc. (NCOA), Washington, D.C., by Louis Harris and Associates, Inc., p. 81.

ents having to be dependent on adult children. When this situation occurs, the adult children are typically in their middle years. However, in many instances the adult children are elderly themselves. Most adults maintain a strong desire to remain independent during their later years of life and express concern over becoming a burden to their children (Troll, 1971).

Single parents.   According to Porter (1978), the single-parent family is the fastest growing family form today. These families include 10 million children under the age of 18. In 1970, 12 percent of all children in the United States lived with one parent; by 1980, this figure had increased to approximately 20 percent (U.S. Bureau of the Census, 1981b). Single parenthood can result from divorce, separation, desertion, death of a spouse, or never having married. Over 85 percent of these parents are women, most of whom are legally divorced or separated. Prior to 1960, a father had to prove the mother "unfit" to care for the children or demonstrate the detrimental nature of the environment in which they were living in order to gain custody of his children (Schlesinger, 1966). Changes in the structure of the divorce laws have increased the number of single-parent families headed by males. Rogers (1979) predicts an even greater increase due to the greater societal emphasis on fathering, the increased number of men enjoying their experiences as fathers, and the equal-rights movement.

While single mothers and single fathers share similar concerns such as adequate day care, some unique problems and adjustments are present for each sex. The single mother usually experiences financial difficulty. In 1979, the median income of families headed by a woman was $9,927 compared with $21,503 for a two-parent family headed by a male (U.S. Bureau of the Census, 1981b). Many divorced women are unprepared in terms of education and training to support their children. In addition, women typically receive lower incomes than men in equivalent positions and often have less secure jobs (Brandwein, Brown & Fox, 1974). Fathers, on the other hand, must contend with the questioning of their ability to raise children alone as well as actual lack of experience in childrearing in some cases. Despite these difficulties, Mendes (1976) has found fathers to be competent single parents.

Single parents use various means to effectively cope with their situations. Many who can afford it hire housekeepers to care for their children. A small percentage join communes which have many of the economic and social advantages of an extended family (Brandwein, Brown & Fox, 1974). Porter (1978) in a presentation at the National Symposium on Building Family Strengths stated that lack of support is one of the most devastating aspects of becoming a single parent at midlife. In urban areas, organizations such as Parents Without Partners are often available and provide support, services and information to single parents. Many divorced parents eventually remarry thus ending some of the unique difficulties stemming from their single-parent status.

Grandparent-Grandchild Relationships

Although we often stereotype grandparents as being elderly, most individuals first become grandparents during midlife when they are highly involved in major life roles (Bornstein, 1980). Thus, most beginning grandparents are likely to be middle aged and employed. Because grandparenthood is associated with advanced age, having a grandchild is often considered a concrete symbol of "getting older." For persons overly concerned with their own aging, adjustment to this new role may be difficult because of the surplus meaning it carries.

The Perspective of the Grandparent

Claven (1978) has commented on the diversity in both the perception and practice of grandparenting in the United States. Indeed, Neugarten and Weinstein (1964) have found considerable variation in the way grandparents perceive this role. After studying middle-class grandmothers and grandfathers in their fifties and sixties, these investigators were able to identify five distinct styles of grandparenting which are described in Table 2–5.

The "formal," "surrogate parent", and "reservoir of family wisdom" roles are fairly traditional grandparenting roles. In this study, grandmothers were more often associated with the surrogate parent role than were grandfathers. "Reservoir of family wisdom" style was demonstrated by only a few of the respondents, the majority of which were grandfathers. In a highly industrialized society, the transmission of knowledge and skills from older family members to younger ones is not seen as an important function of grandfathers. The other two styles, "fun-seeking" and "distant figure," seem to be emerging as new and popular roles for grandparents. Next to the formal role these two styles were the most frequently selected, and Neugarten and Weinstein found them to be more common among younger grandparents (under 65) while the formal role was more frequent among older grandparents.

A second major study on styles of grandparenting was conducted by Robertson (1977); however, she only included grandmothers in her sample. Like Neugarten and Weinstein, she found about one-third of her sample to be remote with regard to grandparenting. Nevertheless, most grandmothers appeared happy with their roles and many re-

Table 2–5. A Typology of Grandparenting.

Style	Characteristics
Formal	Highly interested in grandchild; provides special treats and indulges child; may babysit, but leaves parenting to the parent
Fun-seeker	Informal, playful relationship; authority is irrelevant; expects mutually satisfying emotional relationship; sees grandparenting as leisure activity
Surrogate parent	Grandparent assumes actual care-taking responsibilities
Reservoir of family wisdom	Authoritarian grandparent provides special skills or resources; younger generations are in subordinate position
Distant figure	Contacts are infrequent; visits on holidays and special occasions; benevolent but remote

Based on: B. L. Neugarten and K. K. Weinstein, "The Changing American Grandparent," *Journal of Marriage and the Family,* 1964, 26, 199—204.

ported preferring grandmothering to mothering. In fact, almost all agreed that grandparenting is easier than parenting. The majority of grandparents in the Neugarten and Weinstein study also expressed pleasure and satisfaction in the role of grandparents, frequently mentioning such factors as feeling younger when spending time with their grandchildren ("biological renewal"), the importance of carrying on the family line ("biological continuity"), or being able to do things for their grandchildren they could not do for their own children ("emotional fulfillment"). A few grandparents reported pleasure in being able to provide for their grandchildren by giving of their time, money or experience ("resource person"). Also a small number suggested that the significance of the grandparent role for them lay in their grandchildren being able to achieve goals unattained or unavailable to preceding generations ("vicarious accomplishments").

The Perspective of the Grandchild

The findings of Kahana and Kahana (1970) suggest that the meaning of the grandparent role for the aging grandparent needs to be understood in the context of the changing needs of the developing grandchild. Few studies have examined the grandparent-grandchild relationship from the

The mother-daughter bond frequently brings the maternal grandmother into more involvement with grandchildren, often in the role of surrogate mother. (Don Shafer, photographer)

perspective of the grandchild. Kahana and Kahana found that children of different ages emphasize different aspects of this relationship. Views of grandparents are linked to the child's level of cognitive development: preschool children typically value grandparents for their indulgent qualities and use concrete physical characteristics to describe them, while school-age children tend to discuss their relationships with grandparents in terms of shared activities ("we play ball together"). During adolescence, an abstract interpersonal orientation emerges, but more distance from grandparents is usually shown by adolescents than by younger aged children. When describing interactions with their favorite grandparents, children in this study referred to styles of grandparenting that overlapped with those identified by Neugarten and Weinstein (1964).

In a study of 269 undergraduate females, Hoffman (1979) found that college-age grandchildren usually have more contact and feel closer to their maternal grandparents. Differences in proximity cannot explain the differences in interactions with maternal and paternal grandparents since older adults are equally likely to live close to their sons as they are their daughters (Adams, 1968). The closest grandparent-grandchild bond Hoffman found was with the maternal grandmother. The mother-daughter bond frequently brings the maternal grandmother into more involvement with the grandchildren, often in the role of mother surrogate. Gifford and Black (1972) found that even when grandchildren and grandparents do not see each other often because of geographical separation they are likely to feel close to each other if the parent-grandparent relationship is strong.

An Alternative Approach to Grandparenting

The geographical mobility of contemporary American society has resulted in many grandparents living at a considerable distance from their grandchildren. The organization of adoptive grandparent programs has been one innovative way of dealing with the realities of modern family life. Older persons who either have no grandchildren or who are physically separated from their relatives are adopted (in an informal sense) by younger families who desire grandparent figures in the lives of their children. As Clavan (1978) points out, older persons seeking an active family role do not necessarily need biological grandchildren. A recent newspaper article contained the story of a 78-year-old retired electrician who placed a "grandfather-for-adoption" ad in a South Dade County, Florida newspaper. A Miami divorcee with a nine-year-old daughter and a ten-year-old son contacted him and asked him to become an in-resident granddad. Three years later, the arrangement is still working. In addition to getting the children off to school, this adopted grandfather takes responsibility for a variety of household tasks. He says however that he considers the time he spends with the children to be the highlight of each day. This arrangement appears to be mutually beneficial: while providing an important and meaningful role for the older person, it has direct benefits for single parents who have limited time to spend with their children because of the necessity of full-time employment.

Great-Grandparenting: A Contemporary Family Role

Due to the increasing length of time between departure of the last child from the family and death, more individuals are having the experience of being a great-grandparent. A cross-national study conducted in 1962 found that a significant number of older individuals had great-grandchildren: 40 percent in the United States, 23 percent in Denmark, and 22 percent in Britain (Shanas, Townsend, Wedderburn, Friis, Mihoj & Stehouwer, 1968). As four-generation families became more common, the dynamics of family life will become more complex. According to

Kimmel (1980), it will result in more demands on time and energy as adults are called upon to care for their aging parents while at the same time maintaining their parent and grandparent roles. Intergenerational relationships will be an important focus for future research.

Adult Sibling Relationships

The relationship between a pair of siblings is usually the relationship of longest duration in the human life span; however, little has been written about this aspect of adult family life. Most of the research done on siblings has focused on the childhood years. Sibling relationships begin with the birth of the youngest member of the pair and ends with the death of one of the siblings. As siblings reach young adulthood, they typically move from their family of orientation into separate residences as they seek educational opportunities and careers or begin to establish families of their own. Because of this physical separation, contact becomes largely voluntary and continues to be so throughout the adult life span.

Sibling Interactions During Adulthood

It is not uncommon today for sibling relationships to span 80 to 90 years since the majority of adults have at least one sibling alive and geographically accessible up to the end of their lives (Circirelli, 1979). Adams (1964), in his study of sibling relationships of young and middle-aged adults, found that 88 percent of his sample had at least one living sibling with the average number of siblings being 3.9. About 29 percent had a sibling residing in the same city and 60 percent had a sibling within 100 miles of their homes. Studies among elderly have shown 85 percent (Shanas et al., 1963) to 93 percent (Clark & Anderson, 1967) having at least one living sibling; however, number of living siblings generally declines with age as one might expect. In a recent investigation, Circirelli (1979) found that elderly aged 60 to 69 had 2.88 living siblings, declining to 2.18 in the 70−79 age group, and being only 1.08 for older people over 80 years of age. Approximately 26 percent of the older adults in this study had at least one sibling residing in the same city while an additional 29 percent had a sibling living within 100 miles.

Research also shows that the majority of siblings continue to interact through the adult years; however, frequency of visiting is higher for persons living within 100 miles of their siblings (Adams, 1964). In a study of seven subsamples of Chicago elderly (Bild & Havighurst, 1976), 17 to 30 percent reported seeing their siblings at least weekly, and 31 to 43 percent contacted siblings by telephone weekly. Letter writing was another means by which the elderly siblings reported maintaining contact. Circirelli (1979) found only a few older people who had lost contact with any of their siblings.

The Nature of Adult Sibling Relationships

Despite individual differences, available evidence shows that siblings remain affectionately close to each other during adulthood. Sixty-five percent of the 300 elderly Circirelli (1979) studied said that they felt "close" or "extremely close" to the sibling with whom they had the most contact; only 5 percent reported no feeling of closeness. While both males and females in this study tended to name sisters and middle-born siblings as their closest sibling, Circirelli pointed out that this finding may reflect greater availability of sisters and middle-born children due to differential death rates rather than actual closeness. However, several other studies have supported the closeness of the sister-sister tie as compared to relationships between brothers or cross-sex pairs (Adams, 1968; Cumming & Schneider, 1961). In fact, Adams (1968) found that more than half of the sisters in his study indicated feeling closer in adulthood than they did when they were growing up. Brothers reported the most competitiveness, ambivalence and jealousy in their relationships particularly when a status difference existed. Interaction patterns established early in a sibling relationship can often extend into adulthood. For example, strong sibling rivalry evidenced during childhood can be observed in adult relationships. Troll (1975) suggests that rivalry may be expressed subtly by using the sibling as a yardstick for assessing one's own activities and achievements.

Intense Sibling Loyalties

In some adult sibling relationships, unusually strong bonds of attachment have been observed. Several studies have supported the notion that early parental inaccessibility can promote strong bonds among siblings. Early investigations by Levy (1937) and Sewall and Smalley (1930) found an inverse relationship between sibling rivalry and size of family. In large families, interaction with each child may be limited by constraints of time and energy thus detracting from the parent-child relationship and intensifying siblings' rapport with each other as they look for attention and emotional support. This view has been supported in interviews of siblings from large families (Bossard & Boll, 1956).

Extreme cases of sibling loyalty have been discussed by Bank and Kahn (1979). After studying groups of intensely loyal and caring siblings, they found that many of them had suffered parental loss and grown up under emotionally-trying conditions. These relationships were characterized by intense attachment, devotion and a commitment to "stick together" which developed in early childhood and persisted into middle age (the age of the oldest sibling studied). Among these adults having experienced abandonment or deficiency of care by a parent during childhood, the researchers identified several conditions necessary for the establishment of intensely close relationships between sibling pairs. First of all, all pairs studied by Bank and Kahn had at least one nurturing parent who provided an early example of caring for others. In addition, all of the sibling pairs had been reared together as children rather than being separated thus giving them access to one another, and none had been compared against each other by their natural parents thereby allowing the development of positive interactions. Bank and Kahn suggest that if other supportive adults are available (that is, aunts, uncles, grandparents), the sibling system becomes less influential.

In conclusion, it appears that in general siblings continue to be an important emotional support and influence on behavior during the adult years. The type and quality of these relationships and the frequency of interaction among siblings vary and will be affected by such factors as early experiences, residence patterns, history of interactions, and sex of siblings. More research is needed on changes in sibling relationships during the course of adulthood.

Adult Friendships

The topic of friendship was an important one for ancient thinkers. Homer spoke of it in the *Odyssey*, and Socrates often discussed the subject with his students. Throughout the centuries, numerous poems, essays and intellectual discourses have focused on the nature and merits of friendship. Francis Bacon expressed the view that without true friends "the world is but a wilderness." Indeed, one only has to examine the importance of friends in one's own life to appreciate this statement.

Levels of Friendship

Aristotle differentiated three types of friendships: (1) the first kind is the friendship of utility which centers on the exchange of material goods between friends. Friends in this relationship value each other for what benefits they receive from knowing and interacting with each other. The friends are cared for only as long as they are useful; (2) The friendship of pleasure constitutes a second form. These friendships arise out of the delight and enjoyment the individuals derive from each other's company. The persons are valued as long as they provide and share entertainment and fun. Both friendships of utility and friendships of pleasure are instrumental relationships and are easily dissolved as people's needs and interests change; (3) The highest form of friendship that Aristotle described is the association between persons who love each other primarily for what they are as individuals. These friendships will usually be both useful and pleasant, but the foundation of the relationship is based on a mutual respect of character. Such relationships are infrequent and require time and familiarity to develop (McKeon, 1941).

Patterns of Adult Friendship

Unfortunately, most studies on adult friendship do not specify the type of relationship being studied and often encompass a wide array of friendship levels. In fact, many studies do not distinguish between friends and neighbors. Actually there is some justification for this procedure since several studies of friendship have found physical proximity to be the best single predictor of bonding (Freedman, Carlsmith & Sears, 1974; Whyte, 1956). Neighborhoods tend to be homogeneous and similarity of attitudes promotes the development of friendships (Byrne, 1961).

Several differences in friendship patterns have been found between males and females. A number of studies suggest important differences between the sexes in sociability, intimacy, degree of self-disclosure, empathy, and affiliative styles—all of which play a role in friendship formation. Booth (1972) has noted that while adult males tend to have more friends than females, male friendships tend to be less close and affectionate than female friendships. Other studies have provided additional evidence of greater intimacy in female relationships (Adams, 1968; Troll, 1975). This sex difference has also been observed among adolescents (Douvan & Adelson, 1966). Pleck (1975) suggests that competitiveness and fear of homosexuality have hindered the development of close male friendships.

Lampe (1976) has commented on the lack of friendship between members of the opposite sex among married adults. He contends that it stems from the ideal of exclusivity in traditional marriages, the emphasis on sexual rather than individual traits in women, and the fear that opposite-sex relations may endanger the marriage itself. Lampe believes that having more opposite-sex friendships in adulthood can enrich adult life, promote interpersonal development, and strengthen marital bonds. By having emotional needs satisfied by a wide range of relationships, strain is reduced in marital relations and spouses no longer have to "be all things" for each other.

Adults in their thirties and forties usually have three or four friends to whom they feel very close. This number, however, tends to decrease as one grows older (Haan & Day, 1974). Death can account for the loss of some friendships during late adulthood. Also, it can be more difficult

The companionship of beloved pets can be an important source of emotional gratification for many individuals during their later years. (Priscilla Solomons Davis, photographer)

to develop new friendships or maintain old ones if community participation is restricted because of lack of transportation or poor health. However, a national survey found that 91 percent of persons 65 years of age and older had seen a close friend during the two weeks preceding the study (National Council on the Aging, 1976). A pronounced decline in visiting patterns among older friends is not apparent until advanced old age (Riley & Foner, 1968). Lowenthal and Haven (1968) have found that the presence of a stable, intimate relationship during the later years of life serves as a buffer against many significant losses associated with advancing age (for example, loss of role, spouse, and status) and combat depression. Life satisfaction of older adults appears to be closely connected to contact with friends (Arling, 1976).

Friendships of the Future

In his book *Future Shock*, Alvin Toffler (1970) predicts that friendship patterns of the future will be significantly different and provides the following quote by psychologist Courtney Tall:

> Stability based on close relationships with a few people will be ineffective due to high mobility, wide interest range, and varying capacity for adaptation and change found among the members of a highly automated society. . . . Individuals will develop the ability to form close 'buddy-type' relationships on the basis of common interests or subgroup affiliations, and easily leave these friendships, moving either to another location and joining a similar interest group or to another interest group within the same location. . . . Interests will change rapidly. . . . This ability to form and then to drop, or lower to the level of acquaintanceship, close relationships quickly, coupled with increased mobility, will result in any given individual forming many more friendships than is possible for most at the present. . . . Friendship patterns of the majority in the future will provide for many satisfactions, while substituting many close relationships of shorter durability for the few long-term friendships formed in the past.

While modern life may produce changes in the nature and structure of adult relationships, persons will continue to seek satisfactory avenues for the fulfillment of their need for intimacy.

Suggested Activities and Exercises

1. Who are the significant others in your life? Examine the level of trust and acceptance in your interpersonal relationships. How much do you reveal of yourself? What factors interfere with self-disclosure?
2. If you were to prepare a premarriage contract, what terms would you include? Would you be willing to compromise on any of your views? If so, which ones and under what conditions?
3. During a given week, identify examples of pronatalism which you encounter. How strong are the pressures to have children in your culture?
4. Given the five styles of grandparenting described by Neugarten and Weinstein, identify the interaction style you would prefer (a) as a grandchild and (b) as a grandparent. Do you predict that new patterns of grandparent-grandchild relationships will develop in the future? What factors might influence future grandparenting styles?

5. Consider your relationships with your own siblings. How close would you judge these relationships to be? Have they changed over the years? Would you (a) allow any of them to live with you in your present situation, (b) loan them money, or (c) give them advice on important life decisions? Would they approach you for assistance in any of the above areas? Discuss your responses with several other persons and explore the diversity in sibling interactions.
6. Interview at least three people in young, middle and late adulthood regarding their friendship patterns. Inquire about the following variables: nature and duration of the relationships, frequency of contact and activities shared. Are any developmental trends apparent from your interviews?

References

Adams, B. *Kinship in an urban setting.* Chicago: Markham, 1968.

Adams, M. *Single blessedness.* New York: Basic Books, 1976.

Arling, G. The elderly widow and her family, neighbors and friends. *Journal of Marriage and the Family,* 1976, *38,* 757–68.

Atchley, R. C. *The social forces in later life.* (2nd ed.) Belmont, Ca.: Wadsworth, 1977.

Bank, S., & Kahn, M. D. *Intense sibling loyalties.* Paper presented at the annual meeting of the American Psychological Association, New York, September 1979.

Bayer, A. E. Birth order and college attendance. *Journal of Marriage and the Family,* 1966, *23,* 484.

Berger, M. E. Trial marriage: Harnessing the trend constructively. *The Family Coordinator,* 1971, *20,* 38–43.

Bernard, J. *The future of marriage.* New York: World, 1972.

Berzon, B. Achieving success as a gay couple. In B. Berzon & R. Leighton (Eds.), *Positively gay.* Millbrae, Ca.: Celestial Arts, 1979.

Blake, J. Can we believe recent data on birth expectations in the United States? *Demography,* 1974, *11,* 25–44.

Blake, J. Is zero preferred? American attitudes toward childlessness in the 1970s. *Journal of Marriage and the Family,* 1979, *41,* 245–57.

Booth, A. Sex and social participation. *American Sociological Review,* 1972, *37,* 183–92.

Bornstein, R. Cognitive and psycho-social development in middle-scence. In C. Schuster & S. Ashburn (Eds.), *The process of human development: A holistic approach.* Boston: Little, Brown, 1980.

Bossard, J. H. S., & Boll, E. S. *The large family system.* Philadelphia: University of Pennsylvania Press, 1956.

Bower, D. W. *A description and analysis of a cohabitating sample in America.* Master's thesis, University of Arizona, 1975.

Bradley, B., Berman, J., Suid, M., & Suid, R. *Single: Living your own way.* Reading, Mass.: Addison-Wesley, 1977.

Brandwein, R. A., Brown, C. A., & Fox, E. M. Women and children last: The social situation of divorced mothers and their families. *Journal of Marriage and the Family,* 1974, *36,* 498–514.

Broderick, C. B. Fathers. *The Family Coordinator,* 1977, *26,* 269–75.

Budd, L. S. *Problems, disclosure, and commitment of cohabitating and married couples.* Doctoral dissertation, University of Minnesota, 1976.

Byrne, D. Interpersonal attraction and attitude similarity. *Journal of Abnormal and Social Psychology,* 1961, *62,* 713–15.

Caldwell, J. C. Fertility attitudes in three economically contrasting rural regions of Ghana. *Economic Development and Change,* 1967, *15,* 217–38.

Caldwell, J. C. Fertility and the household economy in Nigeria. *Journal of Comparative Family Studies,* 1976, *7,* 193–253.

Callahan, S. C. *Parenting: Principles and politics of parenthood.* Baltimore, Md.: Penguin Books, 1973.

Campbell, A. The American way of mating: Marriage is, children only maybe. *Psychology Today,* 1975, *8,* 37–42.

Campbell, E. Q. Adolescent socialization. In D. A. Goslin (Ed.), *Handbook of socialization theory and research.* Chicago: Rand McNally, 1969.

Christensen, H. T., & Gregg, C. F. Changing sex norms in America and Scandinavia. *Journal of Marriage and the Family,* 1970, *32,* 616–27.

Cicirelli, V. G. *Sibling influence throughout the life span.* Paper presented at the annual meeting of the American Psychological Association, New York, September 1979.

Clark, M., & Anderson, B. *Culture and aging.* Springfield, Ill.: C. C. Thomas, 1967.

Clavan, S. The impact of social class and social trends on the role of grandparents. *The Family Coordinator,* 1978, *27,* 351–57.

Cook, A. S., West, J. B., & Hammer, T. J. *Changes in attitudes toward parenting among college women: 1972 and 1979 samples. Family Relations,* 1982, *31,* 109–13.

Cooper, P. E., Cumber, B., & Hartner, R. Decision-making patterns and postdecision adjustment of child free husbands and wives. *Alternative Lifestyles,* 1978, *1,* 71–94.

Cormack, M. L. *She who rides a peacock.* New York: Praeger, 1960.

Cozby, P. C. Self-disclosure, reciprocity, and liking. *Sociometry,* 1972, *35,* 151–60.

Cuber, J. F., & Harroff, P. B. *The significant Americans: A study of sexual behavior among the affluent.* New York: Hawthorn Books, 1968.

Cumming, E., & Schneider, D. Sibling solidarity: A property of American kinship. *American Anthropologist*, 1961, *63*, 498–507.

Cutts, N. E., & Moseley, N. *The only child.* New York: Putnam, 1954.

Darling, J. *An interactionist interpretation of bachelorhood and late marriage: The process of entering into, remaining in, and leaving careers of singleness.* Doctoral dissertation, University of Connecticut, 1976.

DeJong, J. F., & Sell, R. R. Changes in childlessness in the United States: A demographic path analysis. *Population Studies*, 1977, *31*, 129–41.

Derlega, V. J., & Chaikin, A. L. *Sharing intimacy.* Englewood Cliffs, N.J.: Prentice-Hall, 1975.

Douvan, E., & Adelson, J. *The adolescent experience.* New York: Wiley, 1966.

Dyer, D. T. Are only children different? *Journal of Educational* Psychology, 1949, *36*, 297–302.

Dyer, E. D. Parenthood as crisis: A restudy. *Marriage and Family Living*, 1963, *25*, 196–201.

Elliott, N. *Sensuality in Scandinavia.* New York: Weybright & Talley, 1970.

Farrell, W. *The liberated man.* New York: Random House, 1974.

Feldman, H. The effects of children on the family. In A. Michel (Ed.), *Family issues of employed women in Europe and America.* Lieden, The Netherlands: Brill, 1971.

Freedman, J. L., Carlsmith, J. M., & Sears, D. D. *Social psychology.* Englewood Cliffs, N.J.: Prentice-Hall, 1974.

Gadlin, H. Private lives and public order: A critical view of the history of intimate relations in the United States. In A. Levinger & H. L. Ravsh (Eds.), *Close relationships.* Amherst: University of Massachusetts Press, 1977.

General Social Science Survey, July 1975. Conducted by the National Opinion Research Center, Chicago.

Gilford, R., & Black, D. *The grandchild-grandparent dyad: Ritual or relationship.* Paper presented at the meeting of the Gerontological Society, San Juan, 1972.

Glick, P. C. A demographer looks at American families. *Journal of Marriage and the Family*, 1975, *37*, 15–26.

Glick, P. C. *Some recent changes in American families.* In U.S. Bureau of the Census (Current Population Reports, Series P-23, No. 52). Washington, D.C.: U.S. Government Printing Office, 1975.

Glick, P. C. Updating the life cycle of the family. *Journal of Marriage and the Family*, 1977, *39*, 5–13.

Goldsen, R. K., Rosenberg, M., Williams, R. M., Jr., & Suchman, E. A. *What college students think.* Princeton, N.J.: Van Nostran, 1960.

Gould, R. Adult life stages: Growth toward self-tolerance. *Psychology Today*, 1975, *8*, 74–78.

Gove, W. R. The relationship between sex roles, marital status, and mental illness. *Social Forces*, 1972, *51*, 34–44.

Greene, G. A vote against motherhood. *The Saturday Evening Post*, January 26, 1963, 10–12.

Griffith, J. Social pressure on family size intentions. *Family Planning Perspectives*, 1973, *5*, 237–42.

Grindstaff, C. F. The baby bust: Changes in fertility patterns in Canada. *Canadian Studies in Population*, 1975, *2*, 15–22.

Gubrium, J. F. Being single in old age. *International Journal of Aging and Human Development*, 1975, *6*, 29–41.

Guilford, R. B. & Worchester, D. A. A comparative study of the only and non-only child. *Journal of Genetic Psychology*, 1930, *38*, 411–26.

Gupta, J. R. Love, arranged marriage, and the Indian social structure. *Journal of Comparative Family Studies*, 1976, *7*, 75–85.

Haan, N., & Day, D. A. Longitudinal study of change and sameness in personality development: Adolescence to later adulthood. *International Journal of Aging and Human Development*, 1974, *5*, 11–39.

Harris, L. and Associates. *The myth and reality of aging in America.* Washington, D.C.: The National Council on the Aging, 1975.

Hawke, S., & Knox, D. *One child by choice.* Englewood Cliffs, N.J.: Prentice-Hall, 1977.

Hawke, S., & Knox, D. The one-child family: A new lifestyle. *The Family Coordinator*, 1978, *27*, 215–19.

Hayes, M. P., & Stinnett, N. Life satisfaction of middle-aged husbands and wives. *Journal of Home Economics*, 1971, *63*, 669–74.

Hetherington, E. M., Cox, M., & Cox, R. Divorced fathers. *Psychology Today*, April 1977, 42–46.

Hill, R. Campus values in mate selection. *Journal of Home Economics*, 1945, *37*, 554–58.

Hobbs, D. F., Jr. Parenthood as crisis: A third study. *Journal of Marriage and the Family*, 1965, *27*, 367–72.

Hobbs, D. F., Jr. Transition to parenthood: A replication and an extension. *Journal of Marriage and the Family*, 1968, *30*, 413–17.

Hobbs, D. F., Jr., & Cole, S. P. Transition to parenthood: A decade replication. *Journal of Marriage and the Family*, 1976, *38*, 723–31.

Hobbs, D. F., Jr., & Patterson, S. B. Transition to parenthood: The "baby honeymoon" hypothesis. *Family Perspective*, 1980, *14*, 47–51.

Hoffman, E. Young adults' relations with their grandparents: An exploratory study. *International Journal of Aging and Human Development*, 1979, *10*, 299–309.

Hoffman, L. W., & Hoffman, M. L. The value of children to parents. In J. T. Fawcett (Ed.), *Psychological perspectives on population.* New York: Basic Books, 1973.

Houseknecht, S. H. Reference group support for voluntary childlessness:

Evidence for conformity. *Journal of Marriage and the Family*, 1977, *39*, 285–94.

Hudson, J. W., & Henze, F. L. Campus values in mate selection: A replication. *Journal of Marriage and the Family*, 1969, *31*, 772–75.

Jacoby, S. 40 million singles can't be all right. *The New York Times Magazine*, February 1974, *13*, 41–49.

Jourard, S. *The transparent self.* Princeton, N.J.: Van Nostrand, 1964.

Jourard, S., & Friedman, R. Experimenter-subject "distance" and self-disclosure. *Journal of Personality and Social Psychology*, 1970, *25*, 278–82.

Kahana, E., & Kahana, E. Grandparenthood from the perspective of the developing grandchild. *Developmental Psychology*, 1970, *3*, 98–105.

Kelly, J. R. Life styles and leisure choices. *The Family Coordinator*, 1975, *24*, 185–90.

Kimmel, D. C. Adjustments to aging among gay men. In B. Berzon & R. Leighton (Eds.), *Positively gay*. Millbrae, Ca.: Celestial Arts, 1979.

Kimmel, D. C. *Adulthood and aging.* (2nd ed.) New York: Wiley, 1980.

Knox, D., & Wilson, K. The differences between having one and two children. *The Family Coordinator*, 1978, *27*, 23–25.

Knupfer, G., Clark, W., & Room, R. The mental health of the unmarried. *American Journal of Psychiatry*, 1966, *122*, 841–51.

Koch, J., & Koch, J. Sex therapy: Caveat emptor. *Psychology Today*, 1976, *9*, 37.

Kurian, J. Marriage and adjustment in a traditional society: A case study of India. In M. A. Kanwar (Ed.), *The sociology of the family*. Hamden, Ct.: Linnett Books, 1971.

Kurian, J. Modern trends in mate selection and marriage with special reference to Kerala. In G. Kurian (Ed.), *The family in India: A regional view*. The Hague: Mouton, 1974.

Lampe, P. E. Adultery and anomie. *Human Behavior*, 1976, *5*, 14–15.

Lavori, N. *Living together, married or single: Your legal rights.* New York: Harper & Row, 1976.

Lee, J. P., & Stewart, A. H. Family or sibship position and scholastic ability. *Sociological Review*, 1957, *5*, 94.

LeMasters, E. E. Parenthood as crisis. *Marriage and Family Living*, 1957, *19*, 352–55.

Levinger, J. Reviewing the close relationship. In J. Levinger & H. L. Raush (Eds.), *Close relationships*. Amherst: University of Massachusetts Press, 1977.

Levy, D. M. Sibling rivalry. *American Orthopsychiatric Association Research Monographs*, No. 2, 1937.

Lewis, R. A., Spanier, J. B., Storm, V. L., & Lettecka, C. F. *Commitment in married and unmarried cohabitation*. Paper presented at annual meeting of the American Sociological Association, San Francisco, August 1975.

Lowenthal, M. F., & Haven, C. Interaction and adaptation: Intimacy as a critical variable. *American Sociological Review,* 1968, *33,* 20–30.

Luckey, E. B., & Nass, G. D. A comparison of sexual attitudes and behavior in an international sample. *Journal of Marriage and the Family,* 1969, *31,* 364–79.

Lyness, J. F., Lipetz, M. E., & Davis, K. E. Living together: An alternative to marriage. *Journal of Marriage and the Family,* 1972, *34,* 305–11.

McGinnis, R. Campus values in mate selection: A repeat study. *Social Forces,* 1958, *36,* 368–73.

McKeon, R. (Ed.). *The basic works of Aristotle.* New York: Random House, 1941.

Macklin, E. D. Heterosexual cohabitation among unmarried college students. *The Family Coordinator,* 1972, *21,* 463–72.

Macklin, E. D. Nonmarital heterosexual cohabitation. *Marriage and Family Review,* 1978, *1,* 1–12.

Macklin, E. D. Unmarried heterosexual cohabitation on the university campus. In J. P. Wiseman (Ed.), *The social psychology of sex.* New York: Harper & Row, 1976.

Martin, D., & Lyon, P. The older lesbian. In B. Berzon & R. Leighton (Eds.), *Positively gay.* Millbrae, Ca.: Celestial Arts, 1979.

Maslow, A. *The Farther reaches of human nature.* New York: Viking, 1971.

Mendes, H. A. Single fathers. *The Family Coordinator,* 1976, *25,* 439–44.

Minnigerode, F. A., & Adams, M. R. Elderly homosexual women and men: Report on a pilot study. *The Family Coordinator,* 1978, *27,* 451–56.

Montagu, A. Introduction. In A. Montagu (Ed.) *The practice of love.* Englewood Cliffs, N.J.: Prentice-Hall, 1975.

Montgomery, J. P. *Commitment and cohabitation cohesion.* Paper presented at the annual meeting of the National Council on Family Relations, Toronto, October, 1973.

Morgenthaler, E. Dads on duty. *The Wall Street Journal,* 1979.

Mousseau, J. The family, prison of love. *Psychology Today,* 1975, *9,* 52–4; 56–8.

Mueller, E. *Attitudes toward the economics of family size and their relation to fertility.* Unpublished manuscript, University of Michigan, 1970.

Murstein, B. *Love, sex, and marriage through the ages.* New York: Springer, 1974.

National Council on the Aging. *The myth and reality of aging in America.* Washington, D.C., 1976.

Neugarten, B. L., & Weinstein, K. K. The changing American grandparent. *Journal of Marriage and the Family*, 1964, *26*, 199–206.

Ory, M. J. The decision to parent or not: Normative and structural components. *Journal of Marriage and the Family*, 1978, *40*, 531–40.

Parke, R., & O'Leary, S. Father-mother-infant interaction in the newborn period: Some findings, some observations, some unresolved issues. In K. Riegal & J. Meacham (Eds.) *The developing individual in a changing world, Vol. II, Social and environmental issues*. The Hague: Mouton, 1975.

Pineo, P. C. Disenchantment in the later years of marriage. *Marriage and Family Living*, 1961, *23*, 3–11.

Pleck, J. H. Is brotherhood possible? In N. Glazer-Malbin (Ed.), *Old family—New family*. New York: Van Nostrand, 1975.

Pleck, J. H., & Sawyer, J. (Eds.) *Men and masculinity*. Englewood Cliffs, N.J.: Prentice-Hall, 1974.

Polit, D. F. Stereotypes relating to family size status. *Journal of Marriage and the Family*, 1978, *40*, 105–14.

Porter, B. R. *Single-parent families*. Paper presented at the National Symposium on Building Family Strengths, Lincoln, May 1978.

Poston, D. L., Jr., & Gotard, E. Trends in childlessness in the United States, 1910 to 1975. *Social Biology*, 1977, *24*, 212–44.

Praelius, A. P. Expected sex role attitudes, expectations, and strains among college women. *Journal of Marriage and the Family*, 1974, *37*, 146–54.

Rainwater, L. *Family design: Marital sexuality, family size, and contraception*. Chicago: Aldine, 1965.

Rao, V. V. P., & Rao, V. N. Arranged marriages: An assessment of the attitudes of the college students in India. *Journal of Comparative Family Studies*, 1976, *7*, 433–53.

Rapoport, R., & Rapoport, R. N. *Leisure and the family life cycle*. London: Routledge and Keagan Paul, 1975.

Rhodes, S. L. A developmental approach to the life cycle of the family. *Social Casework*, 1977, *58*, 301–11.

Riley, M., & Foner, A. *Aging and society. Vol. 1: An inventory of research findings*. New York: Russell Sage Foundation, 1968.

Rindfuss, R. R., & Sweet, J. A. Rural fertility trends and differentials. *Family Planning Perspectives*, 1975, *7*, 264–69.

Robertson, J. F. Grandmotherhood: A study of role conceptions. *Journal of Marriage and the Family*, 1977, *39*, 165–74.

Robey, P. A. Shared parenting: Perspectives from other nations. *School Review*, 1975, *83*, 415–31.

Rockwood, L. D., & Ford, M. E. N. *Youth, marriage and parenthood*. New York: Wiley, 1945.

Rodman, H. Illegitimacy in the Caribbean social structure: A reconsideration. *American Sociological Review*, 1966, *31*, 673–83.

Rogers, D. *The adult years.* Englewood Cliffs, N.J.: Prentice-Hall, 1979.

Rollin, B. Motherhood: Who needs it? *Look*, 1970, *34*, 11–17.

Rollins, B. C., & Cannon, K. L. Marital satisfaction over the life span: A reevaluation. *Journal of Marriage and the Family*, 1974, *36*, 271–83.

Rosenberg, M. *Society and the adolescent self-image.* Princeton, N.J.: Princeton University Press, 1965.

Ross, A. D. *The Hindu family in its urban setting.* Toronto: University of Toronto Press, 1961.

Rossi, A. S. Family development in a changing world. *American Journal of Psychiatry*, 1972, *128*, 106.

Russell, C. S. Transition to parenthood: Problems and gratifications. *Journal of Marriage & the Family*, 1974, *36*, 294 – 302.

Russell, M. G., Hey, R. N., Thoen, J. A., & Walz, T. The choice of childlessness: A workshop model. *The Family Coordinator*, 1978, *27*, 179–83.

Russo, N. F. The motherhood mandate. *Journal of Social Issues*, 1976, *32*, 143–53.

Schlesinger, B. The one parent family: An overview. *The Family Coordinator*, 1966, *15*, 133–38.

Schwartz, M. A. *Career strategies of the never married.* Paper presented at the annual meeting of the American Sociological Association, New York City, August 1976.

Sewall, N., & Smalley, R. Two studies in sibling rivalry. *Smith College Studies in Social Work*, 1930.

Shanas, E., Townsend, P., Wedderburn, D., Friis, H., Milhoj, P., & Stehouwer, J. *Older people in three industrial societies.* New York: Atherton, 1968.

Siddiqui, H. R. *Family, social engineering, and population programs: A study of physicians, government officials, lawyers and professors in Pakistan.* Doctoral dissertation, Cornell University, 1967.

Stafford, R., Blackman, E., & diBona, P. The division of labor among cohabitating and married couples. *Journal of Marriage and the Family*, 1977, *39*, 43–57.

Stein, P. J. (Ed.) *Single life: Unmarried adults in social context.* New York: St. Martin's Press, 1981.

Stein, P. J. The lifestyles and life chances of the never-married. *Marriage and Family Review*, 1978, *1*, 1–11.

Stephens, W. *The family in cross-cultural perspective.* New York: Holt, 1963.

Stevens, D. J. H. *Cohabitation without marriage.* Doctoral dissertation, University of Texas, 1975.

Stevens-Long, J. *Adult life.* Palo Alto, Ca.: Mayfield, 1979.

Stinnett, N., Carter, L. M., & Montgomery, J. E. Older persons' perceptions of their marriages. *Journal of Marriage and the Family,* 1972,
34, 665–70.

Stinnett, N., & Walters, J. *Relationships in marriage and the family.* New
York: Macmillan, 1977.

Stolka, S. M., & Barnett, L. D. Education and religion as factors in wom-
en's attitudes motivating childbearing. *Journal of Marriage and the
Family,* 1969, *31,* 740–50.

Tamashiro, R. J. Developmental stages in the conceptualization of marriage. *The Family Coordinator,* 1978, *27,* 237–44.

The American family: Bent but not broken. *U.S. News & World Report,*
June 16, 1980, 48–61.

Thornburg, H. D. *You and your adolescent.* Tuscon, Ar.: H.E.L.P. Books,
1977.

Toder, N. Lesbian couples: Special issues. In B. Berzon & R. Leighton
(Eds.), *Positively gay.* Millbrae, Ca.: Celestial Arts, 1979.

Toffler, A. *Future shock.* New York: Bantam, 1970.

Troll, L. E. *Early and middle adulthood.* Monterey, Ca.: Brooks/Cole, 1975.

Troll, L. E. The family life cycle: A decade review. *Journal of Marriage
and the Family,* 1971, *33,* 274.

Troll, L. E. Poor, dumb, and ugly. In L. E. Troll, J. Israel & K. Israel (Eds.),
*Looking ahead: A woman's guide to the problems and joys of growing
old.* Englewood Cliffs, N.J.: Prentice-Hall, 1977.

Trost, J. Dissolution of cohabitation and marriage. Unpublished manuscript, Uppsala University, 1977.

Tsoi-Hoshmand, L. Marital therapy and changing values. *The Family* Coordinator, 1976, *25,* 57–63.

Udry, J. *The social context of marriage.* Philadelphia: Lippincott, 1974.

U.S. Bureau of the Census. *Fertility history and prospects of American
women: June, 1975.* (Current Population Reports, Series P-20, No.
288). Washington, D.C.: U.S. Government Printing Office, 1976.

U.S. Bureau of the Census. *Marital status and living arrangements: March
1980.* (Current Population Reports, Series P-20, No. 365). Washington, D.C.: U.S. Government Printing Office, 1981. (a)

U.S. Bureau of the Census. *Population profile of the United States: 1980.*
(Current Population Reports, Series P-20, No. 363). Washington, D.C.:
U.S. Government Printing Office, 1981. (b)

Veevers, J. E. Voluntary childlessness: A review of issues and evidence.
Marriage and Family Review, 1979, *2,* 1–26.

Wainwright, W. H. Fatherhood as a precipitant of mental illness. *American Journal of Psychiatry,* 1966, *123,* 40–4.

Watson, J. A., & Kivett, V. R. Influences on the life satisfaction of older
fathers. *The Family Coordinator,* 1976, *25.* 482–88.

Weitzman, L. J. To love, honor, and obey? Traditional legal marriage and alternate family forms. *The Family Coordinator*, 1975, *24*, 531–48.

Westoff, C. F. Some speculations on the future of marriage and fertility. *Family Planning Perspectives*, 1978, *10*, 79–83.

Whelpton, P. K., Campbell, A. A., & Patterson, J. E. *Fertility and family planning in the United States*. Princeton, N.J.: Princeton University Press, 1966.

Whyte, W. H., Jr. *The organization man*. New York: Simon & Schuster, 1956.

Wilkinson, M. L. Romantic love and sexual expression. *The Family Coordinator*, 1978, *27*, 141–48.

Williamson, N. E., Putnam, S. L., & Wurthmann, H. R. *Future autobiographies: Expectations of marriage, children, and careers*. Honolulu: East-West Center, 1976.

Worthy, M., Gary, A., & Kahn, J. Self-disclosure as an exchange process. *Journal of Personality and Social Psychology*, 1969, *13*, 59–64.

Wrigley, A. P., & Stokes, C. S. Sex-role ideology, selected life plans, and family size preference: Further evidence. *Journal of Comparative Family Studies*, 1977, *7*, 391–400.

Chapter 3

Work, Retirement and Leisure

Let us stop equating work with earning a living, but rather think of it as an important component of making a life.

Ralph C. Weinrich

Bolles (1978) maintains that we tend to segment our lives into three sequential boxes: education, work and retirement. Individuals typically view these periods as isolated from each other. When they are in one stage, they give little thought or attention to the next stage until arriving at the threshold of transition. As a consequence, adequate preparation is typically lacking. In addition to stressing the need for preparation, Bolles advocates life-planning strategies that include learning, work and play throughout adulthood, rather than following the common segmented sequence. In this regard, Bolles uses the concept of balance; while we may be focused on one of the three boxes he describes, we must maintain a balance of activities related to continued growth and learning, effectiveness in a work role, and leisure-time pursuits.

In this chapter, various perspectives on work, retirement and leisure are presented. Decision making, adjustment, development and preparation are the primary themes integrating each topic. Current trends in work and retirement and the effects of these trends on the individual and family are also considered.

Career Decision Making

Work is central to the lives of most adults. A career consists of the occupations and jobs that one has had or will have in a specific field (Vogelsang, 1978). "What Color is Your Parachute?" (Bolles, 1975) is one of several popular books on the market lately in response to the increasing demand for more guidance in career decision making. Faced with a myriad of career options, young adults are often unsure of how to begin this process. Given that most adults spend a significant portion of their lives in occupationally-related activities, vocational choices greatly influence one's overall life satisfaction.

This process of selection becomes more difficult for each successive generation as the occupational structure continues to expand and diversify. The Dictionary of Occupational Titles lists an increasing number of new job titles and areas of specialty each time it is revised. Unfortunately, most people operate under the myth that one ideal job exists for them. Actually, many jobs are suited to a person with particular skills, interests and values. Attempting to identify the "one" is usually a rather fruitless endeavor. Individuals need to realistically examine their range of alternatives, keeping in mind what they want to do, what they can do, and what there is to be done (Shingleton, 1977).

Too often society attempts to force an initial career decision before the individual is ready. Very early in life individuals are presented with the question "What do you want to be when you grow up?" and one of the first questions asked during the first trip home after entering college is "What is your major?" or "What field have you chosen?" To avoid appearing indecisive, some individuals choose a career direction rather arbitrarily without giving sufficient thought to how it really suits them. Elder (1968) has said:

> Vocational choice and commitment might be premature if they are made without self-appraisals, experience, and learning gained from exploration and trial. In some cases, early formation of a vocational identity may precede the crystalization of other identities and thus require considerable adjustment in subsequent years (p. 108).

More opportunity needs to be created for career exploration in the early years of adulthood. For college students, Shingleton (1977) suggests learning about careers in three ways: (1) through media (professional publications from specialized fields, books on career development, periodicals containing descriptions of occupations with information on salaries, et cetera); (2) interviews with professionals in the field you are considering entering; and (3) work experience (such expe-

81

rience can be obtained through part-time or summer jobs, practicum and internship experiences, and work-study programs).

Part of choosing a career is clarifying who you are. In fact, Maslow (1973) viewed finding one's identity as almost synonymous with finding one's career. As he expressed it: "Part of learning who you are, part of being able to hear your inner voices, is discovering what it is that you want to do with your life" (p. 185).

Holland (1973) has proposed a classification scheme consisting of six categories that concurrently describe personality types and model working environments for these types. The six categories are as follows: investigative, artistic, social, enterprising, conventional and realistic. An individual who is intellectual, curious, analytical and rational would fit with a comparable work role (e.g., scientific work). On the other hand, if one tends to be more the artistic type (expressive, introspective, imaginative, original) he or she would do well in a setting in which these traits could find expression. Basically, different personality types require different working environments. Holland uses the term *congruence* to describe appropriate person-environment matches.

Unfortunately, incongruence is present in many situations. For some adults, this results from economic necessity—the individual takes the first available job or the one that meets family economic needs. It can also occur as a consequence of premature vocational choices made by individuals who have had limited perspectives on occupations and their own work-related interests and abilities. External societal and parental pressures to go into certain "status" professions can result in incongruity as well. It is also possible that an occupation that was congruent in early adulthood will cease to be so at middle age. Due to the developmental nature of adult life, a deepening and greater clarification of values, an expansion of interests and abilities, and a reawakening of previous aspirations can result in modification of an original career choice later on in life (Schlossberg, Troll & Leibowitz, 1978).

Box 3–1

For Status Seekers Only

An occupation that is considered prestigious in one society may be looked down upon in another. The status given to occupations is directly related to the value systems of a culture. When students in Czechoslovakia and the United States were asked to rate various occupations in terms of the esteem and honor associated with them, some interesting differences were obtained. The students from Czechoslovakia ranked masons, locomotive drivers, and cabinet makers higher than priests and judges, while the reverse was true for American students. Similar differences were found when they were asked to rank occupations on their utility to society. Young Czechs have obviously internalized the values of socialism with its emphasis on the worth of manual labor, while Americans continue to aspire to white-collar and professional positions. And what about physicians—how are they ranked? Number one in both countries. Apparently, the "I want my son to be a doctor" phenomenon is not a uniquely American invention.

Source: R. Penn, "Occupational Prestige Hierarchies," *Social Forces,* 1975, *54,* 352–64.

Mid-life Career Change

Sheehy (1977b) has described the period between 28 and 32 as a time when adults reappraise the decisions made in their early 20s. This reappraisal can result in a major change in one's present course or a deepening of commitments made in the past. Both paths emerge from more self-directed life goals.

Later on in middle age the reappraisals continue but become more focused on work as individuals move into Erikson's stage of *Generativity versus Stagnation.* Frustration and disappointment may be experienced if one has not attained previously established career goals (Brim, 1976; Levinson, et al., 1974). In the event of a disparity between one's earlier aspirations and what one has achieved, some individuals will simply readjust their career goals. For example, a 56-year-old man in middle management may come to grips with the fact that he will never be president of the company, but nonetheless feel satisfaction in what he has accomplished. Others will not be able to psychologically resolve the discrepancy between what they are and what they wanted to be.

This "time of truth" in middle age often includes asking oneself if the right decisions were made in early adulthood (Gould, 1972). This reassessment at times results in a redirection of one's life in the hopes of improving life satisfaction. Realizing that time is running out, middle-aged adults see the opportunities for achieving their major life goals as decreasing. For some, this process of redirection may be seen in a mid-life career change. In fact, growing numbers of individuals in mid-life are taking this step (Mills, 1970).

Career renegotiation does not only occur as a result of dissatisfaction with self or work. A number of other situations can prompt a start on a second career, including the following (Heddescheimer, 1976):

1. loss of a job due to dismissal
2. need for retraining because of job obsolescence
3. retirement at an early age (prevalent with military careers)
4. desire for more challenge, greater income or increased status
5. discovery of new interests.

For women, mid-life may be a time of starting a first career rather than a second. With the departure of the last child from the home or even before the youngest child enters school, an increasing number of women are pursuing delayed vocational aspirations. Divorce or widowhood may also precipitate entry into the work world, oftentimes of necessity (Heddescheimer, 1976). Unless employed earlier in life, entry into the work force will usually require job training or additional educational preparation. Even if the individual has worked previously, some retraining is usually necessary.

The process of changing careers in middle age appears to have several stages. Stage 1 begins with a struggle over the question of "What do I want to do with my life?" Stage 2 is an assessment of one's achievements and satisfactions. During Stage 3 the individual discusses the potential change with family, friends and work associates, and then in Stage 4 other career possibilities are investigated. The more time spent considering or planning for the career change, the greater chance one has of a positive outcome (Robbins & Harvey, 1977).

Career choice at mid-life is often even more difficult, and certainly more complex, than in early adulthood. Individuals know that this change will probably be their last; while they may change jobs again, their age will probably prevent another major career change. On the more positive side, the middle-aged are usually more in touch with their priorities and values in life, obtained through the introspection and soul-searching that comes with age. They are more likely to set realistic goals and avoid the illusions associated with inexperience. Also they have been in the work force for 15 years or longer and therefore probably have more information and insight about their own particular needs and preferences in a job and the realities of the work world. Sometimes when making a second career choice, the middle-aged build on previously acquired skills and knowledge. At other times they opt to start fresh in a new field.

Work and Education

Mid-life career change usually entails a need for additional technical or educational training. An undergraduate or advanced degree may be necessary for persons moving from skilled labor to a professional career, persons changing from one profession to another, and individuals training for an emerging field. For some, a college education will not necessarily be needed but will be a major life goal in itself.

The Returning Student

Middle-aged adults comprise a significant and growing segment of the student population in higher education. This trend began in the late 1960s and early 1970s. The number of women over the age of thirty who have enrolled in college has more than doubled in the past decade. The percentage of increases in college enrollments for female students from 1970 to 1974 was as follows: 27 percent for ages 20–21, 29 percent for ages 22–24, 108 percent for ages 25–29, and 95 percent for ages 30–34 (Tittle & Denker, 1977a, 1977b). By 1979, students over age 25 (both males and females) accounted for approximately 35 percent of student undergraduate enrollments in the United States (U.S. Bureau of the Census, 1981), and this percentage is expected to increase even more in the 1980's (Kasworm, 1980).

Mature students are different from the traditional-aged college student in several ways. Through the process of maturation, the older adult has become more self-directed and has more clearly defined goals for being in school. Therefore, they tend to look for immediate rather than postponed application of what they are learning. Typically, their goals are related to the developmental tasks appropriate to their age level and their family and work roles. Unlike younger students who are still dealing with the question of "Who am I?", older students have already established an identity and view education as a practical way to meet life goals or needs (Knowles, 1980). However, for some a return or first entry into college may represent a move toward a redefinition of self in terms of new roles and experiences (Astin, 1976). Because of their reservoir of personal and work experience, older students can be a tremendous asset in the college and university classroom. The instructor, however, must recognize the value of the life experiences these students bring to the learning process.

Because the characteristics of returning students are different from those of traditional college age, their needs also vary. Kasworm (1980) has charged undergraduate institutions with ignoring the needs of the adult learner and expecting returning students to adapt to an environment that is designed for full-time, residential students in the 18–22 age range. Other writers have urged institutions of higher education to reconsider their policies in view of the increasing number of older students they are serving. According to Cunningham (1973):

Work, Retirement and Leisure

If a college intends to provide education for the older student, it must build in flexibility and expect variations in the traditional approach to acquiring a degree. The older student cannot (and will not) completely fit into a system molded for an 18-year-old" (p. 10).

Some institutions are recognizing these needs and responding with the development of external degree programs and more flexible curricula and requirements (Astin, 1976), but recent research shows that the needs extend further.

Returning students frequently report apprehension about remembering how to effectively take notes, write papers, use the library and prepare for exams. A need for more vocational counseling is also commonly expressed by older students (Astin, 1976; Lance, Lourie & Mayo, 1979). Lance and his colleagues (1979) suggest the need for a reentry admissions counselor and a specialized credit course for reentry students as means of providing needed support. The need for child care is also often indicated by returning students, especially women (Lance, Lourie & Mayo, 1979; Smallwood, 1980). Smallwood (1980) thinks the issue of adequate child care should receive top priority among college student personnel professionals. In addition to child care, financial needs may be extremely great among recently divorced female students with children (Rice, 1978). Many of these individuals can only study part-time because of other responsibilities, and unfortunately institutional financial support is typically limited to full-time students.

Impact on individuals and families.   Most of the impact research in this area has focused on the older female student. Despite the obstacles, most women who have returned to school report favorable outcomes. Many report increased self-awareness and self-esteem. As one returning female student said, "I am not stupid. I lived with that image for 28 years. In the last three years that image has changed." They also appear to place high value on their newly acquired knowledge and skills (Astin, 1976). Ballmer and Cozby (1975) found that husbands saw their wives as better conversationalists and less dependent on them since their return to school, and children gained greater respect for the mother because of her student role. In addition to the positive effects so frequently reported by women, the return to school can trigger some uncomfortable feelings as well. Venturing out of the home for the first time to seek personal goals produces guilt in some women. Besides the time that they are devoting to their schooling, they may also feel guilty about spending money that could perhaps be used for their children's education (Astin, 1976; Hooper, 1979b). Weighing these costs with the gains can result in internal conflict and feelings of ambivalence.

The decision of a woman to return to school and in many cases to pursue a career impacts her family as well. In her study of returning female students, Astin (1976) found that the majority of husbands had positive feelings about their wives' activities. Positive effects mentioned included the wife's increased happiness and her increased earning potential. Only 10 percent of the husbands thought that the wife's return to school would put a strain on their marriage. More than half thought it would improve their relationship.

Fathers also felt the children benefited. While more household chores were assigned to the children than before the mother's return to school, fathers saw this as making them more independent and responsible. Even though the majority of children reported being able to spend less time with their mothers since they became students, very few expressed disapproval of their mother's expanded role (Astin, 1976).

Research has shown that most married women who are returning to school view verbal support and encouragement from their husbands as very important. In fact, Hooper and Rice (1978) have reported that spouse support is often a determining factor in the decision to return to school in the first place. Student wives, however, do not necessarily interpret lack of assistance with family and household responsibilities as being nonsupportive (Katz, 1976). This is surprising in view of evidence showing that lack of instrumental support is related to the probability of returning women students dropping out of school (Berkove, 1976). Also, these women themselves report that lack of time and role strain are among their greatest problems (Van Meter, 1976).

Consistent with previous findings, Hooper (1979a) found high levels of verbal support in her interviews with 24 husbands of returning female students. However when questioned about instrumental support, a different pattern emerged. A quarter of the husbands said that they shared the majority of household tasks with their wives. The other three-quarters of the sample maintained their roles in the family along traditional sex-role lines and did not assume any responsibility for housecleaning or child care. However, in six families this division of labor was by agreement whereas in the other 12 disagreement and conflict over responsibilities occurred. The latter group also reported the highest anxiety over the marital relationship. Hooper concluded that these families were engaged in on-going struggles related to roles and tasks. Sample comments from husbands in each of the three groups are presented in Table 3–1.

It is interesting to note that the majority of the men in Hooper's (1979a) sample did not view their wives' assumption of a new role as affecting their own family roles. In some cases, even the wives gave no indication that more tangible support should be provided. Others felt that this change automatically necessitated some role shifting within the family. Families are more likely to provide instrumental support if

Table 3–1. Sample Comments by Division of Labor Among Husbands of Returning Female Students (N = 24).

Egalitarian (N = 6)

"We have to do more around here. I do laundry, scrub floors, all the yard work she used to do. [Seventeen-year-old] vacuums, dusts, and does dishes. I suppose it's good for us to be more responsible. Anyway, she couldn't do it alone.

"You should see our chart! It took the kids and me three nights with felt pens to lay it out. It's working pretty well. I don't really enjoy it, but who does?"

Division of Labor by Agreement (N = 6)

"Nothing has particularly changed. She's scheduled her time so the kids and I aren't affected by her absence."

"Well she doesn't get her housework done the way she used to, but I'm proud of her—enjoy her more."

Division of Labor by Disagreement (N = 12)

"Of course she'll tell you how little I do around here. But my Lord, what does she expect? I can't leave patients sitting around the office while I wash the floor. She knew that when she got married. She knew it!"

"I take care of the garage, the car, the sidewalks, and the yard. I also work a 50 or 60 hour week most weeks. Where I'm supposed to find time to help her with her work is beyond me! I wish she'd have thought of all this before she went off to the university."

Source: J. O. Hooper, "My Wife, the Student," *The Family Coordinator*, 1979, 28, 459–64.

role assignments are somewhat nontraditional initially and if the husband agrees with the wife's decision to return to school (Parelman, 1974).

Hooper (1979a) has pointed out that "new research on men at midlife (see Brim, 1976) indicates that men such as those in the present study may be extremely vulnerable to major changes in the attitudes and behaviors of their wives" (p. 464). As the following statement from a 40-year-old man illustrates, role flexibility may be difficult for a husband who at middle age is near the peak of responsibility in his job:

> Her timing is all off. I just got promoted, I'm near the top in my company. I can't just suddenly take time off from my career to start sharing housework. The time is just not right for me (Hooper, 1979a, p. 462).

"We are coming to a point in time when continuing education over the lifespan is not only desirable—it is a necessity" (Birren and Woodruff, 1973, p. 314). (Courtesy of Colorado State University Office of Instructional Development)

Hooper (1979b) emphasizes the role of counselors in helping students and their families understand the demands of the student role, prepare for the impact on the family, and cope with problems that arise.

The Concept of Life-Long Learning

The educational notion that an individual completes his education by receiving the baccalaureate or higher degree and then lives his life on the basis of what he has learned is simply inadequate. Perhaps in the last century it was appropriate to use the inoculation model of education in which an individual received a sufficient dose of education early in his life which would immunize him from the need for additional formal learning . . . we are coming to a point in time when continuing education over the life span is not only desirable— it is a necessity (Birren & Woodruff, 1973, p. 314).

Work, Retirement and Leisure

Birren and Woodruff (1973) suggest that we discard the view that occupational skills will be sufficient for a lifetime. More and more retraining of workers will be necessary as certain jobs become obsolete due to technological innovation. Toffler (1970) predicts that serial careers will be common in the future. The following facts on the rate of change and the information explosion are indeed mind-boggling:

1. In four and a half centuries the publication of new books has increased from 1,000 a year to 1,000 a day.
2. The number of journals and articles appears to be doubling every 15 years, the current output being approximately 20,000,000 pages per year.
3. Between 85 and 95 percent of all scientists who ever lived were alive in 1970.
4. The innovation cycle from the time of the mental conception of a new idea to its application in society has been reduced to only a few years (Toffler, 1970).

Birren and Woodruff (1973) have stated that in order "to cope with the demands of accelerating social change in the twentieth century, the orientation of educational institutions must be altered from one of exclusive concern with the first two decades of life to involvement with education over the entire human life span" (p. 306). In addition to meeting societal needs, it is also in the best interest of educational institutions, especially those of higher learning, to shift their orientation to a life-span focus. Changes in the age structure in the United States have reduced the number of young adults in the total population thus affecting college and university enrollments.

Vocational Development

Contemporary thinking about career development has been greatly influenced by the writings of Donald Super (1963). He views vocational development as a series of developmental experiences and a continuous and patterned process as individuals move toward mastery and competence in work. Super has postulated the following five developmental tasks related to career development:

Crystallization Formulation and crystallizing of ideas about work that are in accord with the individual's self-concept (14–18 years).
Specification Specification of a vocational preference by narrowing one's choice and taking the steps necessary to enter an occupation (18–20 years).

Implementation Implementation of vocational preference by finishing training and entering employment (21–24 years).
Stabilization Seeking stability in a vocation (25–35 years).
Consolidation Advancement and attainment of status (after 35 years).

Abilities of the individual, factors in the external environment, and available opportunities all operate to determine the level of achievement eventually obtained.

Havighurst (1964) has also proposed a model of vocational development which he presents as a life-long process (see Table 3–2). His delineation of stages begins at an early age and goes through the period of retirement. A review of Erikson's list of stage-appropriate psychosocial crises and Havighurst's developmental tasks presented in Chapter 1 will show that Havighurst, in his theorizing about vocational development, has drawn heavily from these more general models. As can be seen in Table 3–2, he places much emphasis on the effect of early experiences on later vocational development. Another important aspect of Havighurst's theory is his inclusion of the task for the 40–70 age group of inducting younger people into Stage III (acquiring identity as a worker) and Stage IV (becoming a productive person)—a function now called *mentoring*.

Table 3–2. Havighurst's Theory of Vocational Development.

Stages of Vocational Development	Age
I. *Identification with a Worker*	
Father, mother, other significant persons.	5–10
The concept of working becomes an essential part of the ego ideal.	
II. *Acquiring the Basic Habits of Industry*	
Learning to organize one's time and energy to get work done (school work, chores).	10–15
Learning to put work ahead of play in appropriate situations.	
III. *Acquiring Identity as a Worker in the Occupational Structure*	
Choosing and preparing for an occupation.	15–25
Getting work experience as a basis for occupational choice and for assurance of economic independence.	

Table 3–2. Havighurst's Theory of Vocational Development. (cont.)

Stages of Vocational Development	Age
IV. *Becoming a Productive Person*	
Mastering the skills of one's occupation.	25–40
Moving up the ladder within one's occupation.	
V. *Maintaining a Productive Society*	
Emphasis shifts toward the societal and away from the individual aspect of the worker's role. One sees oneself as a responsible citizen in a productive society. One pays attention to the civic responsibility attached to one's job. One is at the peak of one's occupational career and has time and energy to adorn it with broader types of activity.	40–70
One pays attention to inducting younger people into stages III and IV.	
VI. *Contemplating a Productive and Responsible Life*	
This person is retired from work or is in the process of withdrawing from the worker's role. One looks back over one's work life with satisfaction, sees that he or she has made a social contribution, and is pleased with it. While one may not have achieved all of one's ambitions, one accepts one's life and believes in oneself as a productive person.	70+

Source: R. J. Havighurst, "Youth in Exploration and Man Emergent," in H. Borow (Ed.), *Man in a World at Work* (Boston: Houghton Mifflin, 1964).

The presence of a mentor appears to be extremely important in career development. In fact, Levinson and his colleagues (1974) view the lack of a mentor as a vocational handicap. Mentors are typically 8 to 20 years older than their younger colleagues and have attained some measure of success in their fields. While serving as role models, mentors show their young colleagues "through the ropes" and act as guides, tutors and sponsors. This sponsorship by the mentor generally leads to greater acceptance and advancement within the organization (Bolton, 1980).

The mentor relationship appears to have a definite developmental progression (Ard, 1973; Dalton, Thompson & Price, 1977). Not only the mere presence of a mentor opens the door to success; the younger individual must move through all the stages of the relationship. The consecutive stages and the roles associated with each stage are as follows (Bolton, 1980):

Stage 1: observer ←——→ role model
Stage 2: mentee ←——→ mentor
Stage 3: protégé ←——→ sponsor
Stage 4: peer ←——→ peer

It should be mentioned that many individuals do not get beyond the first stage in the model. While they may observe and emulate a professional role model, the relationship will not move beyond that point unless the role model chooses to take a personal interest in the younger individual's career. Also, some people never outgrow their dependence on their mentor, and therefore never progress to the final stage in which they view their previous mentor as a peer. The cycle does not have to be complete, however, for the younger individual to become a role model to a newcomer in the field. Thus, a given individual can be at different positions of the cycle concurrently, in one position as a subordinate and in the other as a superior (Bolton, 1980).

Most studies on mentor relationships have been conducted with males. The evidence from investigations on women have shown that women who have gained recognition in their work have had a mentor relationship (Henning & Jardim, 1980; Orth & Jacobs, 1971; Sheehy, 1977a). The anthropologist Frantz Boas persuaded Margaret Mead to change her field from psychology to anthropology, and under his tutelage she began her unorthodox anthropological work. Robert Browning was an established poet at the time he encouraged Elizabeth Barrett to write poetry. Her work is now as well respected as his. Similar mentor relationships existed between film directors Federico Fellini and Lina Wertmüller and philosopher-writers Jean-Paul Sartre and Simone de Beauvoir (Sheehy, 1977a). It has been discovered, however, that in many cases established males do not choose to serve as mentors to young females because of the charge from peers of mere sexual interest. Also, due to biases, older males may fail to perceive the ability and potential in female students and workers (Epstein, 1971).

Bolton (1980) stresses the importance of successful women serving as mentors for other women—"learning the rules requires guidance from those who have made it." The absence of female role models has had an inhibitory effect on career advancement for women in the past. Veiga (1976) suggests that an "old girl" network be established for women that will provide the same rewards and benefits that "old boy" systems have provided for men.

Worker Satisfaction

Increased emphasis is being placed on the right of all workers to meaningful and healthy jobs. In order for this to occur, work incentives and rewards must correspond with the prevailing values of workers. In the past, status and income have been the main criteria by which jobs were evaluated. However current research shows that young workers today have a different set of priorities, and economics is not number one. In a nationwide survey, Yankelovich (1974) found the following job criteria to be the most critical for today's labor force:

1. Friendly, helpful coworkers (70 percent)
2. Interesting work (70 percent)
3. Opportunity to use your mind (65 percent)
4. Work results you can see (62 percent)
5. Good pay (61 percent)
6. Opportunities to develop skills/abilities (61 percent)
7. Participation in decisions regarding job (58 percent)
8. Getting help needed to do the job well (55 percent)
9. Respect for organization you work for (55 percent)
10. Recognition for a job well done (54 percent)

Yankelovich (1978) has also found that work is receiving decreased emphasis by the younger generation in the work force. While the majority of those in his study said they enjoyed their work, only one out of five (21 percent) said that work meant more to them than their leisure activities. Previous generations of American workers have tended to identify to a large extent with their work. Yankelovich reports that European visitors to the United States would react with surprise when Americans commonly introduced themselves with statements such as: "I am a car dealer"; "I'm assistant manager of the local bank"; "I'm a housewife"; "I manage the personnel department at J. C. Penney's." Today adult workers are placing more emphasis on a personal identity that is much broader than their work role. Yankelovich concludes that "perhaps no question will dominate the workplace in the 1980s more than how to revamp incentives to make them a better match for the work motivations of the New Breed."

The Burnout Syndrome

When work values are not actualized, intense dissatisfaction can occur. *Burnout* is the term that has been adopted by investigators to describe the syndrome of physical and mental exhaustion, low morale and despair found frequently among human service workers. Edelwich (1980)

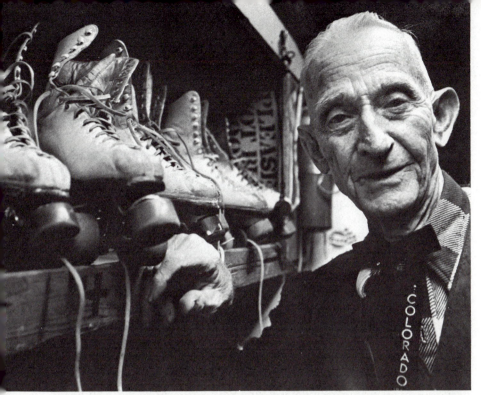

Previous generations of American workers have tended to identify to a large extent with their work. (*The Coloradoan*/Bob Gunter, Photographer)

refers to burnout as a progressive loss of idealism, energy and purpose experienced by those employed in the helping professions. Burnout has been related to conditions commonly found in the work environments of schools, hospitals, nonprofit organizations and government service agencies. These conditions include client overload, too many hours with too little pay, funding uncertainty, excessive paperwork, bureaucratic and political constraints, ungrateful clients and pressure to increase work loads. These conditions often lead to feelings of anxiety, powerlessness, anger and depletion among workers. Also, sufferers of burnout show increased use of alcohol and drugs and a higher incidence of physical illness and absenteeism (Edelwich, 1980; Bramhall & Ezell, 1981; Pines & Maslach, 1979). Pines and Maslach (1978) point out that burnout can have negative consequences for the worker's relationships with family and friends as well. Oftentimes the stress of the job is carried home, and little provocation is required for the venting of work-related frustration. Consequently, the worker's family often ends up being the scapegoat.

What type of person is most vulnerable to burnout? Ironically, the classic burnout victims are usually those who were the most enthusiastic and energetic initially. As is stated in many burnout workshops: "You have to have been on fire in order to burn out" (Bramhall & Ezell, 1981, p. 24). Eventually this initial vigor and idealism gives way to the realization of one's inability to "solve the problems of the world." At the same time, the constant pressure and demand for service provision continues (Freudenberger, 1980).

Edelwich (1980) has identified five stages in the disillusionment process. Stage 1, *Idealistic Enthusiasm*, is characterized by high hopes, high energy and unrealistic expectations. In Stage 2, *Stagnation*, the job begins to lose some of its initial appeal. The person is less willing to sacrifice for the job, and issues of money, working hours and career development become more important. By Stage 3, the *Frustration* stage, individuals begin to question the value of their work and their effectiveness at doing it. Emotional and physical symptoms of burnout may appear at this point. Stage 4, the *Apathy* stage, is the point at which apathy occurs as a natural response against chronic frustration. In this stage, challenges are avoided and workers give less of themselves to their clients. The fifth stage is *Intervention*. Unfortunately, most people go through stage four before they do something to alter their situation. Some decide to change jobs. Others chose to return to school and train for a different field. Alternative solutions include modifying one's job description, restructuring relationships with work associates and forming mutual support networks, and expanding one's life outside of work.

In the last few years, burnout workshops have been conducted all over the country in response to the increased recognition of this problem. If workers and employers learn to recognize symptoms of burnout in the early stages, interventions can be implemented sooner. In fact, Maslach and Pines (1977) support the idea of teaching coping skills prior to observing job-related stress. The current lack of preparation for the unique emotional stresses involved in "people work" results in many professionals being "unable to maintain the caring and commitment they initially brought to the job" (p. 100).

Women and Work

Work experiences of older women typically reflect an uneven employment history punctuated by periodic withdrawal from the labor force to fulfill the roles of wife and mother. Some older women have never worked outside of the home (Lopata & Steinhart, 1981). Today, a different pattern is emerging in which women are engaged in a longer and more consistent pattern of participation in occupational roles. According to estimates by the Urban Institute of Washington, nearly 70 percent of all women between the ages of 16 and 54 will be in the labor market by 1990 (*New York Times*, Sept. 25, 1979).

The Women's Movement of the 1970s raised important issues regarding equality in the work place and women's rights. Consequently, increased occupational opportunities are now available for women. In 1981, Sandra Day O'Connor was appointed as the first female Supreme Court justice in our nation's history. (United Press International)

This increased participation of women has occurred as a result of a number of societal trends and changing family and work patterns. Women now have more time at their disposal. Labor-saving devices in the home have decreased the time spent on household work. Also, improved birth control technology now allows families to more effectively plan the number and spacing of their children, thus affecting time spent in childrearing. In addition to the time factor, today's women appear to have different attitudes toward working. The Women's Movement of the 1970s raised important issues regarding equality in the work place and women's rights. Consequently, increased opportunities are now available for women and the female identity is expanding. Some women, however, are not working by choice. An uncertain economy and high rates of inflation have put many women into work roles, and in some households the woman is the primary breadwinner as the head of a single-parent family.

While more women are working than ever before, they continue to hold the jobs in society that have the lowest status and lowest pay. Only a small number of women are in management positions and most of these tend to be in traditionally "feminine fields" such as nursing, education and retailing. Even in these fields, males commonly are employed in the supervisory positions.

More women are moving into nontraditional occupations but in small numbers. For example, in 1978 women comprised approximately 13 percent of scientists and less than 2 percent of engineers in the United States; however, most of the increase of female workers in these areas did occur in the 1970s (Vetter, 1978). And in examining the percentage of doctorates awarded to women in science between 1920 and 1970, it was found that the percentages actually decreased from 1920 through the 1960s. By the 1970s it had risen, but only to a level approximately equivalent with that of the 1920s (Increasing the Participation of Women in Scientific Research, 1978).

Schlossberg, Troll and Leibowitz (1978) believe one reason few women have reached high level positions is that they have not been encouraged to consider and explore these career possibilities. Barnett (1975) found that the higher the prestige of an occupation, the more likely males were to aspire to it and the more likely females were to have an aversion to it. Lower aspirations of women are derived to a large extent from their early socialization experiences. It has been found that young children learn to link occupation with sex, thus beginning the process of premature occupational foreclosure for females early in life (Goodman & Schlossberg, 1972). Children acquire their attitudes about sex roles from a variety of sources, one such source being the literature they read or is read to them. After examining award-winning children's books, Weitzman and her colleagues (1972) concluded that "the world of picture books never tells little girls that as women they might find fulfillment outside of their homes or through intellectual pursuits" (p. 1146). Also, the children's books examined by Weitzman et al. typically portrayed women as passive beings—as a helper of a worker, as an admirer of a king—rather than active participants of life. Nor was the reality of our changing world reflected—working and divorced women did not appear in these stories. Recently a few writers of children's literature have attempted to convey the message of role flexibility to young children, but sex stereotyping is still strong in most children's books.

These stereotypes, carried over into adulthood, are also partly responsible for the biases and discrimination shown against female workers. Current data from a study conducted by the American Association for the Advancement of Science suggest that women do not have the same opportunities for jobs, promotions and high salaries as men. Statistics show that in 1976 men who did not finish high school earned more than female college graduates. Also, despite equal opportunity and affirmative action laws, the gap between women's and men's wages has continued to widen. In 1975, women with Ph.D.'s had salaries 19 percent below men's; the difference was less—17 percent—in 1973. It was concluded that "women make less than men at every degree level, in every field, in every employment setting, at every age, in every activity—and the difference increases with age" (Increasing the Participation of Women in Scientific Research, 1978, p. 4).

Box 3–2

An Example of Sex Stereotyping in Children's Literature

Do appropriate role models for young female children say nothing, wear disguises and serve moonburgers? While most people would say no to this question, a look at some of the books that are presented to children show that we may be doing a disservice to young girls by providing them with poor female models in the stories they read. Juanita Williams (1977, p. 176) in her book *Psychology of Women* provides an excellent example of inappropriate sex stereotyping in children's literature.

A popular line of children's books sold by the millions in supermarkets and drug stores includes a story of a small boy and girl fantasizing about the future (Vogel, 1968):

1. *He will be a baker, an icing expert. She will be the baker's wife.*
2. *He will be a mailman, delivering surprise packages. She looks, listens, says nothing.*
3. *He will be an explorer in the jungle, and will bring back a lion. She will curl the lion's mane in her beauty shop for animals.*
4. *He will be a policeman. She will wear a disguise and be his helper.*
5. *He will be a doctor. She will be a nurse.*
6. *He will be a fireman. She will be rescued by him.*
7. *He will be a deep-sea diver. She will be a mermaid and serve him tea and ice cream.*
8. *He will be an artist. She will be a singer. As he paints, three of the four people watching him are females. As she sings, all her ad-*
9. *He will be an astronaut and go to the moon. She will be there, prepared to serve him moonburgers.*

99

Work, Retirement and Leisure

> *All nine of his fantasies have the potential to be realized. They are real occupations for which people are trained and paid. Of hers, only three seem to have even the slightest vocational potential: nurse, singer and animal groomer. In the others she marries him, helps him and serves his food. And is a victim if the house catches on fire.*

Dual-Career Marriages

One of the most important questions of the 1980s will be how women can more effectively combine family and work roles. Most working women are married, and over two-thirds of them have children (Van Dusen & Sheldon, 1976). Since the mid-60s, the greatest increase of women workers has been in the 25–35 age group—the time during which women are usually the most intensively involved with childrearing and the age period during which women's participation in the labor force has traditionally been the lowest (U.S. Department of Labor, 1975). Experimenting with different lifestyles, some couples have reversed roles in their families with the woman assuming the position of primary breadwinner while the husband takes responsibility for household and childcare duties; but these situations are rare. Families in which both parents are working outside the home are the norm in our society, and 15 percent of American families are headed by only one adult, with the remaining parent usually employed (Harris, 1981).

Dual-career couples have few role models for successfully combining family and work roles. Margaret Mead has said ". . . we don't know how to have professional marriages because we've had so few of them" (The Participation of Women in Scientific Research, 1978, p. 9). Several investigators have provided evidence that working couples experience role strain as they attempt to meet competing demands and balance the multiple roles of spouse, parent and worker (Eaton, 1981; Hall & Hall, 1979; Hochschild, 1973). Most studies show that women suffer more stress as a result of role conflict and role overload than do men (for example, Ferber & Loeb, 1973; Gove & Tudor, 1973; Havens, 1973; Holmstrom, 1971). In a sample of 1,400 New York families, women employed full-time spent an average of four to eight hours per day, or approximately 26 to 35 hours per week, on household work (Walker, 1973). Women also still have the primary responsibility for child care in most families though, as Figure 3–1 shows, there is a trend toward more equitable sharing of this activity. Eaton (1981) has observed that "many women have assumed a 'superwoman' role by taking on the de-

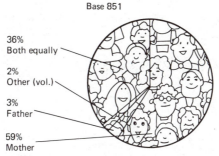

Would you say that, in your family, the children are cared for mostly by the mother, mostly by the father, or that both parents share day-to-day child care equally?

Base 851

36%
Both equally

2%
Other (vol.)

3%
Father

59%
Mother

Figure 3–1. Family member with primary responsibility for child care. (Source: L. Harris and Associates, Inc. The General Mills American Family Report 1980–81. *Families at Work: Strengths and Strains.* Minneapolis: General Mills, Inc., 1981, p. 28.)

mands and pressures of a career without relinquishing any of their former duties as a housewife and mother" (p. 1).

Few institutional adjustments have been made for women's increased participation in the labor force. Therefore, women and their families have had to absorb the pressures that impact on married women's ability to build and sustain careers as well as to feel satisfaction with their accomplishments as mothers and wives.

When DeFrain (1979) asked couples who shared work and family responsibilities to identify their biggest problems, two major difficulties experienced by these families were inadequate day care and job inflexibility. Over half the mothers and fathers in the sample desired day care programs in locations near their work or in the same building if possible. Some indications exist that employers are realizing the need to alter their policies and offer additional worker benefits to reduce the stress on modern families. When 104 human resource executives were interviewed in a nationwide study, only 14 percent said that their organizations presently provided child care for employees at their place of work. However, an additional 67 percent thought that their organization was likely to establish such child-care facilities within the next five years (Harris, 1981).

Several personnel policies have been suggested to allow for more job flexibility. Tables 3–3 and 3–4 show the responses of the same 104 human resource executives to eight such policies. An examination of the tables indicates that the 1980s will most likely be a time of major alteration of personnel practices and experimentation with new models of employment which may better meet the needs of today's workers

Work, Retirement and Leisure

Table 3–3. Policies Already Adopted by Corporations (N = 104).

Organization has already adopted (volunteered):

The right to resume work at the same pay and seniority after a personal leave of absence		60%
The right to refuse a relocation or transfer with no career penalty		48%
A shorter workweek with less pay		34%
A choice between a 7 to 3, 8 to 4, or 9 to 5 workday		28%
A four-day workweek with longer hours each day but with a three-day break		28%
Work schedules that allow one day to work at home		28%
Freedom to set a work schedule, as long as they work 70 hours every two weeks		20%
A single job shared with someone else, so that each person can take more time away from work but the job still gets done		12%

Source: L. Harris and Associates, Inc. *Famililes at Work: Strengths and Strains* (Minneapolis, Minnesota: General Mills, Inc., p. 57).

and their families. While few companies currently have flexible work hours, it appears that it may become a prominent part of our labor scene in the next decade (Harris, 1981). Flexi-time began in Europe in the late 1960s and has been shown to be quite successful. In West Germany, half of the nation's white-collar workers enjoy flexible scheduling of their work hours. In France and Switzerland, the percentage of workers having flexi-time policies where they are employed are 30 percent and 40 percent, respectively (DeFrain, 1979).

In the past, white-collar workers involved in industry have been penalized if they refused a job transfer. For those employees with working wives, relocation usually resulted in a disruption of the woman's career. If the husband refused the offer, his position and further advancement were jeopardized. Recognizing the detrimental effects of forced

Table 3—4. Policies Most Likely to be Adopted by Corporations in the Next Five Years (N = 104).

And which of these policies do you think your organization is most likely to adopt in the next five years?

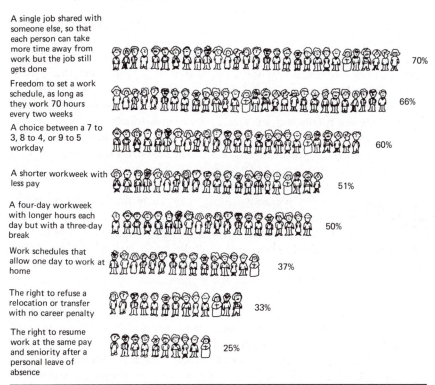

Policy	Percent
A single job shared with someone else, so that each person can take more time away from work but the job still gets done	70%
Freedom to set a work schedule, as long as they work 70 hours every two weeks	66%
A choice between a 7 to 3, 8 to 4, or 9 to 5 workday	60%
A shorter workweek with less pay	51%
A four-day workweek with longer hours each day but with a three-day break	50%
Work schedules that allow one day to work at home	37%
The right to refuse a relocation or transfer with no career penalty	33%
The right to resume work at the same pay and seniority after a personal leave of absence	25%

Source: L. Harris and Associates, Inc. *Families at Work: Strengths and Strains* (Minneapolis, Minnesota: General Mills, Inc., 1981, p. 56).

relocation on families, an increasing number of corporations are relaxing their relocation policies. Harris and his associates (1981) found that nearly half of the 104 organizations represented in their study did not impose a career penalty if a move or transfer was refused, and an additional one-third indicated plans to adopt this policy in the near future.

A more controversial issue is job sharing in which one position is shared by two people. This arrangement typically has the benefits of more job security and opportunities for advancement than with a part-time job, yet it allows more time away from work. While Harris and his research team (1981) found that only 12 percent of the organizations they studied had already implemented job sharing, 70 percent planned to provide this option within the next five years. By instituting many of these policies, employers can play an instrumental role in reducing some of the stress and strain on contemporary American families.

Unemployment

A situation that has an even greater impact on the family than having both parents employed is when neither parent is employed. Unemployment not only results in a drastically reduced income but it can be psychologically devastating as well. In industrialized societies, work and productivity are highly valued. The worth of individuals, especially males, is often judged by their occupational achievements and income. Unemployment can threaten the male's position within the family as well as his respectability outside of it, particularly among members of the middle class (Veil, Barat, Ginault & Sabliére, 1970).

Unemployment is typically followed by fairly predictable reactions and behavior patterns. After the initial reaction of shock, frustration and anger over losing their jobs, individuals casually begin searching for employment and are fairly confident that they will find a new job. However, for most persons, finding another job does not come this easily or quickly. Having initially enjoyed their increased leisure time, the unemployed grow restless after approximately one month and begin engaging in a more systematic and organized job search. If these efforts fail, the individual's optimism declines and self-doubt becomes stronger. At this time, relations with family and friends frequently become strained. Continued unemployment at this point can have further negative effects for the individual and his family as the person begins to experience isolation, apathy and helplessness as well as having increased difficulty envisioning himself in a job (Powell & Driscoll, 1973).

These feelings may be accentuated by the opinions of others. For example, Tausky and Piedmont (1968) have noted that in the United States public opinion is usually antagonistic to the unemployed, somehow placing the blame on the individual for not having a job. In individualistic and equalitarian societies such as the United States, it is assumed that the opportunities exist and it is up to the individual to "make it." These generally unsympathetic attitudes only result in further reducing the self-esteem of the unemployed person.

Veil et al. (1970) have referred to a series of studies conducted in France that examined the wife's reactions to her husband's extended unemployment. According to the findings from these investigations, there is a tendency to deny the situation at first and the word "unemployed" suddenly disappears from the family's vocabulary. Soon the husband's job loss becomes more of a reality as its impact is felt on the family budget and the denial cannot be continued any longer. This stage is followed by growing difficulties in communication between the wife and husband, increased domestic conflict, and efforts to hang onto the past. Middle-class males may feel they have little support from friends since few have had similar experiences, and they begin to avoid their peers due to embarrassment. Gradually the family becomes isolated, and the wife's image of her husband deteriorates as his own self-image is further damaged by his prolonged unemployment.

Unemployment is especially high among minorities. For example, the unemployment rates for blacks are about twice as high as those for whites (Ritzer, 1977). Also unemployment rates are higher for those age forty and over (Kay, 1974), and once unemployed, middle-aged and older adults are likely to stay unemployed for up to 70 percent longer than younger workers (Entine, 1976). According to a Report of the President's Council on Aging (1961), unemployment during the middle years can be particularly disastrous because "family responsibilities are likely to be at their height and the need to accumulate social-security credits for adequate benefits upon retirement and to build up savings for old age are most urgent. Unemployment during these years undermines not only the worker's morale but the security of his dependents as well" (p. 36).

Age Discrimination Among Older Workers

Charlie Smith ran a small store in Bartow, Florida until he was 133 years old. In 1955, he was made to retire from his work on a citrus farm because he was considered too old to be climbing trees. In 1972 he was officially recognized as the oldest person in the United States.

Alex Comfort
A Good Age

Age discrimination appears widespread in the United States not only in dismissals but in hiring policies, promotions, training opportunities and forced retirement as well. Less than one-fifth of American workers are self-employed. Most individuals are employed by others and are therefore greatly affected by age biases held toward older workers. Although in 1967 the Age Discrimination in Employment Act was passed, suits claiming age discrimination were filed against 5,054 establishments as late as 1977 (U.S. Department of Labor, 1978). The earlier act of 1967 was amended in 1974 and 1978 to provide broader coverage. The upper age limit was also extended in 1978 to age 70; prior to that time the law protected only those workers between ages 40 and 65.

What are the reasons for this widespread ageism in the work place?

There appear to be several, all related to economics. Cost of fringe benefits such as pensions, health insurance and life insurance rise as the average age of a company's employees increases. Also salaries tend to increase with age. Younger persons can usually be employed at almost half of what middle-aged individuals earn after twenty years with a company. Young professional workers, while not having the experience of the older workers, usually enter with the latest skills and at no training costs to the employer. In addition, employers often say that too many older employees will limit the opportunities for advancement of their younger colleagues, a situation that will encourage the young to seek employment elsewhere (Kendig, 1978).

Age discrimination is also due to beliefs about characteristics of older workers that have little or no basis in fact. Older employees are viewed as less efficient, slower to retrain, and having higher absenteeism rates than younger workers—factors that can increase the operating costs of an organization. Available evidence, however, provides little or no support for these assumptions. Greenberg (1961) found that the output of many older workers exceeded that of younger workers. Other researchers have found that older employees, when compared to younger ones, are more accurate in their work and have a steadier output (Kelleher & Quirk, 1973). Also older workers are less likely than

Although less than one-fifth of American workers are self-employed, those that are can avoid the age discrimination that exists against older workers. (Bob Harvey, Photographer)

Older workers, when compared with younger workers, have been shown to have a steadier output, less absenteeism, and fewer accidents. (Bob Harvey, Photographer)

younger ones to be absent from work or be involved in occupational accidents (McFarland, 1973; U.S. Department of Labor, 1965). Other studies have found no relationship between age and adaptation to a new job (Birren, 1964; Chown, 1972).

Despite these findings, ageism still continues. When workers are at their peak of job skill, experience and maturity, many are met with a preference for the young. Some organizations have even admitted that they preferred not to have older employees because they want to present a youthful image to the public (Kendig, 1978).

Retirement

What's old? Folks sixty-five don't think sixty-five's old. It's the young people who think sixty-five's creaking age.

James A McCracken
The Company Tells Me I'm Too Old

Harriet Miller (1978), speaking as Director of the American Association of Retired Persons, has charged that "mandatory retirement practices help to put the stamp of respectability on age discrimination" (p. 325). Mandatory retirement at age 65 was adopted by much of private industry following the federal government's decision to use this age as the cutting point at which individuals would be eligible for old age assistance payments. However, it should be noted that the choice of age 65 in the original Social Security Act was rather arbitrary and was based more on consensus of opinion than on any scientific evidence (Cohen, 1957).

In January, 1979, the age when most workers can be compelled to retire was raised from 65 to 70, thus giving protection to older persons who wish to continue in their work role through their 60s (Soldo, 1981). But what about those who want to continue working in the seventh, eighth and ninth decades of their lives? Schultz (1974) has reported that among retired males, 7 percent are able and desirous of work but cannot find employment. As Figure 3–2 shows, these men were forced out of their previous jobs by mandatory requirement rules.

Issues Regarding Mandatory Retirement

There appear to be several arguments on both sides of the issue of mandatory retirement. Among those in favor of compulsory retirement, the following arguments are often made:

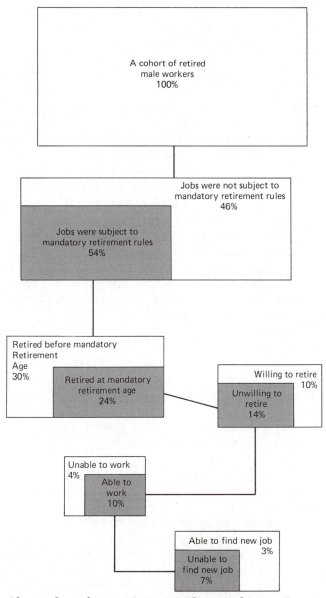

Figure 3–2. Incidence of mandatory retirement in the United States. (Source: J. H. Schulz, "The Economics of Mandatory Retirement," *Industrial Gerontology, 1,* 5.) Reprinted by permission of the National Council on the Aging, Inc.

1. Mandatory retirement provides a predictable situation which allows both employers and employees to plan ahead.
2. It is simple and easy to administer.
3. Compulsary retirement prevents discrimination against individual workers by treating everyone in the same age group similarly.
4. Mandatory retirement saves face for older workers; rather than be told they are no longer performing satisfactorily, they can blame their retirement on compulsory retirement policies.
5. Medical science has not devised an accurate, easy-to-administer test that will determine the physical and psychological competence of older workers on their jobs. If available, such large-scale testing of individuals would be extremely costly.
6. Compulsory retirement forces management to provide retirement benefits at a determined age.
7. Older workers can retire with Social Security or other retirement income, thereby making jobs available to younger unemployed workers who do not have other income potential.
8. It prevents seniority and tenure systems from blocking the hiring and promotion of younger workers.

In addition to the above arguments, reasons such as poor health and impaired work performance are often cited. As was discussed under the topic of age discrimination, the available empirical evidence does not support these latter arguments (Palmore, 1972; Select Committee on Aging, 1977).

Those opposed to mandatory retirement also have persuasive arguments which include the following:

1. Mandatory retirement based on age alone is discriminatory and contrary to equal employment opportunities. They can also be challenged as being unconstitutional because they deny older individuals equal protection under the law.
2. Chronological age alone is a poor indication of ability to perform a job; wide variations exist among individuals of the same age.
3. Flexible retirement policies would better utilize the skills, experience and productive potentials of older persons, thereby increasing the country's output in goods and services. With mandatory retirement, considerable skill and experience is lost from the work force.
4. Mandatory retirement is especially detrimental to many female workers who do not start their careers until they are middle-aged. It not only limits their career potential, but also reduces their ability to accumulate significant pension benefits.

5. It can cause major hardships for older persons by significantly reducing their income and taking away a major life role and source of status and satisfaction.
6. Forced retirement results in an increased expense for government income maintenance programs (that is, Social Security) as well as for numerous social service programs.
7. In the year 2000, a proportionately smaller labor force will be supporting a larger retiree population due to declining birth rates. Raising the retirement age or eliminating compulsory retirement altogether could ease this predicted "economic burden" on the country's finances (Palmore, 1972; Select Committee on Aging, 1977).

Rather than taking a pro or con stance on mandatory retirement, many gerontologists are advocating a plan of flexible retirement. The work role of most employees is abruptly terminated by retirement. After consistently engaging in a work pattern for forty or more years, they are suddenly removed from the work force and left to restructure their lives on their own. It is apparent that a more flexible system is needed to aid the worker in the transition to retired status. As early as 1969, Senator Walter Mondale as a member of the Senate Special Committee on Aging called for experimentation with work and retirement patterns. His suggestions for the near retirement years included sabbaticals, phased retirement, trial retirement and part-time work arrangements (Special Committee on Aging, 1969). To date, few attempts to alter traditional patterns have been undertaken. Sweden, however, is engaged in a nation-wide experiment in which a variety of retirement options are offered to older workers. To ease the transition from full-time work to complete retirement, persons between the ages of 60 and 70 are allowed to work part-time. The ratio between job time and retirement time varies for the individual, depending on his or her personal circumstances. Adjustments on job income and pension payments are made according to the work-retirement ratio of each worker. As long as individuals are employed for at least 17 hours a week, they are eligible not only for pension benefits but fringe benefits as well. Also, they can opt to return to full-time work (Miller, 1977). In the United States, retirees are penalized by having their Social Security benefits reduced if they earn over a pre-determined amount each month—a policy that discourages paid employment among individuals in their later years of life.

Adjustment to Retirement

The research done on effects of retirement has focused primarily on white, middle-class males. Little is known about retirement among ethnic minorities, individuals on either end of the income continuum or women. The available evidence, however, suggests that retirement is a complex process of adaptation for most older persons (Atchley, 1975; Lowenthal, Thurnber, Chiriboga & Associates, 1975; Sussman, 1972; Pollman, 1971).

Withdrawal from the work force is usually followed by a "honeymoon" period in which persons enjoy their freedom from work and their increased leisure time. This stage may be followed by disenchantment as one is confronted with unstructured time and a fixed income. This disenchantment is constructively resolved by reorienting oneself and making the necessary adjustments to fill in the gaps opened up by retirement, after which the individual settles into a fairly stable life pattern until severe illness, disability or death strikes (Atchley, 1975).

Responses to retirement appear to be highly varied. It has been found however that individuals who are more educated and in higher occupational levels tend to resist retirement the most (Monk, 1971; Streib & Schneider, 1971). Perhaps these workers have invested themselves more in their work roles than blue-collar workers.

Role loss.   Retirement creates a discontinuity in roles for males. Kline (1975) suggests that females make a better adjustment to retirement and old age because women have experienced role discontinuity throughout their lives as they move from a work role, to the role of wife and mother, to a work role again. Heyman (1970) has remarked that women "retire" several times during a lifetime, unlike males who typically maintain a consistent work role until old age. As women become a more stable part of the work force, patterns of adjustment to retirement may become more similar for the sexes.

Role adjustment can be also seen within the family setting after retirement. The entrance of the retired husband into the home involves adjustments for both the husband and wife and a redefinition of roles. One study of 52 retired couples found that husbands commonly assumed more household duties following retirement. Furthermore, this involvement in the "wife's domain" did not appear to cause disharmony among the couples. Rather than sharing tasks, the husband tended to assume full responsibility for a select group of tasks, none of which was essential to the wife's role conception. Rather than viewing the husband's participation as an invasion of territory, it was viewed more as a welcome emancipation from tasks willingly relinquished (Ballweg, 1967).

Role transition is eased for some retirees by engaging in volunteer work. Some have begun volunteering earlier in life to provide satisfactions perhaps lacking in their paid work and thus continue this role past their formal retirement from the work force. Others are assuming the volunteer role for the first time after retirement (Babic, 1972). Payne

(1977) has remarked that volunteering is becoming a prestigious role for older persons as more and more agencies incorporate volunteer positions into their formal structures (for example, Foster Grandparents, Retired Senior Volunteer Program, Action). She adds that these new volunteer positions "are especially designed to utilize the skills and resources developed over a lifetime in the delivery of critically needed human services" (p. 356). In 1976 approximately 37 million people were engaged in volunteer work in their communities. The value of this volunteer labor has been estimated to be over $30 billion a year (Allen, 1980).

Continuities are usually maintained in other areas of life (for example, family, friends) which tends to minimize the impact of retirement (Cottrell, 1970). Contrary to popular opinion, relatively few Americans move during the retirement years. Between 1975 and 1979, less than one-fifth of noninstitutionalized persons over 65 relocated, most of whom stayed in the same county (Soldo, 1980). Therefore areas of life other than work tend to remain relatively stable for most retirees. However, adjustment to retirement can be compounded by other losses occurring concurrently such as loss of spouse or declining health. And for most older individuals and their families, retirement brings a loss of income and a need for financial readjustment (Atchley, 1979).

Income reduction.   Personal income is usually reduced by a third to one-half after age 65 (Soldo, 1980). In one study, 40 percent of retirees were found to have difficulty adjusting to a lower income (Atchley, 1975). As is shown in Figure 3–3, income levels are particularly low for Blacks and singles over age 65, with many of them living below the poverty level. These reductions in income at retirement are met with increased expenditures in areas such as health care. The percentage of income spent on health care almost doubles in families in which the age of the family head is over 65 (Brotman, 1978). Social security benefits are adjusted for price increases, but these adjustments have failed to keep pace with inflation. It is estimated that most persons who retire today on a fixed income can expect their purchasing power to be cut 50 percent by the time of their death (*Getting Rid of 65-and-out*, 1976).

And what is the government doing to assist the elderly in maintaining an adequate standard of living? The breakdown of federal dollars spent on the elderly in Figure 3–4 shows that nearly three-quarters of each dollar is currently going toward retirement benefits. Most of these funds go to finance the Social Security program.

Social Security

Rules governing mandatory retirement age, eligibility for retirement income, and level of retirement funding are formulated as part of a na-

Figure 3–3. Median income of couples and individuals 65 and over compared with poverty levels and incomes of young families in 1978. (Source: B. J. Soldo, "America's Elderly in the 1980's," *Population Bulletin*, 1980, *35*, 22.)

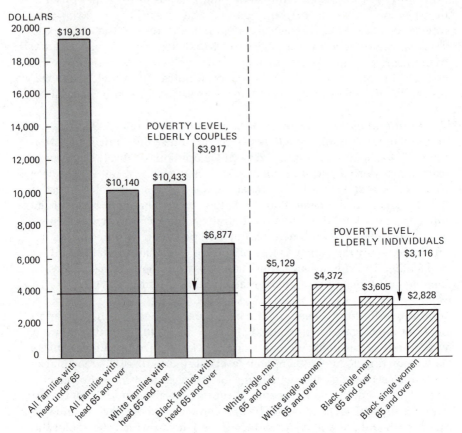

tion's retirement policy. The development of these policies is influenced by societal attitudes toward support of older persons and acceptance of the concept of social insurance. Retirement policies are also influenced by such labor market conditions as layoffs, labor shortages and unemployment (Atchley, 1979).

Most industrialized nations now appear to agree that social insurance is the best method of preventing destitution and providing a minimum of security for older people. Among the developing countries of the world, public assistance and social insurance programs have not received top priority—community development, increased economic production, child and youth services and education have been more pressing issues. In these countries, only a small percentage of individuals, usually government workers, are covered by pension plans, and

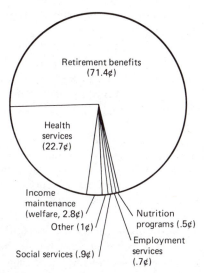

Figure 3–4. Breakdown of the federal dollar spent on the elderly in 1980. (Source: B. J. Soldo, "America's Elderly in the 1980's," *Population Bulletin*, 1980, *35*, 32.)

formal retirement policies for the majority of workers are nonexistent (Friedlander, 1975).

Social insurance benefits were first introduced to the United States in 1935 during the Depression. The program was established to *supplement* income from savings and private pension plans. It was never designed to replace one's former wages (Soldo, 1980). In contrast to this "minimum subsistence" philosophy is the guaranteed "moderate income" approach used in Austria (Friedlander, 1975). Consequently, public spending on the elderly accounts for 5 percent of the gross national product in the United States and 21 percent in Austria (Soldo, 1980).

An examination of the Social Security system of the 1980s shows that it has little resemblance to the program started in 1935. While it has always been financed by payroll deductions, these deductions have progressively increased from a 1 percent tax on earned income up to $3,000 in 1937 to a combined employer-employee tax rate of 13.3 percent on a taxable wage base of $29,700 in 1980. Projections for the future show continued increases (Soldo, 1980).

Part of the need for increased revenues to finance Social Security has come from changes in the coverage and scope of the program. Prior to the 1960s, only a small number of older persons qualified for Social Security benefits. Various occupational groups were gradually included in the program, and today nine out of every ten workers are covered under Social Security. The system has also been expanded over the years

Work, Retirement and Leisure

to include such additional benefits as disability payments and the Medicare program (Soldo, 1980).

In addition to rising costs, the country faces another challenge in financing the Social Security program in the future. Changes in the demography of the nation will result in a sharp increase in the ratio of retirees to workers as the "baby boom" generation begins to turn 65. According to Soldo's (1980) figures:

> In 1980 three workers pay benefits for one retiree. If there are no changes in the present pay-as-you-go system, two workers will be required to support one retired person after 2010 and the combined employer-employee Social Security tax rate could climb to somewhere between 25.4 and 45.3 percent in 2030 (p. 38).

Coupled with these estimates is the growing trend toward early retirement among a significant number of workers. At the beginning of 1974, more than eight million workers retired before age 65, three times the number on early retirement during the previous decade. The "30 and out" plan, whereby full retirement benefits can be received after thirty years of work, has been demanded of companies by the United Auto Workers. Also, Civil Service employees are currently allowed to retire at age 55 provided they have at least thirty years of service behind them (*Why the Big Swing to Early Retirement*, 1974). This trend toward early retirement indicates that more and more workers will be leaving the work force at a time when increased revenues are needed for a swelling over-65 population.

Retirement *is* a complex social institution. As the previous discussion indicates, retirement not only has an impact on individuals and their families but it affects work organizations, other social institutions, and the overall society as well. Social policy experts and gerontologists have stressed the need for retirement planning at governmental, corporate and individual levels.

Preparation for Retirement

While studies have shown that participants in preretirement programs report better adjustment after retirement than nonparticipants, few workers chose to attend preretirement programs (O'Meara, 1977). Also, the programs that are offered vary widely in content. Many programs consist of little more than informing the employee of available benefits.

Workers, however, are becoming more aware of the importance of preretirement planning. Kasschau (1974) cites evidence of the increased desire of employees for more employer-sponsored programs. Currently, even the most basic financial planning is lacking among many middle-aged workers.

Kasschau (1974) suggests that retirement preparation programs should be institutionalized by companies in much the same way that training and retraining programs have been in the past. Most authorities now recommend that preparation should begin 15 to 20 years prior to actual retirement. Financial planning begins earliest with planning in other areas such as housing and use of leisure time occurring later. Kasschau emphasizes the need for flexibility in these programs so that the differing needs of employees can be met.

Leisure

Leisure consists of relatively self-determined activity-experience that falls into one's economically free-time roles, that is seen as leisure by participants, that is psychologically pleasant in anticipation and recollection, that potentially covers the whole range of commitment and intensity, that contains characteristic norms and constraints, and that provides opportunities for recreation, personal growth, and service to others.

> Max Kaplan (1975)
> *Leisure: Theory and Policy*

Retirement brings with it increased time for leisure activities. While some individuals may welcome this newly acquired leisure time, others will be unprepared for it. In a work-oriented society like the United States, developing a positive leisure orientation can be a challenge.

Wall (1975) has pointed out that use of leisure time within a country mirrors cultural values. The Protestant work ethic has strongly influenced Americans' views toward leisure. Among our forefathers, play was seen as an opponent of work and viewed as permissible only for young children. The familiar saying, "Idleness is a devil's workshop" echoes these sentiments. These attitudes have changed considerably over the years, but many adults still feel uncomfortable with too much leisure time.

The topic of leisure is receiving increased attention from researchers as more leisure time becomes available due to such factors as increased longevity, earlier retirement, a shorter work week, and other changes in work resulting from increased automation. Riply and O'Brien (1976) have suggested that "how to live with leisure may become as important for tomorrow's generations as learning to live with work has been for yesterday's" (p. 56). As increased amounts of nonworking time become accessible to members of our society, we will be faced with the question of not only how to spend this time but how it should be distributed across the life span (Kreps, 1972).

It has been suggested that leisure time is given to individuals and their families when they least need it. Older couples in the empty-nest stage often find themselves with an abundance of time, yet they may lack the economic resources to utilize their leisure time in ways they would prefer. Impaired health in the later years can also interfere with

---

Box 3–3

Maintaining the Capacity for Fun

Ira Tanner (1973) has said that ideally as we age the qualities that are childish are cast aside while the qualities that are child-like, such as spontaneity, are maintained. He believes that the manner in which we allow ourselves to continue exercising these characteristics determines the spirit with which we age. According to Tanner, work is valued to such an extent in our culture, that "play" that is not somehow work-oriented is not seen as a legitimate activity for adults. When most adults do play, they concentrate on perfecting what they do rather than just relaxing and enjoying it. Accustomed to striving for mastery and achievement in everyday life, a jogger may be so busy concentrating on improving his time that he may be more aware of the second hand on his watch than the warmth of the sun on his face or the sounds of the birds overhead. Tanner emphasizes that leisure activities do not need to have a purpose; they can be valued simply for the sense of fun and pleasure they bring to the human spirit.

---

full enjoyment of available leisure time. Perhaps it is more reasonable to spread work and leisure more evenly throughout the life cycle so that younger families can have more time to engage in recreational activities. In our modern society, work and family responsibilities consume much of the time and energy of young and middle-aged adults, leaving a comparatively small amount of discretionary time for leisure. Orthner (1975) has indicated that shared leisure time can be beneficial to family members by promoting cohesiveness and strengthening family relationships.

Achieving more of a work-leisure balance early in life can also affect adjustment to retirement. Some individuals reach retirement age without ever having developed meaningful leisure pursuits. Interests and

Preparation for retirement includes the development of fulfilling and satisfying leisure pursuits. (Julie Hanson, Photographer)

preferences established in early adulthood tend to persist into the later years of life (Haan & Day, 1974). Therefore, preparation for retirement can entail the development of fulfilling and satisfying patterns of leisure early in life.

Allen (1980) advocates the inclusion of leisure considerations in vocational counseling. In his view, career guidance must be comprehensive in scope and take into account the growing importance of leisure and its relationship to occupational goals. Leisure activities can contribute directly to health, longevity, happiness and intellectual growth in addition to other needs (Kaplan, 1979). The reader is reminded of the concept introduced at the beginning of this chapter—the need for more integration rather than separation of education, work and leisure over the adult life span.

Suggested Activities and Exercises

1. Career interviews can be a valuable means of obtaining information about jobs. Make an appointment with two or three professionals working in positions to which you aspire. What satisfactions do these individuals receive from their work? What frustrations are present? Using the information and insight gained in the interviews, determine if the nature of the jobs explored are consistent with your abilities, interests and values.
2. Interview someone you admire and inquire about role models in his or her life. Then identify individuals you would like to emulate. What are their special qualities? In what ways can they serve as role models for you?
3. In this chapter, the effects of stress among human service workers have been discussed. What effects could burnout have on community service agencies and the client populations they serve? What can be done to prevent burnout?
4. Talk with older volunteers in your community. How do they view their volunteer work? What are their motivations for engaging in this type of activity, and what needs are being met for the individual and the community?
5. Examine the balance of work and leisure in your life. What patterns are you developing that will facilitate a positive adjustment to the transitions that come with age?

References

Allen, K. K. *Worker volunteering: A new resources for the 1980s.* New York: AMACOM, 1980.

Allen, L. R. Leisure and its relationship to work and career guidance. *The Vocational Guidance Quarterly*, 1980, *28*, 257–62.

Ard, B. N., Jr. Providing clinical supervision for marriage counselors: *A model for supervisor and supervisee. The Family Coordinator*, 1973, *22*, 91–97.

Astin, H. S. Continuing education and the development of adult women. *The Counseling Psychologist*, 1976, *6*, 55–60.

Atchley, R. C. Issues in retirement research. *The Gerontologist,* 1979, *19,* 44–54.

Atchley, R. C. *The sociology of retirement.* Cambridge, Mass.: Schenkman, 1975.

Babic, A. The older volunteer: Expectations and satisfactions. *The Gerontologist,* 1972, *12,* 87–90.

Ballmer, H., & Cozby, P. C. *Changes in family relations when the wife returns to college.* Paper presented at the annual meeting of the Western Psychological Association, Sacramento, California, April 1975.

Ballweg, J. A. Resolution of conjugal role adjustment after retirement. *Journal of Marriage and the Family,* 1967, *29,* 277–81.

Barnett, R. C. Sex differences and age trends in occupational preference and prestige. *Journal of Counseling Psychology,* 1975, *22,* 35–38.

Berkove, G. *Returning women students: A study of stress and success.* Paper presented at the annual meeting of the Western Social Science Association, Tempe, Arizona, 1976.

Birren, J. E. *The psychology of aging.* Englewood Cliffs, N.J.: Prentice-Hall, 1964.

Birren, J. E., & Woodruff, D. S. Human development over the life span through education. In P. B. Baltes & K. W. Schaie (Eds.), *Life-span developmental psychology: Personality and socialization.* New York: Academic, 1973.

Bolles, R. N. *The three boxes of life.* Berkeley, Ca.: Ten Speed Press, 1978.

Bolles, R. N. *What color is your parachute?* Berkeley, Ca.: Ten Speed Press, 1975.

Bolton, E. R. A conceptual analysis of the mentor relationship in the career development of women. *Adult Education,* 1980, *30,* 195–207.

Bramhall, M., & Ezell, S. How burned out are you? *Public Welfare,* 1981, *39,* 23–27.

Brim, O. G., Jr. Theories of the male mid-life crisis. *The Counseling Psychologist,* 1976, *6,* 2–9.

Brotman, H. B. The aging of America: A demographic profile. *National Journal,* 1978, *10,* 1622–27.

Chown, S. M. The effect of flexibility—rigidity and age on adaptability in job performance. *Industrial Gerontology,* 1972, *13,* 105–21.

Cohen, W. *Retirement policies under Social Security.* Berkeley: University of California Press, 1957.

Comfort, A. *A good age.* New York: Crown, 1976.

Cottrell, F. *Technological change and labor in the railroad industry.* Lexington, Mass.: Heath, 1970.

Cunningham, S. M. M. *The older student.* Paper presented at CASC Workshop, August 1973.

Dalton, G. W., Thompson, P. H., & Price, R. L. The four stages of professional careers—A new look at performance by professionals. *Organizational Dynamics*, 1977, *6*, 19–42.

DeFrain, J. Androgynous parents tell who they are and what they need. *The Family Coordinator*, 1974, *28*, 237–43.

Eaton, D. *Coping with the stress of a dual-career marriage.* Paper presented at the annual meeting of the American Psychological Association, Los Angeles, August, 1981.

Edelwich, J., & Brodsky, A. *Burnout: Stages of disillusionment in the helping professions.* New York: Human Sciences Press, 1980.

Elder, G. H. Achievement motivation and intelligence in occupational mobility: A longitudinal analysis. *Sociometry*, 1968, *31*, 327–54.

Entine, A. D. Mid-life counseling: prognosis and potential. *The Personnel and Guidance Journal*, 1976, *55*, 112–14.

Epstein, C. F. *Woman's place: Options and limits in professional careers.* Berkeley: University of California Press, 1971.

Ferber, M. A., & Loeb, J. W. Performance, rewards, and perceptions of sex discrimination among male and female faculty. In J. Huber (Ed.), *Changing women in a changing society.* Chicago: University of Chicago Press, 1973.

Freudenberger, H. J. *Burnout: The high cost of achievement.* Garden City, N.J.: Anchor Press, 1980.

Friedlander, W. A. *International social welfare.* Englewood Cliffs, N.J.: Prentice-Hall, 1975.

Getting rid of 65-and-out. *Business Week*, 1976, March 1, 60–61.

Goodman, J., & Schlossberg, N. K. A woman's place: Children's sex stereotyping of occupations. *Vocational Guidance Quarterly*, 1972, *20*, 266–70.

Gould, R. The phases of adult life: A study in developmental psychology. *American Journal of Psychiatry*, 1972, *5*, 521–31.

Gove, W. R., & Tudor, J. F. Adult sex roles and mental illness. In J. Huber (Ed.), *Changing women in a changing society.* Chicago: University of Chicago Press, 1973.

Greenberg, L. Productivity of older workers. *The Gerontologist*, 1961, *1*, 38–41.

Haan, H., & Day, D. A longitudinal study of change and sameness in personality development: Adolescence to later adulthood. *International Journal of Aging and Human Development*, 1974, *5*, 11–39.

Haenninger, R. *New careers for midlife: May we help you?* Paper prepared for the Board of Directors of the National Vocational Guidance Association, 1974.

Hall, F. S., & Hall, D. T. *The two-career couple.* Reading, Mass.: Addison-Wesley, 1979.

Hansen, L. S. The career development process for women: Current views and programs. In T. Hoshenshil (Ed.), *Career development of women.* (Conference Proceedings) Blacksburg: Virginia Polytechnic Institute, 1974.

Harris, L. and Associates, Inc. *Families at work: Strengths and strains.* Minneapolis, Minn.: General Mills, 1981.

Havens, E. M. Women, work, and wedlock: A note on female marital patterns in the United States. In J. Huber (Ed.), *Changing women in a changing society.* Chicago: University of Chicago Press, 1973.

Havighurst, R. J. Youth in exploration and man emergent. In H. Borow (Ed.), *Man in a world at work.* Boston: Houghton Mifflin, 1964.

Heddescheimer, J. C. Multiple motivations for mid-career changes. *The Personnel and Guidance Journal,* 1976, *55,* 109–11.

Henning, M., & Jardim, A. *The Managerial Women.* New York: Anchor Press/Doubleday, 1980.

Heyman, D. K. Does a wife retire? *The Gerontologist,* 1970, *10,* 54–56.

Hochschild, A. R. A review of sex role research. In J. Huber (Ed.), *Changing women in a changing society.* Chicago: University of Chicago Press, 1973.

Holland, J. L. *Making vocational choices: A theory of careers.* Englewood Cliffs, N.J.: Prentice-Hall, 1973.

Holmstrom, L. Career patterns of married couples. In A Theodore (Ed.), *The professional woman.* Cambridge, Mass.: Schenkman, 1971.

Hooper, J. D. My wife, the student. *The Family Coordinator,* 1979, *28,* 459–64. (a)

Hooper, J. D. Returning women students and their families: Support and conflict. *Journal of College Student Personnel,* 1979, *20,* 145–52. (b)

Hooper, J. O, & Rice, J. K. Locus of control and outcomes following counseling of returning students. *Journal of College Student Personnel,* 1978, *19,* 42–47.

Increasing the participation of women in scientific research. Washington, D.C.: National Science Foundation, 1978.

Kaplan, M. *Leisure: Lifestyle and lifespan.* Philadelphia: Saunders, 1979.

Kaplan, M. *Leisure: Theory and policy.* New York: Wiley, 1975.

Kasschau, P. L. Reevaluating the need for retirement preparation programs. *Industrial Gerontology,* 1974, *1,* 42–59.

Kasworm, C. E. The older student as an undergraduate. *Adult Education,* 1980, *31,* 30–47.

Katz, J. Home life of women in continuing education. In H. Astin (Ed.), *Some action of her own.* Lexington, Mass.: Heath, 1976.

Kay, E. *The crisis in middle management.* New York: AMACOM, 1974.

Kelleher, C. H., & Quirk, D. A. Age, functional capacity, and work: An annotated bibliography. *Industrial Gerontology,* 1973, *19,* 80–98.

Kendig, W. L. The problem of age discrimination in employment. In *Age discrimination in employment.* New York: AMACOM, 1978.

Kline, C. The socialization process of women. *The Gerontologist,* 1975, *15,* 486–92.

Knowles, M. S. *The modern practice of adult education: From pedagogy to andragogy* (rev. ed.). New York: Association Press, 1980.

Kreps, J. The allocation of leisure to retirement. In M. Kaplan & P. Bosserman (Eds.), *Technology, human values, and leisure.* Nashville: Abingdon, 1972.

Lance, L. M., Lourie, J., & Mayo, C. Needs of reentry university students. *Journal of College Student Personnel,* 1979, *20,* 479–85.

Levinson, D. J., Darrow, C. M., Klein, E. B., Levinson, M. H., & McKee, B. The psychosocial development of men in early adulthood and mid-life transition. In D. F. Ricks, A. Thomas, and M. Roff (Eds.), *Life history research in psychopathology* (Vol. 3). Minneapolis: University of Minnesota Press, 1974.

Lopata, H. Z., & Steinhart, F. Work histories of American urban women. *The Gerontologist,* 1971, *11,* 27–36.

Lowenthal, M. F., Thurnber, M., Chiriboga, D., & Associates. *Four stages of life: A comparative study of women and men facing transitions.* San Francisco: Jossey-Bass, 1975.

Maslach, C., & Pines, A. The burn-out syndrome in the day-care setting. *Child Care Quarterly,* 1977, *6,* 100–13.

Maslow, B. J. *The farther reaches of human nature.* New York: Viking, 1973.

McCracken, J. A. The company tells me I'm too old. *Saturday Review,* August, 1976.

McFarland, R. The need for functional age measurements in industrial gerontology. *Industrial Gerontology,* 1973, *19,* 1–19.

Miller, H. Ageism in employment must be abolished. In R. Gross, B. Gross, & S. Seidman (Eds.), *The new old: Struggling for decent aging.* Garden City, N.J.: Anchor Books, 1978.

Miller, H. Flexible retirement—will Sweden make it work? In S. H. Zarit (Ed.), *Readings in aging and death: Contemporary perspectives.* New York: Harper & Row, 1977.

Mills, E. W. Career development in mid-life. In W. E. Bartlett (Ed.), *Evolving religious careers.* Washington, D.C.: Center for Applied Research in the Apostolate, 1970.

Monk, A. Factors in the preparation for retirement by middle-aged adults. *The Gerontologist,* 1971, *11,* 348–51.

O'Meara, J. *Retirement: Reward or rejection.* New York: Conference Board, 1977.

Orth, C. D., & Jacobs, F. Women in management: Pattern for change. *Harvard Business Review,* 1971, *49,* 139–47.

Orthner, D. K. Familia Ludens: Reinforcing the leisure component in family life. *The Family Coordinator,* 1975, *24,* 175–83.

Palmore, E. Compulsory versus flexible retirement: Issues and facts. *The Gerontologist*, 1972, *12*, 343–48.

Parelman, A. *Family attitudes toward the student mother as compared with family attitudes toward working mothers: A pilot study.* Unpublished manuscript, University of California at Los Angeles, 1974.

Payne, B. P. The older volunteer: Social role continuity and development. *The Gerontologist*, 1977, *17*, 355–61.

Penn, R. Occupational prestige hierarchies. *Social Forces*, 1975, *54*, 352–64.

Pines, A., & Maslach, C. Characteristics of staff burnout in mental health settings. *Hospital and Community Psychiatry*, 1978, *29*, 233–37.

Pines, A., & Maslach, C. *Experiencing social psychology.* New York: Knopf, 1979.

Pollman, A. W. Early retirement: Relationship to variation in life satisfaction. *The Gerontologist*, 1971, *11*, 43–44.

Powell, D. H., & Driscoll, R. F. Middle class professionals face unemployment. *Society*, 1973, *10*, 18–26.

Report of the President's Council on Aging. Washington, D.C.: U.S. Government Printing Office, 1961.

Rice, J. K. Divorce and a return to school. *Journal of Divorce*, 1978, *1*, 247–57.

Ripley, T., & O'Brien, S. Career planning for leisure. *Journal of College Placement*, 1976, *36*, 54–58.

Rizger, G. *Working: Conflict and change* (2nd ed.). Englewood Cliffs, N.J.: Prentice-Hall, 1977.

Robbins, P. I., & Harvey, D. W. Avenues and directions for accomplishing mid-career change. *Vocational Guidance Quarterly*, 1977, *25*, 321–28.

Schlossberg, N. K., Troll, L. E., & Leibowitz, Z. *Perspectives on counseling adults: Issues and skills.* Monterey, Ca.: Brooks/Cole, 1978.

Schulz, J. H. The economics of mandatory retirement. *Industrial Gerontology*, 1974, *1*, 1–10.

Select Committee on Aging, U.S. House of Representatives. *Mandating retirement: The social and human cost of enforced idleness.* Washington, D.C.: U.S. Government Printing Office, 1977.

Sheehy, G. The mentor connection. In D. Elkind & D. C. Hetzel (Eds.), *Readings in human development: Contemporary perspectives.* New York: Harper & Row, 1977. (a)

Sheehy, G. *Passages.* New York: Bantam, 1977. (b)

Shingleton, J. *College to career.* New York: McGraw-Hill, 1977.

Smallwood, K. B. What do adult women college students really need? *Journal of College Student Personnel*, 1980, *21*, 65–73.

Soldo, B. J. America's elderly in the 1980s. *Population Bulletin*, 1980, *35*, 1–47.

Special Committee on Aging. *The federal role in encouraging preretire-*

ment counselling and new work lifetime patterns. Hearing before the Subcommittee on Retirement and the Individual of the Special Committee on Aging, U.S. Senate, 91st Congress, First Session, July 25, 1969.

Streib, G. F., & Sneider, C. J., Jr. *Retirement in American society.* Ithaca, N.Y.: Cornell University Press, 1971.

Super, D. E. *Career development: Self-concept theory.* Princeton, N.J.: College Entrance Examination Board, 1963.

Sussman, M. An analytic model for the sociological study of retirement. In F. M. Carp (Ed.), *Retirement.* New York: Behavioral Publications, 1972.

Tanner, I. J. *Loneliness: The fear of love.* New York: Harper & Row, 1973.

Tausky, K., & Piedmont, E. The meaning of work and unemployment: Implications for mental health. *International Journal of Social Psychiatry*, 1968, *1*, 44–49.

Tittle, C. K., & Denker, E. R. Kuder Occupational Interest Survey profiles of re-entry women. *Journal of Counseling Psychology*, 1977, *24*, 293–300. (a)

Tittle, C. K., & Denker, E. R. Re-entry women: A selective review of the educational process, career choice and interest measurement. *Review of Educational Research*, 1977, *47*, 531–84. (b)

Toffler, A. *Future shock.* New York: Bantam, 1970.

U.S. Bureau of the Census. *School enrollment: Social and economic characteristics of students: October, 1979* (Current Population Reports, Series P-20, No. 360). Washington, D.C.: U.S. Government Printing Office, 1981.

U.S. Department of Labor. *Manpower report of the President.* Washington, D.C.: U.S. Government Printing Office, 1975.

U.S. Department of Labor. *The older American workers: Age discrimination in employment, research, materials.* Washington, D.C.: U.S. Government Printing Office, 1965.

U.S. Department of Labor and U.S. Department of Health, Education and Welfare. The aging of America's labor force: Problems and prospects for older workers. *Employment and training report of the President.* Washington, D.C.: U.S. Government Printing Office, 1978.

VanDusen, R. A., & Sheldon, E. B. The changing status of American women—a life cycle perspective. *American Psychologist*, 1976, *31*, 106–16.

Van Meter, M. P. *Role strain among married college women.* Unpublished doctoral dissertation, Michigan State University, 1976.

Veiga, J. F. Female career myopia. *Human Resource Management*, 1976, *15*, 24–7.

Veil, C., Barat, C., Ginault, M., & Sabliére, M. Unemployment and family life. In E. J. Anthony & C. Koupernik (Eds.), *The child in his family* (Vol. 1). New York: Wiley, 1970.

Vetter, B. M. Progress of women in science. In *Increasing the participation of women in scientific research*. Washington, D.C.: National Science Foundation, 1978.

Vogel, I. *When I grow up*. New York: Western, 1968.

Vogelsang, J. *Find the career that's right for you*. New York: Hart, 1978.

Walker, K. E. Household work time: Its implication for family decisions. *Journal of Home Economics*, 1973, *65*, 7–15.

Wall, M. Use of leisure mirrors cultural values. *The Vocational Guidance Quarterly*, 1975, *24*, 7–10.

Weitzman, L. J., Eifler, D., Hokada, E., & Ross, C. Sex role socialization in picture books for preschool children. *American Journal of Sociology*, 1972, *77*, 1125–50.

Why the swing to early retirement. *U.S. News & World Report*, May 13, 1974.

Williams, J. H. *Psychology of women*. New York: Norton, 1977.

Yankelovich, D. *The new morality, a profile of American youth in the 1970's*. New York: McGraw-Hill, 1974.

Yankelovich, D. The new psychological contracts at work. *Psychology Today*, 1978, *11*, 46–50.

Part III
Continuity and Change

Chapter 4

Intelligence, Learning and Creativity

Cognition refers to the process of transforming and interpreting raw sensory information by means of mental operations such as abstracting, problem solving, perceiving relationships, forming concepts, and recall and recognition of previously encountered stimuli. Adults engage in a complex set of cognitive processes as they respond to the demands of their day-to-day existence. In this chapter, we will examine these processes as they are manifest in adult life and address the following questions: What are the components of intelligence and how are they measured? Which aspects, if any, change with age? What are the unique characteristics of the adult learner, and what role does education play in the lives of older adults? How is creativity affected by age?

Adult Intelligence

Cognitive operations cannot be observed directly. They must be inferred on the basis of behavior, which usually takes the form of verbal responses or physical actions. Certain behaviors are considered intelligent while others are not. Our vocabularies contain a myriad of words that describe our casual assessment of behaviors on the dimension of intelligence. In general, "actions of man and other creatures are said to be intelligent when they are more purposive than haphazard, more intentional then accidental, and more insightful and innovative than impulsive and stereotyped" (Bindra, 1976, p. 1).

While there tends to be agreement on the more general descriptions of intelligence such as the one stated above, the debate in this area has come in response to the more specific question of "What is the nature of intelligence?" If one desires to obtain a precise measure of this construct labeled "intelligence," what sorts of abilities should be sampled?

While early theorists such as Spearman (1927) viewed intelligence as an unitary phenomenon, later writers on the subject postulated that intelligence consists of a number of primary abilities all of which form what we refer to as intelligence. Thurstone (1938), however, viewed intelligence as consisting of only seven abilities while Guilford (1967) expanded this number to 120. While there currently is no general agreement about the actual number of primary abilities, a more recent approach has been to look at types of intelligence into which primary abilities can be grouped.

Work initially conducted by Cattell (1963) and later refined by Horn (1970, 1978) has resulted in the specification of two major dimensions of adult intelligence: fluid intelligence and crystallized intelligence. These aspects of intelligence are distinct in individuals yet correlated. Fluid intelligence refers to the basic capacity for learning and problem solving, independent of education and experience. These abilities are used when presented with unfamiliar tasks and novel situations, and they reflect underlying neurological processes. Crystallized intelligence consists of learned knowledge and skills and is developed as an individual interacts with his or her culture throughout life.

Aging and Intelligence

How are intellectual abilities affected by the aging process? Early studies in life-span intelligence conducted during the 30s, 40s and 50s generally employed cross-sectional designs. These studies found that intelligence increased until early adulthood, at which point it was maintained at a plateau level until around the fourth decade of life after which it declined. More recent results from longitudinal studies in which the same subjects were followed over several years reveal quite different results. These studies show that not only does decline occur much later than was previously thought, but some abilities actually improve with age.

Specifically, several investigators have found measures of crystallized intelligence to remain stable or increase with age, while measures of fluid intelligence are more likely to decline (Horn & Donaldson, 1977; Hayslip & Stearns, 1979). Schaie and his associates (Baltes & Schaie, 1974;

Crystallized intelligence, which consists of knowledge and skills acquired from one's culture, can continue to increase throughout life. (Source: Photo of Albert Einstein taken by Ernst Haas and reproduced with his permission.)

Schaie & Labouvie-Vief, 1974) grouped their longitudinal measures into four separate dimensions: (1) *crystallized intelligence* acquired through education and acculturation, (2) *cognitive flexibility*, which refers to the ability to shift from one way of thinking to another, (3) *visuo-motor flexibility*, which includes coordination between visual and motor abilities involved in shifting from familiar to unfamiliar tasks, and (4) *visualization*, the ability to process and organize visual stimuli. This research produced findings that also demonstrated an increase in crystallized intelligence (for example, verbal comprehension, numerical skills, inductive reasoning). In addition, increases in visualization ability were evident with age. No age-related changes were reported for cognitive flexibility, and measures of visual-motor flexibility showed some decline.

The early cross-sectional studies appeared to be measuring generational differences rather than age differences. The generational differences obtained were most likely due to the greater educational achievement of the young as compared to the older subjects. As you will recall from the discussion of cross-sectional studies in Chapter One, this type of design reflects cultural-historical experiences of cohort groups. In contrast, longitudinal studies avoid this type of confounding of the results by measuring the same individuals at different intervals over time. It has been pointed out, however, that while cross-sectional studies have overestimated the effects of aging on intellectual functioning, longitudinal studies may have underestimated them. With repeated testing of individuals, it is more likely that the healthy, able and intelligent subjects will continue to be available for retesting at each measurement interval than those of less ability, thus biasing test results (Botwinick, 1967; Siegler & Botwinick, 1979).

While many questions remain unanswered regarding changes in intellectual abilities with age, it is generally agreed that decline occurs much later in life than was previously assumed and that different abilities show different patterns of change. Rather than asking "What is the effect of aging on intelligence?", we have learned to more appropriately inquire about the *effects* of aging on *intellectual abilities.*

Tests of intelligence have been developed on the assumption that this human attribute can be measured and quantified. Using this psychometric approach, an IQ score is derived that represents how an individual's performance compares to others in his or her age group. Most intelligence tests, however, tap a restricted sample of intellectual abilities (Sattler, 1974).

One of the most widely used instruments for assessing adult intelligence is the Wechsler Adult Intelligence Scale (WAIS). Initially developed several decades ago by David Wechsler, a slightly revised version of the test was published in 1981. The WAIS is administered to individuals on a one-to-one basis by a trained examiner with the testing session usually lasting from 60 to 90 minutes. In addition to an overall IQ score, a Verbal IQ score and Performance IQ score are also obtained. Subtests within both the Verbal and Performance Scales are described in Table 4–1. Items within each subtest represent a range of difficulty levels. Typically, the beginning items are relatively simple and then become progressively more difficult.

The WAIS is a standardized test and therefore the subtests are given in a specified sequence. Prior to the revision of the instrument, all of the verbal subtests were administered first, followed by the Performance subtests. On the revised WAIS, the Verbal and Performance subtests are alternated.

Research has demonstrated the existence of greater age differences for the subtests on the Performance Scale than for the subtests on the Verbal Scale (Botwinick, 1977). The Performance subtests measure aspects of fluid intelligence, whereas the verbal subtests include items that emphasize past learning and are thus measuring crystallized abilities. These findings are therefore consistent with experimental studies that show greater age changes for fluid abilities. Table 4–2 lists the WAIS subtests in rank order according to their sensitivity to age differences. These mean rankings were taken from Botwinick (1967) and were derived from his analysis of findings from ten studies of intelligence.

Difficulty in Assessing Abilities in Older Adults

Intellectual abilities of the aged have been primarily assessed in controlled experimental settings and in clinical situations, and the applicability of these testing procedures has been challenged by numerous critics. Pressey reminds us that intelligence tests were first devised for the purpose of predicting school performance and suggests that the procedures associated with administering these tests and the content contained within them may simply not be appropriate for tapping the wisdom of older individuals (Baltes & Schaie, 1974). Also Satter (1974) has stated that current tests do not provide us with "valid scores for the different kinds of intelligence necessary for a person to function in a mature, responsible, and adequate manner" (p. 415). And Tyler (1971) has noted that IQ scores do not allow us to determine how flexible someone will be in adapting to a new situation, nor do they permit us to accurately predict performance in noneducational settings.

IQ scores reflect a measure obtained by individuals on a particular test at a particular point in time. Carroll and Horn (1981) have recently commented that some unfortunate consequences have resulted from the widespread belief among the general public that an IQ score is an actual equivalent of intellectual ability. The topic of intelligence testing

Table 4–1. Description of the Subtests on the Wechsler Adult Intelligence Scale—Revised.

Scale	Subtest	Description	Sample Items[a]
Verbal	Information	29 questions about knowledge of factual information.	What are the *Vedas*?
	Digit Span	14 series of digits are presented and the examinee is asked to repeat the first half of the series in the same order as read by the examiner. Then the second half of the series must be repeated in reverse order. The number of digits on each series varies from two to nine.	5-1-9-3-7
	Vocabulary	35 words definitions.	What does the word *matriculate* mean?
	Arithmetic	14 items testing the ability to perform basic calculations in arithmetic problems without the aid of paper and pencil (timed).	If a woman is driving her car at a rate of 60 miles an hour, how long should it take her to reach a city 200 miles from her original starting point?
	Comprehension	16 items measuring practical or "common-sense" knowledge.	Why are death certificates required?
	Similarities	14 pairs of words are given and the examinee is asked to indicate how the words in each pair are alike.	How are a sculpture and a poem alike?

Picture Completion Subtest

Picture Arrangement Subtest

Object Assembly Subtest

(lines represent pieces of puzzle)

1	2	3	4	5	6	7	8	9
☰	/	✓	⊏	/	+	▽	⌐	△

5	9	3	1	6	8	3	4	7
□	□	□	□	□	□	□	□	□

Performance	Picture Completion	20 line drawings on small cards with each having a missing part that is to be identified (timed).
	Picture Arrangement	10 series of cards containing line drawings of scenes. Cards in each series are to be placed in sequence so that they tell a logical story (timed).
	Block Design	9 designs are to be replicated using small blocks which have some sides that are red, some that are white, and other sides that are half red and half white (timed).
	Object Assembly	4 puzzle-type problems, each consisting of pieces which when put together correctly resemble a familiar object (timed).
	Digit Symbol	93 blank squares with numbers randomly placed above them are to be filled in with corresponding symbols, the correct correspondence being indicated by the number-symbol pairs which are provided as a model (timed).

[a]The items provided as examples for each subtest were constructed by the author but are similar to actual test items appearing on the WAIS-R.

Intelligence tests do not allow us to accurately predict performance in non-educational settings. (Bob Harvey, Photographer)

Table 4–2. Rank Order of WAIS Subtests by Age Sensitivity.

Subtests	Mean Ranks
Information	1.85 (least)
Vocabulary	2.33
Comprehension	2.75
Arithmetic	4.40
Similarities	5.60
Digit span	6.50
Picture completion	6.65
Object assembly	7.00
Block design	8.55
Picture assembly	9.85
Digit symbol	10.85 (most)

Source: J. Botwinick, *Cognitive Processes in Maturity and Old Age.* (New York: Springer, 1967).

has been one of heated debate during the past decade as particular groups, particularly ethnic minorities, have made the charge of test bias and have challenged the general validity of the use of such instruments as the WAIS (Cole, 1981).

Is there a possibility of a built-in bias against older persons as well? Since many of the subtests on the WAIS are timed, especially those measuring visual-motor performance, individuals with slower response times are penalized. Response time has been found to decline with age (Bischof, 1976), therefore older persons would be more likely to receive lower scores on timed subtests. While the slower response time of older persons is likely to result in a lower assessment of their intellectual ability, Birren (1964) has pointed out that the differences in response time between the old and young are not significant in everyday life and the differences that do exist can be reduced through practice.

Lower scores may also be obtained on older persons because of unique difficulties encountered when testing them. For example, older persons may have had less practice with taking tests. In our modern test-oriented society, young adults are familiar with test-taking procedures and thus usually display a more matter-of-fact attitude than elderly individuals who are not accustomed to this type of evaluation and may therefore be threatened by it. Also, older individuals are more likely than younger ones to have some degree of impairment in one or more of their sense organs. These sensory deficits combined with other age-related physical problems (such as arthritis) can interfere with accurate comprehension of the test instructions and skillful manipulation of the objects used in the visual-motor tasks. Because tests such as the WAIS are normally given in one sitting, difficulties with physical stamina can also influence performance. Although the testing session is not overly strenuous, individuals who fatigue easily may fail to perform to their full capacity on items presented toward the end of the test. Due to these factors and others, an IQ score can reflect many characteristics and conditions of the person other than intelligence.

Box 4–1

The Influence of Health Status on Test Performance

Abrahams (1976) has called attention to the fact that few investigators obtain information on the health status of subjects prior to their participation in research studies. While some types of health conditions are highly visible, others such as hypertension and cardiovascular disease are not. Even the individuals themselves may not be aware of existing health problems.

The relevance of assessing health status prior to testing is clearly demonstrated in the findings of Riegel and Riegel (1972). These scientists demonstrated that health factors that precipitate death are also related to a decline in intellectual functioning even though this decline may not be apparent from mere casual observation. In a longitudinal study, they found a sudden deterioration in performance on an intelligence test by individuals who subsequently died within five years following testing. In other words, lower scores were predictive of impending death. These findings led the Riegels to formulate their so-called "terminal drop" hypothesis.

Since relatively more older individuals die than do younger ones, the average score of an older group of subjects is therefore more likely to be depressed due to this terminal drop phenomenon. While reasons for this intellectual decline as the elderly approach death are not completely clear, these findings nonetheless have important implications for subject selection procedures used in cognitive research.

Siegler (1975) has also stated that the terminal drop data may help explain the wider variability in performance found in older groups when compared to younger groups, and it might also indicate that changes occurring in certain intellectual abilities are minimal until the final years of life. In addition, she has suggested that decreased scores on psychological measures may have value for detecting and thus treating death-causing conditions.

The Stage-Theory Approach

Stage theories of cognitive functioning are based on the notion that the actual nature of cognition undergoes predictable changes over the life span. In other words, not only do individuals increase their knowledge and problem-solving ability as they mature, but certain modes of thinking and processing are linked to particular age periods. Thus, qualitative changes occur along with quantitative changes.

Certainly one of the best known stage theories of intellectual development is that of Jean Piaget (1970). He has postulated the following four stages: (1) the *sensorimotor stage* (birth to two years of age) in which cognition is tied to action and the coordination of motor functions with perceptual functions; (2) the *pre-operational stage* (two to six years of age) in which the child is able to cognitively represent objects and actions previously observed but is not yet able to engage in mental operations involving reversibility and conservation; (3) the *concrete operational stage* (seven to eleven years of age) in which the child is capable of engaging in logical thought yet is tied to his or her concrete reality and can perform operations only on objects or events that can be directly observed; and (4) the *formal operational stage* (twelve to fifteen years of age) in which abstract reasoning emerges and the individual is capable of dealing with hypothetical situations and theoretical postulations.

As is apparent from a description of these stages, Piaget has focused his work primarily on the changes that occur during the years of childhood. Other researchers, however, in their attempts to obtain a better understanding of adult cognition, have questioned some of Piaget's assumptions regarding formal operations and have made attempts to extend his theory beyond the years of adolescence. Interesting findings have emerged from these research efforts—findings that perhaps raise more questions than they answer.

The majority of research conducted on adult subjects does not support the universality of formal operations acquisition during adolescence. In cross-cultural research, differences have been noted between the performance of villagers and urban-educated populations on Piagetian tasks (Ashton, 1975; Kohlberg & Gilligan, 1971). Even in the modern context of the United States, research on college students has shown that only about half or less of those tested have attained the formal operational stage and can be classified as formal thinkers (Arlin, 1975; McKinnon & Renner, 1971; Papalia, 1972; Wason, 1968).

As a response to these challenges of his original observations on the period of formal observations, Piaget (1972) has revised some of his views relative to this stage. While he maintains that formal operations are attained by all persons of normal intelligence at least by 15 or 20 years of age, he adds that this stage will be achieved in different areas and used in different ways depending on an individual's aptitudes and occupational specialization. Piaget has also conceded to the possibility that only the first three stages of his theory are universal and that adolescence is marked by a diversification of aptitudes which continues into adulthood. In addition, he has mentioned the role of environmental conditions and acquired experience as possible factors in the observed variations in development of formal cognitive structures. While he has offered the latter two explanations as alternative hypotheses, he does not favor them.

Once attained, does formal operational thinking continue into advanced old age or does some regression occur? Since biological factors appear to have a significant role in the progressive changes that occur in cognition during the early years, do biological changes occurring in the later years affect cognition in a reverse fashion? Hooper, Fitzgerald and Papalia (1971) were among the first to point to the need for research to determine if qualitative cognitive regression exists in the later years of life.

Several investigations have provided evidence for the life-long maintenance of formal operational skills once they are acquired (Hughton & Protinsky, 1978; Rubin, 1976; Tesch, Whitbourne & Nehrke, 1978). Other studies of older adults have given support for reverse horizontal decalage (intra-stage development), in which skills are lost later in life in the reverse order of which they were acquired (Papalia, 1972; Papalia, Salverson & True, 1973; Storck, Looft & Hooper, 1972). It has been suggested that these reported decrements could represent generational differences rather than true regression on Piagetian task performance, but the paucity of longitudinal data prevents us from drawing final conclusions in this area (Long, McCrary & Ackerman, 1979).

A third aspect of Piaget's theory currently being explored relates to the acceptance of formal operations as the final stage of cognitive development. Do changes in adult cognition warrant the extension of Piaget's work to include additional stages? Some scholars think so.

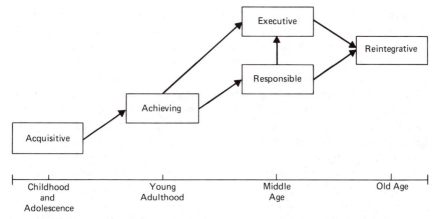

Figure 4–1. Schaie's stage theory of adult cognitive development. (Source: K. W. Schaie, "Towards a Stage Theory of Adult Cognitive Development," *International Journal of Aging and Human Development,* 1977, *8,* 129–128.)

Arlin (1975, 1977) has extended Piaget's theory to include a fifth stage of *problem finding.* The ability to raise questions and define new problems is characteristic of this stage. The attainment of formal operations appears to be a necessary but not sufficient condition for the appearance of problem-finding abilities. Individuals operating at this level demonstrate highly creative thought processes.

Instead of simply extending Piaget's work, Schaie (1977) has proposed his own sequence of qualitative stages that take into account changing goals over the life span and the differing intellectual skills associated with these goals. Figure 4–1 provides an outline of the stages proposed by Schaie and their correspondence to specific age periods. In the *acquisitive stage,* which covers the period of childhood and adolescence, the focus of cognition is on the acquisition of information and the development of culturally-relevant skills. In the *achieving stage,* occurring in young adulthood, the emphasis is shifted from the acquisition of knowledge and skills to the achievement of competence. At this time there is greater concern with the consequences of a solution, and problem-solving activities are more goal oriented than during the acquisitive stage. In young adulthood, cognitive functioning is strongly influenced by the requirements for role performance. As a result, young adults would be expected to demonstrate more efficient cognitive performance on tasks that have role-related achievement value or social implications.

The next stage, termed the *responsible stage,* begins in the early thirties and extends until the late sixties. Individuals in this stage of life assume increased responsibility for others, and they therefore adopt a problem-solving approach that takes into consideration long-range goals and consequences for family members. According to Schaie (1977): "In laboratory situations, this should imply increased skills in relevant problem-solving tasks, shifts in cognitive style to greater flexibility and lessened field dependence, gain in what has been described as the crystallized, but loss in the fluid abilities, the latter being of lowered relevance to the experiential demands upon the individual" (p. 134). Some individuals will also enter the *executive stage* during middle age. Middle-aged persons who have responsibility for complex systems within society have a "corresponding need to develop cognitive strategies which are efficient at integrating complex and high level hierarchical relationships." Both the responsible and executive stages usually require increased integration of acculturated intellectual skills, depending on the extent of an individual's societal involvement and responsibility.

The *reintegrative stage* occurs in the later years of life. As Schaie (1977) points out, this stage:

> . . . completes the transition from the "what should I know," through
> the "how should I use what I know," to the "why should I know"
> phase of life (p. 135).

Cognitive processes are thus more affected by motivational and attitudinal factors in this period than was the case in the earlier stages. Attention is restricted to aspects of the environment that have meaning and purpose within the immediate life situation of the older person. This selective attention may have utility for avoiding a progressive overload of information as one accumulates a lifetime of intellectual input (Schaie, 1979).

While Schaie (1977) thinks that current psychometric techniques may be appropriate for assessing and describing cognitive behaviors central to the early stages of life, he considers them inappropriate for measuring intellectual competence in later stages. He concludes that new strategies need to be developed for assessing abilities in relation to changing experiences and roles throughout life.

Memory and Learning

It is difficult to discuss learning without discussing memory. As Adams (1980) has said: "Learning and memory are two sides of the same coin. Learning is acquisition of a persistent disposition to respond, and memory is its storage over time and its activation when recollection takes place" (p. 7).

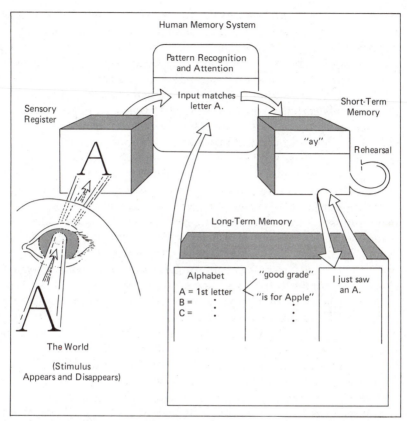

Figure 4–2. A model of the human information-processing system. (Source: R. L. Klatzky, *Human Memory: Structures and Processes* (2nd ed.). San Francisco: W. H. Freeman and Company, 1980, p. 12.)

An Information-Processing Approach to Memory

Since the 1960s, information-processing models have been used to understand the area of human memory (Craik, 1977). This approach emphasizes the active processing involved in the acquisition and retention of information and the mechanisms involved in these cognitive operations. Figure 4–2 presents a model of memory as an information-processing system. As can be seen, information first enters the system through one of the five senses and is held briefly in the sensory register as a literal copy. Most of the sensory information registered by the system is lost through the process of decay, since the sensory impression fades unless processed at a deeper level.

145   Intelligence, Learning and Creativity

Certain input proceeds to the next stage through the processes of selective attention and pattern recognition. This stage is referred to as *short-term memory.* No longer existing as a raw sensory impression, information in short-term memory has been recognized and labeled. While information is usually retained in short-term memory for only a brief period, the retention period can be lengthened by a process known as *rehearsal.* Perhaps you can remember trying to retain a telephone number or a grocery list temporarily by repeating the numbers or items to be remembered over and over again? Without the occurrence of rehearsal, the information in short-term memory is soon lost.

A more permanent storehouse is located in *long-term memory.* But, in order for information from short-term memory to be transferred into the more permanent storage structure of long-term memory, the information must be transformed and given meaning. This transformation is made by the use of control processes which determine the flow of information through the system. Just as attention and pattern recognition were used for the transfer of information from the sensory register to short-term storage, other processes are used to make a similar transfer from short-term memory to long-term memory. These processes are extremely complex and consist of various coding and elaboration strategies. For example, when asked to remember pairs of words, adults often use mental images as mnemonic devices. If one of the pairs was "dog-bicycle," a person might form a mental image of a dog riding a bicycle. Other individuals might use natural language mediators to aid memory by forming a sentence such as "The dog is chasing the bicycle." Organizing material through the use of categories is also a means of coding information in a way that will facilitate storage and later retrieval (Klatzky, 1980).

From our discussion, the sensory register, short-term memory and long-term memory may appear to be separate and discrete structures within the information-processing system. Rather than viewing them as different structural components, it is perhaps more accurate to interpret these features as indicating depth of processing. Qualitative changes occur in the material to be remembered as it is transferred from one storage structure to another. Because these structures more precisely represent memory processes rather than retention intervals, Waugh and Norman (1965) have argued that the terms short-term and long-term memory be replaced by primary memory and secondary memory, respectively.

Aging and Memory

For the purposes of discussing age differences, Fozard (1980) has further differentiated memory structures to include tertiary memory. While primary and secondary memory are associated with newly acquired information, tertiary memory stores information that has been well learned over a period of time.

Craik (1977) has concluded that age differences in primary memory capacity are minimal. Even in the small number of studies in which differences have been found, they have been minimal.

Clear age differences, however, are apparent in secondary memory. When presented with a large amount of new information, older people are usually unable to recall as much as younger individuals. In order to understand these age-related differences in secondary memory, many researchers have formulated hypotheses about acquisition and retrieval decrements in the elderly. They have been interested in finding out if the observed age differences indicate acquisition deficiencies among older persons or an inability to effectively retrieve recently-stored information from memory. Researchers have also focused on age differences in encoding as it relates to depth of processing. Semantic processing of material facilitates recall (Hartley, Harker & Walsh, 1980). Are older individuals engaging in less semantic processing or are they just less able to maximize the mneumonic benefits of this processing? Investigators are now attempting to answer these questions.

Tertiary memory does not appear to decline with age. In fact when age differences have been found, they have been in favor of older groups. While knowledge generally increases with age, the efficiency for remembering stored information remains constant across age. Thus older individuals are retrieving information from memory as effectively as their younger counterparts while at the same time drawing from a larger repertoire of stored information (Lachman & Lachman, 1980). Findings also show that this recall ability is not restricted to idiosyncratic material (Fozard, 1980).

Box 4–2

Oral Histories: Tapping the Memory of the Old Ones

According to Baum (1980), oral histories can be an important way of "gathering and preserving significant historical information by tapping the memories of those who have lived through the historical events or periods" (p. 51). Obtaining oral histories can have additional benefits such as encouraging contact between the young and the old and providing a greater awareness of the changes that have occurred in our society. As a project for their English class, students Tami Ashmead and Darren Lougree (1981) of Douglas,

Wyoming interviewed residents of a local nursing home about their past. The following description of the Depression given by one elderly resident provides insight into the impact of this historical event on the lives of Americans:

Faye Swanbom

I remember the great Depression of the 1930s. I'm sure everybody who lived during that period remembers the great Depression that altered, sometimes devastated, so many hopes and dreams.

I trained to be a teacher and taught in Nebraska for several years. After World War I, I married my husband who had graduated from the University of Nebraska Dental School. My intended began his practice at Dentistry at Crete, Nebraska, and shortly thereafter we were married.

What beautiful hopes and dreams we had of our life together. Our first born was a beautiful and very welcomed baby girl, and we were very proud and happy young parents. Before our second child, a boy, was born, we were well along with building our family home. The times were good, the country was confident, and we thought 'prosperous.' Little did we suspect the impending economic danger. In 1926 another baby girl was born and again in 1929. 1929, the year of the stock market crash, how devastating. Young dreamers could scarcely comprehend the meaning of the danger awaiting this country and them.

Little by little, like an economic cancer, individuals succumbed. Once proud working men, who fully intended to provide for their families, found that there were no jobs to be had and no money to reward their labor. Some wandered in search of work; some were fortunate, most were not!

In Crete, Nebraska, not only did we experience the depression that inflicted the whole nation, we also experienced drought; times were tough! There was little money that exchanged hands.

Few people had dental work done, and most patients came only when the pain became so severe they had to go to the dentist. How we worried about keeping food on the table. Our garden was large. We provided for the chickens in the backyard and were blessed with fruit trees of plums and cherries as well as grapes in the vineyard and a large strawberry patch. We were fortunate that farmers who owed for their dental bills delivered milk. The children received piano lessons from a patient that needed a great deal of dental work done. We counted our blessings when we were able to pay the interest on the loan for our large brick dream house.

The dreams we dreamed were beyond reason for many years for us and for just about everyone else. Mostly, it was very, very hard doing the wash, ironing, cleaning, canning and gardening, and with

Continuity and Change

everyone working as hard as possible, we were only barely able to survive.

The country began to pull out of the depression as it geared up to fight World War II. For many it was too late, and the agony of the great depression is still carried by many of us to this day.

Hartley, Harker and Walsh (1980) have raised the issue of ecological validity in psychological research saying, "We do not know how relevant or how ecologically valid various experimental tasks are to adult life. There has been no systematic examination of the kinds of learning required in the typical adult's daily life" (p. 244).

They have also observed that most of the current research has focused on the initial acquisition of simple learning tasks rather than studying changes in capacity and use of strategies as one engages in practice and accumulates knowledge about a particular task. They suggest that the processes and strategies used in the later stages of learning may be qualitatively different, and they provide the following example to demonstrate their point:

> . . . the performance of adults learning to play chess goes through a series of qualitatively different stages. The novice learns first the possible moves of each playing piece. The need and method for defending one's important pieces and attacking those of the opponent must also be mastered. Eventually, the more talented players learn to perceive the playing board as a set of configurations. The advanced player learns complicated strategies that begin with the first move and unfold across longer periods of play. Clearly, the nature of the learning process changes dramatically as one's experience with chess increases (Hartley, Harker & Walsh, 1980, p. 249).

Older Learners

A study sponsored by the National Council on the Aging found that older Americans are generally viewed as inactive, inflexible and limited in their ability to learn new skills (Harris & Associates, 1975). In contrast, Mead (1967) has observed that in Bali, continued learning among the old is not only encouraged but expected. She states:

> The Balinese have no idea that age has anything to do with the ability to learn. If a man who has never carved before wants to start carving at 60, no one has the slightest objection or shows any surprise.

Certainly, expectations influence our approach to learning new skills and knowledge as we age.

Many older adults in the United States have grown up hearing the old adage, "You can't teach an old dog new tricks." This common belief can lead to the avoidance of new learning tasks by the elderly. Environments that are stimulating and challenging are important for continued cognitive growth. By limiting their opportunities for learning, older persons become victims of this self-fulfilling prophecy.

While attitudes are important, other noncognitive factors influence learning as well. In exploring alternative explanations for the poor performance of older learners when compared to the young, some researchers have examined personality differences. It has been shown that older learners are less likely to give a response unless they are certain it is accurate. Okun, Siegler & George (1978) have shown that these age differences in cautiousness were at least partially responsible for the lower performance of the elderly in their particular study.

Also, many older adults approach experimental learning tasks with apprehension. They may fear that their abilities are declining and find the situation threatening. Whitbourne (1976) found that older men were more anxious than younger men following a memory task. High levels of anxiety have been shown to impair performance in learning situations, and this observed anxiety among the elderly may account for their lower performance on learning tasks.

Adult Education

Malcolm Knowles (1977) has introduced the term *andragogy* for the art and science of helping adults learn, and he advocates lifelong, self-directed learning for adults. At the 1971 White House Conference on Aging, education of the elderly was identified as a top priority. As chairperson of the section on education, Howard Y. McClusky stated:

> Education is a basic right for all persons of all age groups. It is continuous and henceforth one of the ways of enabling older people to have a full and meaningful life, and as a means of helping them develop their potential as a resource for the betterment of society (see Kobasky, 1974).

Continued learning is even more important for older adults today than in the past because the quickened pace of change in our society necessitates learning new information and skills for adaptation (Aker, 1974). Davis (1974) has proposed the following educational goals for today's elderly:

150

1. Enrich free time with educational pursuits and retain mental alertness.
2. Continue employment as long as desired or find new occupations.
3. Expand mental horizons through interactions with others.
4. Keep in touch with the surrounding world.
5. Meet the challenges, opportunities and problems that come with age.

While only a small percentage of the elderly are currently participating in educational programs, Goodrow (1975) found that over half of the elderly he interviewed were interested in such opportunities. Reasons given for lack of participation varied considerably. Transportation and fear of going out alone were mentioned by some, especially females. Others felt that they were too old to be in a classroom and thought they would not be adequately prepared. It must be remembered that most older Americans have had limited formal education. In fact, only about half of all Americans age 65 and over are high school graduates (U.S. Bureau of the Census, 1979). They may therefore have little confidence and many doubts about their ability to succeed in an educational setting.

Older persons in other studies have cited the following additional reasons for not taking advantage of available educational opportunities: courses offered are too expensive; they are too busy or have conflicting responsibilities; no interest; and poor health (Graney & Hays, 1976; Harris & Associates, 1975). Many of these barriers to learning among the elderly can be overcome with appropriate planning and structuring of adult educational programs. Requirements for entrance should be flexible and should take into consideration the full range of educational backgrounds typically represented. In addition, costs and scheduling should receive careful attention. When selecting instructional aids, sensory impairment (especially in vision and hearing) needs to be considered and appropriate modifications made. Also, an optimally designed program will pace learning in a manner that maintains interest and attention while avoiding fatigue.

The use of effective instructional strategies is also important. Okun (1977) reviewed available experimental research on older learners and translated the findings into specific guidelines that can be used by instructors of older adults. The implications he has extrapolated from the laboratory to the classroom are presented in Table 4–3 and are organized by salient instructional variables.

With increased improvement in instructional strategies, adult learning will be enhanced. Greater participation in educational endeavors

Table 4–3. Instructional Implications of Laboratory Experimental Geropsychological Research.

Instructional Variable	Researchers	Implications
Rate of Presentation of Information	Canestrari (1963); Monge & Hultsch (1971)	1. Present new information at a fairly slow rate. 2. Let adult learner proceed at his/her own rate whenever feasible. 3. Provide adult learner with ample time to respond to questions. 4. Present a limited amount of material in any single presentation to prevent swamping effects.
Organization of Information	Hultsch (1969, 1971); Laurence (1967); Rabbitt (1968)	5. Present new information in a highly organized fashion. 6. Use section headings, handouts, summaries, etc., so that adult learner can get a "handle" on material. 7. If memory processes are taxed in a learning project, encourage adult learner to use retrieval plans. 8. Avoid introduction of irrelevant information in order to prevent confusion. 9. If visual displays are used, employ simple stimulus configurations.
Mode of Presenting Information	Denney & Denney (1974); Taub (1972); Taub & Kline (1976)	10. Use auditory mode of presentation when presenting discrete bits of information to be used immediately. 11. Use visual mode when presenting textual materials to capitalize on opportunity for review during reading. 12. Utilize models to facilitate strategy development.

Category	References	Strategy
Covert Strategies	Cannestrari (1963); Hulicka & Grossman (1976)	13. Encourage adult learner to generate his/her own mediators.
	Labouvie-Vief & Gonda (1976); Robertson-Tchabo et al. (1976); Treat & Reese (1976)	14. Supply adult learner with mediators when necessary.
		15. With concrete material, imagery mediators are superior to verbal mediators and interacting images are better than conjunctive images.
		16. Whenever feasible, train adult learner in use of mnemonic devices.
		17. Encourage adult learner to generate covert monitoring verbalizations and provide training when necessary.
Meaningfulness of Material	Arenberg (1968)	18. Present information which is meaningful to the adult learner.
		19. Assess cognitive structure of adult learner to insure that material is introduced at appropriate level.
		20. Use examples, illustrations, etc., which are concrete.
Degree of Learning	Hulicka & Weiss (1965)	21. Provide ample opportunity for adult learner to overlearn material before moving on to new material.
		22. Remove time constraints from instructional and evaluation process.
Introduction of New Material	Christensen (1968); Heglin (1956); Lair et al. (1969); Sanders et al. (1975, 1976)	23. As an initial step in learning, identify and eliminate inappropriate responses which may "compete" with the appropriate response.
		24. Organize instructional units so that potentially interfering materials are spaced far away from each other.

	25. Stress differences between concepts before similarities.
	26. Make instructional sequence parallel hierarchy of knowledge in any given area.
	27. Instructional procedures should be premised on knowledge of conditions required for a type of learning based on task analysis.
	28. Introduce a variety of techniques for solving problems.
Transfer Effects Hultsch (1974)	29. Take advantage of experience the adult learner possesses.
	30. Relate new information to what adult learner already knows.
	31. Develop learning sets which maximize opportunity for positive transfer effects (i.e., learning to learn effects).
Feedback Effects Bellucci & Hoyer (1975); Hornblum & Overton (1976); Schultz & Hoyer (1976)	32. Provide verbal feedback concerning correctness of responses after each component of task is completed.
	33. Do *not* assume that initially poor performance on a novel, complex task is indicative of low aptitude.
Climate Birkhill & Schaie (1975); Leech & Witte (1971); Ross (1968)	34. Establish a supportive climate.
	35. Engage adult learner in information-oriented, collaborative evaluation.
	36. Encourage adult learner to take educated guesses.

Source: M. A. Okun, "Implications of Geropsychological Research for the Instruction of Older Adults," *Adult Education*, 1977, 27, 139–55.

among the old, however, will only occur if the program content meets their needs. With more input from older community residents and an appreciation of the diversity of interests among the older generation, adult educators can be instrumental in promoting continued growth in the later years of life.

Creativity and Aging

Wisdom and experience are necessary to make the world go round; creative ability to make it go forward.

David Wechsler

Our society places a heavy emphasis on learning and memorization, paying less attention to the development of divergent thinking. As we attempt to deal with the problems of modern-day life, creative minds will be needed to develop novel approaches and solutions to situations occurring in our changing world. On a day-to-day basis, individuals who can be adaptive and employ new strategies for dealing with life transitions will have the strongest coping potential.

Despite its importance, creative thought has received little attention in the aging literature. The few studies that have been conducted have not been consistent in their definition or measurement of creativity.

A frequently cited investigation by Lehman (1953) concluded that individuals reach a peak in creative output during their thirties with the proportion of high-quality work declining thereafter. Rather than focusing on peak production of high-quality works, Dennis (1966) examined total productivity of creative persons in the arts, sciences and humanities. He found that while patterns differed for the various specializations, the decade of the forties was generally the most productive.

It is apparent from casual observation that many highly creative persons do some of their finest work in their later years of life. One has only to consider Picasso, Frank Lloyd Wright and Michelangelo for examples of creative genius active into advanced old age. Our history books are replete with many other examples as well. Perhaps our empirical measures of creativity do not tell the full story. The following passage from the autobiography of the Japanese artist Hokusai, written at age seventy-five, may tell us as much:

I have been in love with painting ever since I became conscious of it at the age of six. At fifty I had published innumerable drawings, but nothing I did before the age of seventy was of any value at all. At seventy-three I have at last caught nearly every aspect of nature— birds, fish, animals, insects, trees, grass, all. Thence at eighty, I shall

155

have developed still further, and shall at ninety really enter the mystery of reality. When I reach a hundred I shall be truly sublime, and at the age of one hundred and ten, every line and dot I draw will be imbued with life.

Suggested Activities and Exercises

1. What reactions do the following situations typically elicit? How are these behaviors interpreted?
   a) a 75-year-old man forgetting his hat
   b) a 25-year-old man forgetting his hat
   a) a 70-year-old woman desiring to learn a foreign language for the first time
   b) a 20-year-old woman desiring to learn a foreign language for the first time
2. Interview at least five older people regarding their views on what they have learned in life and how their perspectives have changed.
3. Visit a local adult education office, and talk to staff members about the philosophy and structure of their program. What do they perceive the educational needs of older community members to be?

References

Abrahams, J. P. Health status as a variable in aging research. *Experimental Aging Research*, 1976, *2*, 63.

Adams, J. A. *Learning and memory* (rev. ed.). Homewood, Ill.: Dorsey, 1980.

Aker, G. F. Learning and the older adult. In A. Hendrickson (Ed.), *A manual on planning educational programs for older adults*. Tallahassee: Florida State University, 1974.

Arlin, P. K. Cognitive development in adulthood: A fifth stage? *Developmental Psychology*, 1975, *5*, 602–6.

Arlin, P. K. Piagetian operators in problem finding. *Developmental Psychology*, 1977, *13*, 297–98.

Ashmead, T., & Lougee, D. *I remember when . . .* Douglas, Wy.: Douglas High School, 1981.

Ashton, P. T. Cross-cultural Piagetian research: An experimental perspective. *Harvard Educational Review*, 1975, *45*, 475–506.

Baltes, P. B., & Schaie, K. W. Aging and IQ—The myth of the twilight years. *Psychology Today*, 1974, *7*, 35–38, 40.

Baum, W. Therapeutic value of oral history. *International Journal of Aging and Human Development*, 1980, *12*, 4953.

Bindra, D. *A theory of intelligent behavior*. New York: McGraw-Hill, 1976.

Birren, J. E. *The psychology of aging.* Englewood Cliffs, N.J.: Prentice-Hall, 1964.

Bischof, L. J. *Adult psychology.* New York: Harper & Row, 1976.

Botwinick, J. *Cognitive processes in maturity and old age.* New York: Springer, 1967.

Botwinick, J. Intelligence and aging. In J. E. Birren & K. W. Schaie (Eds.), *Handbook of the psychology of aging.* New York: Van Nostrand, 1977.

Carroll, J. B., & Horn, J. L. On the scientific basis of ability testing. *American Psychologist,* 1981, *36,* 1012–20.

Cattell, R. B. Theory of fluid and crystallized intelligence: A critical experiment. *Journal of Educational Psychology,* 1963, *54,* 1–22.

Cole, N. S. Bias in testing. *American Psychologist,* 1981, *36,* 1067–77.

Craik, F. I. M. Age differences in human memory. In J. E. Birren & K. W. Schaie (Eds.), *Handbook of the psychology of aging.* New York: Van Nostrand, 1977.

Davis, G. E. Background paper on education for aging. In R. D. Gordon (Ed.), *Learning process in aging and adult education.* Washington, D.C.: U.S. Department of Health, Education and Welfare, 1974.

Dennis, W. Creative productivity between the ages of 20 and 80 years. *Journal of Gerontology,* 1966, *21,* 1–8.

Fozard, J. L. The time for remembering. In L. W. Poon (Ed.), *Aging in the 1980s: Psychological issues.* Washington, D.C.: American Psychological Association, 1980.

Goodrow, B. A. Limiting factors in reducing participation in older adult learning opportunities. *The Gerontologist,* 1975, *15,* 418–22.

Graney, M. J., & Hays, W. C. Senior students: Higher education after age 62. *Educational Gerontology,* 1976, *1,* 343–59.

Guilford, J. P. *The nature of human intelligence.* New York: McGraw-Hill, 1967.

Harris, L., & Associates. *The myth and reality of aging in America.* Washington, D.C.: National Council on the Aging, 1975.

Hartley, J. T., Harker, J. O., & Walsh, D. A. Contemporary issues and new directions in adult development of learning and memory. In L. W. Poon (Ed.), *Aging in the 1980s: Psychological issues.* Washington, D.C.: American Psychological Association, 1980.

Hayslip, B., & Sterns, H. L. Age differences in relationships between crystallized and fluid intelligences and problem solving. *Journal of Gerontology,* 1979, *34,* 404–14.

Hooper, F. H., Fitzgerald, J., & Papalia, D. E. Piagetian theory and the aging process: Extensions and speculations. *Aging and Human Development,* 1971, *2,* 3–20.

Horn, J. L. Human ability systems. In P. B. Baltes (Ed.), *Life-span development and behavior* (Vol. 1). New York: Academic, 1978.

Horn, J. L. Organization of data on life-span development of human abilities. In L. R. Goulet & P. B. Baltes (Eds.), *Life-span developmental psychology: Research and theory.* New York: Academic, 1970.

Horn, J. L., & Donaldson, G. Faith is not enough. *American Psychologist,* 1977, *32,* 369–73.

Hughton, G. A., & Protinsky, H. O. Conservation abilities of elderly men and women: A comparative investigation. *Journal of Psychology,* 1978, *98,* 23–26.

Klatzky, R. L. *Human memory: Structures and processes* (2nd ed.). San Francisco: Freeman, 1980.

Knowles, M. S. *The modern practice of adult education.* New York: Association Press, 1977.

Kobasky, M. B. Educational opportunities for the elderly. In S. Grabowski & W. D. Mason (Eds.), *Learning for aging.* Washington, D.C.: Adult Education Association of the USA, 1974.

Kohlberg, L., & Gilligan, C. F. The adolescent as philosopher: The discovery of the self in a postconventional world. *Daedalus,* 1971, *100,* 1051–86.

Lachman, J. L., & Lachman, R. Age and the actualization of world knowledge. In L. W. Poon, J. L. Fozard, L. S. Cermak, D. Arenberg, & L. W. Thompson (Eds.), *New directions in memory and aging: Proceedings of the George A. Talland Memorial Conference.* Hillsdale, N.J.: Lawrence Erlbaum, 1980.

Lehman, H. C. *Age and achievement.* Princeton, N.J.: Princeton University Press, 1953.

Long, H. B., McCrary, K., & Ackerman, S. Adult cognition: Piagetian-based research findings. *Adult Education,* 1979, *30,* 3–18.

McKinnon, J. W., & Renner, J. W. Are colleges concerned with intellectual development? *American Journal of Physics,* 1971, *39,* 1047–52.

Mead, M. Ethnological aspects of aging. *Psychosomatics,* 1967, *8,* 33–37.

Okun, M. A. Implications of geropsychological research for the instruction of older adults. *Adult Education,* 1977, *27,* 139–55.

Okun, M. A., Seigler, I. C., & George, L. K. Cautiousness and verbal learning in adulthood. *Journal of Gerontology,* 1978, *33,* 94–97.

Papalia, D. E. The status of several conservation abilities across the life span. *Human Development,* 1972, *15,* 229–43.

Papalia, D. E., Salverson, S. M., & True, M. An evaluation of quantity conservation and performance during old age. *International Journal of Aging and Human Development,* 1973, *4,* 103–9.

Piaget, J. Intellectual evolution from adolescence to adulthood. *Human Development,* 1972, *15,* 1–12.

Piaget, J. Piaget's theory. In P. H. Mussen (Ed.), *Carmichael's handbook of child psychology.* New York: 1970.

Riegel, K. F., & Riegel, R. M. Development, drop, and death. *Developmental Psychology,* 1972, *6,* 306–19.

Rubin, K. H. Extinction of conservation: A life span investigation. *Developmental Psychology*, 1976, *13*, 51–56.

Sattler, J. M. *Assessment of children's intelligence*. Philadelphia: Saunders, 1974.

Schaie, K. W. The primary mental abilities in adulthood: An exploration in the development of psychometric intelligence. In P. B. Baltes & O. G. Brim, Jr. (Eds.), *Life-span development and behavior* (Vol. 2). New York: Academic, 1979.

Schaie, K. W. Toward a stage theory of adult cognitive development. *International Journal of Aging and Human Development*, 1977, *8*, 129–38.

Schaie, K. W., & Labouvie-Vief, G. Generational versus ontogenetic components of change in adult cognitive behavior: A fourteen-year cross-sequential study. *Developmental Psychology*, 1974, *10*, 305–20.

Siegler, I. C. The terminal drop hypothesis: Fact or artifact? *Experimental Aging Research*, 1975, *1*, 169.

Siegler, I. C., & Botwinick, J. A long-term longitudinal study of intellectual ability of older adults: The matter of selective subject attrition. *Journal of Gerontology*, 1979, *34*, 242–45.

Spearman, C. *The abilities of man*. New York: Macmillan, 1927.

Storck, P. A., Looft, W. R., & Hooper, F. H. Interrelationships among Piagetian tasks and traditional measures of cognitive abilities in mature and aged adults. *Journal of Gerontology*, 1972, *27* 461–65.

Tesch, S., Whitbourne, S. K., & Nehrke, M. F. Cognitive egocentrism in institutionalized adult males. *Journal of Gerontology*, 1978, *33*, 546–52.

Thurstone, L. L. *Primary mental abilities*. Chicago: University of Chicago Press, 1938.

Tyler, L. E. *Tests and measurements* (2nd ed.) Englewood Cliffs, N.J.: Prentice-Hall, 1971.

U.S. Bureau of the Census, *Social and economic characteristics of the older population: 1978*. (Current Population Reports, Series P-23, No. 85). Washington, D.C.: Government Printing Office, 1979.

Wason, P. C. Reasoning about a rule. *Quarterly Journal of Experimental Psychology*, 1968, *20*, 273–81.

Waugh, N. C., & Norman, D. A. Primary memory. *Psychological Review*, 1965, *72*, 89–104.

Whitbourne, S. K. Test anxiety in elderly and young adults. *International Journal of Aging and Human Development*, 1976, *7*, 201–10.

Chapter 5

Adult Sexuality

Adults are sexual beings. Our sexuality allows us to express love and affection, enjoy physical gratification and engage in procreation. While sexuality is definitely linked to the human anatomy and specific physiological responses, the psychological aspects are equally as important. It is not only the physical stimulation and response that we experience, but how we view and interpret these experiences that determine their significance. Sexuality involves attitudes, behaviors and feelings as well as physiological processes and mechanisms. Among adults, sexuality can take many forms ranging from solitary to interactive activities and encompassing heterosexual, bisexual and homosexual preferences.

In this chapter, the topic of sexuality will be examined within a developmental framework. With the issue of consistency and change in mind, the following questions will be addressed: What changes in sexual attitudes and behaviors occur with age? What factors are responsible for these changes? And what are the predominant areas of sexual concern at each stage of adulthood?

Sexual Attitudes and Behaviors

Young Adulthood

Young adulthood is a time for assuming adult status for the first time. It involves developing a personal value system and making one's own

160

Adults are sexual beings. Our sexuality allows us to express love and affection, enjoy physical gratification, and engage in procreation.

judgments rather than relying on directives from parents. This process, which begins in adolescence and becomes more firmly established in young adulthood, is an important point of transition in life.

The thread of sexuality appears throughout the developmental tasks of young adulthood. Young adults are faced with many decisions regarding their view of appropriate and inappropriate sexual behavior. During this time of life, individuals must work out personally acceptable patterns of sexuality that will allow them to express their affection and caring for others. In addition, they must clarify their views on premarital sex, contraception, abortion and homosexuality. Sexual values are part of an individual's larger value system. Hettlinger (1974) believes that the search for values is related to the search for identity and that young adults have few guideposts for sexual decision making.

In young adulthood, developmental tasks not only revolve around the consolidation of one's identity and the formulation of a personal value system, but they also relate to interactions with others. Young adulthood is a time for establishing the capacity for true intimacy and learning to give and receive affection in a mature and meaningful way. For most people, emotional intimacy is eventually pursued in the context of marriage. As part of sexual adjustment, marriage partners must build and maintain mutually satisfying and rewarding sexual relations. Haeberle (1978) charges that in our society youth "are raised on a steady diet of sexual shame and guilt until some magic wedding ceremony supposedly transforms them into passionate, sensuous and satisfied husbands and wives." Unfortunately, in real life this often does not happen. Positive sexual adjustment is related to acceptance of our sexuality and is based on healthy attitudes developed earlier in life.

Sexual mores in our country have changed, making premarital intercourse more acceptable among today's young adults. Katz (1976) has estimated that 70 percent of all students have engaged in sexual intercourse by their senior year in college. Other research shows that only about one-fifth of college students view premarital sexual intercourse as immoral (King, Balswick & Robinson, 1977). It appears that the younger generation, however, expects that these sexual experiences be meaningful rather than casual encounters (Calderone & Burleson, 1976).

Most of the change in sexual patterns of young unmarried adults appears to have occurred in the 1970s, although beginning trends were apparent in the previous decade. The data reflect some increase in male sexual behavior, but the increases are most dramatic for women. King et al. (1977) found no real differences between sexual attitudes of males and females in their 1975 sample, suggesting that the traditional "double standard" for men and women is weakening. They note that with greater liberalization in female behavior and attitudes, the differences between the sexes with regard to premarital sexual behavior have largely disappeared.

Along with this increase in sexual activity, young people have needed reliable information on birth control and other aspects of sexuality. In some cases when institutional support has been lacking, college students have established their own programs (Hamberg, 1976) and even written, financed and published their own sexuality handbooks (Stanley & Reed, 1976). The Guttmacher Institute (1976) reports that venereal disease, pregnancy and abortion have seen dramatic increases in the college population within the last ten years. The failure of student health services to keep pace and accept the changes that have occurred among the student population has resulted in sexually active persons often operating with limited and inaccurate knowledge about the prevention of pregnancy and venereal disease. Wasserman (1976) believes that this situation has resulted in a serious health crisis in our country. Sarrel (1973), one of the designers of a model sex education program at Yale University, reports that campus sex education programs can be instrumental in reducing pregnancy, facilitating interpersonal relationships through counseling, and helping students with sexual concerns. He states:

> Unquestionably, sexuality is a particularly crucial and evolving issue in the years between 17 and 21. Our colleges are in a unique position to affect this aspect of personal development, for good or ill. The Yale experience suggests that a multi-faceted program, combining sex education and sex counseling, can have a profound influence for maturation on a student population. Hopefully, more colleges and universities will see the value of such programs and will tailor them to meet their own needs and circumstances.

Middle Age

The younger generations, while enjoying greater sexual freedom themselves, seem to have difficulty thinking of the middle-aged in sexual terms, especially their parents. A study of 646 undergraduate students at Illinois State University found that a quarter of the respondents believed their middle-aged parents never had sexual intercourse anymore or only had it once a year. Only 4 percent estimated that their parents had sexual intercourse three to four times a week, and none of the students thought it occurred with any greater frequency. Nonetheless, 90 percent still felt their parents were happily married and still in love with each other. Many students refused to answer questions dealing with premarital and extramarital intercourse, oral-genital sex and masturbation, although their responses were anonymous (Poes, Godow, Tolone & Welsh, 1977). In contrast to the expectations of the younger generation, human sexuality studies have found that middle-aged adults engage in regular and frequent patterns of sexual activity (Pfeiffer, Verwoerdt & Davis, 1972).

At middle age, many events occur which require readjustment of one's self-concept. As physiological changes associated with aging become more and more pronounced during middle age, individuals may question their sexual attractiveness. In a society that places a high value on a youthful appearance, adjustment to the changes that come with age are accentuated. Many primary relationships are also disrupted during the middle years. Children grow up and leave home which means loss of a primary role for most middle-aged adults, especially women. Aged parents often die during this time as well, reminding the middle-aged of their own mortality and adding to their loss of meaningful relationships. Retirement is also anticipated, which presents the threat of another major role loss. Sexuality during the middle years may serve to reassure persons not only of their physical attractiveness and desirability but also of their sustained ability for physical pleasuring and intimacy.

Menopause, the time at which menstruation ceases and a woman loses her reproductive capacity, occurs during middle age. Menopause can threaten a woman's feelings of self-esteem and her concept of herself as a female. While it is a biological event, its symbolic significance may have a greater psychological than physiological impact on women who have invested much of their identity in the mother role.

The research on psychological reactions to menopause indicate, however, that the assumed traumas associated with this event have been exaggerated. A survey conducted by the Boston Women's Health Collective (1976) found that younger women viewed menopause much more negatively than older women who had actually experienced it; only about one third of the older women felt negative about the changes occurring with menopause. Approximately half reported no change in their sexual desires, while the remainder of the sample were evenly divided in their reports of an increase or a decrease in this area. When asked if they felt differently about themselves sexually, two thirds said no. A significant number of women in fact expressed relief that their child-bearing years were over and looked forward to relaxed intercourse without having to be concerned about pregnancy. Neugarten (1967) studied 100 women between the ages of forty-three and fifty-three and discovered that only 4 percent viewed menopause as a major source of worry. More frequent concerns were widowhood, getting older and cancer. When asked to identify the worst thing about menopause, 26 percent replied "not knowing what to expect."

Among middle-aged males, fears of waning virility and declining sexual attractiveness are common. This anxiety over sexual abilities is due in part to the realization that one is growing older and having misconceptions about the effects of the aging process on sexual functioning. The high rates of extramarital relationships during the middle years reflect these sexual concerns. Needed to be assured of their sexual prowess, middle-aged males may pursue sex outside of their marriage, many for the first time. The choice of one's sexual and marriage partner may also be questioned at mid-life as part of the larger process of re-evaluation that typically occurs at this stage of life.

Late Adulthood

Sexual expression in late adulthood, as at any age, is dependent upon factors such as cultural mores, one's sexual history, actual physiological capacities and an available partner. While our culture as a whole tends to be more open about sexuality than in the past, we must remember that most older people were raised in an atmosphere very different from today's. Their early sexual attitudes were developed in an environment permeated by Victorian values, which made it difficult for sexual drives, fantasies and impulses to be freely enjoyed without some sense of shame or wrongness. Women especially were taught to be passive sex objects rather than active participants in sexual activity. Thus, it is difficult for older persons to completely reorient themselves and accept "the new sexuality."

Despite these factors which can potentially interfere with sexual enjoyment, the results of a longitudinal investigation at the Duke University Center for the Study of Aging and Human Development showed that 80 percent of aging men in their sample continued to be interested in sex. While there was a gradual decline in the frequency of sexual intercourse with advancing age, patterns of regular sexual activity were reported by 70 percent of the males at age 68. One out of every five women in their sixties was sexually active. Interestingly, 15 percent of the group showed increased patterns of sexual activity as they grew older (Pfeiffer, Verwoerdt & Davis, 1972; Verwoerdt, Pfeiffer & Wang, 1969).

While sexual activity may decline, there is no clear age-related ending to sexual behavior. Most older people continue to have sexual interests and remain capable of engaging in sex. Cessation of sexual behavior is more related to social circumstances, attitudes of significant others, and ill health than age (Masters & Johnson, 1966, 1970).

For older widowed women, lack of an available partner influences their sexual behavior, resulting in a marked decrease in sexual functioning. Christenson and Gagnon (1965) found that while 70 percent of older married women were having sex, the figure decreased to 12 percent for unmarried women. Women tend to live longer on the average than men and therefore compose the majority of the widowed population. Availability of a sexual partner is further affected by the smaller proportion of older men still living and society's condemnation of elderly women becoming involved with younger males.

Masters and Johnson (1966) and other researchers of human sexuality have found that the likelihood of having an active sex life in the later years is greater if persons have engaged in regular sexual activity earlier in life. Patterns developed in the younger years tend to be maintained. Individuals who have never shown high levels of sexual interest or involvement are not likely to do so in their later years. Therefore, sexual history is a strong determinant of later sexual behavior patterns.

When assessing sexuality and aging, frequency of intercourse provides data on only one dimension of sexuality. Recent studies show that

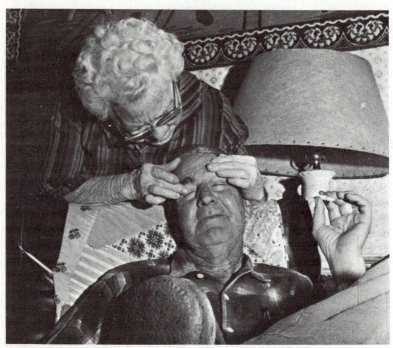

"Love and sexuality in the later years are an affirmation of present aliveness and past shared experiences" (Reedy, 1978, p. 194). (Bob Harvey, photographer)

many older persons report that their lovemaking has actually improved over the years. Relieved from the pressures of childbearing and fear of pregnancy, older couples can be more relaxed. Also, with retirement and children leaving home more privacy, time and opportunity for intimacy exists (Brody, 1980).

When lovers grow old together, a deepening of the relationship can occur. While physical and sexual attraction to each other continues to be important, the nature of sexual intimacy among older couples appears to have "less to do with intense excitement and more to do with tenderness, affection, understanding, touching, warmth, and physical closeness. Love and sexuality in the later years are an affirmation of present aliveness and past shared experiencs" (Reedy, 1978, p. 194).

Many myths about sexual behaviors of older adults prevail in our society. In general, views of sexuality among the aged are dominated by irrational fears, stereotypical thinking and a lack of knowledge. It is commonly thought that older people do not have sexual desires and are incapable of engaging in sex because of their fragile physical state. The elderly are also labeled by younger generations as sexually undesirable, and sexual interest in the later years is often viewed with humor or disgust (Butler & Lewis, 1982). Kass (1981) suggests that societal taboos against "geriatric sexuality" are perhaps the greatest threat to continued sexual expression in the later years. Such terms as "dirty old man" are based on the widespread belief that sexuality is not a natural part of old age, and they serve to convey negative messages to the elderly regarding their sexual needs.

Box 5–1

The Functional Significance of Sex in Later Life

In addition to providing for pleasure, release, communication and shared intimacy, sex during the later years of life can have several other important functions. Butler and Lewis (1978) have suggested that love and sex during late adulthood can also provide:

1. The opportunity for expression of passion, affection, admiration, loyalty and other positive emotions.
2. An affirmation of one's body and its functions—reassurance that our bodies are still capable of working well and providing pleasure.
3. A way of maintaining a strong sense of self-identity, enhancing self-esteem and feeling valued as a person.
4. A means of self-assertion—an outlet for expressing oneself when other outlets for doing so have been lost.
5. Protection from anxiety as "the intimacy and the closeness of sexual union bring security and significance to people's lives, particularly when the outside world threatens them with hazards and losses."
6. Defiance of the stereotypes of aging.
7. The pleasure of being touched and caressed.
8. A sense of romance.
9. An affirmation of a life that has been worthwhile because of the quality of intimate relationships that have been developed.
10. An avenue for continued sensual growth and experience.

Source: R. N. Butler and M. I. Lewis, "The Second Language of Sex," in R. L. Solnick (Ed.), *Sexuality and Aging* (Los Angeles, Ca.: The University of Southern California Press, 1978).

The sexuality of the aged, or assumed lack of it, has often been used as a source of humor in novels, plays and cartoons. Smith (1979) examined 2,217 cartoons published in eight national magazines and found that approximately a quarter of the cartoons that focused on older people had negative themes. These negative themes frequently dealt with the topic of sexuality and portrayed the older person as sexually inadequate, having a sexual dysfunction or diminished sexual interest or ability. For example, one cartoon analyzed by Smith showed "an obviously bewildered elderly man being undressed by a group of pixie-like characters, and was captioned 'At your age you should be grateful for anything you can get' " (p. 409).

To the degree that the elderly accept these messages from society, sexual expression is altered more by psychological than physical factors. With no affirmation of their sexual identity from others, they may reject this aspect of their being. To prevent this from occurring, Kass (1981) recommends better sex education. The major goals of such educational efforts would be "to help society recognize the normality of sexual feelings in later life, to allow the aged to express their sexuality with dignity, to expose the myths of sexlessness, and to provide accurate information about sex and aging to health care professionals who work with the elderly" (p. 75).

The Sexual Response

The hardened, armorlike resistance of the unwanted touch, or the exciting, ever-changing textures of the skin during love-making, and the velvet quality of satisfaction afterward are messages from one body to another that have universal meaning.

Ashley Montagu
*Touching: The Human Significance of
the Skin*

The sexual response involves specific changes in physiologic functioning. It is common knowledge that a sexual experience typically begins with mounting excitement, culminates in an orgasm, and ends in a state of relaxation accompanied by feelings of sexual gratification. Sex researchers however have been interested in investigating the detailed changes that occur in the body during sexual intercourse.

Based on their extensive research on the human sexual response, Masters and Johnson (1966) have divided the sexual experience into the following four phases: excitement, plateau, orgasm and resolution. While these divisions are useful in the study and understanding of adult sexuality, it should be stated that in real life, sexual activity does not occur in such discrete stages but rather "proceeds in a continuous manner with manifestations of various phases overlapping and merging into one another imperceptibly (Katchadourian & Lunde, 1980a, p. 37).

The Sexual Response Cycle

Figures 5–1 and 5–2 summarize the sexual response patterns observed by Masters and Johnson (1966) for males and females, respectively. In-

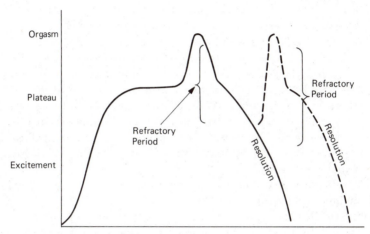

Figure 5–1. The male sexual response cycle. (Source: W. H. Masters and V. E. Johnson. *Human Sexual Response*. Boston: Little, Brown and Company, 1966, p. 5.)

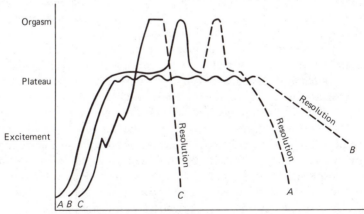

Figure 5–2. The female sexual response cycle. (Source: W. H. Masters and V. E. Johnson. *Human Sexual Response*. Boston: Little, Brown and Company, 1966, p. 5.)

169   Adult Sexuality

dividual variations from these patterns occur typically in the duration, rather than the sequence, of the responses. As can be seen in the figures, the range of variability is greater in the female. While a single pattern is illustrated for the male, three alternative patterns are presented for the female. A refractory period is present in the male cycle, during which a period of time must elapse before a second erection can be achieved. Women, however, are capable of having multiple orgasms in rapid succession (Figure 5-2, line A). In less common patterns among women, arousal may fail to lead to an orgasm (line B) or an orgasm may begin before excitement is stabilized at the plateau stage (line C). In the latter pattern, resolution is achieved rather swiftly.

The length of each phase can vary considerably, with the total cycle occurring in only a few minutes to much longer. Generally, the excitement and resolution stages are the longest of the four phases. These response patterns are independent of the type or source of the stimulation producing them. While the intensity of the responses may vary, the specific body and sex organ reactions associated with the phases in the sexual response cycle will be basically the same regardless of whether they are produced by masturbation, homosexual activities or heterosexual activities.

The first stage in the sexual response cycle begins with sexual excitement and arousal. All of the senses can be involved in sexual arousal but touch is the predominant mode of erotic stimulation followed by vision. There are a wide variety of sexual stimulants to which people respond, some of which are mainly psychological while others are primarily physiological. Many of the psychological stimulants to which we respond sexually are learned through association and conditioning and have no physiological basis. Humans are also capable of responding to stimuli that do not exist in the physical reality, such as mental images and sexual fantasies (Katchadourian & Lunde, 1980a).

In response to effective sexual stimulation, a sensation of arousal is experienced. The response of the sex organs to arousal include erection of the penis and elevation of the testes within the scrotum among males, and lengthening and expansion of the vagina as well as the secretion of vaginal fluid in the female. If stimulation is sustained, the level of arousal is stabilized at a high point and the plateau phase is entered. An orgasmic response soon follows. During orgasm, penile ejaculation occurs and the female experiences rhythmic contractions in the vaginal walls. The resolution phase begins as the neuromuscular tension built up during arousal is gradually dispersed. During this stage the sex organs return to their normal size and shape, and feelings of relaxation and satiation are generally experienced (Katchadourian & Lunde, 1980a).

During the sexual response cycle, many other changes in the body take place, most of which are associated with vasocongestion and myotonia. Vasocongestion occurs when the blood vessels become engorged and an increased blood supply flows into the tissues. Congested tissues become enlarged, flushed and warm due to the excess blood content. Its most dramatic manifestation is in the erection of the penis, but it occurs in other sex organs as well in varying degrees and at different phases of the response cycle. Sexual excitement, however, is always accompanied by widespread vasocongestion. Myotonia refers to increased muscle tension. During sexual activity, myotonia is also widespread and affects both the smooth and skeletal muscles (Katchadourian & Lunde, 1980a).

The Sexual Response in Older Adults

As individuals age, the physiological correlates of the sexual response cycle are not altered in any fundamental way. However, certain physical changes do occur with age, such as decreased muscle tone and strength, loss of elasticity and slower response time which affect the organs and tissues involved in the sexual response. These changes usually do not impair sexual functioning, but they do alter particular aspects of the sexual response (Ludeman, 1981).

Among males the following changes have been identified by Masters and Johnson (1970):

1. An erection takes longer to develop and may not be as full.
2. Ejaculatory control is increased.
3. Ejaculation is not as forceful, and the volume of semen is reduced.
4. The orgasm is usually of shorter duration.
5. The erection subsides more rapidly following ejaculation.
6. The refractory period is lengthened and several hours are usually required before another full erection can be achieved.

Women also experience some sex-related changes with age. Masters and Johnson (1970) have found that the following changes typically occur among older women:

1. Response to sexual stimulation takes longer.
2. Vaginal lubrication is reduced.
3. The vagina is less elastic and loses some of its ability to expand.
4. The vaginal walls become thin, which may cause discomfort for some older women during intercourse.
5. Orgasms are generally briefer and less intense.
6. The length of the resolution stage is considerably reduced.

While these changes do not generally interfere with pleasurable lovemaking, they can be a cause for alarm if couples do not understand that these are normal, age-related changes. For those who do not feel they are sexually impaired, these changes can present some distinct advantages. For example, the increased ejaculatory control of the male allows more time to be spent in foreplay and sexual stimulation of his partner. Therefore, the sexual experience may even be enhanced with age for some couples.

The Climacteric

Middle age is the period of the climacteric, or "change of life," characterized by definite morphologic and physiologic changes in the body. In women, menopause occurs as part of the climacteric. Timiras (1972) has drawn the following analogy: "Climacteric is the counterpart of puberty, and menopause is the counterpart of the menarche" (p. 531).

Estrogen and progesterone secretion begin to decline in the fourth decade of a woman's life and decrease rapidly in the fifth and sixth decades whereupon their production level stabilizes. The major site of estrogen production in the female are the follicles of the ovary, and the loss of these follicles is characteristic of the aging process. The reduction in progesterone production is another sign of endocrine changes in the aging ovary. With these hormonal changes in the aging female, the ovaries stop producing a monthly ovum (egg) and menstruation no longer occurs. Most women become aware that menopause is approaching as their menstrual periods become shorter, have a reduced flow, are farther apart, or are skipped altogether (Timiras, 1972; Williams, 1977).

Decreased estrogen production is associated with specific physical changes in the body during the climacteric, such as decreased firmness of the breasts and loss of subcutaneous fat, as well as the symptoms that often accompany menopause. The sensations experienced by women during this time of hormonal change vary greatly, but common symptoms reported include "hot flashes" in which a sudden sensation of heat is felt followed by perspiration or chills, headaches, dizziness, heart palpitations and pains in the joints (Katchadourian & Lunde, 1980b). Menopausal women also sometimes report psychological symptoms such as anxiety, depression, restlessness and irritability. Neugarten and Kraines (1965), however, found that the incidence of psychological symptoms reported by menopausal women was not significantly higher than for women in other age groups. In fact, adolescents reported the highest incidence of many of the psychological symptoms commonly assumed to be related to menopause.

While the symptoms described above will affect approximately three-quarters of menopausal women to some degree, they will be a major problem for only about ten percent. Estrogen replacement therapy is recommended by some physicians as an effective means of alleviating some of the unpleasant menopausal symptoms. The long-term use of this type of therapy does involve some possible risks and side effects. In 1976, the U.S. Food and Drug Administration issued a statement that linked increased risk of uterine cancer with taking female hormones to relieve menopausal symptoms, and physicians were urged to use caution in prescribing estrogen for this purpose (Katchadourian & Lunde, 1980b).

Box 5–2

What Does the Word "Menopause" Mean to You?

Menopause is often more of a negative experience than it needs to be. Lacking factual information about this life transition, women can be adversely affected by negative societal stereotypes. Our expectation of the experience can be a powerful influence on how the experience actually turns out. What associations do you have to the word "menopause"? One woman described her reactions this way:

> I usually think of geriatric types: little old white-haired women in wheelchairs in nursing homes. It's such an ugly word and image. Dried-up womb—bloodless insides. I'll never forget a man's description of an elegant hotel in the Virgin Islands as "menopause manor"! It made me glad at that time that I was still menstruating and didn't qualify for his derogatory observation. Now, ten years (and Women's Liberation) later, I can see the folly of his remarks and his machismo. But the word by itself still gives me a chill. It seems so final—as if an important bodily function had ceased, and with it all the fun of youth—which, of course, isn't true (Boston Women's Health Collective, 1976).

Among males, no single event is comparable to menopause in women. The testes continue to function indefinitely, although the rates of testosterone secretion and sperm production decline gradually with age. The ejaculatory fluids of older males usually contain viable sperm,

173

therefore allowing them to maintain their reproductive capacity into advanced old age (Katchadourian & Lunde, 1980b).

Sexual Concerns

While some sexual concerns have already been referred to in earlier sections of this chapter, this topic deserves further elaboration. While most sexual dysfunctions can exist at any stage of adulthood, some sexual concerns are linked to specific developmental periods.

Feelings of guilt, fear and shame are responsible for many of the sexual dysfunctions found among college students. While active sexuality may be sanctioned in the permissive campus environment, the larger culture continues to impart its traditional taboos which can produce conflict and confusion about the norm of sexual openness. Peer group pressure may also be felt by those who wish to remain sexually conservative. At this age, social supports are important for sexual decisions and choices (Kaplan, 1974; Sarrel & Sarrel, 1971).

Unable to solve their sexual dilemmas, a large number of students seek professional counseling. Stanley and Reed (1976) have reported that the majority of their college-age clients come to them because of concerns related to sexual orientation and identity, masturbation, frigidity, impotence and general relationship problems. While their active sex life may be a source of guilt and conflict, masturbation appears to cause even more anxiety. While statistics show that it is widely practiced, the majority of the population still expresses strong disapproval of masturbation (Kinsey Institute for Sex Research, 1973). Many students leave campus without adequately resolving these sexual conflicts (Greenberg & Archambault, 1973). Researchers Vacalis, Langston and Molchanov (1977) have found that persons harboring guilt feelings about their sexuality are unable to fully engage in mutual, self-giving interpersonal relationships. Sexual conflicts must be overcome before complete intimacy can be attained.

Frequently these sexual concerns are carried over into the marital arena. Self-reports from a study of 100 married couples (none of which were currently receiving counseling) demonstrate the prevalence of sexual concerns among young adults and the middle-aged. Over a third of the women in this study reported the following sexual problems: difficulty getting excited and maintaining excitement, difficulty in reaching an orgasm, inability to relax and lack of interest in sex. Thirty-eight percent also perceived too little foreplay before intercourse as a problem. The only sexual problem consistently mentioned by one third of the males was "ejaculating too quickly." The data clearly show that while sexual concerns are typically different for the sexes, dysfunction in one's partner will affect the total sexual experience. Despite the concerns expressed by the couples in this study, the majority reported being satisfied with their sexual relations (Frank, Anderson & Rubinstein, 1978).

As has been pointed out earlier in this chapter, the ability to engage in satisfying sexual relations is not necessarily affected by hormonal or other physiological, age-related changes. Sexual performance is usually more affected by anxiety about the changes than the actual physiological changes *per se*. Lack of accurate information is one of the greatest deterrents to effective sexual functioning at all stages of adulthood, yet it may be the most damaging to the elderly.

In our society, the belief that impaired sexuality automatically follows other changes that occur with age is widespread. For example, over half of older men experience discomfort associated with the swelling of the prostate, a small gland located just below the bladder. Removal of this gland is sometimes necessary, a procedure that is commonly assumed to result in impotency in males. However, it has been discovered that almost all impotence occurring after a prostatectomy results from psychological rather than physical factors (Finkle & Prian, 1966). Lack of information and attitudes based on misconceptions can have adverse effects on sexual functioning and should be considered in any type of sex therapy (Annon & Robinson, 1978).

Kass (1981) has emphasized the role of education in preventing sexual dysfunction. Appropriate sex education for the elderly includes teaching them not to equate changes of aging with loss of sexuality, preparing them for the specific physiological changes that do occur, and helping them to cope with their personal feelings and fears. Also, educational programs should include information on the influence of medications on sexual responsiveness and effective sexual techniques for those with physical handicaps.

Positive sexual adjustment throughout life is part of the quality of an overall relationship. One of the essentials for effective sexual functioning at any age is to have open communication with one's sexual partner within an atmosphere of trust in which needs, preferences and concerns can be freely expressed.

Suggested Activities and Exercises

1. What sex education programs are available on your campus? Request information from your student health center regarding the changing incidence of pregnancy and veneral disease on your campus over the past decade.

2. If you had a serious sexual concern, to whom would you go for help? What taboos exist in our culture that result in strong inhibitions against discussing sexual matters?
3. Look at a sample of commercial birthday cards aimed at middle-aged and older adults. How frequently are sexual themes presented? What messages are they conveying?
4. Examine your own reactions to the topic of sexuality among the aged population. How would you describe your attitudes? What factors do you think have influenced your current perceptions?
5. Talk with employees of a nursing home and ask what provisions are made for the privacy of married residents.
6. Talk to human service professionals who work with the aged and find out their perceptions of the sexual needs of the elderly? How do their responses compare with the factual information presented in your text?

References

Annon, J. S., & Robinson, C. H. The use of vicarious learning in the treatment of sexual concerns. In J. LoPiccolo & L. LoPiccolo (Eds.), *Handbook of sex therapy.* New York: Plenum, 1978.

Boston Women's Health Collective. *Our bodies, ourselves.* New York: Simon & Schuster, 1976.

Brody, J. E. Survey of aged reveals liberal views on sex. *New York Times,* April 22, 1980, C1–C2.

Butler, R. N., & Lewis, M. I. *Aging and mental health: Positive psychosocial and biomedical approaches* (3rd ed.). St. Louis: Mosby, 1982.

Butler, R. N., & Lewis, M. I. The second language of sex. In R. L. Solnick (Ed.), *Sexuality and aging* (rev.). Los Angeles: The University of Southern California Press, 1978.

Calderone, M. S., & Burleson, D. A statement of need. In C. E. Rapp, Jr., & M. S. Calderone (Eds.), *Sexual health services for academic communities.* Philadelphia: George F. Stickley, 1976.

Christenson, C. V., & Gagnon, J. H. Sexual behavior in a group of older women. *Journal of Gerontology,* 1965, *20,* 351–56.

Finkle, A. L., & Prian, D. V. Sexual potency in elderly men before and after prostatectomy. *Journal of the American Medical Association,* 1966, *196,* 125–29.

Frank, E., Anderson, C., & Rubinstein, D. Frequency of sexual dysfunction in "normal" couples. *New England Journal of Medicine,* 1978, *299,* 111–15.

Greenberg, J. S., & Archambault, F. X. Masturbation, self-esteem and other variables. *Journal of Sex Research,* 1973, *9,* 41–51.

Guttmacher Institute. *11 million teenagers.* New York: Planned Parenthood Federation of America, 1976.

Haeberle, E. J. *The sex atlas.* New York: Seabury Press, 1978.

Hamburg, M. V. Student health services and sex education: An interdisciplinary approach. In C. E. Rapp, Jr. & M. S. Calderone (Eds.), *Sexual health services for academic communities.* Philadelphia: George F. Stickley, 1976.

Hettlinger, R. *Human sexuality: A psychosocial perspective.* Belmont, Ca.: Wadsworth, 1974.

Kaplan, H. S. *The new sex therapy.* New York: Brunner-Mazel, 1974.

Kass, M. J. Geriatric sexuality breakdown syndrome. *International Journal of Aging and Human Development,* 1981, *13,* 71–77.

Katchadourian, H. A., & Lunde, D. T. *Biological aspects of human sexuality.* New York: Holt, 1980. (a)

Katchadourian, H. A., & Lunde, D. T. *Fundamentals of human sexuality.* New York: Holt, 1980. (b)

Katz, J. Evolving male-female relations and their nurturance. *NASPA Journal,* 1976, *13,* 38–43.

King, K., Balswick, J. A., & Robinson, I. E. The continuing premarital sexual revolution among college females. *Journal of Marriage and the Family,* 1977, *39,* 455–59.

Kinsey Institute for Sex Research. *Report of current sexual standards.* Bloomsfield: Indiana University, 1973.

Ludeman, K. The sexuality of the older person: A review of the literature. *The Gerontologist,* 1981, *21,* 203–8.

Masters, W. H., & Johnson, V.E. *Human sexual response.* Boston: Little, Brown, 1966.

Masters, W. H., & Johnson, V. E. *Human sexual response.* Boston: Little, tle, Brown, 1970.

Montagu, A. *Touching: The human significance of the skin.* New York: Columbia University Press, 1971.

Neugarten, B. L. A new look at menopause. *Psychology Today,* 1967, *1,* 42–49, 70–71.

Neugarten, B. L., & Kraines, R. J. Menopausal symptoms in women of various ages. *Psychosomatic Medicine,* 1965, *27,* 266–73.

Pfeiffer, E., Verwoerdt, A., & Davis, G. C. Sexual behavior in middle life. *American Journal of Psychiatry,* 1972, *128,* 1262–2167.

Poes, O., Godow, A., Tolone, W., & Welsh, R. Is there sex after 40? *Psychology Today,* 1977, *11,* 54–56.

Reedy, M. N. What happens to love? Love, sexuality, and aging. In R. L. Solnick (Ed.), *Sexuality and aging* (rev.). Los Angeles: The University of Southern California Press, 1978.

Sarrel, L. J. Sex counseling on a college campus. *SEICUS Report,* 1973, *1,* 1–2.

177

Sarrel, L. J., & Sarrel, P. M. Birth control services and sex counseling at Yale. *Family Planning Perspectives*, 1971, *3*, 39–42.

Smith, M. D. The portrayal of elders in magazine cartoons. *The Gerontologist*, 1979, *19*, 408–12.

Stanley, E., & Reed, D. *Sex counseling.* In C. E. Rapp, Jr., & M. S. Calderone (Eds.), *Sexual health services for academic communities.* Philadelphia: George F. Stickley, 1976.

Timiras, P. S. *Developmental physiology and aging.* New York: Macmillan, 1972.

Vacalis, T. D., Langston, R. D., & Molchanov, E. The relationship between sex guilt and self-actualization and the implications for sex education. *Journal of Sex Education and Therapy*, 1977, *3*, 14–18.

Verwoerdt, A., Pfeiffer, E., & Wang, H. S. Sexual behavior in senescence. *Geriatrics*, 1969, *24*, 137–53.

Wasserman, S. Sex is a student affair. In C. E. Rapp, Jr., & M. S. Calderone (Eds.), *Sexual health services for academic communities.* Philadelphia: George F. Stickley, 1976.

Williams, J. H. *Psychology of women.* New York: Norton, 1977.

Chapter 6

Personality and Mental Health Issues

While there are numerous definitions of personality, most of them state that personality represents behavioral predispositions that vary from one individual to another and are manifest through interactions with the environment. Personality also includes attitudes, traits and values—components which in totality comprise the system known as "self." These unique combinations of attributes can be thought of as the "me" in each of us.

In this chapter, the self system will be considered as it interacts with the environment over time. Life circumstances often bring incongruence in the fit between an individual and his or her environment. In order to achieve congruence, adjustment and adaptation are necessary. Some adults respond to changes in their lives in maladaptive ways, while others bring a lifetime of effective coping skills to each critical life transition or event. Failure to adapt has important implications for life satisfaction, mental health and physical health.

The Self System: Continuity and Change

The sense of self is a stable personality characteristic. We tend to have considerable consistency in our views toward ourselves. Woodruff and

Birren (1972) found in their longitudinal study that men and women described themselves in very similar terms over a twenty-five year period. While subjectively we feel as though we have changed, our self-descriptions change very little. Individuals, however, vary widely in the strength of their identities upon entering into adulthood.

Adult Identity

Most of the early work on identity concentrated on the years of adolescence. According to Erikson's theory (1959), at this stage the question of identity is first confronted and individuals begin to ask "Who am I?" Erikson views the establishment of a stable and coherent sense of identity as a major task of adolescence.

Depending on the outcome of this search to find oneself in adolescence, individuals will reach the end of this stage with a particular status relative to identity formation. Marcia (1966) sees this process as having four possible outcomes. The ideal status is *"Identity Achieved"* in which the older adolescent has a fairly secure sense of who he or she is as a person. Others will be in a *"Foreclosed"* status. These individuals never really deal with critical identity issues but simply adopt parental beliefs and values. Since personal confrontation on issues critical to the development of the sense of self are avoided, the individual fails to develop true ego identity. Next is the *"Moratorium"* status. Most adolescents go through a period of trying out different roles, discarding some while maintaining others. The moratorium status refers to individuals who are unable to make decisions and remain intensely preoccupied with questions of identity. The final status, *"Identity Diffusion,"* is similar to the moratorium status. These individuals remain indecisive about themselves and what they want from life, but they do not engage in the intense self-questioning and identity struggle of those in the moratrium status.

Rather than describing types, these categories describe styles of dealing with identity issues central to adolescence. While individuals emerge from adolescence in one of these categories, Marcia (1976) suggests that identity in the adult years be viewed as a process rather than a status. She states:

> The problem with statuses is that they have a static quality and identity is never static, not even for the most rigid Foreclosure, who must somehow accommodate himself to each new life cycle issue (p. 153).

The adult years can be characterized by further refinement and clarification of one's identity. As new experiences are encountered and new roles are assumed, they are integrated into one's sense of self. While interactions with the environment alter and expand identity, at the same time one's identity provides direction for a life path. How one sees oneself as a person serves as an organizing factor by influencing choices that are made as well as the interpretation of the outcomes of these choices. As we age, our identities become more complex and differentiated.

A firm sense of self can be critical for successfully facing the later years of life (Lowenthal & Chiriboga, 1973). Old age is associated with physical changes and the loss of roles and relationships that help define the self system. A strong feeling of who we are can provide a sense of stability and internal consistency and make us less vulnerable to external change. Having an identity as an unique individual is essential if one is to end life with integrity.

The elderly have been found to frequently engage in reminiscence, talking and thinking about events in the past. This process can have value for reaffirming one's identity in old age and validating who one is and has been in life. As the elderly take stock of the past, ego integrity is enhanced by recalling experiences and relationships that have given meaning and significance to life.

Old photographs can cue memories of the past and remind the elderly of life experiences that have helped define who they are as individuals. (Holly Haywood, photographer)

Box 6–1

The Life Review

Butler (1963) has used the term "life review" to describe the process of stock taking among the elderly as they reminisce about the past. He views the life review as useful for facing unresolved conflicts which, if successfully reintegrated, can help one face death. For individuals with guilt or pain surrounding past events, Lewis and Butler (1982) have recommended life-review therapy. With assistance from a confidant, hurtful recollections can be placed in perspective within the larger scope of a lifetime. Lewis and Butler have observed that genealogies, scrapbooks and pilgrimages to significant places can be effective means of cueing memories as the older person engages in an autobiographical search.

Literature often gives us deeper insights than we can obtain elsewhere. To gain a real understanding of the life review as a natural and therapeutic process, it is necessary to share this experience with someone. In the book *The Memory of Old Jack*, Wendell Berry (1974) allows us to do this through the mind of an old man approaching death. Following is a brief passsage from this novel:

> He knows too well the way his mind is taking him—his mind that, like a hunting dog backtracking through the country, keeps turning back and turning back, tracing out the way it has come. As if it will be any help to it to know. His mind, he thinks, would do well to settle down and be quiet, for pretty soon he is going up on the hill for the long sleep that most people he knows have already gone off to, and there is not a lot that a man's mind can do about that. He has no fear of death. It is coming, there is nothing to be done about it, and so he does not think about it much. It is the unknown, and he has come to the unknown before. Sometimes it has been very satisfying, the unknown. Sometimes not. Anyhow, what would a man his age propose to do instead of die? He has been around long enough to know that death is the only perfect cure for what ails mortals. After you have stood enough, you die, and that is all right (p. 30).

Maturity

The development of self throughout life can also be related to the concept of maturity. Mature individuals can accept and adapt to the demands and responsibilities of life. In addition, Allport (1961) views mature adults as having the following characteristics:

> The mature personality will (1) have a widely extended sense of self; (2) be able to relate oneself warmly to others in both intimate and nonintimate contacts; (3) possess a fundamental emotional security and accept oneself; (4) perceive, think, and act with zest in accordance with outer reality; (5) be capable of self-objectification, of insight and humor; (6) live in harmony with a unifying philosophy of life (p. 307).

It should be emphasized that a move toward greater maturity can occur throughout life; it is not simply a state at which one arrives at some point in the life course.

Sequences in Adult Life

Even in stable, mature individuals, life brings changes that require some restructuring of the assumptions one has made about oneself and the world. Levinson (1978) has suggested that each decade of life represents a unique period in which life structures are either stabilized or reorganized. Restructuring typically occurs during periods of transition which alternate with periods of relative calm and stability. The reappraisals, changes, and choices made during these times of transition serve as the basis for life structures in the immediately following stages. Levinson places life transitions within the framework of five major eras which form the life-cycle macrostructure. These eras are: (1) preadulthood (age 0 to 22); (2) early adulthood (age 17 to 45); (3) middle adulthood (age 40 to 65); (4) late adulthood (age 60 to 85); and late late adulthood (age 80 and above). Based on in-depth interviews with forty men, Levinson has identified a sequence of eight periods within these eras. Diagrammed in Figure 6-1, these periods can be summarized as follows:

Early adult transition (age 17–22). This period involves modifying the relationship with one's parents and becoming more psychologically and financially independent as the adolescent life structure is terminated. Corresponding with this is an inner exploration of choices for adult life while maintaining a place "on the boundary between adolescence and adulthood" (p. 57). During this stage, life dreams are usually formed—an inner vision of what one wants in life.

Entering the adult world (age 22–28). This is a period of adventure and exploration as young people enter into adulthood. Also during this time, initial commitments are usually made in the areas of work and

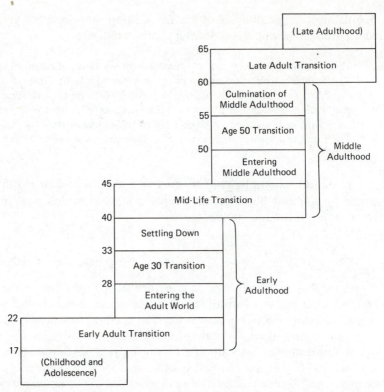

Figure 6–1. Eras and periods in adult male development. (Source: D. J. Levinson, *The Season's of a Man's Life.* New York: Knopf, 1978, p. 57.)

personal relationships. This process of getting established in the adult world includes a shift away from the family of origin. An adult self-image replaces the earlier one of child as adult roles and responsibilities are assumed. As can be seen, this period consists of two somewhat contradictory tasks—the task of exploring possibilities and the task of making commitments and assuming some responsibility. Levinson states: "Finding a balance between these tasks is not an easy matter. If the first predominates, life has an extremely transient, rootless quality. If the second predominates, there is the danger of committing oneself prematurely to a structure without sufficient exploration of alternatives" (p. 58).

Age 30 transition (age 28–33). During this period there is considerable appraisal of previous choices and usually some degree of modification in life structures. At this age comes the realization that the person will become "locked in" to existing life patterns if desired changes are not made soon. For some individuals this transitional phase is rel-

During the "Early Adult Transition" period, life dreams are usually formed—an inner vision of what one wants in life. (Alicia Cook, photographer)

atively smooth, but for others it poses a moderate or severe crisis. Divorce and occupational change are often associated with this age-30 transition. Gould (1978) refers to the years around thirty as a time of self-discovery. Previously occupied with the choices and commitments of the twenties, individuals at the beginning of their third decade become more aware of their feelings, interests and attitudes, which may have previously been ignored or undisclosed. According to Levinson: "The shift from the end of the Age-Thirty Transition to the start of the next period is one of the crucial steps in adult development. At this time a man may make important new choices, or he may reaffirm old choices. If these choices are congruent with his dreams, talents and external possibilities, they provide the basis for a relatively satisfactory life structure. If the choices are poorly made and the new structure is seriously flawed, he will pay a heavy price in the next period" (p. 59).

Settling down (age 33–40). About the age of 33, the males whom Levinson studied began to settle into a stable and secure life pattern. At this point, individuals have made deeper commitments. A deeper sense of rooting comes with such events as buying a house, having children and advancing at work. This is a time of deciding what is really important in life and individuals become more serious about what Levinson refers to as "making it." Long-range planning now includes specific goals, usually related to vocational advancement, and a timetable for achieving these goals. A male's sense of well-being at this stage is strongly related to the progress being made toward these goals. Levinson has identified a phase toward the end of the settling-down period called "Becoming One's Own Man" in which more autonomy and independence from authority are sought. If a man has had a mentor, he will often relinquish that relationship during this phase.

Mid-life transition (age 40–45). Acting as a link between early and middle adulthood, this transition begins the second half of life when more time is stretched out behind than ahead. Individuals become increasingly aware of the time squeeze at mid-life, which results in the soul-searching so characteristic of this period. Previous choices and accomplishments are reevaluated with the urgent realization that time is running out for fulfilling earlier dreams and aspirations. For some, reappraisal will reveal a life lacking in the elements considered important to the person. Depending on the gap between what was attained and what was desired, mid-life can be a difficult and tumultuous time. However, this varies greatly among individuals. As a result of this reassessment of life goals and circumstances, some adults make major changes in their lives. Others simply shift priorities as they take a closer look at what they want from life.

Entering middle adulthood (age 45–50). At around age forty-five the mid-life transition subsides, and the person enters a period of relative stability after the inner turmoil and strife of the previous three or four years. The life structure formed at this time will grow out of new perspectives gained during the previous period. Changes may occur during this period, but they will be more subtle. The experience of middle age will vary considerably from one individual to another depending on the outcome of the mid-life transition. From his interviews, Levinson has concluded: "Some men have suffered such irreparable defeats in childhood or early adulthood, and have been so little able to work on the tasks of their Mid-life Transition, that they lack the inner and outer resources for creating a minimally adequate structure. They face a middle adulthood of constriction and decline. Other men form a life structure that is reasonably viable in the world but poorly connected to self. Although they do their bit for themselves and others, their lives are lacking in inner excitement and meaning. Still other men have started a middle adulthood that will have its own special satisfactions and fulfillments. For these men, middle adulthood is often the fullest and most creative season in the life cycle" (pp. 61–62).

Currently, Levinson does not have empirical data on periods beyond "Entering Middle Adulthood." However, he has proposed transitional periods in both the early fifties and sixties separated by more stable periods. Some modification of life structure can continue to be made during these later stages. "The Late Adult Transition" sets the stage for life structures in the final years of life. Using a similar stage approach, Gould (1972, 1978) has observed that individuals in their fifties accept themselves and others more than at younger ages, and they exhibit a new serenity and relaxed outlook which continues into late adulthood.

Age-Related Personality Trends

Individuals develop characteristic ways of responding that become resistant to change. While one's roles and status may be altered throughout life, personality structures tend to remain stable. Neugarten (1964) describes it this way: "In a sense, the self becomes institutionalized with the passage of time . . . as individuals age they become more like themselves . . ." (p. 198).

Although most studies have underscored the continuity of personality traits over the adult years, some aspects of personality change in a predictable direction as one ages. Characteristics showing age-related change seem to primarily involve the intrapsychic dimensions of personality. Also, major differences in gender characteristics occur with age.

Intrapsychic dimensions. Some of our most valuable information on personality continuity and change has come from the Kansas City Study of Adult Life. Based at the University of Chicago, Bernice Neugarten and her colleagues interviewed nearly 700 noninstitutionalized adults between the ages of 40 and 90 living in Kansas City during the 1950s. Over a ten-year span, numerous studies on personality and adjustment were completed by this Chicago research group (Neugarten & Associates, 1964).

Neugarten (1977) reports that a consistent finding from her research and that of other investigators relates to the increase in introversion in the second half of life. This trend toward greater introversion, referred to as *interiority*, begins in middle age and becomes more pronounced in late adulthood. This trait of interiority among the old has been demonstrated most convincingly in the areas of personal orientation and self-environment relations.

As individuals in the Kansas City sample aged, Neugarten and her colleagues observed a shift from *active mastery* to *passive mastery*. Basically, these observations reflect changes in the perception of the self in relation to the environment. Forty-year-olds saw themselves as being in charge, having the energy required to meet the demands of the outside world, and engaging in self-assertion. In contrast, sixty-year-olds viewed themselves in more passive terms. They perceived themselves as accommodating to an environment that was extremely complex and sometimes even dangerous (Neugarten, 1964; Neugarten & Datan, 1973). Similar age-related trends have been found in other cultures (Gutmann, 1964).

Associated with this change is the occurrence of greater introspection and self-reflection with age, which represents a shift from an outerworld orientation to an inner-word orientation. Older individuals appear to have less ego energy for dealing with the tasks of the outside world, while at the same time becoming more responsive to their own inner processes (Rosen & Neugarten, 1964). This transition has been interpreted in various ways by gerontologists. Some view it as a natural exploration of a rich inner self and an interest in spiritual concerns as one gets nearer to death. Others interpret it as a sign of depression and hopelessness in old age.

Box 6–2

Old Age: A Time for Personal Growth

A theoretical model that reflects the natural tendency of humans toward growth is Abraham Maslow's (1954) theory of human motivation. According to Maslow, individuals are instinctually self-motivated and have a psychological need for growth, development and utilization of potential. An individual placing priorities on self-actualizing values will strive to achieve the following: 1) a sense of wholeness with unity and integration within the person; 2) a feeling of aliveness, functioning to the fullest of one's present capabilities; 3) a quality of existence that includes experiences of richness, fullness and beauty; 4) a sense of playfulness, maintaining a capacity for fun, joy, gaiety and humor; 5) a recognition and acceptance of one's uniqueness and individuality; and 6) a sense of fulfillment in one's life.

In the early 1970s, Gay Luce, a Berkeley psychologist, observed that few programs for the elderly in the United States recognized this stage of life as an important time of growth. Influenced by traditions of the East in which old age is seen as an ideal period for inner growth and contemplation, Luce founded SAGE (Senior Actualization and Growth Explorations). She started her pilot project with the belief that people can "grow as much at 75 as at 25, if given the same conditions that inspire growth in the young—nur-

turance, support, challenge, freedom, and continued activity"
(Fields, 1978, p. 389). Interest in SAGE has now spread all across
the country.

SAGE groups typically meet once or twice a week, and participants engage in a variety of activities designed to promote relaxation, self-awareness, and mental and physical health. Nontraditional methods such as meditation, yoga and T'ai Chi are among
the techniques explored. These techniques for self-realization are
widely practiced in Eastern societies where "old age is looked at
developmentally as a time to look inward, to examine oneself, and
one's relationship to the universe. Insomnia, for example, which
we label as a disease, is looked upon as natural, not something to
erase with a pill. People wake up early for meditation and think
about spiritual matters . . ." (Fields, 1978, p. 388). Luce views the
SAGE program as being effective for extending methods of preventive medicine and allowing individuals to take more responsibility
for their personal well-being.

Sex differences.   Some of the more interesting findings of Neugarten
and her associates (1964) pertained to changes in gender characteristics
with age. As they grew older, individuals in the Kansas City sample became more androgynous (androgyny refers to the manifestation of both
male-typed and female-typed characteristics within a single individual).
Specifically, males became more nurturant and affiliative with age, characteristics typically considered to be "feminine," and older women
demonstrated more assertiveness and independence, traits associated
with "masculinity." In cross-cultural investigations using widely divergent cultures, Gutmann (1977) has obtained similar results.

Several decades before these research findings were obtained, Carl
Jung had reached a similar conclusion from his clinical observations:

> We might compare masculinity and femininity and their psychic com-
> ponents to a definite store of substances of which, in the first half of
> life, unequal use is made. A man consumes his large supply of mas-
> culine substance and has left over only the smaller amount of femi-
> nine substance, which must now be put to use. Conversely, the woman
> allows her hitherto unused supply of masculinity to become active
> (Jung, 1933, p. 16).

This reduction in sex-role differentiation has been related to successful aging (Reichard, Livson & Peterson, 1962). Sinnott (1977) has pos-

tulated that life-span variations in sex roles may indicate a more generalized flexibility and may therefore be an adaptive response which has survival value. The manifestation of stereotyped "masculine" and "feminine" roles in late adulthood may in fact be maladaptive.

Indeed, different life structures may permit and encourage expression of different aspects of the self. In this regard, Sinnott (1977) has noted:

> The relationship between androgyny and successful aging appears to be part of a larger pattern of increasing and deceasing sex-role differentiation at points in the life span. At birth, the individual behaves androgynously. Sex roles diverge in middle childhood, converge again in the working period of the early twenties, and diverge again during the child-raising period. When children have grown, roles again *converge*. This changing lifetime pattern suggests that sex roles are not central to identity and that the adaptive individual usually functions with the ability to modify sex roles and other roles when needed.

Box 6–3

The Case Study Approach

Robert Havighurst (1973) believes that sources of nonscientific literature can offer us useful life-span perspectives on personality. Particularly well-written and documented biographies and auto-biographies provide excellent opportunities for gaining insight into the change and continuity in behaviors, attitudes and values over a lifetime. In addition, he feels that these works can be used as a legitimate source of data on personality development: "Case studies, where the data on the subjects are intensive and extend over a period of time, are valuable, assuming a skillful analysis and a representative sample of cases, in providing a substantial basis for generalization" (p. 22). He points out that Bühler in her work in Vienna relied heavily on biographies, preferring them over autobiographies because they allowed study up to the very end of life rather than only the late periods. Included among the literary works which Havighurst cites as being outstanding psychological portraits of individual personalities are the following:

Jonçich, G. *The Sane Positivist: A Biography of E. L. Thorndike.* Middletown, Conn.: Wesleyan University Press, 1968.
Simmons, L. (Ed.) *Sun Chief: The Autobiography of a Hopi Indian.* New Haven: Yale University Press, 1942.

Roosevelt, E. *The Autobiography of Eleanor Roosevelt*. New York: Harper & Row, 1961.

Adjustment and Adaptation in Later Life

There is nothing which for my part I like better, Cephalus, than conversing with aged men; for I regard them as travellers who have gone on a journey which I too may have to go, and from whom I ought to inquire whether the way is smooth and easy or rugged and difficult. And this is a question which I should like to ask of you who have arrived at that time which the poet calls the threshold of old age: is life harder at the end, or what report do you give of it?

Socrates

As one passes through middle age, the temporal ordering of life events is gradually seen from a different vantage point. Rather than viewing life from time since birth, time comes to be perceived as time left to live (Neugarten, 1968). Accompanying this change in time perspective is an expanded view of the life cycle, which is attained only when one has experienced it. As Butler and Lewis (1982) describe it: "An inner sense of the life cycle . . . produces a profound awareness of change and evolution . . . and therefore a profound but nonmorbid realization of the precious and limited quantity of life. For older people it is not the same as 'feeling old'; it is instead a deep understanding of what it means to be human" (p. 173).

Despite the commonalities of the aging experience, considerable variation occurs among individuals in their adjustment to aging. What factors are related to positive adjustment? Which personality types appear to adapt best in the later years of life?

Theories of Adjustment to Aging

Adjustment occurs when there is a balance among needs, stimuli and opportunities offered by the environment. When these elements are in balance, personal well-being and life satisfaction are experienced. Older individuals can be said to be in a state of well-being if they (1) take pleasure from activities in daily life; (2) view life as meaningful and accept their present life circumstances; (3) feel that they have achieved their major life goals; (4) have a positive image of themselves; (5) primarily experience happy and optimistic attitudes and moods (Havighurst,

191   Personality and Mental Health Issues

Disengagement theory portrays aging as a process of gradual physical, psychological, and social withdrawal from the mainstream of society. (Alicia Cook, photographer)

Neugarten & Tobin, 1968). Persons characterized as successfully adjusting to aging display many of these attributes and characteristics. Several
theories have been advanced in an attempt to explain the process of
adjustment in old age. Perhaps the best known are the *disengagement
theory* and the *activity theory.*

First proposed in 1961 by Cumming and Henry, disengagement theory portrays aging as a process of gradual physical, psychological and
social withdrawal from the mainstream of society in preparation for
eventual physical decline and death. According to this theory, disengagement is a mutual process whereby society relinquishes the elderly
from their roles at the same time that older individuals are beginning
to shift their attention away from work, social and civic activities. Disengagement is seen as mutually advantageous to both older persons
and the larger society.

Advanced as an alternative interpretation of successful aging, the
activity theory maintains that the most successful agers are those who
maintain a high degree of involvement in life. Although some reduction
in activity is expected with age, healthy older persons maintain fairly

stable patterns of activity (Neugarten, 1973) and declines in activity are associated with lower levels of satisfaction, contentment and happiness (Garney, 1975; Maddox, 1963; Neugarten & Associates, 1964). According to activity theorists:

> Except for the inevitable changes in biology and in health, older people are the same as middle-aged people, with essentially the same psychological and social needs. In this view, the decreased social interaction that characterizes old age results from withdrawal by society from the aging person; and the decrease in interaction proceeds against the desires of most aging men and women. The older person who ages optimally is the person who stays active and who manages to resist the shrinkage of his social world. He maintains the activities of middle age as long as possible and then finds substitutes for those activities he is forced to relinquish (Havighurst, et al., 1968, p. 161).

Neither the disengagement nor the activity theory seem to adequately explain successful adaptation during the later years of life. Empirical evidence seems to be against the major tenets of the disengagement theory as it was originally proposed (Maddox, 1969), and the activity theory has been criticized as an oversimplification of the questions involved in adjustment in old age. Based on data from their Kansas City

The activity theory maintains that the most successful agers are those who continue to have a high degree of involvement in life. (The Coloradoan/Bob Gunter, photographer)

sample, Neugarten et al. (1968) have proposed that personality may be more of a pivotal factor in predicting which individuals age successfully than activity and disengagement considered alone. They maintain that with age "patterns of overt behavior are likely to become increasingly consonant with the individual's underlying personality needs and his desires," thus explaining the wide variations observed in adaptation.

To further elucidate the diversification among aged individuals, Neugarten et al. (1968) identified four major personality types each with its own subdivisions. Based on different combinations of role activity and life satisfaction, their topology reveals eight unique patterns of aging: the Reorganizer, the Focused, the Disengaged, the Holding-on, the Constricted, the Succorance-seeking, the Apathetic, and the Disorganized. Table 6–1 provides descriptions of each of these life patterns.

As Havighurst (1968) has concluded:

> From a social psychological perspective aging is better viewed, not as a process of engagement or disengagement, but as a process of adaptation in which personality is the key element. The aging individual not only plays an active role in adapting to the biological and social changes that occur with the passage of time but in creating patterns of life that will give him greatest ego involvement and life satisfaction.

Additional Variables Related to Life Satisfaction

Rather than looking at life satisfaction and aging *per se*, Elwell and Maltbie-Crannell have focused on role loss which commonly accompanies the aging process. After reviewing the available literature, they have concluded that role loss affects coping resources and life satisfaction of the elderly both directly and indirectly. Although our discussion will extend beyond the consideration of role loss, their model presented in Figure 6–2 is a useful organizing framework for examining factors which mediate adjustment and either diminish or contribute to life satisfaction.

Personal characteristics. Elwell and Maltie-Crannell (1981) cite research indicating that age and education are inversely related to life satisfaction. The older the elderly person and the less education he or she has, the more likely they will undergo role loss. In addition, the less likely they will be to have good health, an adequate income and sufficient social supports. Nonwhites are also more apt to suffer role loss than whites. When rural-urban status is examined, rural elderly report significantly higher rates of physical ailments and lower incomes than their urban counterparts (Youmans, 1977).

Table 6–1. Patterns of Aging.

Personality Type	Characteristics of the Type	Role Activity	Life Satisfaction
1. Integrated	Well-adjusted persons with high self-regard who maintain a comfortable degree of control over life's impulses		
a. Reorganizer	Competent people, engaged in many activities, who substitute new activities for lost ones	High	High
b. Focused	Persons selective in their activities and who concentrate on one or two roles	Medium	High
c. Disengaged	Those who voluntarily move away from role commitments and social relations; they are calm, contented, and withdrawn	Low	High
2. Armored-Defended	Striving and ambitious persons with high defenses against anxieties associated with aging		
a. Holding-on	Those who try to maintain patterns of middle age as long as possible; to them old age is a threat	High or medium	High
b. Constricted	Persons who defend themselves against aging by limiting their social contacts and trying to conserve their energies	Low or medium	High or medium
3. Passive-Dependent			
a. Succorance-seeking	Those people who are dependent on others for emotional support	High or medium	High or medium
b. Apathetic	Persons who are passive and submissive	Low	Medium or low
4. Unintegrated			
a. Disorganized	Persons with defects in psychological functions	Low	Medium or low

Source: Based on B. L. Neugarten, R. J. Havighurst, and S. S. Tobin, "Personality and Patterns of Aging," In B. L. Neugarten (Ed.), *Middle Age and Aging* (Chicago: The University of Chicago Press, 1968, p. 174).

Multiple role losses during late adulthood can deplete coping resources and reduce life satisfaction. (Bob Harver, photographer)

Personal resources. When placed in situations that require adjustment, individuals have been found to rely heavily on their own resources (Gurin, Veroff & Feld, 1960). Two important resources an individual can possess are income and health. Several studies have shown that financial security and good health are among the best predictors of life satisfaction among the elderly (Edwards & Klemmack, 1973; Lar-

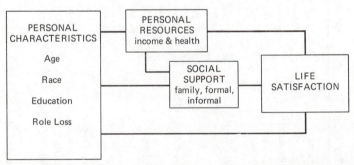

Figure 6–2. Impact of role loss. (Source: F. Elwell and A. D. Maltbie-Crannell, "The Impact of Role Loss upon Coping Resources and Life Satisfaction of the Elderly." *The Geronotologist*, 1981, *36*, p. 227.)

son, 1978; Markides & Martin, 1979). Personal coping strengths can also be considered a resource of the individual. These inner resources can include a philosophy of life as well as religious values and beliefs. Listening to church services on the radio and television, praying, Bible reading and meditating have all been shown to increase with age. Also, beliefs in God and immortality are greater among the elderly (Moberg, 1971). Cutler (1976) found in his investigation of the elderly's participation in voluntary associations that only church membership was consistently related to higher levels of life satisfaction.

Support systems. What support systems are available to older persons to facilitate their adjustment to role loss and increase their life satisfaction? The family system ranks high as a primary source of support for the elderly. As you learned in Chapter Two, high levels of interaction among generations are prevalent in American families. Frequent and meaningful contacts with family members can be important for reaffirming the worth and value of the aging individual.

Informal support networks consist of relatives, friends and neighbors. Mutual support is provided in these systems and requests for assistance are often made for emotional, practical and even financial matters (Cantor, 1979). These informal networks are particularly strong in rural areas and are thought to have contributed significantly to the sur-

Religious values and beliefs can be an important personal resource for the elderly. (DENVER POST/© John Sunderland, photographer)

vival of older families in geographically isolated regions (Collins & Pancoast, 1976). Personal relationships play a large part in the formation of these loosely knit systems. Studies of older people have found that availability of a close friend or confidant—whether a family member, friend or neighbor—frequently differentiated those who were coping effectively from those who were not (Lowenthal & Haven, 1968).

In contrast, formal helping systems are usually composed of agencies, institutions and programs. Human service programs aimed toward the elderly have grown considerably over the past decade. Other services with a more generalized age focus, such as health care and transportation, can also have special significance for the elderly and their adjustment in later life. In rural areas, formal services tend to be fragmented and often located far from the client population, thus interfering with effective service delivery. Also, professionals working in rural areas tend to be generalists since the population is not large enough to support more specialized services (Ginsberg, 1977). Older rural residents may therefore be underserved by formal helping systems in areas critical to their well-being.

Mental Health Concerns

Adults are continually coping with changes in their life space. Some types of change are gradual while others are more abrupt. According to Parkes (1971):

> If change takes place gradually and the individual has time to prepare, little by little, for the restructuring, the chances that this will follow a satisfactory course are greater than they would be if the change was sudden and unexpected. Thus the transitions of maturation—growing in size, changing in appearance, becoming gradually older and more frail—are barely recognized as changes at all, whereas the unexpected loss of a job or wife is more likely to be recognized as a major transition (p. 103).

Based on the concept that any type of change whether positive (changing jobs) or negative (death of a close friend) can be stressful, Holmes and Rahe (1967) developed the Social Readjustment Rating Scale. Containing a list of 43 common life events, the scale provides a stress weighting (referred to as life-change units) for each item. These assigned values were obtained empirically by asking a diverse group of persons to rate each life event according to its stressfulness and the degree of readjustment it required. An examination of the scale in Table 6 – 2 shows that many of the life events with the highest stress ratings commonly

Table 6–2. The Social Readjustment Rating Scale.

Rank	Life Event	Mean Value
1	Death of spouse	100
2	Divorce	73
3	Marital separation	65
4	Jail term	63
5	Death of close family member	63
6	Personal injury or illness	53
7	Marriage	50
8	Fired at work	47
9	Marital reconciliation	45
10	Retirement	45
11	Change in health of family member	44
12	Pregnancy	40
13	Sex difficulties	39
14	Gain of new family member	39
15	Business readjustment	39
16	Change in financial state	38
17	Death of a close friend	37
18	Change to different line of work	36
19	Change in number of arguments with spouse	35
20	Mortgage over $10,000	31
21	Foreclosure of mortgage or loan	30
22	Change in responsibilities at work	29
23	Son or daughter leaving home	29
24	Trouble with in-laws	29
25	Outstanding personal achievement	28
26	Wife begins or stops work	26
27	Beginning or end of school	26
28	Change in living conditions	25
29	Revision of personal habits	24

Table 6-2. The Social Readjustment Rating Scale (*continued*).

Rank	Life Event	Mean Value
30	Trouble with boss	23
31	Change in work hours or conditions	20
32	Change in residence	20
33	Change in schools	20
34	Change in recreation	19
35	Change in church activities	19
36	Change in social activities	18
37	Mortgage or loan less than $10,000	17
38	Change in sleeping habits	16
39	Change in number of family get-togethers	15
40	Change in eating habits	15
41	Vacation	13
42	Christmas	12
43	Minor violations of the law	11

Source: T. H. Holmes and R. Rahe, "The Social Readjustment Rating Scale," *Journal of Psychosomatic Research*, 1967, *11*, 216.

occur in late adulthood, such as death of a spouse or close family member, personal injury and illness, retirement, change in financial status and change in living conditions. Rather than being viewed individually, these stressors are seen as having a cumulative effect. Therefore, an older individual would have a high probability of accumulating a large number of life-change units in a relatively short period of time.

This instrument may have predictive validity for identifying "high-risk individuals," that is, individuals with a higher than normal probability of developing mental or physical health problems. Research has shown a significant effect for stressful life events occurring concurrently during the six months prior to the onset of a physical illness (Rahe, 1974). Significant associations have also been found between reports of life changes and reports of psychophysiological symptoms and signs of depression (Markush & Favero, 1974; Vinokur & Selzer, 1975), as well as scores on several trait measures of anxiety (Reavley, 1974).

Sometimes stressful events tax individuals beyond their ability to cope. Responses to stress can be grouped into three main categories:

(1) physiological responses (for example, physical illness), (2) behavioral responses (for instance, impaired performance) and (3) self-reported subjective states (such as anxiety and depression) (Moos, 1973). It has been postulated that events producing stress reactions may eventually have a "wear and tear" effect upon the indivdual. Indeed, this conception fits with Selye's (1956) well-known model of the physiologic response to stress which consists of the following three stages: the alarm reaction, the stage of resistance involving an increased capacity for the individual to respond, and exhaustion characterized by a loss of functional capacity to continue.

Box 6–4

Suicide in Later Life

For some individuals, depression surrounding life events leads to suicide. The suicide rate for the white male in the United States is the highest of any group, and this rate rises steadily with age. Interestingly, suicide rates for women actually decline after age 65 (see Table 6–3). Although difficult to interpret, perhaps this trend indicates that many of the lossses that occur with age—status, employment, income, physical ability—may be more difficult for males to accept than for females.

Lower rates have also been observed among nonwhites than among whites. The lower rates among ethnic minorities may be due to the fact that many have lived with adverse conditions all of their lives and having a lower status and restricted income is not unique to their later years.

Older individuals contemplating suicide appear less likely than younger people to seek help. The percentage of older callers at suicide prevention centers is much lower than would be anticipated from the suicide statistics. The Suicide Prevention Center in Los Angeles has reported that only 2.6 percent of the calls which they receive are from people over the age of 60 (Farberow & Moriwaki, 1975).

While the parameters of the situation as well as the personalities involved will determine the appropriateness of specific coping strategies, Caplan (1964) has identified the following characteristics of effective coping behaviors that cut across different types of life transitions and crises:

Table 6–3. Suicide Rates in the United States, 1976 (per 100,000).

Age Range	White Males	White Females	Nonwhite Males	Nonwhite Females
5–14	0.7	0.2	0.3	0.4
15–24	19.2	4.9	14.7	4.0
25–34	23.7	8.6	22.8	6.5
35–44	23.6	11.0	16.8	4.7
45–54	27.7	13.8	13.5	4.3
55–64	31.6	12.1	12.3	2.8
65 and over	39.7	8.3	14.5	3.2

Source: U.S. Bureau of the Census. *Statistical Abstracts of the United States* (Washington, D.C.: U.S. Government Printing Office, 1978, p. 183).

1. Active exploration of reality issues and search for information.
2. Free expression of both positive and negative feelings and a tolerance of frustration.
3. Active invoking of help from others.
4. Breaking problems down into manageable bits and working them through one at a time.
5. Awareness of fatigue and tendencies toward disorganization with pacing of efforts and maintenance of control in as many areas of functioning as possible.
6. Active mastery of feelings where possible and acceptance of inevitability where not possible. Flexibility and willingness to change.
7. Basic trust in oneself and others and basic optimism about outcome.

Lieberman (1971, 1975), however, has suggested that traditional views of mental health may not apply to those who have lived a long time and that different processes of coping with crises may be specific to different life stages. Using survivorship as a measure of adaptation, he found that among the elderly he studied "those who were *aggressive, irritating, narcissistic,* and *demanding* were the individuals found to be most likely to survive crisis. Certainly they were not the most likeable elderly. It would seem that the thought of 'growing old gracefully' is more of a comfort to the young than an adequate guide to surviving generally inescapable stresses of longevity" (1975, p. 155). As a result of these findings, Lieberman postulated the trait of combativeness to have survival value. Interestingly, Gutmann (1971) found this same pattern of combativeness to be characteristic of the longest-lived men in the preliterate societies he studied.

Many questions remain to be answered. As we further explore the topic of stress and coping in the later years of life, exciting possibilities may emerge for intervention and prevention of many of the mental health problems prevalent in adulthood.

Suggested Activities and Exercises

1. Interview four older persons and obtain information on their approaches to old age. How would you classify each of them according to the typology proposed by Neugarten and her associates?
2. Ask your parents to relate incidents of your behavior as a child. How did you typically respond to stressful situations? Do you recognize any predispositions in your earlier behavior that are still present today?
3. How do you define yourself as a person? Write a brief essay in which you examine the various facets of your self-identity.
4. Read a well-written biography or autobiography and consider the topic of individual change and continuity in view of what you have learned in this chapter.

References

Allport, G. W. *Pattern and growth in personality*. New York: Holt, 1961.

Berry, W. *The memory of old Jack*. New York: Harcourt, 1974.

Butler, R. N. The life review: An interpretation of reminiscence in the aged. *Psychiatry*, 1963, *26*, 65–76.

Butler, R. N., & Lewis, M. I. *Aging and mental health: Positive psychosocial and biomedical approaches* (3rd ed.). St. Louis: Mosby, 1982.

Cantor, M. H. Neighbors and friends: An overlooked resource in the informal support system. *Research on Aging*, 1979, *1*, 434–63.

Caplan, G. *Principles of preventive psychiatry*. New York: Basic Books, 1964.

Collins, A. H., & Pancoast, D. L. *Natural helping networks: A Strategy for prevention*. Washington, D.C.: National Association of Social Workers, 1976.

Cumming, E., & Henry, W. *Growing old: The process of disengagement*. New York: Basic Book, 1961.

Cutler, S. J. Membership in different types of voluntary associations and psychological well-being. *The Gerontologist*, 1976, *16*, 335–39.

Edwards, J. N., & Klemmack, D. L. Correlates of life satisfaction: A reexamination. *Journal of Gerontology*, 1973, *28*, 497–502.

Elwell, F., & Maltbie-Crannell A. D. The impact of role loss upon coping resources and life satisfaction of the elderly. *Journal of Gerontology*, 1981, *36*, 223–32.

Erikson, E. H. Identity and the life cycle: Selected papers. *Psychological Issues*, Monograph No. 1, 1959.

Farberow, N. L., & Moriwaki, S. Y. Self-destructive crises in the older person. *The Gerontologist*, 1975, *15*, 333–37.

Fields, S. Senior actualization and growth explorations (SAGE). In R. Gross, B., Gross, & S. Seidman (Eds.), *The new old: Struggling for decent aging*. Garden City, N.J.: Anchor Press, 1978.

Ginsburg, L. H. Rural social work. In *Encyclopedia of social work*. Washington, D.C.: National Association of Social Workers, 1977.

Gould, R. L. The phases of adult life: A study in developmental psychology. *American Journal of Psychiatry*, 1972, *129*, 33–43.

Gould, R. L. *Transformations*. New York: Simon & Schuster, 1978.

Graney, M. J. Happiness and social participation in aging. *Journal of Gerontology*, 1975, *30*, 701–6.

Gurin, G., Veroff, J., & Feld, S. *Americans view their own mental health*. New York: Basic Books, 1960.

Gutmann, D. L. An exploration of ego configurations in middle and later life. In B. L. Neugarten & Associates (Eds.), *Personality in middle and later life*. New York: Atherton, 1964.

Gutmann, D. L. Dependence, illness and survival among Navajo men. In E. Palmore & F. C. Jeffers (Eds.), *Prediction of life span*. Lexington, Mass.: Heath, 1971.

Gutmann, D. L. The cross-cultural perspective. In J. E. Birren & K. W. Schaie (Eds.), *Handbook of the psychology of aging*. New York: Van Nostrand, 1977.

Havighurst, R. J. A social-psychological perspective on aging. *The Gerontologist*, 1968, *8*, 67–71.

Havighurst, R. J. History of developmental psychology: Socialization and personality development through the life span. In P. B. Baltes & K. W. Schaie (Eds.), *Life-span developmental psychology: Personality and socialization*. New York: Academic, 1973.

Havighurst, R. J., Neugarten, B., & Tobin, S. Disengagement and patterns of aging. In B. Neugarten (Ed.), *Middle age and aging*. Chicago: University of Chicago Press, 1968.

Holmes, T. H., & Rahe, R. The social readjustment rating scale. *Journal of Psychosomatic Research*, 1967, *11*, 216.

Jung, C. T. The stage of life (translated by R. F. C. Hull). In J. Campbell (Ed.), *The portable Jung*. New York: Viking, 1971.

Larson, R. Thirty years of research on the subjective well-being of older Americans. *Journal of Gerontology*, 1978, *33*, 109–25.

Levinson, D. J. *The seasons of a man's life.* New York: Knopf, 1978.

Lewis, M., & Butler, R. N. Life review therapy: Putting memories to work in individual and group therapy. *Geriatrics*, 1974, *29*, 165–73.

Lieberman, M. A. Adaptive processes in late life. In N. Datan & L. Ginsberg (Eds.), *Life-span developmental psychology: Normative life crises.* New York: Academic, 1975.

Lieberman, M. A. Some issues in studying psychological predictors of survival. In E. Palmore & F. C. Jeffers (Eds.), *Prediction of life span.* Lexington, Mass.: Heath, 1971.

Lowenthal, M. F., & Chiriboga, D. Social stress and adaptation: Toward a life-course perspective. In C. Eisdorfer & M. P. Lawton (Eds.), *The psychology of adult development and aging.* Washington, D.C.: American Psychological Association, 1973.

Lowenthal, M. F., & Haven, C. Interaction and adaptation: Intimacy as a critical variable. *American Sociological Review*, 1968, *33*, 20–30.

Maddox, G. L. Activity and morale: A longitudinal study of selected elderly subjects. *Social Forces*, 1963, *42*, 195–204.

Maddox, G. L. Disengagement theory: A critical evaluation. *The Gerontologist*, 1969, *4*, 80–83.

Marcia, J. E. Development and validation of ego-identity status. *Journal of Personality and Social Psychology*, 1966, *3*, 551–58.

Marcia, J. E. Identity six years after: A follow-up study. *Journal of Youth and Adolescence*, 1976, *5*, 145–160.

Markides, K. S., & Martin, H. W. A causal model of life satisfaction among the elderly. *Journal of Gerontology*, 1979, *34*, 86–93.

Markush, R. E., & Favero, R. V. Epidermiologic assessment of stressful life events, depressed mood, and psychophysiological symptoms— A preliminary report. In B. S. Dohrenwend & B. P. Dohrenwend (Eds.), *Stressful life events: Their nature and effects.* New York: Wiley, 1974.

Maslow, A. H. *Motivation and personality.* New York: Harper & Row, 1954.

Moberg, D. O. *Spiritual well-being* (White House Conference on Aging). Washington, D.C.: U.S. Government Printing Office, 1971.

Moos, G. E. *Illness, immaturity and social interaction.* New York: Wiley-Interscience, 1973.

Neugarten, B. L. The awareness of middle age. In B. L. Neugarten (Ed.), *Middle age and aging.* Chicago: University of Chicago Press, 1968.

Neugarten, B. L. Personality and aging. In J. E. Birren & K. W. Schaie (Eds.), *Handbook of the psychology of aging.* New York: Van Nostrand, 1977.

Neugarten, B. L. Personality change in late life: A developmental perspective. In C. Eisdorfer & M. P. Lawton (Eds.), *The psychology of adult development and aging*. Washington, D.C.: American Psychological Association, 1973.

Neugarten, B. L., & Associates. *Personality in middle and late life*. New York: Atherton, 1964.

Neugarten, B. L., & Datan, N. Sociological perspectives on the life cycle. In P. B. Baltes & K. W. Schaie (Eds.), *Life-span developmental psychology: Personality and socialization*. New York: Academic, 1973.

Neugarten, B. L., Havighurst, R. J., & Tobin, S. S. Personality and patterns of aging. In B. L. Neugarten (Ed.), *Middle age and aging*. Chicago: The University of Chicago Press, 1968.

Parkes, C. M. Psycho-social transitions: A field for study. *Social Science and Medicine*, 1971, *5*, 103.

Rahe, R. H. The pathway between subjects' recent life changes and their near-future illness reports: Representative results and methodological issues. In B. S. Dohrenwend & B. P. Dohrenwend (Eds.), *Stressful life events: Their nature and effects*. New York: Wiley, 1974.

Reavley, W. The relation of life events to several aspects of anxiety. *Journal of Psychosomatic Research*, 1974, *18*, 421–24.

Reichard, S., Livson, F., & Peterson, P. *Aging and personality*. New York: Wiley, 1962.

Rosen, J. L., & Neugarten, B. L. Ego functions in the middle and later years: A thematic apperception study. In B. L. Neugarten (Ed.), *Personality in middle and late life*. New York: Atherton, 1964.

Selye, H. *The stress of life*. New York: McGraw-Hill, 1956.

Sinnott, J. D. Sex-role inconstancy, biology, and aging: A dialectical model. *The Gerontologist*, 1977, *17*, 459–63.

U.S. Bureau of the Census. *Statistical abstract of the United States*. Washington, D.C.: U.S. Government Printing Office, 1978.

Vinokur, A., & Selzer, M. L. Desirable versus undesirable life events: Their relationship to stress and mental distress. *Journal of Personality and Social Psychology*, 1975, *32*, 329–37.

Woodruff, D. S., & Birren, J. E. Age changes and cohort differences in personality. *Developmental Psychology*, 1972, *6*, 252–59.

Youmans, E. G. The rural aged. *Annals of the American Academy of Political and Social Science*, 1977, *429*, 81–90.

Chapter 7
Physical Health and Longevity

Good health is often taken for granted by young adults. They usually do not even think about their health until they become ill. This attitude changes somewhat during late adulthood when one observes increasing health problems among peers. At this time in life, adults are more cognizant of the devastating effects of physical illness and the importance of good health.

The key health problems affecting most middle-aged and older adults today are related to chronic rather than acute illnesses. Chronic illnesses are generally long-term, irreversible and progressive in nature. Treatment is geared toward control and management of symptoms. With some diseases, rehabilitation is an important part of the treatment program as well (Kart, Metress, Metress, 1978). Examples of chronic illnesses prevalent during the adult years are heart disorders, diabetes, arthritis, multiple sclerosis and long-term forms of cancer. These diseases can vary widely in their symptoms and degrees of debilitation.

Impaired health can have developmental implications for persons in all stages of adulthood. In some cases, the threat of disability or death may forestall the completion of developmental tasks. For example, young adulthood is a time when most individuals are beginning a career, establishing intimate relationships, and starting a family. Following a diagnosis of chronic illness, life goals are often reconstructed in view of unforeseen restrictions on abilities, activities and social relationships.

Mages and Mendelsohn (1979) found that the development of intimacy was affected by the uncertainty faced by young adults with cancer. At mid-life, diseases such as cancer pose more of a threat in terms of established work and family roles. Self-sufficiency, financial security, and care of children and dependent spouse become critical issues for the ill adult at this stage of life. For older persons, disease means loss—loss of independence, ability and control at a time when they are already experiencing loss of status, loss of role and loss of spouse in many cases.

In this chapter, we will first examine chronic illness and its effects on the individual and family. Next, physical changes that occur with age will be discussed, followed by a section on the role of nutrition and exercise in the maintenance of health and prevention of disease. In our society, institutionalization has become an option for providing care for elderly persons suffering from severe physical impairments. Both historical and current perspectives will be provided on long-term care of the elderly in the United States, along with a consideration of the needs of the institutionalized elderly. As one studies health and physical change during the adult years, many questions inevitably come to mind about the nature of the aging process and the prevalence of disease and deterioration in a modern, technologically-advanced age. This chapter will conclude with a look at theories of aging, directions of current research efforts in this area, and the possibilities for the extension of life.

Chronic Health Problems

Adjustment of the Individual

Following diagnosis of an illness or disability, a period of mourning occurs in which the person grieves for his or her loss. The loss may represent a function already impaired or a part of life that will not be experienced in the future because of the illness. This mourning is a necessary psychological function that, if successfully resolved, will lead to a realistic acceptance of limitations and a redefinition of self. According to Crate (1965), this grief reaction may vary depending on the severity of the illness, the meaning of the lost function to the person, and the degree to which he or she has adapted to other crises in life. Each new loss or change in body function can be expected to cause grief for the current loss as well as reactivate the grieving process of earlier episodes. Burnfield and Burnfield (1978) recommend that this reaction should be neither discouraged or overindulged.

Moos (1977) views the maintenance of a satisfactory self-image as

Mandated wheel-chair accessibility to public building has expanded educational and work opportunities for many diabled persons. (Bob Harvey, photographer)

an adaptive task accompanying the onset of a chronic illness. Changes in physical functioning or appearance can trigger an "identity crisis." Self-images must be revised to incorporate the person's existing physical condition. In some cases, a change in personal values and lifestyle is necessary. Despite sometimes drastic changes in physical functioning and appearance, chronically-ill persons must be able to think of themselves in positive terms in order to achieve a positive adjustment.

In the case of physical disability, the attitudes of society may interfere with an individual's adjustment. Wright (1960) has compared the attitudes toward the disabled to the prejudice shown toward many ethnic and religious minorities. In her book on the psychological aspects of physical disability, Wright cites the results of a study that demonstrated strong stereotyping of the disabled. When asked to assign personality characteristics to photographs of six boys, one pictured in a wheel-chair, high school students perceived the disabled child as more conscientious, feeling more inferior, a better friend, obtaining better grades, more even-tempered, more religious, enjoying parties less, and more unhappy than the other youths. When a negative evaluation of a disability affects the evaluation of other nonimpaired characteristics of the person with the disability, it can interfere with the individual's adjustment. We have seen increased efforts aimed at protecting the rights of the disabled in the past few years. Legislation mandating wheel-chair accessibility to public buildings has helped remove some of the barriers to adjustment and has expanded educational and work opportunities for many diabled persons.

Unfortunately, health status is usually seen as a dichotomous rather than a continuous variable. Our tendency to view a person as either "sick" or "well" can cause problems for adults with a chronic illness or disability. In many diseases of adulthood, symptoms such as fatigue and pain are often not visible to others. Burnfield and Burnfield (1978) report that multiple sclerosis patients are sometimes regarded as hypochrondriacs by family members and employers because they appear fit and healthy. Bruhn (1977) has used the term "marginal men" to describe the efforts of renal failure patients to set expectations and goals for themselves. Realistically, they are usually functioning somewhere between the "world of the sick" and the "world of the well." However, because they did not fit into the traditional "sick" role, these individuals were often expected to resume all of their former responsibilities—an expectation that could further jeopardize their health.

Effects on Families

The effects on families of the chronically ill are far-reaching and affect all family members. As chronic illnesses progress, there is usually a need for role adjustment and task reallocation as ill persons become unable to perform some or all of their roles (Cleveland, 1980; McDaniel, 1976). Marra and Novis (1959) have identified the following changes that typically occur within families of disabled husbands/fathers: (1) the wife assumes greater responsibility for home management, (2) social and recreational activities are reduced, (3) children assume more household responsibilities, (4) debt increases, (5) plans of having a large family are altered, (6) wife becomes employed, (7) marital discord increases, and (8) living accommodations change.

Parsons' (1958) role theory is useful when considering the effects of chronic illness on the family. According to Parsons, a role is defined as an individual's performance of various differentiated tasks within his or her own social system. A chronic illness or a disability, depending on its nature and severity, can interfere with the performance of accustomed tasks. However, the extent of the disability may not be the most important variable affecting family relationships—in some cases role issues may be more salient. Role ambiguity was found by Peterson (1979) to have a greater detrimental effect on the marital relationship than severity or degree of disability.

In examining adjustment styles of males who were chronically ill with multiple sclerosis, Power (1979) found that these individuals tended to be either spectators or participants in their family life. Those assuming the spectator role were largely inactive and demonstrated dependency on others even though they were physically capable of working at their jobs part-time and performing household tasks. Their social interactions decreased, and they spent much of their time watching television. They seldom participated in family discussions, and they were primarily observers rather than participants of family activities. Their conversations revolved around physical complaints and rarely included any reference to the future. Power reported that these men seemed confused, depressed and anxious. Feeling deprived of their traditional role in the family, these men displayed their anger by withdrawing and refusing to assume new tasks. On the other hand, men who were categorized by Power as being in a participant role remained active. Even though their physical limitations were similar to those of the "spectator" men, individuals in the participant role continued to work part-time or found new avocational interests, and they remained highly involved in activities with family and friends. While their role in the family was modified since they were not earning most of the family income, they assumed responsibility for other tasks such as assisting with food preparation and helping children with schoolwork.

Why do individuals respond so differently to the same illness? Power (1979) found that both family expectations of role complementarity and the person's view of the illness were strong influences on adjustment. In families of the "spectator" men, the husbands were relieved from responsibilities while the spouse took over their usual tasks. As a result, power and influence in the family shifted to the well partner. By being placed in a sick role by family members, these men were unable to effectively adopt a new role in the family. Unlike these families, the families of men in the participant role had high expectations for role performance in spite of the illness and felt that family life should proceed as normally as possible. When differences in perceptions of the illness were examined, Power found that "spectator" men put more emphasis on their physical limitations rather than their residual abilities. In contrast, those men who were active as husbands and fathers did not view their disease as an insurmountable obstacle. At the time of diagnosis, these men had received information and encouragement from their physicians regarding their involvement in marital, family and occupational roles. In addition, family members were encouraged to learn as much as possible about their husband's/father's disease. The results of

---

Box 7–1

What Is Multiple Sclerosis?

Multiple sclerosis is a disease of the central nervous system which can be seriously disabling. Typically occurring in young adulthood, it is a slow, deteriorating illness with an unpredictable course. It is, however, a progressive illness characterized by periods of remission alternating with intervals when the symptoms of the disease are exacerbated. Persons with multiple sclerosis commonly experience difficulty with vision, speech, coordination, sensation, use of extremities, and bowel and bladder control, but the degree of impairment in these areas will vary from individual to individual. Despite these physical limitations, persons with multiple sclerosis usually have the functional capacity for many years of active life. While incidence of the disease varies by geographical area, it is estimated that one out of every 2,500 people in the United States is afflicted with this disease, with a higher incidence occurring among women than men.

Source: B. Matthews, *Multiple Sclerosis* (Oxford: Oxford University Press, 1978).

---

this study strongly point to the need for family-oriented counseling to facilitate adjustment to a chronic illness such as multiple sclerosis.

Jacobson and Eichhorn (1964) studied the effects of heart disease on farm families. When the husband was disabled, it was easier for younger wives to obtain employment and assume the "breadwinner" role than it was for older wives. It was also easier for husbands to change careers (provided their disability did not preclude involvement in a work role) if they were young. However, other studies have shown that disabled individuals, no matter how qualified, may have difficulty obtaining employment due to biases of employers toward disabled workers (Rickard, Triandis & Patterson, 1963). Jacobson and Eichhorn (1964) also found that older families were usually more financially secure than younger ones, therefore having retirement as an option. In addition, the age of children was important in their ability to adapt to role shifts within the family. Older children were able to help more with farm work, and mothers of older children were more likely to seek nonfarm employment.

Several studies have discussed the financial concerns of families of the chronically ill. Jacobson and Eichhorn (1964) found that a large percentage of wives worried about money and their future financial security. In another study in which male myocardial victims were asked to identify their family difficulties in order of importance, financial problems headed the list followed by depression, curtailment of activities, and fear of recurrent attack. Bruhn (1977) found that the greater the financial difficulty, the more negative were the family reactions to the disability and the changes it produced.

In conclusion, while severe chronic illnesses affect a small percentage of adults during young and middle adulthood, they require major adjustment when they do occur—an adjustment not only for the individual but for significant others as well. Now let us turn our attention to more normative physical changes that occur during adulthood. Even in the absence of disease, we must learn to cope with the physical decline that accompanies advanced age.

Age-Related Physical Changes

Why is a male with graying temples considered distinguished while this trait in women is often thought to be unattractive? This double standard of aging, as it has been referred to by Susan Sontag (1977), is a reflection of the greater emphasis placed on physical attractiveness for women in American society. When combined with the tendency in our society to equate beauty with youth, these conditions result in an "aging crisis" among many adults, especially women, as they begin to notice changes in their physical appearance.

It is not easy to grow old in a culture that worships youth. The American obsession with "looking young" has led to the development of a billion-dollar cosmetic industry claiming to have potions that will erase the signs of age. Our reluctance to accept the physical changes that come with time is further exploited by advertisers. A glimpse through advertisements in almost any leading magazine will reveal page after page of youthful images extolling the virtues of their products. The message? Youth is the desired status; to be anything other than young is undesirable.

Box 7–2

Face Lifts: Elixirs for Youth?

Today the patients who go to a plastic surgeon's office are among the ranks of the middle class. No longer are face lifts and other surgical attempts to maintain a youthful appearance confined to only celebrities and jet setters. The use of cosmetic surgery as a means of avoiding the changes that occur with age is becoming more and more acceptable among the general public. The procedure for a face lift (technically called a rhytidoplasty) is a fairly simple one which involves separating the skin on the temple, cheek and neck from the underlying muscle and stretching it until the wrinkles disappear. The excess skin is then removed and sutures are made around the ears and hairline. The improved tautness resulting from this operation will generally last from five to seven years. The price for a more youthful appearance? A complete face lift can cost from $1,500 to $3,500 and up for the surgeon's fee alone.

Skin

The changes that occur in the skin and hair are usually the most noticeable of the age-related physical changes. Graying of the hair and wrinkling of the skin are therefore most often associated with advancing age. The parts of the body that have been most exposed to the sun, such as the face and hands, tend to show the most pronounced skin changes. While many view the beginning of wrinkles (usually in the 20s) with alarm, some view it as our body's way of recording our personal experiences:

> The human face, because of its musculature, is capable of tremendous movement and expression of emotions. Indeed, facial expressions represent an extremely important component of human communication. Smiles, laughter, frowns, disappointment, anger, rage and surprise are all recorded. The hand of time captures our expressions and outlines them on our faces. Lines begin to form in areas of greatest movement, proliferate and become deeper as the years pass. By the age of 40 years, most of us bear the typical lines of our expressions (Kart, Metress & Metress, 1978, p. 33–34).

Changes in the skin with age are due primarily to the loss of skin elasticity, reduction of subcutaneous fat, and atrophy of sweat and oil-secreting glands. Also, reduced blood supply to the skin contributes to thickened nails and a reduction or loss of body hair. A change in skin pigmentation can also be noted. While a decrease in the number of functioning, pigment-producing cells alters skin and hair color, some pigment cells enlarge resulting in the dark spots frequently seen on the hands and faces of older persons.

Skeletomuscular Structure

Changes in the skeletomuscular system are generally characterized by diminished bone and muscle mass. In most cases, the skeletomuscular structure is capable of performing its functions of providing structure for the body and protecting vital organs. However, mobility can be restricted with progressive degenerative diseases. The incidence of *osteoarthritis*, a degenerative joint change that can cause pain and joint stiffness, is significantly correlated with age (Timiras, 1972). While approximately 90 percent of all people demonstrate some joint deterioration by the age of forty, often little or no discomfort will be experienced. Also linked to the aging process is *osteoporosis* in which skeletal mass is reduced without disrupting the proportion of minerals and organic materials. While many persons may not detect these changes, a reduction in bone mass can result in such problems as chronic backache and susceptibility to fractures. It can also contribute to diminished height and slumped posture among older persons (Kart et al., 1978).

Circulatory System

With age comes a progressive reduction of strength in the heart muscles and diminished cardiac output. Despite these changes, adequate blood flow is sustained in the absence of disease (Rodstein, 1971). The heart's ability to respond to stress, however, does decline with age.

Rates of coronary artery disease are very high in the United States, as it is in most industrialized nations, making it difficult to separate the effects of the disease from the aging process. With this disease, the amount of blood supplied to the heart is deficient because of blood-vessel constriction. In a particular condition known as *atherosclerosis*, the passage way of the large arteries are narrowed due to build-up of plaques on the interior walls. These plaques, composed of fat and cholesterol in combination with other elements, can eventually result in total occlusion of the artery. Occlusion can also be the result of a blood clot becoming wedged in the narrowed vessel. *Arteriosclerosis*, sometimes confused with atherosclerosis, refers to the loss of elasticity of the arterial walls and can also contribute to reduced blood flow to an area of the body. Arteriosclerosis is commonly referred to as "hardening of the arteries" and is age-related. When arteriosclerotic or atherosclerotic changes occur in blood vessels which lead to brain tissue, malfunction and death of brain cells can occur due to lack of nourishment from the restricted blood flow. A stroke (or cerebrovascular accident) occurs when the blood is not reaching a portion of the brain. The severity of a stroke depends on the area of the brain affected and the total amount of brain tissue involved. Individuals surviving a stroke may be left with paralysis, speech disorders and sensory disturbances.

Blood pressure tends to increase with age (Master & Lasser, 1964), thereby explaining why the normalcy of your blood pressure reading is determined in relation to your age. Hypertension, or high blood pressure, also tends to increase with age in our society unlike the case in some of the less developed areas of the world (Lowenstein, 1961). A significant correlation exists between hypertension and the risk of coronary artery disease. In older persons, arteriosclerotic and atherosclerotic changes in the arteries decrease their diameter, distensibility and capacity causing the heart to work harder in order to pump blood through them.

Respiratory System

Several changes in the respiratory system occur with age. The tissues and airways of the respiratory tract become less elastic, thus reducing the maximum amount of air that can be expelled from the lungs. As a consequence, less air is available for oxygen-carbon dioxide exchange. Also the muscles involved in inhalation and exhalation decrease in strength, and changes in the bone structure can limit rib cage expansion. Collectively, these changes reduce one's maximum breathing capacity. While usually not affecting an older person in a resting state, it will cause older persons to fatigue faster than younger persons when engaging in physical activity (Saxon & Etten, 1978).

In addition to age-related changes, an adult's lungs can be adversely affected by long-term exposure to harmful environmental agents such as cigarette smoke and air pollution. Respiratory diseases such as chronic bronchitis, emphysema and lung cancer are more prevalent in older persons than in the general population, and the threat of serious respiratory infection increases with age (Kart et al., 1978).

Digestive System

A large majority of older people have dental problems which affect their eating habits. Difficulties can stem from both loss of teeth as well as ill-fitting dentures. Of perhaps more concern are peridontal diseases, such as pyorrhea, which can lead to chronic infections and tooth loss. Hope-

216   Continuity and Change

fully through the improved dental care available today, the aged of the future will have fewer problems in this area.

Changes occurring in the gastrointestinal tract related to the aging process include reduction of strength and tone in the muscular tissue, some atrophy of mechanisms responsible for the secretion of enzymes used in digestion, and decreased motility within the system. The implications of these changes on the absorption and utilization of nutrients are especially important. Changes in the bacterial flora in the small intestine of older people can lead to the rapid growth of foreign organisms which can result in lowered resistance and inflammation. Also, important vitamins may be lost. For example, abnormal bacterial growth can bind vitamin B_{12} and reduce its availability as a nutrient for the body (Kart et al., 1978).

Urinary System

The bladder of an elderly person has a capacity of less than half (250 ml) that of a young adult (600 ml) which leads to the need for more frequent urination, often causing older persons to awaken during the night. Also as a person ages, recognition of the need to urinate does not occur until the bladder is near capacity, requiring urgency in some situations. Diminished muscle tone may also result in incomplete emptying of the bladder. In fact, the bladder of an elderly person often contains as much as 100 ml of residual urine (Kart et al., 1978).

The kidneys are also altered by age. They become smaller and the number of nephrons, the functional units of the kidneys, is reduced. Age-related changes in the arteries can impair kidney function when blood flow is reduced.

Renal complications accompany a number of pathologic conditions that are common among the elderly. For example, inability to urinate is often associated with prostate gland enlargement in older men, however in some cases increased urination may occur. Other disorders that can cause urinary tract disturbance include diabetes mellitus, multiple sclerosis and Parkinson's disease (Kart et al., 1978).

Endocrine System

The endocrine system serves as a regulator of metabolic and homeostatic functions of the body during adulthood. Timiras (1972) states that it is best to view the entire endocrine system as a unit rather than a group of independent structures since changes in one endocrine gland usually affect others.

It should be remembered that the sex hormones discussed in Chapter 5 are also part of this system. While, as we have seen, some changes do occur in the endocrine system with age, major disorders of this system do not appear to be common in old age. In fact, when these disorders do occur the probability is higher that the onset will be during the early or middle years of adulthood rather than the later years. Even so, diseases such as diabetes and thyroid dysfunction are severe health risks for the older person (Kart et al., 1978).

Sensory Loss

In all of the sense organs, aging produces a lowered sensitivity in the sense receptors, thereby requiring higher levels of stimulation in order to obtain a response. Changes in vision and hearing are perhaps the most pronounced. These changes are significant because of the important role of visual and auditory input in communication and as a link to the external environment.

Vision. During middle age, individuals commonly have difficulty with near-point vision, thus necessitating the use of corrective lens when engaging in activities that require focusing on an object a short distance from the face (for example, reading). This decreased ability with age of the eye's lens to focus is known as *presbyopia*. Without the aid of glasses, older persons often have to hold objects such as newspapers at a distance in order to see them clearly (Kart et al., 1978). Other changes in the eye occurring with age affect color perception (Dalderup & Fredericks, 1969), visual adaptation to darkness (McFarland, Domey, Warren & Ward, 1960), and sensitivity to glare (Wolf, 1960). In most cases, however, these changes do not impose major limitations on day-to-day living. Disability can result when other visual conditions are present, the most notable being cataracts and glaucoma.

Cataracts account for much of the visual disability occuring among the elderly. With this condition, the normally transparent lens of the eye becomes opaque, which interferes with the passage of light rays to the retina. The older person with cataracts will experience blurred vision. When interfering significantly with vision, cataracts are usually removed surgically (Kart et al., 1978). Researchers believe that everyone would eventually develop cataracts if they lived long enough (Timiras & Vernadakis, 1972).

Glaucoma, an eye disease causing increased pressure on the optic nerve, is the most serious of visual problems associated with late adulthood. If untreated it can cause total blindness. Symptoms often include severe headaches, blurred vision and the appearance of halos around objects of light, pain and tearing of the eyes, nausea, and loss of peripheral vision (Kart et al., 1978).

Hearing. *Presbycusis* is the progressive loss of hearing associated with aging caused by degenerative changes occurring in the auditory system. These changes begin during middle age but are not usually apparent until the later years of life. When hearing loss does occur it usually involves high-frequency tones, common examples of which are the ringing of a telephone or doorbell, the whistle of a kettle, and the song of a robin. This type of loss can also make it more difficult for an older person to hear a female's voice than a male's voice and more difficult to perceive consonant sounds than vowel sounds. Obviously when speech perception is impaired it can interfere with effective communication. The ability to hear high-frequency sounds is still possible with amplification from a hearing aid. Increasing the volume from the source of the sound can also help, but shouting usually has a negative psychological impact and typically only raises the frequency of the speech sounds being delivered (Kart et al., 1978). Interestingly, presbycusis appears to be more common among males (Birren, 1964). Exposure to greater environmental noise in the work milieu may be a plausible explanation for this observed sex difference.

Nutrition and Exercise

The physical changes described here do not occur at the same rate or to the same degree in all individuals. Both genetic and environmental factors influence the occurrence of age-related physical changes. Many gerontologists have emphasized the important role of nutrition and exercise in maintaining good health.

Nutrition

From food we obtain necessary substances for the maintenance and repair of body tissue. We also meet our body's energy needs through our caloric intake. From the available evidence, good nutrition appears to be vital for the physical health of adults. As the slogan goes: "You are what you eat."

Adequate nutrition can be a special problem for older people. In addition to changes in the digestive system, several other factors can interfere with a proper diet during this period of life. With a reduced income, older people may not be able to purchase certain preferred foods. Also, they may tend to eat more carbohydrates because of the lower cost. Factors such as living alone or having chronic physical disabilities can result in less motivation to prepare complete meals, and changes in smell and taste in the later years as well as difficulties in

Government-funded meal sites can provide older persons with nutritional meals as well as an opportunity to socialize with peers. (John Buffington, photographer)

chewing due to the loss of teeth can affect food choices (Harrill, Erbes & Schwartz, 1976; Howell & Loeb, 1969).

Diet is becoming more of a focus in health-oriented programs. In fact, dietary intake is thought to be directly linked with many degenerative diseases prevalent in our society. While we still do not know the exact role nutrition plays in many major illnesses, excessive sodium intake has been associated with hypertension, and diets high in animal products have been studied in relation to atherosclerosis. Other researchers are investigating the effects of refined sugar consumption and low fiber intake, both of which are common in the typical American diet.

The quantity as well as the quality of food you eat is important. It has been suggested that obesity is much more of a problem among the elderly than poor nutrition (Bender, 1971). The human body has a lower caloric requirement with age, and obesity may result unless diets are adjusted as one grows older. Excess body weight has been associated

Many Americans are currently exploring alternative forms of exercise for physical vitality and well-being. The adults in this photograph are practicing the meditative movements of T'ai Chi Ch'uan, an ancient Chinese system of development. (Bob Harvey, photographer)

with lowered life expectancy (Timiras, 1972) as well as hypertension and cardiovascular disease (Weg, 1978).

Exercise

Timiras (1972) has pointed out that it is difficult to differentiate the effects of exercising on aging from the effects of aging on exercising. While physical exercise cannot prevent aging, individuals who have good control over their bodies and who build up reserves of physical strength through a regular exercise program do appear to be in a much better position to cope with physically stressful conditions.

De Vries (1977) argues for vigorous physical exercise as a preventive measure. A sedentary lifestyle can lead to obesity and other health problems, and in general adults tend to become less active with age. According to De Vries, vigorous physical conditioning in the healthy older organism can bring about significant improvements in the cardiovascular and respiratory systems, body musculature and body composition. He also recommends exercise as an effective relaxant for older persons and as an alternative to tranquilizers.

No one form of exercise is appropriate for everyone. An exercise program must take into account each person's health status, body condition, and personal goals. From the available evidence, however, it is clear that incorporating some type of exercise into one's lifestyle is necessary for physical and mental well-being and vitality.

Health Care of the Elderly

Geriatrics is a field of medicine specializing in the care of the elderly. Unfortunately, this area has failed to attract large numbers of physicians. Many doctors do not view geriatrics as having the status or offering as much challenge as other specialties. Several studies have shown evidence of age bias among the medical profession. Miller and his associates (1976) found that only 38 percent of the medical profession said that they would put forth equal effort on the young and the old, and the same percentage viewed nursing homes as places to die. Gruber (1977) has used the terms "defeatism, negativism, and professional apathy" to describe the attitudes of physicians toward medical care of the aged. Certainly attitudes such as these interfere with the delivery of quality health care to the elderly.

The rising cost of health care is another legitimate concern of older people in this country. Moss and Halamandaris (1977) report a 2,000 percent increase in the expenditures for care in nursing homes between 1960 and 1976, while during this same period there was only a 245 percent increase in the number of residents in these facilities. Medicare, a national health insurance program designed for the elderly and administered by the federal government, was passed by Congress in 1965 as part of the amendments to the Social Security law. Financed through the social security tax, the Medicare program fails to cover many common health-related needs of the elderly, such as glasses and hearing aids, thus increasing their out-of-pocket expenses. Medicaid, a separate program, is for the medically indigent and is not restricted to those over 65. Nonetheless, in 1979 more than one out of every three Medicaid dollars was spent for skilled nursing home care (U.S. Department of Health and Human Services, 1980b). Albert and Zarit (1977), after examining the legislative provisions for health care in this country, concluded that "when catastrophic situations arise, Americans discover that these programs encourage hospitalization, fail to provide many needed services, and often result in a depletion of resources before one can qualify for Medicaid" (p. 127).

As we have seen, every major system in the body is altered to some degree by age. For most individuals, these changes will not interfere with their day-to-day functioning; for others, it will mean disability and incapacitation. Improved medical technology has resulted in more individuals surviving diseases associated with late adulthood. Of these survivors, many have been left with severe mental and physical impairments which reduce their functional capacity, prohibit solitary residence, and affect the need for long-term care.

Institutional facilities for the elderly are a reality of twentieth-century America. There are presently over 23,000 nursing homes in the United States. While only approximately 5 percent of persons over sixty-five are institutionalized, this figure represents approximately 1,000,000 older Americans. This 5 percent figure was derived from cross-sectional rather than longitudinal data. While this seemingly small percentage of the elderly population is actually living in institutions at any point in time, Kastenbaum and Candy (1973) provide evidence that the probability of older persons entering a long-term care facility during their life time is at least one in five. The current status of nursing homes in the United States can best be understood by reviewing the origins of this industry and the social, economic and political factors that have shaped its development.

History of Long-Term Care in America

. . . but their generation is the first to fade like this, not at home but assigned to a numbered frequent ward, stowed out of conscience as unpopular luggage.

W. H. Anden
Old People's Home

Early facilities providing care for the elderly consisted of county homes and almshouses ("poorhouses") and provided for such diverse groups as the disabled, the aged, widows with children, orphans, the mentally and chronically ill, and the unemployed. The common element among all of these groups was poverty. The almshouse concept continued during most of the nineteenth century, given impetus in 1834 by the Poor Law of England (Brody, 1977).

The notion of providing adequately for aged persons unable to care for themselves and without family or assets developed slowly in America. Only in the latter half of the nineteenth century were any attempts made to reform institutions for the sick and aged. In 1883 Connecticut was the first state to establish a state board of charities, but no clean line of demarcation identifying the purposes of almshouses, asylums and hospitals was made until World War I. Finally, because of social pressures and growing recognition of the conditions prevailing in public facilities for the elderly, many almshouses were closed in the 1920s. As institutions became more specialized and different groups of patients and residents began to be separated, an apparent need existed for a facility for elderly persons unable to reside in their homes but not in need of hospital care. Although the concept of such a facility had considerable support at that time, government funds were not available for the development of these facilities (Moss & Halamandaris, 1977).

One of the most significant catalysts for the development of the nursing home industry in the United States has been legislation enacted by Congress. As influential legislation was passed, the elderly population shifted from multi-purpose institutions into institutions specifically designed to care for elderly persons whose functional capacities were chronically impaired.

The passage of the Social Security Act in 1935 provided the first major impetus for the establishment of nursing homes. The act was proposed in an effort to provide financial security for the aged. Through the Social Security Act, funds were made available to persons over 65, although individuals housed in public institutions were excluded from receiving these funds because of the strong reactions to conditions in public poorhouses. This exclusion encouraged tremendous growth of private facilities. As a result, thousands of elderly persons were transferred from public facilities to privately owned, profit-oriented boarding houses. Eventually such facilities began to add medical personnel and call themselves nursing homes. Thus, today's nursing home industry began in those early facilities organized as a result of the restrictions of social security legislation (Moss & Halamandaris, 1977).

The growth of new facilities was encouraged in the 1950s by several legislative acts. In 1954 the Hill-Burton Act was amended to provide federal grant assistance for the construction and equipping of public and nonprofit long-term care institutions. In 1958, small loans were made available to nursing homes through the Small Business Act and the Small Business Investment Act. The following year, the National Housing Act was amended to provide mortgage insurance for the construction and renovation of nursing homes.

Another major expansion in the nursing home industry occurred as a result of the Social Security Act Amendments of 1965 (Acts XVIII and XIX) which provided substantial financial coverage for nursing home care through Medicare and Medicaid programs. With this increase in financial base, nursing homes changed from family enterprises to sizable businesses and began attracting the investments of large corporations (Moss & Halamandaris, 1977).

Concurrent with the increase in facilities available to older people were changes in American family structure and residence patterns. The Industrial Revolution greatly influenced the American family structure. Intergenerational families were not uncommon in early rural America because of the demands of an agrarian existence. Most older people lived with or close to their children, and early American neighborhoods were composed largely of related households. With the influx of immigrants into this country, the United States became more industrialized and the American family structure evolved to accommodate the realities of an urban, mobile society. Factors related to the trend toward smaller nuclear families were difficulties in supporting large families in cities with small quarters and low wages, the geographical mobility often demanded by industrial employment and made possible through developments in transportation, and the diminishing roles of children and the elderly related to the economic functioning of the family. These changes were augmented by the passage of the Social Security Act which provided elderly persons with their own funds and allowed them some degree of financial independence. However, special problems were presented for the elderly unable to live independently, resulting in an increase in institutional placements.

Recent changes in family roles have made it increasingly difficult for families to care for disabled elderly relatives at home. The traditional role of the woman in American society has included providing care for dependent family members. Expansion of traditional sex roles and an increase in single-parent families have resulted in more women entering the work force. In 1900, the percentage of women participating in the labor force was 17 percent, while in 1980 it increased to 51.6 per-

Intergenerational families were not uncommon in early America because of the demands of an agrarian existence. (Courtesy of John Cook)

cent (U.S. Bureau of the Census, 1981). The percentage of employed women is usually high during periods when aging parents are most likely to need their care. Factors such as family dependence on the joint income of both husband and wife for economic survival and the unwillingness of many women to sacrifice a rewarding career for more traditional roles have increasingly influenced decisions regarding care of older relatives.

The Institutionalized Elderly and Their Families

Despite these social and economic trends, Brody (1977) found that placement of an elderly individual in a nursing home is the last reasonable alternative used by most stable families. The stereotype of "families putting their old away in institutions" can be psychologically damaging to families who wish to avoid institutionalization but feel they have few alternatives. Families need more information and support from professionals not only in making the decision regarding placement, but in locating an adequate facility once the decision is made. York and Calsyn (1977) found that families are not very thorough in their search for nursing homes for older relatives; 51 percent of the families in their study did not even visit the facility prior to the placement. Availability of a bed and location were the principal criteria used by families in their selection of a facility. Quality of care in old-age institutions can vary tremendously along a variety of dimensions such as staff-residence ratio, physical care, cleanliness and adequacy of meals (Kart & Manard, 1976). Also, media articles condemning safety conditions in nursing homes have increasingly appeared. Physical dangers such as fire hazards and inadequate facilities as well as actual instances of abuse and neglect have been reported. Moss and Halamandaris (1977) recommend more effective legislation, improved monitoring, and legal action against substandard facilities as ways to alleviate these conditions. Helpful guidelines for families selecting a nursing home have been established by the U.S. Department of Health, Education and Welfare (see Box 7–3).

The resident's subjective perception of the facility is also important. Noelker and Harel (1978) found that the primary predictors of personal well-being for the sample of nursing-home residents in their study were the older persons' perceptions of the facility and staff. These subjective factors were more important than the more objective characteristics, such as availability of activities and physical conditions. A positive perception of the facility and staff by the residents was significantly associated with morale, life satisfaction and satisfaction with treatment which in turn were found to be predictors of physical survival. While these investigators believe that efforts aimed at the improvement of the phys-

Continuity and Change

ical characteristics of long-term care centers are needed, they also think that more attention should be given to the subjective reactions of potential residents. Noelker and Harel recommend involving the older person to the fullest possible extent in discussions of the need for entry, realistic alternatives, and selection of a long-term care facility.

According to Tobin and Lieberman (1976), the three variables most likely to affect admittance of elderly persons to a nursing home are increasing physical deterioration, the inability or unwillingness of their families to provide care for them, and the lack of community service organizations to provide the services needed for independent living. The chances of entering an institution increase with age. While only 2 percent of the 65 to 75 year olds are institutionalized, this figure increases to 10 percent for those 80 and over. Of the institutionalized elderly, women outnumber men by more than 2 to 1 which is not surprising considering their longer life expectancy (U.S. Bureau of the Census, 1979; U.S. Department of Health, Education and Welfare, 1975).

Box 7–3

Evaluating Long-Term Care Facilities

Carry this checklist when you visit nursing homes. It will help you compare one with another. As a rule of thumb, the best home is the one for which you check the most "yes" answers. However, remember that different kinds of homes offer different types of services. You should compare skilled nursing homes with skilled nursing homes and residential homes with residential homes.

If the answer to any of the first four questions is "no," do not use the home.

	Yes	No
1. Does the home have a current license from the State?	____	____
2. Does the administrator have a current license from the State?	____	____
3. If you need and are eligible for financial assistance, is the home certified to participate in government or other programs that provide it?	____	____

4. Does the home provide special services such as a specific diet or therapy which the patient needs?   _____ _____

Physical Considerations

5. Location   _____ _____
   a. Pleasing to the patient?   _____ _____
   b. Convenient for patient's personal doctor?   _____ _____
   c. Convenient for frequent visits?   _____ _____
   d. Near hospital?   _____ _____

6. Accident Prevention   _____ _____
   a. Well-lighted inside?   _____ _____
   b. Free of hazards underfoot?   _____ _____
   d. Warning signs posted around freshly waxed floors?   _____ _____
   e. Handrails in hallways and grab bars in bathrooms?   _____ _____

7. Fire Safety   _____ _____
   a. Meets Federal and/or State codes?   _____ _____
   b. Exits clearly marked and unobstructed?   _____ _____
   c. Written emergency evacuation plan?   _____ _____
   d. Frequent fire drills?   _____ _____
   e. Exit doors not locked on the inside?   _____ _____
   f. Stairways enclosed and doors to stairways kept closed?   _____ _____

8. Bedrooms   _____ _____
   a. Open onto hall?   _____ _____
   b. Window?   _____ _____
   c. No more than four beds per room?   _____ _____
   d. Easy access to each bed?   _____ _____
   e. Drapery for each bed?   _____ _____
   f. Nurse call bell by each bed?   _____ _____
   g. Fresh drinking water at each bed?   _____ _____
   h. At least one comfortable chair per patient?   _____ _____
   i. Reading lights?   _____ _____
   j. Clothes closet and drawers?   _____ _____
   k. Room for a wheelchair to maneuver?   _____ _____
   l. Care used in selecting roommates?   _____ _____

9. Cleanliness   _____ _____
   a. Generally clean, even though it may have a lived-in look?   _____ _____

b. Free of unpleasant odors? _____ _____
c. Incontinent patients given prompt attention? _____ _____

10. Lobby _____ _____
    a. Is the atmosphere welcoming? _____ _____
    b. If also a lounge, is it being used by residents? _____ _____
    c. Furniture attractive and comfortable? _____ _____
    d. Plants and flowers? _____ _____
    e. Certificates and licenses on display? _____ _____

11. Hallways _____ _____
    a. Large enough for two wheelchairs to pass with ease? _____ _____
    b. Hand-grip railing on the sides? _____ _____

12. Dining Room _____ _____
    a. Attractive and inviting? _____ _____
    b. Comfortable chairs and tables? _____ _____
    c. Easy to move around in? _____ _____
    d. Tables convenient for those in wheelchairs? _____ _____
    e. Food tasty and attractively served? _____ _____
    f. Meals match posted menu? _____ _____
    g. Those needing help receiving it? _____ _____

13. Kitchen _____ _____
    a. Food preparation, dishwashing and garbage areas separated? _____ _____
    b. Food needing refrigeration not standing on counters? _____ _____
    c. Kitchen help observe sanitation rules? _____ _____

14. Activity Rooms _____ _____
    a. Rooms available for patients' activities? _____ _____
    b. Equipment (such as games, easels, yarn, kiln, etc.) available? _____ _____
    c. Residents using equipment? _____ _____

15. Special Purpose Rooms _____ _____
    a. Rooms set aside for physical examinations or therapy? _____ _____
    b. Rooms being used for stated purpose? _____ _____

16. Isolation Room _____ _____
    a. At least one bed and bathroom available for patients with contagious illness? _____ _____

17. Toilet Facilities _____ _____
    a. Convenient to bedrooms? _____ _____
    b. Easy for a wheelchair patient to use? _____ _____
    c. Sink? _____ _____
    d. Nurse call bell? _____ _____
    e. Hand grips on or near toilets? _____ _____
    f. Bathtubs and showers with nonslip surfaces? _____ _____

18. Grounds _____ _____
    a. Residents can get fresh air? _____ _____
    b. Ramps to help handicapped? _____ _____

Services

19. Medical _____ _____
    a. Physician available in emergency? _____ _____
    b. Private physician allowed? _____ _____
    c. Regular medical attention assured? _____ _____
    d. Thorough physical immediately before or upon admission? _____ _____
    e. Medical records and plan of care kept? _____ _____
    f. Patient involved in developing plans for treatment? _____ _____
    g. Other medical services (dentists, optometrists, etc.) available regularly? _____ _____
    h. Freedom to purchase medicines outside home? _____ _____

20. Hospitalization _____ _____
    a. Arrangement with nearby hospital for transfer when necessary? _____ _____

21. Nursing Services _____ _____
    a. RN responsible for nursing staff in a skilled nursing home? _____ _____
    b. LPN on duty day and night in a skilled nursing home? _____ _____
    c. Trained nurses' aides and orderlies on duty in homes providing some nursing care? _____ _____

22. Rehabilitation _____ _____
    a. Specialists in various therapies available when needed? _____ _____

23. Activities Program   _____   _____
    a. Individual patient preferences observed?   _____   _____
    b. Group and individual activities?   _____   _____
    c. Residents encouraged but not forced to   _____   _____
       participate?
    d. Outside trips for those who can go?   _____   _____
    e. Volunteers from the community work   _____   _____
       with patients?

24. Religious Observances   _____   _____
    a. Arrangements made for patients to   _____   _____
       worship as they please?
    b. Religious observances a matter of   _____   _____
       choice?

25. Social Services   _____   _____
    a. Social worker available to help residents   _____   _____
       and families?

26. Food   _____   _____
    a. Dietitian plans menus for patients on   _____   _____
       special diets?
    b. Variety from meal to meal?   _____   _____
    c. Meals served at normal times?   _____   _____
    d. Plenty of time for each meal?   _____   _____
    e. Snacks?   _____   _____
    f. Food delivered to patients' rooms?   _____   _____
    g. Help with eating given when needed?   _____   _____

27. Grooming   _____   _____
    a. Barbers and beauticians available for   _____   _____
       men and women?

Attitudes and Atmosphere

28. General atmosphere friendly and
    supportive?   _____   _____

29. Residents retain human rights?   _____   _____
    a. May participate in planning treatment?   _____   _____
    b. Medical records are held confidential?   _____   _____
    c. Can veto experimental research?   _____   _____
    d. Have freedom and privacy to attend to   _____   _____
       personal needs?
    e. Married couples may share room?   _____   _____
    f. All have opportunities to socialize?   _____   _____

g. May manage own finances if capable or obtain accounting if not? ———— ————

h. May decorate their own bedrooms? ———— ————

i. May wear their own clothes? ———— ————

j. May communicate with anyone without censorship? ———— ————

k. Are not transferred or discharged arbitrarily? ———— ————

30. Administrator and staff available to discuss problems? ———— ————

    a. Patients and relatives can discuss complaints without fear of reprisal? ———— ————

    b. Staff responds to calls quickly and courteously? ———— ————

31. Residents appear alert unless very ill? ———— ————

32. Visiting hours accommodate residents and relatives? ———— ————

33. Civil rights regulations observed? ———— ————

34. Visitors and volunteers pleased with home? ———— ————

Source: U.S. Department of Health, Education, and Welfare, *Nursing Home Care* (Washington, D.C.: Medical Services Administration, 1976).

Minority groups are generally underrepresented in long-term care facilities. Gottesman and Hutchinson (1974) suggest that lifestyle and hardiness of those minorities who do survive to an advanced age may partially account for their low rates of placement in long-term care facilities, but Jackson (1973) charges that minorities have probably been unable to obtain institutional care due to their poor economic status and discriminatory practices.

For anyone, regardless of age, sex or race, moving into a long-term care facility constitutes a major adjustment. Thus, the availability of social supports is crucial for individuals experiencing this transition. The involvement of families with nursing home residents has been studied by York and Calsyn (1971). Most of the families in their study visited institutionalized relatives despite the presence in some cases of severe mental and physical deterioration. The number of visits after placement was related to the amount of family interaction with the resident prior to the placement. A more problematic issue than the frequency of visits appeared to be the enjoyment of the visits; 42 percent of the families reported enjoying less than half of their visits to the nursing home. Enjoyment of the visit was more related to the amount of mental deterioration than the presence of physical and sensory impairments. One of the major problems cited was lack of anything to do on visits; the families felt that they just sat and stared at their relatives for an hour. Many family members expressed feelings of guilt, frustration and resentment. York and Calsyn concluded that families could benefit from education about the aging process (especially behavior changes and mood disturbances associated with organic brain syndrome) and ways to make visits more beneficial and rewarding for both the family and the resident. Strong interest was expressed by families in the study for participating in these types of programs.

Nursing home employees can also play an important role in meeting social and emotional needs of residents. However, factors such as low wages and heavy work loads interfere with staff members fulfilling this role. Nurses' aides, who comprise the largest percentage of staff employed in nursing homes and have four times as much contact with residents as the professional staff, also have the highest turnover rate (Handschu, 1973). Institutional policies that will encourage staff stability and commitment are needed.

Taboos against touching combined with little opportunity for privacy in institutions work against the development of intimate relationships among residents. Even the physical contact that occurs between residents and staff members tends to be functional touching like that involved in moving residents from one location to another (Loeb & Watson, 1975). Acceptance of more open displays of affection in long-term care facilities can serve to reassure residents of their self-worth, compensate somewhat for other sensory losses, and communicate feelings of concern. Cook (1981) has stressed that the human component of caregiving needs more emphasis.

Therapeutic Intervention

Residents of long-term care facilities need the opportunity to use their remaining competencies and abilities. Environments that reinforce dependency and encourage the "helpless role" of residents promote continued deterioration. Schulz (1976) has demonstrated that loss of control among institutionalized elderly is at least partially responsible for depression, physical decline and early death. Kahn (1977) has suggested that disability can actually be induced in institutional environments. He used the term "excess disability" to describe the discrepancy between the actual physiological impairment of the individual and the degree of disability demonstrated in day-to-day functioning. According to his re-

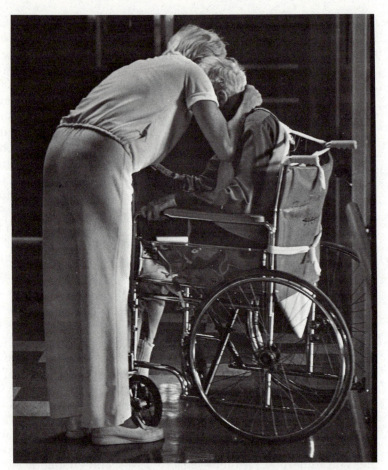

Acceptance of more open displays of affection in long-term care facilities can serve to reassure residents of their self-worth, compensate somewhat for other sensory losses, and communicate feelings of concern. (DENVER POST/© John Sunderland, photographer)

search, signs of "excess disability" can be found in 40 percent of the institutionalized aged.

The term "senility" is commonly used to refer to the confused and disoriented behaviors sometimes exhibited by older people, many of whom are institutionalized. These behaviors can be a function of organic changes in the brain or the arteries leading to the brain (organic brain syndrome) which in many cases are irreversible. They can also result from such factors as metabolic disorders, malnutrition, and drug intoxication and should be treated accordingly (Saxon & Etten, 1978). In some cases, however, the condition has more of a psychological basis than a physiological one and can be environmentally induced. According to Hyams (1969), disorientation may result from the elderly person's reaction to the loss of identity and dignity in a nursing home environment.

Cora

Her hands move ceaselessly in nervous fidgeting,
their fingers drawn and twisted with age.
Her eyes open wide in wonder at inexplicable happenings
that refuse to fit into her confusion.

She is tired but not allowed to rest,
she is angry but cannot rage.

I look at her and retreat into fond memories
of her kindness and gentle nurturing,
of finger plays made with strong straight hands,
of stories told softly in clear exciting whispers.

Where is the hickory stick on which she leaned so trustingly?
Where is the quick determined gait in her walk?

Her brow is drawn in a perpetually troubled look
and she mumbles a senseless repetitious cadence.
Sometimes I hear her say, "I don't know, I don't know,"
and other times I hear only meaningless syllables.

She seems to be lost much of the time,
not recognizing suddenly unfamiliar faces.

She wants to go home much of the time,
and escape these strange and unfamiliar places.

John T. Cook
July 7, 1980

Therapeutic intervention has been shown to be effective in reversing behavior deterioration in a variety of situations. Irene Burnside (1978), in her book *Working with the Elderly: Group Processes and Techniques*, describes group intervention techniques ranging from remotivation therapy to art and music therapy. The goals and techniques used vary as much as the therapies themselves, yet all approaches aim to improve the lives of the institutionalized elderly.

Alternatives to Placement

Berg and his colleagues (1970) have commented on the high incidence of unnecessary institutionalization of older persons. It is estimated that approximately 15 to 40 percent of persons living in institutions could be residing in the community if supplemental home care could be obtained (Hendricks & Hendricks, 1977). Increased recognition of the need for a continuum of care, as opposed to the dichotomous choice of totally independent living versus institutionlization, has led to the development of a wide range of community services. In order to provide assistance to older people who live in their own homes but cannot provide fully for themselves, programs such as Meals on Wheels and Homemaker Services have been established. Also, organizations such as Visiting Nurses Association offer valuable services to noninstitutionalized elderly in need of regular medical care (Harbert & Ginsberg, 1979). Although not widespread, geriatric day care programs have recently received a lot of attention in the United States (Beattie, 1977). An important component of many European health care programs, the day care approach avoids institutionalization yet provides for the changing needs of families.

Unfortunately, many families are not aware of the programs available in their communities. More effort needs to be devoted to the linkage aspect of service delivery, or rather, how to establish contact between the person having a need and the agencies that offer services specific to that need. In some situations, the problem is primarily unavailability of services rather than lack of awareness. For example, in rural areas with a small population scattered over a large geographical area, the full range of support services will not usually be available.

Despite the increase in community programs serving the elderly, federal legislation has presented several obstacles to the provision and utilization of alternative services, thereby making institutional placement the most feasible choice for many families (Kaufman, 1980). Troll and others (1979) have demonstrated that families in the United States are actually penalized financially for their efforts to care for their aging parents. Barber (1980) believes that tax relief and reinbursement for financial support of aged family members should be seriously considered by political decision makers if we wish to support families in assuming the caretaking function of the elderly.

Box 7-4

Ashrams: A Place for the Old in India

Ashrams are religious centers in India which are usually open to Hindus on their journeys to places of religious significance. Some of these centers are also designed to meet the long-term needs of older persons who wish to retire from active participation in the outside world and devote the rest of their lives to spiritual pursuits. In some ashrams, food and accommodations are provided at no charge. At others some type of payment is required for persons to share in this collective living arrangement. Some facilities simply accept an older person's remaining assets in return for life-time shelter and care. In the Indian society, the elderly who choose to spend their final stage of life in religious contemplation at an ashram are greatly admired.

Source: S. Vatuk, "Cultural Perspectives on Social Services for the Aged in India." A paper presented at the annual meeting of the Gerontological Society, San Diego, California, November, 1980.

Understanding the Aging Process

When a textbook is written on the aging process fifty years from now, it will probably be very different from this text. Many questions currently remain unanswered regarding the mechanisms producing physical change with age. Although much progress has been made in understanding the process of aging, many paths have been taken in order to arrive at our present position.

History is full of examples of the search for the proverbial fountain of youth. In Greek mythology, the sorceress Medea is reported to have emptied the veins of King Aeson and then filled them with a mixture of grasses, roots and herbs, the blood of a black ram, the flesh of an owl, and the skin of a snake. According to legend, upon receiving the potion the old King jumped from his bed full of vim and vigor. Throughout the middle ages, various techniques were tried to retain the vital energy of youth. These techniques ranged from the inhalation of the breath of young maidens to drinking the blood of young lambs, but no effective remedy for the aging dilemma was found. Even Ponce de León in his search for the fountain of youth in the New World only ended up with Florida (deRopp, 1960).

Palmore (1971) attributes the universality of this search for longer life to the instinctual drive for self-preservation, which no individual or group can survive for long without. This search continues today in modern scientific laboratories, rather than in the milieus of explorers and alchemists.

Biological Theories of Aging

Current biological theories of aging guide most of the research in this area today. Theories serve several purposes. First of all, an adequate theory will help us *understand* the process being studied. A theory provides a conceptual framework which gives order to our empirical findings. If we understand the mechanisms involved in the process and how they operate, we should then be able to *predict* and *control* the functioning of these mechanisms. Thus in the context of our present discussion, biological theories of aging combined with empirical data can potentially take us a long way toward altering the course of aging. Unfortunately, the current theories appear to be lacking in several respects. In Hayflick's (1974) view, "there is probably no other area of scientific inquiry that abounds with as many untested and untestable theories as does the biology of aging." Despite these limitations, the work that has been done is still impressive and worthy of our attention.

While numerous theories have been proposed, the most prominent ones can be classified into one, or some combination, of the following four categories: wear and tear theory, programmed-aging theory, error-accumulation theory, and autoimmunity theory.

Wear and tear theory. Some of the earliest theories of the aging process were based on the assumption that aging occurs as a consequence of continued use, or wear and tear, of the body as one progresses through life. In other words, parts of the body simply wear out, contributing to a decreased capacity to resist stress (Timiras, 1972). With improved medical technology, replacement of organs now often extends life; however, it is generally recognized that this approach cannot adequately alter the decreasing efficiency of the systems of the body and the homeostatic mechanisms. This theory also fails to take into account the fact that use of body parts in some cases actually leads to increased strength (for instance, use of muscles).

Programmed-aging theory. Many current theories are based on the assumption that the aging process is genetically determined and aging and death are built into the genetic "program" from the time of conception (Wilson, 1974). The observation that the lifespan appears to be relatively fixed from species to species supports this view. Also, Hayflick (1968) has demonstrated that cells grown in laboratory tissue culture only divide a finite number of times, and a relationship exists between the number of cell divisions and the age of the organism from which the cell was taken. Cells taken from young animals normally divide 40 or 50 times, whereas those from older animals divide only about 20 or 25 times. Bernard L. Strehler (1977), another scientist working in this

Many current theories of aging are based on the assumption that the aging process is genetically determined and built into the genetic "program" from the time of conception. (Courtesy of Nancy Houser)

field, believes that the key to understanding the aging process is to be found in the mechanisms that control and prevent the division of cells.

Other scientists have linked the genetic clock of aging to the release of hormones during critical periods in the lifespan. While the particular hormone (or group of hormones) involved has not been identified in humans, animal experiments have shown the release of specific hormones to be related to the aging process. By removing the adrenal gland in the Pacific salmon and the optic gland in the female octopus, scientists have been able to significantly increase longevity (Rosenfield, 1976).

Other research on the genetics of aging has focused on diseases in which accelerated aging is present, with the belief that if the genetic program can be speeded up by mistake then perhaps it can be slowed down scientifically. Two rare diseases, *progeria* and *Werner's syndrome*, have received attention from researchers. In progeria, aging is accelerated to the point that a three-year-old child can show physical changes characteristic of an older person. With this condition, the cells of the body go through fewer divisions and death usually occurs by age twelve. This disease appears to be genetically based, but this has not been confirmed. Werner's syndrome, however, is known to be a single-gene disease. While similar to progeria, accelerated aging does not occur until the teens (Rosenfeld, 1976).

Is it possible to reset our biological clock of aging? Perhaps so. According to Strehler (1977), we need only to unlock the information hidden in the DNA molecules, and now it appears that only a few critical genes or gene clusters may be involved. Also, recent discoveries in the field of genetics have greatly expanded our understanding of the genetic code, and thus, the potential for genetic engineering.

Error-accumulation theory.   The error theory actually encompasses several theories of aging, but all are based on the notion of the accumulation of errors or "noise" within the cell. A strong relationship has been established between aging and cellular mutations (Curtis, 1965). In fact, it has been estimated that probably one error exists in every cell of the body by the age of ninety (Hershey, 1974). These errors are known to affect cell functioning and are capable of causing cell death (Curtis, 1965). Mutations can occur spontaneously or result from radiation exposure or imperfect cell division.

Evidence shows that collagen and elastin (both composed of protein) undergo significant changes with age. Specifically, this connective tissue has a tendency to become cross-linked or bound to other protein substances in the body. Bjorksten (1974) has suggested that cross-linkage with DNA could also account for cell mutations as well as the accumulation of metabolic waste products, such as lipofuscin, within the cell.

Autoimmunity theory. When functioning properly, the immune system of the body protects against foreign organisms. According to the autoimmunity theory, antibodies in older organisms begin attacking normal cells (as in the case of rheumatoid arthritis) and become insufficient to destroy foreign cell bodies (Alder, 1974). Several leading causes of death (such as cancer and diabetes) have been linked to malfunctions of the immune system (Blumenthal & Berns, 1964). These changes in immune response may be related to the atrophy of the thymus gland in the aging organism (Makinodan, 1977).

Difficulties in Conducting Research on Biological Aging

Research on biological aging must contend with the unique problem of time. To study age-related change longitudinally, research must be conducted during a large portion of an organism's lifespan. This presents some obvious practical problems when the investigators are of the same species as the objects of investigation. In much of the research on aging and longevity, investigations have been conducted on subhuman species such as mice and fish because of their shorter lifespans. Questions have been raised, however, about the generalizability of the findings from this research to humans.

Methods that will allow scientists to complete studies on humans within a short time span are needed. Some progress has been made in this direction; several procedures are now available by which changes in the rate of aging can be detected within three to five years (Comfort, 1969). While these developments are promising, much more refinement is needed in order to obtain conclusive data on humans.

Another obstacle to research in this area has been the limited availability of funds. Despite the wide array of current research efforts, Strehler (1977) has expressed dismay over the fact that society has not invested more in trying to understand and control the aging process. He points out that "to date, less has been spent on the entire spectrum of research efforts in biological aging than on a single moon shot."

Longevity

As we have seen, the research on biological aspects of aging is closely tied to efforts to extend longevity. Once the tools are found that can alter the course of aging, this discovery will have direct implications for the length of human life.

Life expectancy refers to the average number of years that persons of a given age are expected to live. It is related to the nutrition, disease,

Table 7–1. Life Expectancies in Selected Countries.

Country	Male	Female	Country	Male	Female
Sweden	72.1	77.5	West Germany	67.6	74.1
Norway	71.3	77.6	Australia	67.6	74.2
Canada	69.3	76.4	U.S.S.R.	64.4	74.0
Italy	69.0	74.9	Mexico	62.8	66.6
East Germany	68.9	74.2	People's Republic of China	59.9	63.3
England	68.9	75.1	Brazil	57.6	61.1
United States	68.7	76.5	Iran	50.7	51.3
France	68.6	76.4	India	41.9	40.6

Source: United Nations Bulletin of Statistics, 1977.

sanitation, and health care present in a country. These factors have improved historically, but much variation still exists among countries. Table 7–1 shows the average life expectancies calculated for selected countries around the world in 1977.

Large gains in the life expectancy of Americans have been made during this century. With the elimination of many infectious diseases and a reduction in infant mortality, more and more people are surviving childhood and living to a ripe old age. In 1900 one could expect a newborn child to live approximately 47.3 years; by 1978 this figure had increased to 73.3 (U.S. Department of Health and Human Services, 1980a). However, fewer strides have been made in the ability to alter the human lifespan—the maximum length of life potentially attainable. In the Bible, the ninetieth Psalm puts the natural lifespan at three score and ten years, a figure highly similar to our average life expectancies today.

Each individual's longevity is determined by a variety of environmental and genetic factors. The quiz provided in Table 7–2, while being only a rough guide to your personal longevity, will aquaint you with factors shown to be related to length of life.

Table 7–2. How Long Will You Live?

This is a rough guide for calculating your personal longevity. The basic life expectancy for males is age 68 and for females is age 76. Write down your basic life expectancy. If you are in your 50s or 60s, you should add ten years to the basic figure because you have already proven yourself to be quite durable. If you are over age 60 and active, add another two years.

Basic Life Expectancy ____

1. Family history
   Add 5 years if 2 or more of your grandparents lived to 80 or beyond. ____
   Subtract 4 years if any parent, grandparent, sister, or brother died of heart attack or stroke before 50. Subtract 2 years if anyone died from these diseases before 60. ____
   Subtract 3 years for each case of diabetes, thyroid disorders, breast cancer, cancer of the digestive system, asthma, or chronic bronchitis among parents or grandparents. ____

2. Marital status
   If you are married, add 4 years. ____
   If you are over 25 and not married, subtract 1 year for every unwedded decade. ____

3. Economic status
   Subtract 2 years if your family income is over $40,000 per year. ____
   Subtract 3 years if you have been poor for the greater part of life. ____

4. Physique
   Subtract one year for every 10 pounds you are overweight. ____
   For each inch your girth measurement exceeds your chest measurement deduct two years. ____
   Add 3 years if you are over 40 and not overweight. ____

5. Exercise
   Regular and moderate (jogging 3 times a week), add 3 years. ____
   Regular and vigorous (long distance running 3 times a week) add 5 years. ____
   Subtract 3 years if your job is sedentary. ____
   Add 3 years if your job is active. ____

6. Alcohol
   Add 2 years if you are a light drinker (1–3 drinks a day). ____
   Subtract 5 to 10 years if you are a heavy drinker (more than 4 drinks per day). ____
   Subtract 1 year if you are a teetotaler. ____

7. Smoking
   Two or more packs of cigarettes per day, subtract 8 years. ____
   One to two packs per day, subtract 4 years. ____
   Less than one pack, subtract 2 years. ____
   Subtract 2 years if you regularly smoke a pipe or cigars. ____

8. Disposition
   Add 2 years if you are a reasoned, practical person. ____
   Subtract 2 years if you are aggressive, intense and competitive. ____
   Add 1–5 years if you are basically happy and content with life. ____
   Subtract 1–5 years if you are often unhappy, worried and often feel guilty. ____

9. Education
   Less than high school, subtract 2 years.   ____
   Four years of school beyond high school, add 1 year.   ____
   Five or more years beyond high school, add 3 years.   ____

10. Environment
    If you have lived most of your life in a rural environment, add 4
    years.   ____
    Subtract 2 years if you have lived most of your life in an urban
    environment.   ____

11. Sleep
    More than 9 hours a day, subtract 5 years.   ____

12. Temperature
    Add 2 years if your home's thermostat is set at no more than 68°F.   ____

13. Health care
    Regular medical checkups and regular dental care, add 3 years.   ____
    Frequently ill, subtract 2 years.   ____

Source: R. Schulz, *The Psychology of Death, Dying and Bereavement* (Reading, Mass.: Addison-Wesley, 1978, pp. 97—98). Reprinted with permission.

Cross-cultural studies have given us additional insight into the effects of lifestyle variables on longevity. Anthropologists have revealed cases of extreme longevity in several rather remote areas of the world—in the Soviet Republic of Abkhasia, in the Andean villages of Ecuador, and among the inhabitants of Hunza in West Pakistan (Leaf, 1975). Confirmation of these reports, however, has been difficult because of the lack of verifiable records.

Box 7–5

Abkhasia: Land of Long-lived People

I raised my glass of wine to toast a man who looked no more than 70. "May you live as long as Moses (120 years)," I said. He was not pleased. He was 119.

This incident and other similar ones have been related by Sula Benet, an anthropologist, who has studied the living patterns of the Abkhasians in their villages. In the Soviet republic of Abkhasia, an unusually large number of the population live to be over a hundred years of age. Not only do they seem to live longer, but many of the ailments we associate with old age are not present among this group of people. An examination of their lifestyle shows a high activity level and involvement in physical labor (there is no concept of retirement); a diet high in fruit and vegetables and low in meat with no consumption of coffee, tea or sugar; and continued sexual activity in the later years of life. Their attitudes are also of importance. Abkhasians do not view sickness as natural or normal even in advanced age. In fact, their vocabulary does not even have a term for "old people"; those who live to be over one hundred are simply called "long-lived people."

Source: S. Benet, *Abkhasians: The Long-living People of the Caucasus* (New York: Holt, 1974).

Based on the documented evidence currently available, the highest age obtained by any individual appears to be 120 years (Timiras, 1978). But not all scientists agree that there are limits to the human lifespan. In an interview several years ago, Bernard Strehler boldly argued for the possibility of immortality. In his opinion, death is capable of being conquered. "There is no absolute principle in nature," states Strehler, "which dictates that individual living things cannot live for indefinitely long periods of time in optimum health" (Rosenfeld, 1976, p. 4). Many other scientists do not accept this position. Nonetheless, the research activity in this area will certainly be interesting to follow over the next several decades.

Suggested Activities and Exercises

1. Conduct a survey of long-term care facilities in your community. Include interviews with nursing home administrators regarding factors influencing the establishment and development of their particular facilities.
2. Write a case study on an older person residing in a long-term care facility. Discuss specific needs of the resident and identify factors in the environment interfering with satisfaction of these needs.
3. Interview several older persons in your community regarding the care of the functionally impaired elderly in the early 1900s. What is their perspective on changes that have taken place in the American health care system?
4. Consider the occurrence of a breakthrough in research on aging. If the human life expectancy was increased by 50 years or more, what would be the implications for (a) social relationships, (b) work patterns, and (c) family systems?

5. Examine your family records and note the age and cause of death of your relatives over several generations. What observations did you make regarding changes in health and disease patterns? What conclusions can you draw about your family's health history?
6. Some writers have stated that the absence of death would completely transform the meaning of life. What are your thoughts on the subject? Do you think the elimination of death is a realistic, or even desirable, goal?
7. Examine your daily routine. What are you doing to promote healthy living during your adult years?

References

Albert, W. C., & Zarit, S. H. Income and health care of the aging. In S. H. Zarit (Ed.), *Readings in aging and death: Contemporary perspectives.* New York: Harper & Row, 1977.

Alder, W. An autoimmune theory of aging. In M. Rockstein (Ed.), *Proceedings of a symposium on the theoretical aspects of aging.* New York: Academic, 1974.

Barber, C. E. Adult children and aged parents: Proposals for strengthening family relationships in later life. *Family Perspectives*, 1980, *14*, 111–17.

Beattie, W. Aging and the social services. In R. Binstock & E. Shanas (Eds.), *Handbook of aging and the social sciences.* New York: Van Nostrand, 1977.

Bender, A. E. Nutrition of the elderly. *Royal Society of Health Journal* (England), 1971, *91*, 115–21.

Benet, S. *Abkhasians: The long-living people of the Caucasus.* New York: Holt, 1974.

Berg, R. S., Browning, F. E., Hill, J. G., & Wenkert, W. Assessing health care needs of the aged. *Health Services Research*, 1970, *5*, 36–59.

Birren, J. E. *The psychology of aging.* Englewood Cliffs, N.J.: Prentice-Hall, 1964.

Bjorksten, J. Cross-linkage and the aging process. In M. Rockstein (Ed.), *Proceedings of a symposium on the theoretical aspects of aging.* New York: Academic, 1974.

Blumenthal, H. J., & Berns, A. W. Autoimmunity in aging. In B. L. Strehler (Ed.), *Advances in gerontological research.* Vol. 1. New York: Academic, 1964.

Brody, E. M. The aging of the family. *The Annuals of the American Academy of Political and Social Science*, 1978, *438*, 13–27.

Brody, E. M. *Long-term care of older people: A practical guide.* New York: Human Scienes Press, 1977.

Bruhn, J. G. Effects of chronic illness on the family. *The Journal of Family Practice,* 1977, *4,* 1057–60.

Burnfield, A., & Burnfield, P. Common psychological problems in multiple sclerosis. *British Medical Journal,* 1978, *6121,* 1193–4.

Burnside, I. M. (Eds.) *Working with the elderly: Group processes and techniques.* North Scituate, Mass.: Duxbury, 1978.

Cleveland, M. Family adaptation to traumatic spinal cord injury: Response to crisis. *Family Relations,* 1980, *29,* 558–65.

Comfort, A. Test battery to measure aging rate in man. *Lancet,* 1969, *2,* 1411–15.

Cook, A. S. A model for working with the elderly in institutions. *Social Casework,* 1981, *62,* 420–5.

Crate, M. A. Nursing functions in adaptation to chronic illness. *American Journal of Nursing,* 1965, *65,* 72–76.

Curtis, H. J. The somatic mutation theory. In R. Kastenbaum (Ed.), *Contributions to the psychobiology of aging.* New York: Springer, 1965.

Dalderup, L. M., & Fredericks, M. L. C. Color sensitivity in old age. *Journal of the American Geriatic Society,* 1969, *17,* 388–90.

deRopp, R. S. *Man against aging.* New York: St. Martin's, 1960.

De Vries, H. A. Physiology of exercise and aging. In S. H. Zarit (Ed.), *Readings in aging and death: Contemporary perspectives.* New York: Harper & Row, 1977.

Gottesman, L. E., & Hutchinson, E. Characteristics of the institutionalized elderly. In E. M. Brody and contributers, *A social work guide for long-term care facilities.* Washington, D.C.: U.S. Government Printing Office, 1974.

Gruber, H. W. Geriatrics—Physical attitudes and medical school training. *Journal of American Geriatrics Society,* 1977, *25,* 494–99.

Handschu, S. S. Profile of the nurse's aide: Expanding her role as psycho-social companion to the nursing home resident. *The Gerontologist,* 1973, *13,* 315–17.

Harbert, A. S., & Ginsberg, L. H. *Human services for older adults: Concepts and skills.* Belmont, Ca.: Wadsworth, 1979.

Harrill, I., Erbes, C., & Schwartz, C. Observations on food acceptance by elderly women. *The Gerontologist,* 1976, *16,* 349–55.

Hayflick, L. Cytogerontology. In M. Rockstein, *Theoretical aspects of aging.* New York: Academic, 1974.

Hayflick, L. Human cells and aging. *Scientific American,* 1968, *218,* 32–37.

Hendricks, J., & Hendricks, C. D. *Aging in mass society: Myths and realities.* Cambridge, Mass.: Winthrop, 1977.

Hershey, D. *Life span and factors affecting it.* Springfield, Ill.: Charles C. Thomas, 1974.

Howell, S. C., & Loeb, M. B. Nutritional needs of the older adult (in Part

247

1, Nutrition and aging: A monograph for practitioners). *The Gerontologist*, 1969, *9*, 17–30.

Hyams, D. E. Psychological factors in rehabilitation of the elderly. *Gerontologica Clinica*, 1969, *11*, 129–36.

Jackson, J. Really, there are existing alternatives to institutionalization for aged blacks. In E. Pfeiffer (Ed.), *Alternatives to institutional care for older Americans: Practice and planning*. Durham: Center for the Study of Aging and Human Development, Duke University, 1973.

Jacobson, M. M., & Eichhorn, R. L. How farm families cope with heart disease: A study of problems and resources. *Journal of Marriage and the Family*, 1964, *26*, 166–73.

Kahn, R. L. Excess disabilities in the aged. In S. H. Zarit (Ed.), *Readings in aging and death: Contemporary perspectives*. New York: Harper & Row, 1977.

Kart, C. S., & Manard, B. B. Quality of care in old age institutions. *The Gerontologist*, 1976, *16*, 250–56.

Kart, C. S., Metress, E. S., & Metress, J. F. *Aging and health: Biologic and social perspectives*. Menlo Park, Ca.: Addison-Wesley, 1978.

Kastenbaum, R., & Candy, S. The 4 percent fallacy: A methodological and empirical critique of extended care facility program statistics. *Aging and Human Development*, 1973, *4*, 15–21.

Kaufman, A. Social policy and long-term care of the aged. *Social Work*, 1980, *25*, 133–37.

Leaf, A. *Youth in old age*. New York: McGraw-Hill, 1975.

Lowenstein, F. Blood pressure in relation to age and sex in the tropics and subtropics. *Lancet*, 1961, *1*, 389.

Mages, N. L., & Mendelsohn, G. A. Effects of cancer on patients' lives: A personological approach. In G. C. Stone, F. Cohen, N. E. Alder & Associates (Eds.), *Health psychology—A handbook*. San Francisco: Jossey-Bass, 1979.

Makinodan, T. Immunity and aging. In C. E. Finch and L. Hayflick (Eds.), *Handbook of the biology of aging*. New York: Van Nostrand, 1977.

Marra, J., & Novis, F. Family problems in rehabilitation counseling. *Personnel and Guidance Journal*, 1959, *38*, 40–42.

Master, A., & Lasser, R. Blood pressure elevation in the elderly person. In A. Brest and J. Moyer (Eds.), *Hypertension*. Philadelphia: Lea and Ferbiger, 1964.

McDaniel, J. W. Physical disability and human behavior (2nd ed.). New York: Pergamon, 1976.

McFarland, R. A., Domey, R. J., Warren, A. B., & Ward, D. E. Dark adaptation as a function of age: A statistical analysis. *Journal of Gerontology*, 1960, *15*, 149–54.

Miller, D. B., Lowenstein, R., & Winston, R. Physicians' attitudes toward the ill aged and nursing homes. *Journal of American Geriatrics Society*, 1976, *24*, 498–505.

Moos, R. H. *Coping with physical illness.* New York: Plenum, 1977.

Moss, F. E., & Halamandaris, V. J. *Too old, too sick, too bad: Nursing homes in America.* Germantown, Md.: Aspen Systems Corporation, 1977.

Noelker, L., & Harel, Z. Predictors of well-being and survival among institutionalized aged. *The Gerontologist*, 1978, *18*, 562–67.

Palmore, E. The promise and problems of longevity studies. In E. Palmore & F. C. Jeffers (Eds.), *Prediction of life span.* Lexington, Mass.: Heath, 1971.

Parsons, J. Definitions of health and illness in the light of American values and social structure. In E. J. Jaco (Ed.), *Patients, physicians, and illness.* New York: Glencoe, 1958.

Peterson, Y. The impact of physical disability on marital adjustment: A literature review. *The Family Coordinator*, 1979, *28*, 47–51.

Power, P. W. The chronically ill husband and father: His role in the family. *The Family Coordinator*, 1979, *28*, 616–21.

Rickard, T., Triandis, H., & Patterson, C. Indices of employer prejudice toward disabled applicants. *Journal of Applied Psychology*, 1963, *47*, 52–55.

Rodstein, M. Heart disease in the aged. In I. Rossman (Ed.), *Clinical geriatrics.* Philadelphia: Lippincott, 1971.

Rosenfeld, A. *Prolongevity.* New York: Knopf, 1976.

Saxon, S. V., & Etten, M. J. *Physical change and aging.* New York: Tiresias, 1978.

Schulz, R. Effect of choice and predictability on the physical and psychological well-being of the institutionalized aged. *Journal of Personality and Social Psychology*, 1976, *33*, 563–73.

Sontag, S. The double standard of aging. In L. R. Allman and D. J. Jaffe (Eds.), *Readings in adult psychology: Contemporary perspectives.* New York: Harper & Row, 1977.

Strehler, B. L. A new age for aging. In S. H. Zarit (Ed.), *Readings in aging and death: Contemporary perspectives.* New York: Harper & Row, 1977.

Timiras, P. S. Biological perspectives on aging. *American Scientist*, 1978, *66*, 605–13.

Timiras, P. S. *Developmental physiology and aging.* New York: Macmillan, 1972.

Timiras, P. S., & Vernadakis, A. Structural biochemical, and functional aging of the nervous system. In P. S. Timiras, *Developmental physiology and aging.* New York: Macmillan, 1972.

Tobin, S. S., & Lieberman, M. A. *Last home for the aged.* San Francisco: Jossey-Bass, 1976.

Troll, L. E., Miller, S. J., & Atchley, R. C. *Families in later life.* Belmont, Ca.: Wadsworth, 1979.

U.S. Bureau of the Census. *Population profile of the United States: 1980.* (Current Population Reports, Series P-20, No. 363). Washington, D.C.: U.S. Government Printing Office, 1981.

U.S. Bureau of the Census. *Social and economic characteristics of the older population: 1978.* (Current Population Reports, Series P-23, No. 85). Washington, D.C.: U.S. Government Printing Office, 1979.

U.S. Department of Health and Human Services. *Health, United States: 1979.* Hyattsville, Md.: National Center for Health Statistics, 1980. (a)

U.S. Department of Health and Human Services. National health expenditures, 1979. *Health Care Financing Review,* 1980, 2, 1–36. (b)

U.S. Department of Health, Education and Welfare. *Nursing home care.* Washington, D.C.: Medical Services Administration, 1976.

U.S. Department of Health, Education and Welfare. *Tables from 1973–74 national nursing home survey.* Hyattsville, Md.: National Center for Health Statistics, 1975.

Vatuk, S. Cultural perspectives on social services for the aged in India. A paper presented at the annual meeting of the Gerontological Society, San Diego, California, November 1980.

Wasow, M., & Loeb, M. B. Sexuality in nursing homes. In R. L. Solnick (Ed.), *Sexuality and aging.* Los Angeles: University of Southern California Press, 1978.

Weg, R. B. *Nutrition and the later years.* Los Angeles: University of Southern California Press, 1978.

Wilson, D. The programmed theory of aging. In M. Rockstein (Ed.), *Proceedings of a symposium on the theoretical aspects of aging.* New York: Academic, 1974.

Wolf, E. Glare and age. *Archives of Opthalmology,* 1960, 64, 502–14.

Wright, B. *Physical disability: A psychological approach.* New York: Harper & Row, 1960.

York, J. L., & Calsyn, R. J. Family involvement in nursing homes. *The Gerontologist,* 1977, 17, 500–05.

Chapter 8

Death and Dying

"Death belongs to life as birth does. The walk is in the rising of the foot as in the laying of it down." This quote from the Indian poet Tagore illustrates the importance of including a chapter on death and dying in an adult development textbook. Coping with the loss of significant others and facing one's own death are major issues of adult life. An omission of this topic would indicate failure to acknowledge that death is indeed a natural part of living.

While death is universal, death-related experiences and attitudes are strongly influenced by the general orientation toward death of the society in which one lives. This orientation may vary during different historical periods. Kastenbaum (1981) contends that individual reactions to death cannot be fully understood unless they are viewed in the context of time, place and culture.

Death has been labled a taboo subject in Western culture (Pattison, 1977). However, the prevalence of death themes in European paintings, statues and carvings indicate that death was more openly acknowledged in previous times. Feifel (1963) has documented an increasing denial of mortality in America since about 1900. Several factors account for this alienation from death. After 1900 Americans observed and experienced fewer deaths due to the absence of wars fought on our soils, the banning of public executions, and the tremendous decrease in infant mortality. In addition, we have tended to segregate those who are

251

Elisabeth Kübler-Ross has been a pioneering figure in the area of death and dying (Ann Ring, photographer)

approaching death into nursing homes and retirement centers, thus allowing us to further deny the reality of decline and eventual death (Parson & Lidz, 1967).

Robert Fulton (1980), Director of the Center of Death Education and Research at the University of Minnesota, has asserted that ours is the first "death-free" generation. People in modern American society are increasingly likely to grow to maturity without ever witnessing the natural death of a close friend or relative. In fact, the majority of young adults in the United States report never having seen a person die.

Since the mid-1960s, we have begun to shift from being a death-denying culture toward a more open, death-integrating one (Pattison, 1977). Dr. Elisabeth Kübler-Ross, who is known for her work with the terminally ill, has been a key influence in the death-awareness movement. The heightened awareness and interest resulting from this movement have helped to address the modern dilemmas and problems related to care of the dying

Knott (1979), in discussing the expanding interest in death education, says that training programs in human services and medical sciences have significantly increased their course offerings in topics related to death and bereavement. Currently over a thousand courses on death and dying exist at the post-secondary level in the United States, most of which have been added during the past ten years. We will examine the topic of death and dying within this cultural and historical context.

First, we will discuss contemporary issues surrounding death. Modern societies in our age are faced with the difficult tasks of providing new criteria of death, deciding who will set these criteria, and determining individual rights regarding death. We will explore the complexities of each of these issues. The following section will focus on the dying process, including discussions of impact of a terminal diagnosis, needs of the dying, and the institutionalization of death. The final part of this chapter will consider responses to death: the meaning and function of rituals and customs (cultural responses), the mourning process (personal responses), and adjustment to widowhood (role change as a response to death).

Death: The Contemporary Scene

Attitudes Toward Death

As humans, we alone know that death is inevitable. We have been endowed with the ability to anticipate and contemplate our own death and the death of others, internalize belief systems regarding the significance of death, and speculate about events occurring after death. Humans have also developed the means to alter the course of death somewhat with our sophisticated strategies of medical intervention. Despite these abilities that clearly separate us from other forms of life, we are caught in a paradox regarding death. Although intellectually we know that death is an inevitable and universal event, most of us have difficulty conceiving of our own personal death and we resist thinking of death as a common, everyday happening (Gurthrie, 1969).

While several studies on adult attitudes toward death have been conducted, unfortunately most of these investigations have focused primarily on the fear of death and have failed to measure a broad range of death attitudes (Marshall, 1980). Also, these studies have been generally criticized for viewing "fear of death" as a unitary phenomenon. Indeed, fear of death appears to be very complex and multidimensional in nature. Simpson (1979) identified the following four components of death fear: (1) fear of the dying process including associated biological and social processes of pain, dependency, loneliness, impairment and loss of body functions; (2) fear of loss of self and nonexistence; (3) fear of the consequences of death such as outcome of plans and projects, effects on survivors, and the uncertainty regarding an afterlife; and (4) fear of separation and loss of loved ones.

Despite problems with measurement and conceptualization of fear of death, a consistent finding relating to age differences has been reported. Older persons appear to be significantly less fearful of death than younger individuals (Bengston, Cuellar & Ragan, 1977; Kalish & Johnson, 1972; Kalish & Reynolds, 1976; Riley, 1970). Kalish and Reynolds (1976) found that persons in the 20–39 age category were most likely to indicate fear of death, however, few persons of any age said that they felt terrified of death. Kalish (1976) has offered three possible explanations for the decreased fear of death found among older persons. First of all, older persons may perceive the costs of giving up life to be lower because they view their lives as having less value than when younger. Secondly, older persons may feel justified by having lived to an old age. The third possible explanation is that older persons may become socialized to accept their own deaths through repeated experiences with the deaths of others. Marshall (1980) has added that some of these age-related findings may be due to cohort or historical influences since they were derived from cross-sectional data.

It has been argued that fear of death is universal and operates as an important survival mechanism. However, cross-cultural data challenges this position. Howard and Scott (1965) found a marked contrast in their comparison of American attitudes toward death with the attitudes of the Rotumans, a Polynesian group. The investigators argued that death conflicts with the American value system and results in a high degree of death anxiety among Americans. First of all, at the core of the American value system is the belief that nature can be controlled; death is therefore viewed as defeat. Also, Americans highly value productivity, and death is usually associated with inactivity. Thirdly, death means separation for Americans who typically develop close interpersonal attachments in the context of the nuclear family. In contrast, the Rotumans generally view death with acceptance. Individuals in this society tend to accept nature rather than attempt to control it, display much passivity, and have an extensive kin network consisting of many diffuse relationships which results in less trauma from separation.

While attitudes toward death are strongly influenced by the cultural milieu, it should be noted that wide variations exist among individuals. The attitudes of any single individual will be determined by a multiplicity of factors including personal experiences with death, attitudes of parents and other significant persons, religious beliefs, and situational variables. Modern life forces us to confront these attitudes as we face contemporary issues concerning death.

Death: What Is It?

With the advent of new medical technology, the problem of determining acceptable criteria of death has emerged. In previous times, little question existed whether someone was actually dead. Death was determined simply by the absence of heartbeat and respiration. Now with the possibility of maintaining heart and lung functions by artificial means, questions such as "When is someone actually dead?" have become extremely complex. Human intervention in the dying process have led us to seek clearer guidelines for defining death.

The debate over what definition to use and the approach to be used in arriving at an acceptable definition of death involves medical, philosophical, legal, ethical and religious concerns. Veatch (1979) has asserted that practical empirical questions ("What technical test should be applied in the determination of death?") must be separated from the philosophical issues ("What essential aspect of life is lost at the time of death?"). He says that the conceptual question must be resolved because differing concepts of death will suggest different criteria for determining death, and he adds that medical training is not necessary in order to address the broader philosophical issue. According to Veatch, terms such as *brain death* and *heart death* should be avoided because they obscure the question of when the death of the individual as a whole occurs.

In modern medical facilities today, physicians typically use one of the following definitions of death: (1) irreversible brain damage, with no possible recovery of consciousness; (2) no possibility of restoring a spontaneous heartbeat; or (3) electroencephalogram (EEG) brain death (Mant, 1968). The third definition, proposed by the Ad Hoc Committee to Examine the Definition of Brain Death of Harvard Medical School, is the most widely accepted in the United States. In its report published in 1968, this interdisciplinary committee presented the following criteria for determining the complete and irreversible loss of brain activity:(1) unreceptivity and unresponsivity, (2) no movements or breathing, (3) no reflexes, and (4) a flat electroencephalogram. The report calls for repetition of these tests after a period of 24 hours. Patients are excluded from these criteria when hypothermia (body temperature is below 90°F) or central nervous system depressants (that is, barbiturates) are present. These guidelines enable surgeons to remove organs for transplants while the donor's heart is still beating and the organs remain viable.

Analogous sets of criteria have been proposed by Europeans (Wolstenholme & O'Connor, 1966). However, Veatch (1979) has pointed out that even among those who generally agree on the types of measurement, disagreement on levels of measurement may exist. For example, the 24-hour period proposed by the Harvard committee has been criticized for being too conservative. In states that have not adopted specific legislation, physicians cannot be assured of legal protection if they use the criteria of the Harvard committee. Veatch emphasizes that "some order must be brought out of this confusion. A public policy must be developed that will enable us to know who should be treated as alive and who should be treated as dead." The problem is obvious in situations in which resuscitative efforts have left individuals in comatose states. If one set of criteria is used the person will be pronounced dead, and if a second set is used the person will be considered alive. The task is to reexamine and clarify the meaning and definition of death in order to more adequately resolve contemporary life and death dilemmas. However, our criteria for death will continually require reassessment as progress is made in the technical aspects of medicine.

Box 8–1

Brain Death: Welcome Definition . . . or Dangerous Judgment?

On May 25, 1968, at the beginning of the era of organ transplants, a 56-year-old black laborer was brought to the operating room of a Virginia hospital having suffered massive brain damage from a fall. The court case ensuing from the events following his admittance raised important questions regarding acceptable definitions of "brain death." The following timetable is taken from the summary of the actual court case:

6:05 p.m.   Admitted to the hospital

11:00 p.m.   Emergency right temporoparietal craniotomy and right parietal burr hole.

2:05 a.m.   Operation complete; patient fed intravenously and received "medication" each hour.

11:30 a.m.   Placed on respirator, which kept him "mechanically alive."

11:45 a.m.   Treating physician noted "prognosis for recovery is nil and death imminent."

1:00 p.m.   Neurologist called to obtain an EEG with the results showing "flat lines with occasional artifact. He found

	no clinical evidence of viability and no evidence of cortical activity."
2:45 p.m.	Mr. Tucker taken to the operating room. From this time until 4:30 p.m. "he maintained vital signs of life, that is, he maintained, for the most part, normal body temperature, normal pulse, normal blood pressure and normal rate of respiration."
3:30 p.m.	Respirator cut off.
3:33 p.m.	Incision made in Joseph Klett, heart recipient.
3:35 p.m.	Patient pronounced dead.
4:25 p.m.	Incision made to remove Tucker's heart.
4:32 p.m.	Heart taken out.
4:33 p.m.	Incision made to remove decedent's kidneys.

Following removal of the heart and kidneys by the surgical team, the heart was transplanted to a donor who died one week later. The brother of the deceased charged the transplant team with deliberately hastening the death in order to obtain the needed organs and carrying out the transplant procedure without permission from the patient's family.

Source: R. M. Veatch, "Brain Death: Welcome Definition . . . or Dangerous Judgment?", *Hastings Center Report,* 1972, 2, No. 5.

Many argue that physicians should be allowed to use the definition they choose, while others think that physicians should be required by law to use the definition of death adopted by the state in which they reside. Veatch (1979) suggests that allowing the patient or relatives of the patient to decide their own criteria for death may be the most workable solution since there exists such a diversity of religious, moral and philosophical perspectives on the issue. Others have also agreed that the individual, rather than the physician or state, has the right to decide on the criteria to be used for his or her own death (Sullivan, 1973).

The Right to Die

The right to die has also been a topic of considerable discussion. Technological advances in the field of medicine have provided means to pro-

Death and Dying

long life through sophisticated drugs and mechanical devices. These life-sustaining techniques and procedures have kept alive, oftentimes at large personal and financial costs, persons who in the past would have died.

Many individuals hold the view that life is desirable only if it can be lived with some measure of dignity, and mere continuation of life by machines and drugs is a violation against human integrity. Neurosurgeon Milton D. Heifetz (1975), who wrote *The Right to Die*, has said, "The man who cannot speak, who cannot think, who would live as a vegetating mass of protoplasm without any hope of recovery should not be forced to live." However, a *Psychology Today* article entitled "Our Failing Reverence for Life" reported that our culture no longer values human life as it once did. According to the authors of this article, "faced with the mounting population and diminishing world resources, we have moved from talking about the value of life to talking about its worthlessness under certain conditions . . ." (Hall & Cameron, 1976). Other writers have made stronger statements on the subject suggesting that death legislation is being introduced because the very ill and infirmed are considered too great a burden on society.

At what point is a life no longer worth living and who should make this determination? These questions are basic to the issue of euthanasia. The term *euthanasia*, a Greek word meaning "good death," refers to deliberate attempts to relieve pain and suffering of persons for whom there is no hope by hastening death.

Americans appear to be changing their views toward the practice of euthanasia. Only 36 percent of Americans sampled in Gallup polls in 1947 and 1950 were willing to grant doctors the power to end the life of a patient suffering from an incurable illness, even if both the patient and family requested it. When asked the same question in 1973, 53 percent indicated acceptance. If the death occurred as a result of withholding treatment (passive euthanasia) rather than actively ending life (active euthanasia), this percentage increased to 72 percent (Hall & Cameron, 1976).

In a study of physicians' views toward euthanasia, nearly two-thirds of the doctors sampled said they would use "extraordinary means" if a member of their family were suffering from a terminal illness with no hope of recovery (Rice, 1974). Fletcher (1977) has argued that ethics based on the sanctity of life must be replaced by a code of ethics on the quality of life which will apply to the peculiarities of death in the twentieth century. Current patterns of death are very different from those of earlier times when many individuals died untimely deaths due to infectious diseases. Patients who did survive were usually able to recover completely and live long, productive lives. With the dramatic reduction in infectious diseases due to improved sanitation, routine immunization, and the use of antibiotics, death is now more often associated with chronic diseases from which recovery is unlikely under most circumstances. Perhaps the earlier medical approach of preserving life at all costs needs to be reevaluated in view of the modern circumstances of death (Morison, 1973).

**Box 8–2

The Story of "Gramp"

Frank Tugend was our grandfather. He was born in Scranton, Pennsylvania, in 1892. Although he went into the mines as a slatepicker when he was 11 years old, he had a happy childhood.

After his retirement, Gramp was cursed with an infirmity that's lumped under titles like senility or hardening of the arteries or generalized arteriosclerosis. On February 11, 1974, Frank Tugend, age 81, removed his false teeth and announced that he was no longer going to eat or drink. Three weeks later, to the day, he died.

Dan wrote, "It is probably the feeling that Gramp is patiently waiting for death that fascinates me the most. He lies there not stirring, not even calling for enough of substance to keep away the pain of thirst." He was through with the intolerable problems that living had forced upon him. He was ready to be conquered.

What Gramp did want was somebody to be with him all the time. His bony but still-strong fingers clutched the hand of whoever was with him. Gramp finally slipped into a coma. Doctor Ben Kline found that his heart and lungs were still functioning. The doctor said that the term for a person being kept alive by tubes was "a heart-and-lung case." Family opinion was resolute. If Gramp had stoically endured his tongue cracking and the roof of his mouth flaking off from lack of liquid, no way were we going to sneak nourishment into him now.

One night in March, Nink walked into the kitchen and said, "I think Dad's gone." We could find no pulse. After the funeral director left, Mark wrote in his journal: "For three years, through babysitting, 'accidents', hassles, much of our lives had revolved around this room. I felt no sense of relief that Gramp was gone. There was a tinge of emptiness. I thought "You pulled it off, Gramp. You really pulled it off."

Source: M. Jury and D. Jury, *Gramp* (New York: Grossman, 1975).

The euthanasia issue has been complicated by the controversy over the definition of death. Also, the distinction between passive and active euthanasia is often unclear. Physicians are often hesitant to publicly acknowledge their support of euthanasia for fear of potential charges of malpractice or homicide. However, in a poll of the Association of American Physicians, over two-thirds of the physicians admitted having practiced passive euthanasia ("Euthanasia and the law," 1974). Carson (1979) has stressed that the following factors should be considered when determining the ethics of withdrawing treatment or administering medication that will hasten death: (1) the physical, mental and emotional condition of the patient; (2) the intent of those persons attending the patient; and (3) the expressed wishes of the patient.

Individuals are becoming more assertive about their right to control the manner in which they die. In a national poll, 78 percent of respondents believed that terminally-ill patients had a right to tell their doctors to allow them to die (Harris Poll, 1982). Schulz (1978) suggests several reasons why terminally-ill patients may want to end their lives including the belief that life is no longer meaningful; the desire for a dignified death; the opportunity to control when and how they die; and relief from pain and mental distress. He adds that patients may wish to die because they feel they are emotional and financial burdens on their families. It is important to recognize a sincere desire for death and distinguish it from a choice made because of subtle or direct cues conveyed by relatives.

Oftentimes the wishes of dying persons cannot be known if they are comatose. California, passing the Natural Death Act in 1976, was the first state to deal with this problem through legislative action. This act allows persons to sign living wills (see Box 8–3) in advance of a terminal illness requesting that extraordinary means not be used to extend their lives. It also provides legal protection for physicians and paramedical personnel from criminal prosecution when they act according to the provisions of the bill. Many other states have enacted right-to-die legislation since the passage of the California act.

Box 8–3

A Living Will

To My Family, My Physician, My Lawyer and All Others Whom It May Concern

Death is as much a reality as birth, growth, maturity and old age—it is the one certainty of life. If the time comes when I can no longer take part in decisions for my own future, let this statement stand as an expression of my wishes and directions, while I am still of sound mind.

If at such a time the situation should arise in which there is no reasonable expectation of my recovery from extreme physical or mental disability, I direct that I be allowed to die and not be kept alive by medications, artificial means or "heroic measures." I do, however, ask that medication be mercifully administered to me to alleviate suffering even though this may shorten my remaining life.

This statement is made after careful consideration and is in accordance with my strong convictions and beliefs. I want the wishes and directions here expressed carried out to the extent permitted by law. Insofar as they are not legally enforceable, I hope that those to whom this Will is addressed will regard themselves as morally bound by these provisions.

Signed: _____

Date: _____

Witness: _____   Witness: _____

Copies of this request have been given to: _____

Source: Concern for Dying, 250 W. 57th Street, New York, N.Y. 10019.

Box 8–4

Death with Dignity Isn't Easy

DEAR ABBY: Recently you ran a letter from a woman who had signed a "Living Will," and was relieved to know that should she ever fall victim to an incurable illness, she would be allowed to die in dignity. I think you should warn your readers that merely signing a Living Will is no guarantee that one's wishes will be carried out. It will also take perseverence on the part of the family.

Last May, my husband died of lung cancer after a very short illness. He had a history of heart disease, and the previous year had suffered a severe stroke that left him partially paralyzed. I feared that, should he suffer heart failure, "heroic measures" might be taken, and he would be "saved" only to suffer more from the cancer.

The doctors who had treated him previously were aware that he had signed a Living Will. However, one specialist seemed to view my husband more as a pair of diseased lungs than a whole man, and was determined to save him should heart failure occur. It took days of arguing and button-holing every responsible person I could reach for the instructions of "No Code" to be included on his chart. (The "No Code" signified that no resuscitation team would be summoned.)

If your spouse (or family member) has signed a Living Will, my advice would include:

(1) Talk the situation over thoroughly with your family so that there is no doubt in anyone's mind as to your intentions.

(2) Discuss this philosophy at length with your family doctor, who will be the admitting doctor and responsible for any instructions to be included on the patient's chart regardless of any specialists who might be called in. Doctors are trained to save lives, and some are unable to make the mental adjustment to a passive course of no action. If the doctor seems reticent or unwilling to follow your wishes, CHANGE DOCTORS.

(3) Once the patient is admitted to the hospital. Make sure the instructions on the chart are in accord with your wishes; keep pestering the doctor until they are.

(4) If treatment is being prescribed that is offensive to the patient and family, the family CAN check the patient out of the hospital without the doctor's release.

Abby, we CAN die with dignity, but it might take great perseverance on the part of our spouse and family to make sure we are given the opportunity.—BEEN THERE.

Source: Reprinted with permission of Abigail Van Buren.

The Final Phase of Life

Although each of us is somewhat closer to our final hour with the passage of each day, the actual time that death will occur in the life course of any one individual is unknown. Statistics show that greater numbers of Americans are now surviving to late adulthood. In fact, a dramatic shift in leading causes of death has taken place since the turn of the century with the major communicable diseases being replaced by diseases associated with the aging process (see Table 8–1). With the increased control of communicable diseases, young adults have a greater

Table 8–1. The Ten Leading Causes of Death: United States, 1900 and 1977.

1900

Rank	Cause of Death	Percent of All Deaths
1	Influenza and pneumonia	11.8
2	Tuberculosis	11.3
3	Gastroenteritis	8.3
4	Diseases of heart	8.0
5	Cerebral hemorrhage	6.2
6	Chronic nephritis	4.7
7	Accidents, total	4.2
8	Malignant neoplasms (cancer)	3.7
9	Certain causes of mortality in early infancy	3.6
10	Diphtheria	2.3

1977

Rank	Cause of Death	Percent of All Deaths
1	Diseases of the heart	37.8
2	Malignant neoplasms (cancer)	20.3
3	Cerebrovascular diseases	9.6
4	Accidents, total	5.4
5	Influenza and pneumonia	2.7
6	Diabetes mellitus	1.7
7	Cirrhosis of the liver	1.6
8	Arteriosclerosis	1.5
9	Suicide	1.5
10	Certain causes of mortality in early infancy	1.2

Source: U.S. Department of Health and Human Services, *Vital Statistics of the United States 1977: Volume II—Mortality* (Part A). Hyattsville, Ma.: National Center for Health Statistics, 1981.

Determining the meaning one's life has had appears to be the main task of the elderly facing death. (DENVER POST/© John Sunderland, photographer)

probability of living a full lifespan. Death, however, continues to strike individuals of all ages. Each year, a significant number of adults in their young and middle years die prematurely (Lerner, 1980).

Facing Death

Young adulthood is a time for expansion. Most young adults are in the process of establishing intimacy, building meaningful relationships, and starting families and careers. It is a period of excitement, adventure, intensity and hope. When death confronts the young adult, the resulting reactions are usually rage, frustration and disappointment. Just when one's abilities are emerging, life is cut short. Dreams of what might have been must be reconciled with the reality of impending death. The middle years are characterized by increasing responsibilities and commitments to family members, friends, neighbors and work associates. For the middle aged, coping with dying centers around those interpersonal involvements which will be interrupted. As persons in their later years approach the end of their lives, it is a time for reflection and for evaluation of the uniqueness of their existence. Determining the meaning one's life has had appears to be the main task of the elderly facing death (Pattison, 1977).

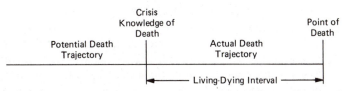

Figure 8–1. The dying trajectory. (Source: E. M. Pattison. *The Experience of Dying*. Englewood Cliffs, N.J.: Prentice Hall, Inc., 1977.)

Most individuals conduct and plan their lives with an anticipated lifespan as a frame of reference. When faced with the crisis of knowledge of impending death, this potential death trajectory is suddenly altered. The period between the crisis knowledge of death and the actual point of death has been referred to as the living-dying interval, illustrated in Figure 8–1 (Pattison, 1977).

Kübler-Ross (1969) has conceived of the living-dying interval in terms of five sequential stages. In the first stage, patients react to the news of their terminal illness with shock and disbelief. *Denial* is the prominent feature of this stage. Persons often seek additional medical opinions in the hope that a mistake has been made. Kübler-Ross describes one woman who in her denial insisted that God would heal her despite her rapidly progressing cancer. The next stage is one of *anger*. The patient asks "Why me?" and experiences hostility and resentment. These feelings can be displaced in all directions including family, friends, the medical staff and God for allowing it to happen. *Bargaining* begins in the following stage as the anger subsides. Attempts to postpone the inevitable are made by bidding for more time. The person may promise to repent if allowed to live until Christmas. Yet when the holiday passes, the dying person proposes yet another bargain. The fourth stage in the dying process is one of *depression*. The person has faced the reality of impending death and is grieving for the anticipated loss of life. Feelings of sadness and a great sense of loss are present. In the fifth and final stage, *acceptance* is the main theme. Despair and remorse are absent as the person achieves a quiet peace prior to death.

While the stages proposed by Kübler-Ross have served an important role in generating interest in psychological aspects of the dying process, they have been misinterpreted by many as representing "the correct way to die." Kübler-Ross (1974) herself has warned against viewing the five stages as invariant, universal steps to a mature death. Her model of the dying process has been criticized by Simpson (1979) for its overgeneralization and simplicity. According to him such approaches do not adequately consider "the patient's previous personality, ethnic and cultural context, earlier life experiences, the nature of the particular disease and treatment, nor the interrelationships with significant others in the family and the caring team."

Pattison (1977) believes that a dying person can demonstrate a wide variety of emotions during the living-dying interval, and that emotional responses emerge in an ebb-and-flow fashion rather than appearing in a certain order. While questioning the existence of *stages* of dying, he suggests a *phase* approach consisting of an initial acute phase, a chronic living-dying phase, and a terminal phase. The *acute phase* occurs at the onset of knowledge of death and is associated with high levels of anxiety. In acute diseases that progress rapidly to death, the patient only experiences this phase. The *chronic living-dying phase* begins when the anxiety starts to diminish as the person adjusts to the severity of the illness. The patient's withdrawal from the external world marks the transition to the *terminal phase*. In cases of sudden unexpected death after a long illness, no terminal phase will occur. Pattison stresses that use of the phase concept is primarily to aid in the understanding of the mechanisms involved; it is in actuality an artificial division of a dynamic life process.

The dying process will vary somewhat for each individual in terms of length, certainty, and pattern and symptoms of the specific diseases involved. Four basic death trajectories have been described by Glaser and Strauss (1965, 1968):

1. *Certain death at a known time* (for example, a patient with a brain tumor is given the prognosis of death within six months).
2. *Certain death at an unknown time* (a person with a chronic heart problem is presented with the ambiguous time frame of between one and ten years).
3. *Uncertain death and a known time when the question will be resolved* (a patient will learn following radical surgery if she will recover).
4. *Uncertain death and an unknown time when the question will be resolved* (a young adult with multiple sclerosis).

Anxiety is decreased when the death knowledge is provided within a relatively specific time frame. It is easier to cope with certainty, however unpleasant, than to try to adjust your life to an uncertain future. The length of the living-dying interval also produces differential effects. When this interval is greatly extended, it results in prolonged emotional stress for the dying person and for the family.

Treatment of the Dying

Should persons be informed of their terminal condition? Prior to 1970, most investigations showed that physicians overwhelmingly favored not telling patients that they were dying (Fitts & Ravdin, 1953; Oken, 1961; Feifel, 1965). More recent studies show a greater willingness of physicians to disclose a terminal diagnosis (Rea, Greenspoon & Spilka, 1975; Carey & Posavoc, 1978). Perhaps this shift has been in response to demands made by patients. In a Gallup Poll in which a representative sample of the adult population in the United States was interviewed, 90 percent said that they would want to be told if they had a fatal illness (Blumenfield, Levy & Kaufman, 1979). Hinton (1980) advocates that questions of the patient be answered openly and honestly, but he emphasizes that the patient should be allowed to control the pace of the communication. Opposition to the practice of giving a prognosis of death using *specific* units of time (days, weeks, months, etc.) has been voiced by Kübler-Ross (1974). She believes that such estimates undermine hope and are not usually very accurate.

Evidence suggests that individuals know when they are dying even when not told directly. Weisman (1972) has described a state of "middle knowledge" in which one suspects but is not really sure about his or her condition. Ways in which suspicions are often confirmed include overhearing comments of physicians, nurses, and others; observations of unusual behavior (for example, a brother who lives 1500 miles away drops in for a casual visit); changes in medical care procedures (the patient is given narcotics and pain medication more readily); a change to another physical location (the patient is transferred to another ward); self-diagnosis through reading of medical books and comparisons with symptoms of others; signals from within the body as pain and discomfort increase; and altered responses to future-oriented statements (visitors avoid discussing future plans of the patient) (Kalish, 1970).

Erickson and Hyerstay (1975) suggest that attempts to conceal information from the dying patient can be psychologically destructive. They conclude that an abundance of time and effort goes into the deception of persons who usually do not want to be deceived and who already suspect the seriousness of their illness. These elaborate systems of deception may include misleading explanations for medical decisions, hints and fabrications to suggest favorable progress, discounting symptoms, encouraging the patient to make optimistic interpretations, giving undue attention to irrelevant statements and events, reducing the range of expression and conversational topics, and focusing conversation on the present (Glaser & Strauss, 1965). In a study by Kastenbaum and Aisenberg (1972), over 200 attendants and nurses in a geriatric hospital were asked how they responded to patients' statements about death. Their answers typically fell into one of the following categories:

1. *Reassurance* ("You're doing much better.")
2. *Denial* ("You're not going to die. You'll live to be a hundred.")

Death and Dying

3. *Changing the Subject* ("Let's talk about something more cheerful.")

4. *Fatalism* ("We're all going to die sometime.")

5. *Discussion* ("Why do you feel that way?")

Over 82 percent reported that they avoided discussion of the patients' thoughts and feelings about death. Avoidance of the topic may be due to the belief that it is in the patient's best interests, or it may result more from the inability of the staff or family member to cope with the situation.

Sometimes the individual enters into this conspiracy of silence and finds himself or herself engaged in a mutual pretence situation with hospital staff, family and friends. While everyone knows that death is approaching, no one acknowledges the possibility of it happening. In fact, extreme measures are taken by all parties to stay on safe topics and refrain from emotional outbursts. If they should occur, they are simply ignored (Glaser & Strauss, 1965).

This avoidance of the topic of death can generalize and include avoidance of the terminally-ill person altogether. One study found that it took nurses significantly longer to respond to terminal patients' bedside calls than to those of less severely ill patients (LeShan, reported in Kastenbaum & Aisenberg, 1972). This tendency to avoid interaction with the dying can apply to family members and friends as well. According to Epley and McCaghy (1978) "in a future-oriented society interaction with one who lacks a future becomes both frustrating and problematic." This emotional and physical withdrawal from the terminally ill may result in a social death prior to actual biological death (Glaser & Strauss, 1968). Death itself is frequently neither the most important nor the most difficult issue for dying patients. Issues of isolation, dependency and fear of abandonment are usually more disturbing (Koenig, 1973).

Kübler-Ross (1974) has found that most dying persons want to talk to someone about their feelings and fears. She emphasizes the importance of having a compassionate listener who will respond openly and honestly. The companion will do much more listening than talking as the dying person attempts to gain closure on his or her life. This time can be one of reaffirming important relationships, resolving old conflicts, putting one's affairs in order, and completing other unfinished business.

Three of the most important needs of terminally-ill persons are the need for pain control, the need to retain feelings of dignity and self-worth, and the need for love and affection. Saunders (1980), a leading authority in the care of the dying, advocates that analgesics be given regularly to persons with malignant pain. Through an appropriate match between level of analgesia and the intensity of the pain, a person can be virtually pain-free yet still alert. Some professionals have questioned if death with dignity is possible in situations in which the dying person is experiencing high levels of pain and discomfort. Dignity will certainly be lessened when the dying are made to feel powerless and are given little or no control in their daily lives. Having a terminal illness does not necessarily imply that persons are any less capable of making important decisions that concern their lives (and deaths). Feelings of self-worth are sustained when one's opinions and preferences are considered. It is all too easy to cast the dying into a dependent, passive "patient role," rather than viewing them as active participants in the dying process. Weisman and Kastenbaum (1968) stress that all the important interpersonal roles (spouse, parent, etc.) of a person should be given an avenue for expression. These roles have helped to shape each person's identity and removal of them will result in a diminished sense of self. A supportive environment for the terminally ill includes the presence of persons who have shared other life experiences with the dying individual and who can respond with genuine love and concern. Sharing this time of transition with a loved one can often strengthen and enhance existing family relationships.

Dying in a hospital.   While the majority of persons indicate that they would prefer to die at home, approximately 80 percent of all deaths in the United States occur in institutions (Loether, 1975). Carson (1979) has stated that those caring for the dying should respect the person's right to be involved in decision making, acknowledge and support individual preferences, and assist in keeping meaningful relationships intact during this period of stress. Unfortunately, the institutional context of death in modern America is at odds with these objectives. Kübler-Ross (1975) feels that "dying in a hospital too often means stripping away all that is personally defining and meaningful." The hospital climate of dependency and institutional routine can be demoralizing to the dying. Mauksch (1978) claims that although hospitals are well designed for the challenge of healing, they are ill-equipped to meet human needs of those whose physical condition is beyond their capacity for successful intervention. He also contends that dying patients represent medical failure and produce feelings of inadequacy in those trained to heal.

The intensive care unit (I.C.U.) of a hospital is designed for the care of the critically ill. It contains features which may create special psychosocial problems for dying patients and their families. The I.C.U. is usually equipped with respirators, electrocardiograph machines, and other sophisticated apparatus. This area is structurally and spatially organized to maximize the application of life-sustaining medical technology. Sherizen and Paul (1977) found that this physical setting makes family members uneasy while in the unit visiting a dying loved one, and this uneasiness often results in avoidance of the unit and minimal visitation of the patient. In addition, they found that the structure of the I.C.U. can interfere with the ability of the family to face the death of the patient. Intensive care units usually have strict rules regarding appropriate behaviors during the limited visitation periods. Role switching between the family and medical staff occurs with staff members assuming responsibility in areas family members have previously dominated (for example, trust, companionship, nourishment). Only limited forms of family interaction are allowed at a time when the support and presence of significant others are needed.

Hospice: An alternative. There has been a growing interest in the United States and other countries in providing alternative settings for the intensely personal experience of death. Hospice care has become an increasingly viable alternative for many Americans. Dr. Cecily Saunders founded the first hospice facility in London in 1948 with a donation from a dying patient. The hospice movement in the United States began in 1974 when a hospice program was started in New Haven, Connecticut (Holden, 1976). Today there are over 150 hospices in operation in the United States.

The focus of hospice care is on the quality of remaining life. Persons who have a terminal illness *are* still living and deserve to be responded to as whole human beings with emotional, social, spiritual, and physical needs and concerns. The entire family (not just the dying member) is considered the primary unit of care. The emphasis is on humanizing the experience of death which includes providing comfort and appropriate pain control by a skilled medical staff, involving family members in direct care of the patient, and giving emotional support through the period of bereavement. Sylvia Lack, director of the hospice program in New Haven, Connecticut, has observed that families who have been involved in caregiving usually have less difficulty adjusting to the death (Lack, 1978).

In addition to providing facilities in which people can go to die, hospice also supports care of the dying at home. We have noted earlier that most persons want to die in the familiar setting of their home surrounded by people that have given meaning to their lives. Lack (1978) has found that a large number of families in both the United States and Britain prefer to care for their dying relatives at home. However, many families have never considered home care as a possibility. With the shift away from home care of the dying during the twentieth century, we have become largely dependent on professionals for skills that were previously a part of every family's repertoire. This shift has left most families largely ignorant of the skills required in the care of the terminally ill and lacking the confidence to choose home care as an option

(Hime, 1979). The hospice team teaches family members the practical aspects of caregiving and is available to provide additional medical support if it is needed. Volunteers have an important role in most home care hospice programs. The volunteer component facilitates home care by offering services to the family in a variety of areas (for instance, child care, meal preparation, and emotional support).

"My wife after enduring radiation, chemotherapy, and three major operations decided against the depersonalization of hospitals and chose to die at home with her family attending her. My daughter and I tried to provide the care she needed but found that it was an overwhelming task. When the situation and our stamina was at the breaking point, an organization gave all the care and advice we needed to make my wife comfortable and considerably happy during the last few weeks she was alive. I must admit that I had a dim view of volunteer organizations, but Hospice restored my faith in the goodness and caring of my fellow human beings. In addition to caring for my wife's needs, they also took time to listen and counsel me when my whole world was coming apart."

Source: Statement of a Hospice family member, August 22, 1980.

With the rapid proliferation of hospices in the 1970s, the need to set standards for hospice care became apparent. To eliminate confusion among those seeking services, organizations calling themselves "hospices" must reflect the basic hospice philosophy. The National Hospice Organization was formed in 1978 and soon adopted a set of guidelines and standards for hospices across the country. This organization has been actively seeking legislative changes that will facilitate the continued provision of hospice care and promote development of additional hospice programs. It appears that the hospice movement may well restore death with dignity to the American scene.

Responses to Death

The death of an individual in society involves a configuration of personal, cultural and occupational responses. The death event itself sets many small processes into motion. In our modern society, "the florist, the clerk in the office of vital statistics, the linotype operator who prepares the death notice, and the home office that will demand an explanation of what has happened to holder of charge card #32674-8814-007" are all part of this complex configuration (Kastenbaum, 1975).

Cultural Responses: Rituals and Customs

Perhaps the most visible responses to death are societally-determined rituals and customs. In most societies, both primitive and modern, ceremonies are used to mark important life transitions such as birth, marriage and death. These public ceremonies referred to as *rites of passage* facilitate the transition from one status to another and serve as social recognition that the transition has in fact occurred. In the case of death, rules of appropriate conduct are usually established for persons closely related to the deceased as well as for other members of society. While these rules tend to have much structure and be strictly regulated in nontechnical societies, they are deemphasized in industrial societies in which the death of any one individual will have little impact on the culture as a whole (Pine, 1972).

Cross-cultural research has shown that cultural mechanisms for reacting to bereavement (funeral ceremonies, dress customs, specified norms for behavior, et cetera) serve several important functions (Rosenblatt, Walsh & Jackson, 1977). They represent a way for a society to give meaning to the incomprehensibility of death, they aid in reducing death-related fears, and they provide for emotional catharsis of the bereaved. Pine and Phillips (1970) have noted that Americans lack the ceremonial and social mechanisms that once existed to help them cope with death. In the United States, prescribed mourning dress is now rare, fewer persons cancel social engagements for a specified period following a death, and the practices of viewing the body and visiting the home of those in mourning have decreased. Several writers have suggested that this reduction in acceptable ways to publicly express sentiment for the deceased may explain the willingness of Americans to spend large sums of money on funerals (Pine, 1972; Williamson, Munley & Evans, 1980).

Funerals. Lamers (1969) has defined funerals as an organized, purposeful, time-limited, flexible, group-centered response to death. The term *funeral* includes any ceremony connected with burial or cremation of the dead. Funeral customs are extremely diverse and are influenced by many factors including the physical environment, existing social structures, economic factors and religious traditions. Funerals represent the values of a society and tend to reinforce its norms.

Raether and Slater (1977) have identified five common phases of funerals: removal of the body from place of death, the visitation period, funeral rites, the procession, and the committal of the body. In most

272   Continuity and Change

Funeral customs are strongly influenced by the cultural context in which they occur. (Alicia Cook, photographer)

modern societies there is widespread acceptance of the funeral service practitioner role of coordinating the funeral activities and providing the necessary staff, facilities and equipment for the funeral process. The funeral rituals begin with removal of the body from the place of death. Usually the body is taken to a mortuary by a representative of the funeral industry. The funeral home staff then makes detailed funeral arrangements with the family of the deceased and begins the preparation of the body. Preparation of the body in the United States usually includes embalming and the use of cosmetics when the body is to be viewed. (In many countries of the world, the practice of cosmetology applied to the dead is unknown.) Next is a visitation phase during which community members visit the family of the deceased to express their sympathy and support. The length of the formal visitation period may vary from a few hours to several days depending on ethnic, religious and local customs. Funeral rites or services are usually next in the sequence of funeral activities. Approximately 75 percent of funeral services conducted in the United States have a religious component with clergy officiating. This type of service is usually preferred when the deceased or the survivors have a religious affiliation. Becoming increasingly accepted are humanist or secular services for those who do not find religious services meaningful. The officiant of these services is usually a friend of the family or a respected person in the community. In some cases two services, one religious and one secular, may be conducted to meet the varying needs of family members. An alternative to the funeral service is a memorial service in which the body of the deceased is not present. Special acknowledgement has been given in most cultures to the following phase—the procession. The procession involves movement of the deceased from the place of the funeral service (or the place of death in some cultures) to the place of final disposition. The final phase of the funeral process is the actual act of committing the body to its place of final disposition. The committal underscores the finality of the death. For the bereaved, it clearly marks the beginning of a life without the presence of a loved one. Strong preference for burial as the means of final disposition exists among most Americans. Less than 5 percent of American families favor cremation, whereas over half of those who die in England and Japan are cremated (National Funeral Directors Association of the United States, 1974).

The funeral not only recognizes that a death has occurred, it also acknowledges that a life has been lived. Funerals can provide comfort and consolation to the friends and family of the deceased by providing a supportive atmosphere in which to remember the life of one they loved. It can facilitate the adjustment to the loss by encouraging the release of strong emotions, relieving guilt and emphasizing the finality of the death. Accepting the reality that the person has died is essential in the resolution of grief. A public ceremony also allows the community some form of participation in the family's sorrow. It can promote community solidarity and cohesion and reaffirm family ties (Lamers, 1969; Pine, 1972).

Much controversy, however, has surrounded the issue of funeral practices in the United States. American funerals have been criticized for being unnecessarily costly and extravagant. In her book *The American Way of Death*, Jessica Mitford (1963) charges the funeral industry with exploiting bereaved families by pressuring them to purchase expensive funerals. Unfortunately, most families are ill-prepared to make decisions regarding funerals. They have little information regarding average funeral costs, state laws and options available to them. For example, most people believe that embalming is required by law. While it is routinely done by funeral home staffs without consulting the family, in most states it is only legally required if the death is due to a communicable disease, if the body is to be transported to another state, or if there is a delay of several days until final disposition. Still in shock from news of the death, families can easily make hasty funeral arrangements they later regret. A way to reduce one's vulnerability and confusion during this time is to engage in preneed planning. Many funeral directors welcome visits and inquiring telephone calls from persons prior to a death. Providing services to an informed public protects the funeral industry from unwarranted criticism. Families who make decisions together before the crisis of a death avoid the undesirable consequences of naive decision making. Box 8−5 presents some basic facts regarding funeral costs. How do these figures compare with your assumptions about the expense of funerals?

Box 8−5

Facts About Funeral Costs

Q. What are the major expenses associated with most American funerals?

A. The funeral director's services are the most costly. These services usually include embalming and cosmetology, use of the chapel for the funeral service, use of a viewing room, provision of a casket, and use of a hearse for transporting the deceased. For an additional charge, the funeral director can also arrange for obituary notices, flowers, an honorarium for the clergy, death certificates, and the use of limousines. Other expenses include the purchase of a cemetery plot and related cemetery charges (e.g., open and closing of the grave, fees for maintenance and regular care of the gravesite). Also, most cemeteries require a receptacle (concrete liner or burial vault) to enclose the casket. These can usually be purchased from a mortuary. The cost of a marker or monument for the grave is extra.

Q. What is the average cost of a funeral?

A. The average cost is approximately $2,000 ("Facts worth knowing about funeral costs," 1975) for the standard American funeral with cemetery burial. However, the price can vary widely from one mortuary to another. Also, the cost of different funerals at any one mortuary can vary considerably. The major factor in cost variations is the price of the casket. Insist on seeing all types of caskets available before selecting one. Variations in other aspects of the funeral service can also influence the cost. While most states do not require that mortuary charges be itemized, it is appropriate to request a complete list of charges in advance.

Q. What are ways to reduce funeral expenses?

A. In addition to selection of a low-cost casket, certain elements of the standard funeral can be omitted (embalming and cosmetology if viewing is not going to be part of the service, use of limousines, chapel, etc.). The choice of cremation can be less expensive than burial unless other aspects of the standard funeral are followed. Another alternative is donating your body to medical science. With the possible exception of transportation costs if long-distance travel is involved, receiving medical institutions usually pay all the expenses and take responsibility for final disposition of the body. Medical institutions however usually have strict requirements for the cadavers they accept. Persons interested in this alternative should inquire about the regulations at local medical schools.

Q. How are funerals usually financed?

A. Usually funeral bills are paid primarily from the estate of the deceased. Also, most persons are eligible for funeral expense benefits from one or more source. Social security provides a small sum for this purpose. Some veterans are also eligible for benefits. Other sources of funeral benefits include insurance policies, trade unions, and fraternal organizations.

In summary, funerals can serve important social and psychological needs during bereavement. The funeral exists in many forms. Decisions of cremation versus burial, open casket versus closed casket, and low-cost versus moderate- or high-cost funerals can oftentimes be very difficult for a family in grief. Whatever decisions are made, it is important that the funeral be planned to meet the needs of the bereaved and ease their transition to life without the deceased.

Grief and Bereavement

The bustle in a house
The morning after death
Is solemnest of industries
Enacted upon earth,

The sweeping up the heart,
And putting love away
We shall not want to use again
Until eternity.

Emily Dickinson

Losing significant others through death is an experience most persons have to face at least once and usually several times during their lives. Some deaths will be anticipated as persons reach advanced ages and develop chronic health problems. For others, death will come quite suddenly and unexpectedly. In all cases, the survivors will experience grief.

Grief is a natural response to loss. The grief response can be experienced with many different types of loss (for example, loss through divorce, loss of job, loss of physical abilities). While life is full of many losses, the loss of personal relationships through death is the most traumatic (Kübler-Ross, 1976). In societies such as ours in which families tend to be small and nuclear rather than part of an extended kin network, death of a family member is experienced more intensely by survivors. Death in this context not only causes a disruption of close relationships, but it also leaves an unfilled role. In extended families, larger emotional support systems exist with surrogate parents, siblings, and children being readily available. These systems therefore have a greater capacity to take over roles left by the deceased (Blauner, 1966; Williams, Munley & Evans, 1980).

Sanders (1980) concluded from her research that bereaved individuals, especially those who have lost a child, are in a physical "high-risk" category. The findings from her study of 102 recently bereaved persons demonstrated their increased physical vulnerability during the bereavement period. The bereaved had significantly more physical symptoms and more frequently reported sleep disturbances and appetite loss than did a control group.

The increase in health problems among bereaved individuals has been well documented. Parkes (1972) found a 63 percent increase in visits to physicians and a higher incidence of hospitalization among the recently widowed. The physical stress associated with bereavement can also lead to an early death. In a study in Wales, Rees and Lutkins (1967) found the mortality rate among relatives of the deceased during their first year of bereavement to be seven times greater than that of a control group. Additional studies in both England and the United States have consistently found that the risk of dying is at least twice as high for the bereaved (Schulz, 1978).

The high-risk status of the bereaved appears to be related to more than general stress factors. Fredrick (1977) has obtained evidence to show that grief may be accompanied by an increased secretion of corticosteroids. Corticosteroids are very powerful hormones which can suppress the functioning of the body's immune system thus explaining the increase in infectious and malignant diseases among the bereaved.

The resolution of grief. Only a small minority of persons require professional assistance in coping with their loss. Those who do seek help usually display delayed, inhibited or chronic grief reactions. Delayed grief is characterized by a shallow grief response. Apparently unaffected at first, a person will manifest grief reactions weeks and sometimes years after the death. Grief can also be inhibited and never find direct expression. However, it usually appears indirectly, often in the form of illness or maladaptive behaviors. Chronic grief is demonstrated by persons who continue to experience intense grief years after a death. Mention of the deceased can elicit emotional responses similar to those expressed shortly after the loss (Marris, 1975).

Prolonged pathological grief can occur in cases of sudden death when survivors are not given the opportunity to view the body (for example, a drowning in which the body is never found or war casualties whose corpses are not sent home). Kübler-Ross (1976) has found that the bereaved in these situations have an extremely difficult time facing the reality of the death.

Personality characteristics of the bereaved can sometimes interfere with the resolution of grief and cause aborted grief reactions. For example, persons who tend to overuse the mechanism of denial in their lives may have difficulty overcoming the initial shock and disbelief following a death. Behavior patterns and defense mechanisms that have developed as a result of other life experiences may be maladaptive when coping with loss (Schmale, 1972).

Kastenbaum (1969) has used the term *bereavement overload* to refer to the common experience among older people of having to cope with numerous deaths with little time in between for working through their grief. Grieving can become a constant companion at a stage in life when one has the fewest support systems and the least amount of physical stamina.

Gorer (1965) has described the resolution of grief as having three components: (1) termination of the bond that holds the bereaved to the deceased, (2) adjustment to a life that does not include the deceased, and (3) the establishment of new relationships. Social supports are extremely important in the process of relinquishing one's attachment to the deceased and reinvesting oneself in other relationships. In our society, we often fail to acknowledge the continuing needs of survivors. Immediately after a death friends and neighbors concentrate their attention on the bereaved only to abandon them during the most difficult stages of grief. Kübler-Ross (1969) says that the worst time for the bereaved is usually after the funeral is over when all the relatives have gone. While the overt signs of grief may not be evident, the painful work of mourning has just begun. Various support groups for the bereaved have been organized throughout the United States. Compassionate Friends, a group composed of parents who have experienced the death of a child, is one such group. It can be reassuring to know that others have survived the grief process and have emerged to find life meaningful again.

Not only are the bereaved oftentimes isolated in their grief, but they are denied expression of their sorrow as well. In our death-denying society, discussions of death remind us of our own mortality. Therefore, we usually feel uncomfortable in the presence of someone openly expressing grief. In fact, we admire persons who can control their emotions and often interpret not doing so as a sign of weakness. The common phases of "bouncing back," "keeping a stiff upper lip," and "getting on with life" all reflect our attitudes toward self-control and adjustment. We emphasize outward appearance and behavior without fully considering the inner experiences of the bereaved. Males especially are limited in their display of emotion due to stereotyped concepts of appropriate "masculine" behavior. Our socialization does not permit the uncontrolled emotional outbursts that are encouraged in many tribal societies (Schmale, 1972).

Through the expression of grief, persons are freed to restore their inner harmony and resume their lives. Maddison and Walker (1967) found the ease with which acquaintances accepted crying and other outlets of emotional expression to be a significant influence on health outcomes for widows. Kübler-Ross (1976) has observed that grief is much shorter when people are allowed to express their pain and anguish, and she advocates having screaming rooms in hospitals where survivors can go to "scream, cry, bang the walls, and question the absurdity of the tragedy." Several writers have voiced opposition to the widespread practice of giving medication to the bereaved to calm them. Kübler-Ross

Grief needs to be recognized, accepted, and given expression more than it needs to to be treated, managed, or controlled. (Source: Elliot Erwitt, Magnum Photos.)

(1976) warns that use of sedatives usually only serves to delay the grief response, and Rees (1972) adds that consideration of psychopharmaco-logic management should be reserved for those reactions that interfere with the grieving process.

It is important to remember that grief is healing. While it is painful, it is a necessary psychological process. If an individual is unable to successfully complete this process, then therapeutic intervention may be appropriate. However, in most cases grief needs to be recognized, accepted and given expression more than it needs to be treated, managed or controlled.

> Thoughts of a son watching his mother die: "This was my mother; the word 'mother' brings on a flow of feeling and past experiences and years of living together, loving together, and hating, too. The fighting and conflicts do not seem important anymore, the arguments and intense pains and emotions that clouded the relationship have evaporated. This was my mother, and I realize the uniqueness of our relationship. It was not an impersonal fact of someone having cancer and dying, but it was a basic relationship that can never be repeated, a piece of eternity, never to be the same anymore."
>
> C. C. Moustakas
> *Loneliness*

The grieving process. While no two people will grieve in exactly the same way, common patterns of grief have been demonstrated (Parkes, 1972; Glick, Weiss & Parkes, 1974). Immediately following the death is a period of shock during which survivors report feeling numb and dazed. Shock serves as a protection against the intense psychological pain resulting from the loss. After a few weeks the shock and disbelief are usually replaced by marked mental anguish and an overwhelming sense of sorrow. It is common during this phase, which frequently lasts up to a year, for the bereaved to review the death and search for reasons to explain it. "If only . . ." statements are often combined with behaviors that psychologically evoke a sense of the deceased person's presence. Figure 8–2 shows the incidence of various psychological and physical reactions associated with bereavement. These data were obtained from interviews with 109 widowed persons during their first month of their bereavement. The most common reactions were crying, depressed feelings and difficulty in sleeping. More than half the sample also indicated that they had difficulty concentrating or remembering, lacked appetite or had lost weight, and used sleeping pills or tranquilizers (Clayton, Halikes & Maurice, 1971). Eventually most bereaved persons are able to resolve their grief and recover from their loss. In fact, Glick et al. (1974) found that most of the bereaved they studied had achieved functional stability within a few months and had almost completely resolved their grief by the end of the first year. Specific occasions, however, such as

281

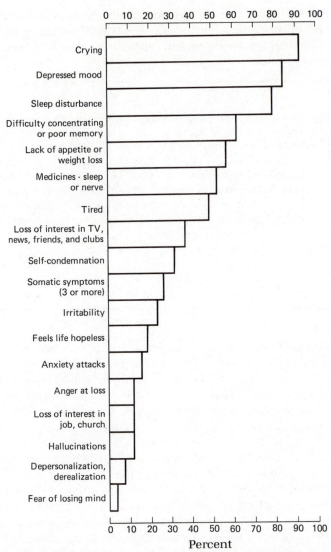

Figure 8–2. Reported symptoms of bereavement. (Source: P. J. Clayton, J. A. Halikes, and W. L. Maurice. "The Bereavement of the Widowed." *Diseases of the Nervous System*, 1971, 32, 597–604.)

anniversaries and holidays may continue to elicit grief responses and instill a renewed sense of loss.

Death of a child appears to cause the most difficult and prolonged grief (Gorer, 1965; Sanders, 1980). Sanders (1980) found that adults experiencing the death of a child had greater depression and more guilt, anger and somatic problems than those experiencing either the death of a spouse or a parent. Regardless of age of the child (they ranged from age six to forty-nine), parents had difficulty accepting the fact that they had outlived their child.

When death is anticipated, persons usually begin the grief process prior to the actual death thus deintensifying the post-death grief reaction. With the benefit of forewarning, it is possible to share feelings and concerns with the dying person and begin to adjust to the anticipated consequences of the impending death. A deep sense of loss and sadness will still accompany the death even though it may be mixed with feelings of relief when a long and difficult illness has ended (Fulton, 1970).

Sudden death deprives friends and family of the opportunity to say goodbye and finish unfinished business. Kübler-Ross (1976) differentiates between grief and grief work. While *grief* is a normal and healthy response to loss, *grief work* includes coping with "hurts never healed, love unexpressed, regrets unresolved." This unfinished business of most sudden deaths results in additional pain and remorse for the bereaved. In a study of the bereaved from the Coconut Grove fire in Boston, Lindemann (1944) found high levels of guilt, hostility and anxiety. The survivors were preoccupied with images of the deceased and experienced physical symptoms such as tightness of the throat, shortness of breath and loss of muscular strength.

Of all possible types of death, suicide is probably the most difficult for the bereaved. Tremendous feelings of failure, despair and guilt often follow a suicide. Cain (1972) has estimated that 750,000 each year are intimately affected by the self-inflicted death of a friend or relative. In addition to their personal loss, family members must face the negative reactions of society toward a person taking his or her own life which often causes feelings of shame and lowered self-esteem. There is also a tendency for one member of the family to be singled out and blamed for the suicide. Because of these factors, survivors may have problems fully resolving their grief (Lindemann & Greer, 1972).

Box 8–6

The Grief of Widows

Since every death diminishes us a little, we grieve—not so much for the death as for ourselves. And the widow's grief is the sharpest of all, because she has lost the most. But few people understand that grief can represent emotional growth, an enrichment of the self. It is cruel that women are not educated in the process of grief, since so many of us face the absolutely inevitable prospect of widowhood. Other cultures, other ages laid down protocols of behavior which, no matter how rigid they may seem to us, were at least a guideline for widows to grasp as they suffered through the various stages of grief. But today, widows have little to guide them. The various efforts to help bereaved women—widow-to-widow services, funeral home booklets, efforts of banks and brokerage houses looking for "widow's mite" accounts, even the courses in death now offered by some universities and colleges are nothing but a Hansel and Gretel trail of bread crumbs. They are no guide to grief. Society's distaste for death is so great that widows tend to become invisible women. They are disturbing reminders of mortality and grief. Yet we are all mortal. And grief is a healing process, not a disease.

If only someone whom I respected had sat me down after Martin died and said, "Now, Lynn, bereavement is a wound. It's like being very, very badly hurt. But you are healthy. You are strong. You will recover. But recovery will be slow. You will grieve and that is painful. And your grief will have many stages, but all of them will be healing."

Source: L. Caine, *Widow,* (New York: Morrow, 1974).

Widowhood: Role Change as a Response to Death

Widowhood involves both personal and social disorganization. While grieving over a personal loss, the widowed individual is also confronted with the loss of a major societal role. Reorganization of social roles is required whenever roles are removed, added, or when the relative importance of existing roles is altered. The degree of change experienced by individuals following the death of a spouse varies widely among different societies. The former practice in India of *suttee* whereby widows committed suicide on their husband's funeral pyre represents the greatest degree of change resulting from the death of a marriage partner. In societies which guarantee immediate remarriage of the widowed within the kin group, little disruption in roles will occur (Lopata, 1972b).

Evidence from Lopata'a study of widows in the Chicago area indicates that widowhood in the United States is a very disorganizing experience. In the context of the nuclear family, the husband-wife relationship assumes added significance. Being the only two adults in the household, most marital partners are highly dependent on one another for emotional and social support (Lopata, 1972b). Loneliness has been reported as a major problem of the widowed (Lopata, 1973; Carey, 1979). Not only do the widowed lose a companion and significant source of emotional support, other relationships are altered as well. The couple orientation among the middle class in our society often makes those who do not have a partner feel like a "fifth wheel" in social situations. Lynn Caine (1974) in her book *Widow* provides an excellent illustration of the social difficulties of middle-class widows:

> I met my friends for lunch. Someone suggested going to the theatre with our husbands that evening. It was awful—I felt so alone. My husband's name came up, because he would have enjoyed this play. They got embarrassed. Imagine—I had to comfort them. When we left there was some discussion about picking me up. I wanted to drive myself even though I had never gone out alone at night. Then they got into this kind of nonsense. I'll never agree to that again, and I'm not sure they want me anymore either.

Having an "available" male or female in social groups composed primarily of married couples can also be very threatening during middle age when divorce rates are high.

Families in which there is much interdependence among family members are more seriously disrupted by the crisis of death than are families whose family members are more independent of each other. In many American families, a clear division of labor exists. Husbands have traditionally assumed the responsibility of providing for the family financially while the wife performed household tasks and child-care functions. In family systems with specialized and well-defined roles, loss of an adult family member can seriously impair the functioning of the family unit. In order to effectively cope with the situation and reestablish equilibrium within the system, the remaining family members (primarily the surviving spouse) will be required to assume responsibility for tasks unfamiliar to them.

Widows and widowers. Due to the longer life expectancy of women and the custom in our society for men to marry women younger than themselves, widowhood is largely a female phenomenon. Almost four times as many women as men are widowed during the later years of their lives. Table 8–2 shows the difference in marital status between the sexes during late adulthood. By the age of 75, 68 percent of American women are widowed.

Many women have invested themselves in the roles of wife and mother to the exclusion of a career role. Death of a spouse often forces women to enter the labor market yet most are ill-equipped to become economically self-sufficient. In one study of 300 urban widows, Lopata

Table 8–2. Marital Status of the Older Population by Sex.

Marital Status	Age 65–74 (Percent)	Age 75 and Over (Percent)
Male		
Single	5.4	4.4
Married	81.7	69.4
Widowed	8.5	24.0
Divorced	4.4	2.2
Female		
Single	5.6	6.4
Married	50.1	23.3
Widowed	40.3	68.0
Divorced	4.0	2.3

Source: U.S. Bureau of the Census, *Marital Status and Living Arrangements: March 1980.* (Current Population Reports, Series P-20, No. 365). Washington, D.C.: U.S. Government Printing Office, 1981.

(1977) found that 26 percent had never worked and 40 percent did not work during marriage, but almost half had to seek jobs after their husbands died. After thirty years or more with little or no work experience outside the home, most widows have difficulty finding adequate employment in an already crowded job market. Many must settle for unskilled, low-paying positions.

The poverty that follows loss of the family breadwinner can also be demoralizing. Lopata (1972a) found that the majority of older widows that she studied were living on less than $3,000 a year. Younger women do not seem to fare much better than older ones because they usually have to provide for their children as well as themselves. A nationwide survey of widowed mothers with dependent children who were receiving Social Security survivor benefits showed their median income to be only slightly above poverty level (Palmore, Stanley & Cormier, 1966). In addition to a dramatic reduction in income, many women must assume responsibility for managing the family finances for the first time.

For a woman who has invested herself in the role of wife, death of a spouse can cause an identity crisis. Accustomed to deriving her status and identity from her relationship with her husband, she is faced with redefining who she is in the absence of this relationship. Lopata (1973) found that widows who assigned highest priority in their lives to a wife role, rather than the mother role or an occupational role, had the most difficulty adjusting to widowhood. Current societal trends which show some shift in women's role expectations may make transition to wid-

Continuity and Change

owhood easier as women develop more independence and decrease their reliance on their families for their definition of self.

Widowers have their own unique problems after the death of a spouse. Loss of a wife will cause a definite change in their home situation. The majority of husbands have had little experience in managing household tasks and sometimes must depend on relatives or hired assistance in such areas as meal preparation and house cleaning. The difficulties are compounded if dependent children are involved. Without the support of a wife and with the demands of a job, males may find the task of single parenting overwhelming.

While financial problems are usually less serious for males than females who have lost a spouse, social isolation may be greater. The female is more likely to have been involved in the maintenance of kinship ties thus facilitating continued involvement during widowhood. Townsend (1963) in fact found that adult children were more likely to make frequent visits to a widowed mother than to a widowed father. Widows are also more likely than widowers to participate in community organizations and seem to have less difficulty forming new same-sex relationships (Bernado, 1970). In addition to the social differences already mentioned, Bedell (1971) found a strong tendency among widowers to get rid of pets and discontinue entertaining in their homes following the death of their wives. If widowhood occurs during retirement, the social life of widowers can be further curtailed as they lose their associations with coworkers in conjunction with a loss of their occupational role.

Adjustment to widowhood. Widowhood represents an abrupt role loss. The role of husband or wife must be replaced with other roles and relationships if an adjustment is to be made. The availability of acceptable roles for the widowed will vary among societies. In some societies, expectations for the behavior and position of widows is well defined. Widows in the United States are presented with a variety of options but with no clear direction provided by the culture. They must make their own adjustment to their new status.

One means of adjusting is to regain the familiar marital role through marriage. Remarriage rates, however, are much higher for older males than for females. Men are much more likely to remarry for several reasons. Due to differential mortality rates, there are more available partners for men in their age group. Also, while it is acceptable in our society for men to marry younger women the reverse is not true. Societal taboos against older women marrying younger men interfere with the remarriage of widows.

Other role shifts are also available. From her research on outcomes of widowhood, Lopata (1975) was able to identify five major lifestyles of

Widowhood represents an abrupt role loss. After the death of her husband, a widow must redefine who she is in the absence of this relationship. (Alicia Cook, photographer)

widows. (1) The first category included the *liberated widows*. Although extremely few in number, these women led multi-dimensional lives and had self-identities that were not linked to familial roles. These widows had less difficulty with adjustment because most had not been dependent on their husbands for their sense of self. (2) The term *merry widows* was applied to women who were very actively involved in social activities with friends and persons of the opposite sex. Only a small percentage of widows fit into this category. (3) The *working widows* comprised another group. The working widow was characterized by having a job, after many years of not working in most cases. These widows tended to be less dependent than traditional widows. (4) A fourth classification was the *widow's widow*. Women in this group usually joined social groups of other widows. The companionship of other widows seemed to offer considerable independence. In fact, many women found this arrangement so satisfying that they reported an unwillingness to alter it by remarriage or by more involvement with their families. (5) The *traditional widows* represented the fifth type of lifestyle. These widows were immersed in family roles devoting themselves to their children and grandchildren. Women in this category tended to live with one of their adult children and have their emotional, social and sometimes financial needs met by relatives.

The degree of change experienced following the death of a spouse will be related to the investment one has made in the marital role. For some it will have provided the main source of their life satisfaction; for others the marital role will have been just one of a complex set of roles. A person's orientation to life following widowhood will also be strongly influenced by factors such as presence of children, economic factors, marketable skills, ability to develop new relationships, health, geographical location, social class and mobility (Lopata, 1976).

Age is related to several of the abovementioned factors and will determine many of the avenues available to the widowed. The probability of remarriage is high for the small percentage of persons widowed under the age of 35 (Cleveland & Gianturco, 1975). For the young who do not remarry, they are more likely to experience role strain as they combine the roles of parent and worker. Although young widows may find it easier to find employment, they may also have been less prepared financially due to an unexpected death. Older couples have had more opportunity to plan for the consequences of death. Older women also have the benefit of widows in their peer group who can serve as role models for effective coping (Silverman, 1972).

Silverman (1972) has proposed an organized network of widow-to-widow aid in which previously widowed individuals can assist the newly widowed in exploring new roles. Lopata (1970) has referred to the lack of societal supports for widows going through role transition. She points out that while we have institutionalized courtship and engagement to ease the transition into marriage, no similar rituals assist persons in psychologically preparing for the role shift which is necessary upon the death of a marriage partner. Perhaps through channels like Silverman's Widow-to-Widow program, we can begin to offer more support to individuals during this difficult time of transition.

Suggested Activities and Exercises

1. What does the phrase "death with dignity" mean to you? Do you believe that death can be dignified? If so, describe your criteria for this type of death.
2. In a small group, discuss the issue of euthanasia and speculate about future trends regarding death in modern society.
3. What is your experience with death? Review your feelings when you have attended funerals or visited the dying. If you have not had these experiences, what would you anticipate your response to be?
4. Investigate funeral costs and practices in your geographical area. What is the average cost of a funeral? What types of services are preferred by most of the survivors? How frequently is cremation selected as a means of disposition? Compare your findings with the information presented in the text.

5. Do you know any individuals who have been widowed? If so, consider their current lifestyle. With Lopata's classification in mind, describe the specific adjustments you think they have made to their role loss.
6. Mention to several of your friends and relatives that you are studying the topic of death in one of your classes. Observe their reactions and consider what factors have influenced their views on death.

References

Bedell, J. W. *The one-parent family: Mother absent due to death.* Unpublished doctoral dissertation, Case Western Reserve University, 1971.

Bengtson, V. L., Cuellar, J. B., & Ragan, P. K. Stratum contrasts and similarities in attitudes toward death. *Journal of Gerontology*, 1977, *32*, 76–88.

Bernado, F. M. Survivorship and social isolation: The case of the aging widower. *The Family Coordinator*, 1970, *18*, 11–25.

Blauner, R. Death and the social structure. *Psychiatry*, 1966, *29*, 378–94.

Blumenfield, M., Levy, N. B., & Kaufman, D. The wish to be informed of a fatal illness. *Omega*, 1979, *9*, 323–25.

Cain, A. C. (Ed.) *Survivors of suicide.* Springfield, Ill.: Charles C. Thomas, 1972.

Caine, L. *Widow.* New York: Morrow, 1974.

Carey, R. G. Weathering widowhood: Problems and adjustments of the widowed during the first year. *Omega*, 1979, *10*, 163–74.

Carey, R. G., & Posavac, E. J. Attitudes of physicians on disclosing information and maintaining life for terminal patients. *Omega*, 1978, *9*, 67–77.

Carson, R. A. Euthanasia or the right to die. In H. Wass (Ed.), *Dying: Facing the facts.* New York: Hemisphere, 1979.

Clayton, P. J., Halikes, J. A., & Maurice, W. L. The bereavement of the widowed. *Diseases of the Nervous System*, 1971, *32*, 597–604.

Cleveland, W. P., & Gianturco, D. T. Remarriage probability after widowhood: A retrospective method. *Journal of Gerontology*, 1975, *32*, 99–103.

Epley, R. J., & McCaghy, C. H. The stigma of dying: Attitudes toward the terminally ill. *Omega*, 1978, *8*, 379–93.

Erickson, R. C., & Hyerstay, B. J. The dying patient and the double-bind hypothesis. *Omega*, 1975, *5*, 287–98.

Euthanasia and the law. *Newsweek*, January 28, 1974.

Facts worth knowing about funeral costs. *Changing Times*, 1975, *29*, 51–52.

Feifel H. The function of attitudes toward death. *GAP report on death and dying: Attitudes of patient and doctor,* 1965, *5,* 632 – 41.

Feifel, H. The taboo on death. *American Behavioral Scientist,* 1963, *6,* 66–67.

Fitts, W. J., & Ravdin, I. S. What Philadelphia physicians tell patients with cancer. *Journal of the American Medical Association,* 1953, *153,* 901–04.

Fletcher, J. Ethics and euthanasia. In J. P. Carse & A. B. Dallery (Eds.), *Death and society.* New York: Harcourt, 1977.

Fredrick, J. F. Grief as a disease process. *Omega,* 1977, *7,* 297–305.

Fulton, R. Attitudes changing on death. In Courses by Newspaper series, *Death and dying: Challenge and change.* San Diego: University of California Extension, 1980.

Fulton, R. Death, grief, and social recuperation. *Omega,* 1970, *1,* 23–28.

Glaser, B. J., & Strauss, A. L. *Awareness of dying.* Chicago: Aldine, 1965.

Glaser, B. J., & Strauss, A. L. *Time for dying.* Chicago: Aldine, 1968.

Glick, I. O., Weiss, R. S. & Parkes, C. M. *The first year of bereavement.* New York: Wiley, 1974.

Gorer, G. *Death, grief, and mourning.* Garden City, N.J.: Doubleday, 1965.

Gurthrie, J. P. The meaning of death. *Voices: The art and science of psychotherapy,* 1969, *5,* 43–46.

Hall, E., & Cameron, P. Our failing reverence for life. *Psychology Today,* 1976, *10,* 104 – 13.

Harris Poll reveals support for "helping to die." *Concern for Dying,* 1982, *8,* 1.

Heifetz, M. D., & Mangel, C. *The right to die.* New York: Putnams, 1975.

Hime, V. H. Dying at home: Can families cope? *Omega,* 1979, *10,* 175–87.

Hinton, J. Speaking of death with the dying. In E. Schneidman (Ed.), *Death: Current perspectives* (2nd end.). Palo Alto, Ca.: Mayfield, 1980.

Holden, C. Hospices: For the dying, relief from pain and fear. *Science,* 1976, *193,* 389–91.

Howard, A., & Scott, R. A. Cultural values and attitudes toward dying. *Journal of Existentialism,* 1965, *6,* 161–74.

Jury, M., & Jury, D. *Gramp.* New York: Grossman, 1975.

Kalish, R. A. The onset of the dying process. *Omega,* 1970, *1,* 57–69.

Kalish, R. A. Death and dying in a social context. In R. H. Binstock and E. Shanas (Eds.), *Handbook of aging and the social sciences.* New York: Van Nostrand, 1976.

Kalish, R. A., & Johnson, A. I. Value similarities and differences in three generations of women. *Journal of Marriage and the Family,* 1972, *34,* 49–54.

Kalish, R. A., & Reynolds, D. K. *Death and ethnicity: A psycho-cultural study.* Los Angeles: University of Southern California Press, 1976.

Kastenbaum, R. Death and bereavement in later life. In A. H. Kutscher (Ed.), *Death and bereavement.* Springfield, Ill.: Charles C. Thomas, 1969.

Kastenbaum, R. *Death, society and human experience* (2nd ed.). St. Louis: Mosby, 1981.

Kastenbaum, R. Is death a life crisis? On the confrontation with death in theory and practice. In N. Datan and L. H. Ginsberg (Eds.), *Lifespan developmental psychology: Normative life crises.* New York: Academic, 1975.

Kastenbaum, R., & Aisenberg, R. *The psychology of death.* New York: Springer, 1972.

Knott, J. E. Death education for all. In H. Wass (Ed.), *Dying: Facing the facts.* New York: McGraw-Hill, 1979.

Koenig, R. Dying vs. well-being. *Omega,* 1973, *4,* 181–94.

Kübler-Ross, E. The child will always be there. Real love doesn't die. *Psychology Today,* 1976, *10,* 48–52.

Kübler-Ross, E. *Death: The final stage of growth.* Englewood Cliffs, N.J.: Prentice-Hall, 1975.

Kübler-Ross, E. *On death and dying.* New York: Macmillan, 1969.

Kübler-Ross, E. *Questions and answers on death and dying.* New York: Macmillan, 1974.

Lack, S. A. New Haven—Characteristics of a Hospice program of care. In G. W. Davidson (Ed.), *The hospice: Development and administration.* Washington, D.C.: Hemisphere, 1978.

Lamers, W. M., Jr. Funerals are good for people—M.D.'s included. *Medical Economics,* 1969, *46,* 144–48.

Lerner, M. When, why, and where people die. In E. S. Shneidman (Ed.), *Death: Current perspectives* (2nd ed.). Palo Alto, Ca.: Mayfield, 1980.

Lindemann, E. Symptomatology and management of acute grief. *American Journal of Psychiatry,* 1944, *101,* 141–48.

Lindemann, E., and Greer, J. M. A study of grief. In A. C. Cain (Ed.), *Survivors of suicide.* Springfield, Ill.: Charles C. Thomas, 1972.

Loether, H. J. *Problems of aging.* Belmont, Ca.: Dickenson, 1975.

Lopata, H. Z. Don't cry in front of your friends. *Human Behavior,* 1972, *1,* 45–57. (a)

Lopata, H. Z. Role changes in widowhood: A world perspective. In D. O. Cowgill & L. D. Holmes (Eds.), *Aging and modernization.* New York: Appleton-Century-Crofts, 1972. (b)

Lopata, H. Z. The social involvement of American widows. *American Behavioral Scientist,* 1970, *14,* 41–57.

Lopata, H. Z. *Widowhood in an American city.* Cambridge, Mass.: Schenkman, 1973.

Lopata, H. Z. Widowhood: Societal factors in life-span disruptions and alternatives. In N. Datan & L. H. Ginsberg (Eds.), *Life-span developmental psychology: Normative life crises*. New York: Academic, 1975.

Mant, A. K. Definition of death. In A. Toynbee, A. K. Mant, N. Smart, J. Hinton, C. Yudkin, E. Rhode, R. Heywood, & H. H. Price, *Man's concern with death*. New York: McGraw-Hill, 1968.

Marris, P. *Loss and change*. Garden City, N.J.: Anchor Books, 1975.

Marshall, V. M. *Last chapters: A sociology of aging and dying*. Belmont, Ca.: Wadsworth, 1980.

Mitford, J. *The American way of death*. New York: Simon & Schuster, 1963.

Morison, R. S. Dying. *Scientific American*, 1973, *229*, 54–62.

National Funeral Directors Association of the U.S., Inc. *Considerations concerning cremation*. Philadelphia: Fortress Press, 1974.

Oken, D. What to tell cancer patients. *Journal of the American Medical Association*, 1961, *175*, 1120–28.

Palmore, E., Stanley, J. L., & Cormier, R. H. *Widows with children under social security*. U. S. Department of Health, Education and Welfare. Washington, D.C.: Government Printing Office, 1966.

Parkes, C. M. *Bereavement: Studies of grief in adult life*. New York: International Universities Press, 1972.

Parsons, T., & Litz, V. M. Death in American society. In E. S. Shneidman (Ed.), *Essays in self-destruction*. New York: Science House, 1967.

Pattison, E. M. *The experience of dying*. Englewood Cliffs, N.J.: Prentice-Hall, 1977.

Pine, V. R. Social organization and death. *Omega*, 1972, *3*, 149–53.

Pine, V. R., and Phillips, D. The cost of dying: A sociological analysis of funeral expenditure. *Social Problems*, 1970, *17*, 405–17.

Polls show rise in public approval of euthanasia. *Euthanasia News*, April 1977, 1.

Raether, H. C., & Slater, R. C. Immediate postdeath activities in the United States. In H. Feifel (Ed.), *New meanings of death*. New York: McGraw-Hill, 1977.

Rea, M.P., Greenspoon, S., & Spilka, B. Physicians and the terminal patient. *Omega*, 1975, *6*, 291–302.

Rees, W. D. Bereavement and illness. *Journal of Thanatology*, 1972, *2*, 814–19.

Rees, W. D., & Lutkins, S. G. Mortality of bereavement. *British Medical Journal*, 1967, *4*, 13–16.

Rice, B. Euthanasia: A time to live and a time to die—How physicians feel. *Psychology Today*, 1974, *8*, 29–32.

Riley, J. W., Jr. What people think about death. In O. J. Brim, Jr., H. E. Freeman, S. Levine, & N. A. Scotch (Eds.), *The dying patient*. New York: Russell Sage Foundation, 1970.

Rosenblatt, P. C., Walsh, R. P., & Jackson, D. A. *Grief and mourning in cross-cultural perspective.* New York: Human Relations Area File Press, 1977.

Sanders, C. M. A comparison of adult bereavement in the death of a spouse, child, and parent. *Omega,* 1980, *10,* 303–22.

Saunders, C. St. Christopher's hospice. In E. S. Shneidman (Ed.), *Death: Current perspectives* (2nd ed.). Palo Alto, Ca.: Mayfield, 1980.

Schmale, A. H., Jr. Normal grief is not a disease. *Journal of Thanatology,* 1972, *2,* 807–13.

Schulz, R. *The psychology of death, dying, and bereavement.* Reading, Mass.: Addison-Wesley, 1978.

Sherizen, S., & Paul, L. Dying in an intensive care unit: The social significance for the family of the patient. *Omega,* 1977, *8,* 29–40.

Silverman, P. Widowhood and preventive intervention. *The Family Coordinator,* 1972, *21,* 95–102.

Simpson, M. A. Social and psychological aspects of dying. In H. Wass (Ed.), *Dying: Facing the facts.* New York: McGraw-Hill, 1979.

Sullivan, M. S. The dying person—his plight and his right. *New England Law Review,* 1973, *8,* 197–216.

Townsend, P. *The family life of old people.* Baltimore, Md.: Penguin, 1963.

U.S. Department of the Census. *Marital status and living arrangements: March 1980.* (Current Population Reports, Series P-20, No. 365). Washington, D.C.: U. S. Government Printing Office, 1981.

U.S. Department of Health and Human Services. *Vital statistics of the United States 1977: Volume II-Mortality* (Part A). Hyattsville, Ma.: National Center for Health Statistics, 1981.

Veatch, R. M. Brain death: Welcome definition . . . or dangerous judgment? *Hastings Center Report,* 1972, *2,* No. 5.

Veatch, R. M. Defining death anew. In H. Wass (Ed.), *Dying: Facing the facts.* New York: McGraw-Hill, 1979.

Weisman, A. D. *On dying and denying.* New York: Behavioral Publications, 1972.

Weisman, A. D., & Kastenbaum, R. *The psychological autopsy: A study of the terminal phase of life.* New York: Behavioral Publications, 1968 (*Community Mental Health Journal* Monograph 4).

Williamson, J. B., Munley, A., & Evans, L. *Aging and society.* New York: Holt, 1980.

Wolstenholme, J. E. W., & O'Connor, M. (Eds.), *Ethnics in medical progress: With special reference to transplantation.* Boston: Little, Brown, 1966.

Zarit, S. A. (Ed.), *Readings in aging and death: Contemporary perspectives.* New York: Harper & Row, 1977.

Part IV
Cultural Variations in Aging

Chapter 9

Aging as a Cultural Experience

"The study of aging must be *comparative*, because only by comparing its variations to one another and to their respective conditions shall we assess what in aging is universal and constant, what is particular and changing, what comes from nature and what from nurture, what is manageable and what is not" (Philibert, 1979, p. 380).

Throughout this textbook cross-cultural examples have given you an appreciation of the tremendous variation in the experience of aging—variation not only in biological and sociological aspects of aging, but also in the meaning different cultures give to this stage of life. A student of gerontology must not only learn about these differences, but more importantly, must understand why they exist. In this chapter, we will be concentrating on the "whys" as we explore historical and cultural forces that have resulted in differences among countries, as well as within countries, over time. Social, economic, political and religious influences will be examined in this process.

Aging and Modernization

Modernization is the process whereby a country is transformed from a primarily rural way of life to a predominately urban one through the application of highly developed technology. Health technology, mobility patterns and educational opportunities are all affected by modernization. Cowgill (1974) contends that this process results in a decrease in the status of older persons.

Increased longevity usually accompanies advances in health technology. Thus, more people live longer which results in an increase in the proportion of the population in the upper age brackets. With increased longevity in the context of a modern society, competition for jobs will occur among the generations. Introduction of the concept of "retirement" within a culture is the most likely solution to this problem, although the societal status of the older person will decline with the loss of the worker role and the associated income.

Along with these shifts come changes in the economic scene. These changes include increased application of inanimate sources of power; improvement of transportation, communication, and distribution systems; the development of industry and large-scale economic operations; the creation of new jobs requiring specialized and professional skills; and greater separation of the home setting from the work setting. The young are usually selected to fill these new work roles. Because the new jobs typically have greater status and provide a higher income than traditional occupations, an inversion of status between the old and young occurs. According to Cowgill (1974), this trend "not only leaves the parents in older, less prestigious, perhaps static and sometimes obsolete positions, it also deprives them of one of the most traditional roles of older people—that of providing vocational guidance and instruction to their children."

Many of the new jobs are in urban areas resulting in the migration of large numbers of the young to the cities. This geographical separation of generations promotes the development of nuclear families and the breakdown of extended families. Interdependence in daily activities is therefore reduced, and more emphasis is placed on independent households. Urbanization also accelerates social mobility. When adult children achieve a social status higher than their parents, they may view their parents as "backward" and fail to hold them in high esteem.

In modernization efforts, measures are also taken to promote literacy and improve and expand educational opportunities. The educational programs are always targeted toward the young with an emphasis on mass public education for children and vocational training for adolescents and young adults. Because of this focus, children in countries undergoing modernization are always more educated than their parents, which further devaluates the older person.

Cowgill's theory is illustrated in Figure 9–1. This diagram outlines the process whereby improved health and economic technology, urbanization, and advances in education lead to lowered status of the aged.

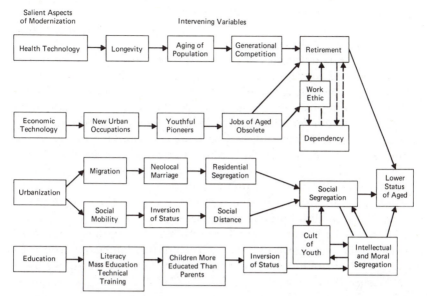

Figure 9–1. The impact of modernization on the status of the aged. (Source: D. Cowgill, "Aging and Modernization," in J. Gubrium (Ed.), *Late Life: Communities and Environmental Policies.* Springfield, Illinois: Charles C. Thomas, 1974.)

The Asmat: An Example

An examination of recent changes among the Asmat of New Guinea further illustrates the effects of modernization on the status of the aged. Van Arsdale (1980) reports that elderly Asmat males have seen their cultural system, developed over several thousand years, disintegrate within two decades.

Traditionally the Asmat have been involved in hunting and gathering activities. This work, however, was not perceived as a constant activity but one varying greatly on a weekly, monthly and seasonal basis. In fact, work of all kinds has been found to occupy only 47.8 percent of a man's waking time and 54.5 percent of a woman's in this society. The remaining time has traditionally been used for recreation and ritual, the latter being extremely important in the Asmat culture. Many of their rituals in the past have revolved around warfare. *Tesmaypits*, who were usually older members of the tribe, was the term given to those responsible for deliberating which war ornaments to wear and deciding on the most appropriate time to strike the enemy—activities that consumed many hours. Elder males also had the responsibility for planning and carrying out the preparations for rituals involving initiations, festivals, headhunting raids and the appeasement of their ancestors. The Asmat customarily relocated their villages every two to five years. In addition to their other duties, *Tesmaypits* also made decisions regarding resettlement and arranged for these moves.

Observations of the Asmat culture during the 1970s show dramatic shifts associated with rapid economic, educational and political change (Van Arsdale, 1980). Just twenty years after the first permanent mission and government posts were established in Asmat, the power has shifted from the old to the young. According to Van Arsdale, "Headhunters who prided themselves in recounting their battle feats and the names of slain enemy now are old men, rarely listened to by the younger generations." While once relatively autonomous, the Asmat are now greatly influenced by the policies of the Indonesian national government and the process of modernization in that part of the world. Van Arsdale reports that by 1976, headhunting and cannibalism had been suppressed and village moves had been stopped. Also, single community houses had replaced buildings designated for each major residential kin group; and the irregular huts of the villages were replaced by straight rows of houses, some designed by Indonesian officials unfamiliar with the Asmat culture.

Other changes created by the Indonesian political structure and economy have resulted in the aged no longer being regarded as decision makers. To accommodate the changes their people are experiencing, younger Asmat men developed new rituals to "arrange things" and produce goods for the community. The traditional rituals operated in a simple economy characterized by informal education and local leadership by the elder *Tesmaypits;* the new rituals are a response to a new way of life which includes a partial cash economy, an emphasis on formal education, and hierarchical leadership within the Indonesian system. Thus, younger tribesmen have become the leaders and serve as liasons with the Indonesian government. Today, most Asmat men being selected for local government offices are less than 40 years of age. They are the ones who are the most likely to be fluent in Indonesian, to have received some formal education, and to be capable of conversing with government officials on problems occurring as a result of political and economic change. Although the specifics vary, this process of change described for the Asmat parallels experiences of many other countries.

After Modernization: What?

The obvious question at this point is: "Does modernization bring a permanent loss of status or are the trends outlined by Cowgill reversible?"

As a result of their study of the relative socioeconomic position of the aged versus the nonaged in thirty-one countries, Palmore and Man-

Cultural Variations in Aging

ton (1974) postulated that the relative status of the aged may rise after the initial stage of rapid modernization. According to these investigators:

> The most obvious explanation for this reversal is that during the early stages of modernization there are the greatest changes which produce the greatest discrepancies between the aged and non-aged, but that when societies 'mature,' the rates of change level off and the discrepancies between the aged and non-aged decrease. There may be other factors such as the growth of new institutions to replace the farm and family in maintaining the status of the aged such as retirement benefits, more adult education and job retraining, policies against age discrimination in employment, etc. (p. 210).

As more countries move "beyond modernization," the results of longitudinal studies on the status of the elderly should prove to be interesting.

Aging: East and West

While the process of modernization seems to have predictable effects on the status of the elderly, the values and traditions of a culture can serve to moderate these effects. All persons develop in the context of a culture containing certain values, practices, beliefs and traditions. These aspects of culture largely influence the views toward older members of a particular society as well as the aging process itself. Dominant societal values are learned very early in life through socialization. In some cultures the young are taught to value the aged for their wisdom; in other cultural groups the old are regarded as having little to offer modern life.

In Cooley's (1956) looking-glass theory, humans perceive and define themselves as they believe others perceive and define them. While the self-concepts of older persons are determined to a large extent by their past experiences, elements of culture also have a strong influence on their self-images. As individuals age, they evaluate their worth and that of others in their age group by their personal values as well as those of the larger culture. Certain values can lead to feelings of high self-esteem in old age, while others contribute to feelings of worthlessness in the later years of life (Clark & Anderson, 1967).

To illustrate the uniqueness of cultural experiences, aging will be compared in both eastern and western countries. The dominant values of countries in both these parts of the world are somewhat in opposition to each other and present an interesting contrast for study.

Aging in the United States

In some ways American values typify views of the western world, but the United States has its own unique historical and cultural heritage. North America was founded and settled by European immigrants who were willing to leave the familiarity of their own cultures to seek adventure and opportunity in a strange new land. Since many different backgrounds were represented among the early settlers, those who arrived in the New World encountered a variety of beliefs and customs. Among these differences, however, several common traits emerged. Because of the challenges and difficulties inherent in their day-to-day existence, these immigrants all shared a strong belief in the value of hard work and perseverance; the personal traits of independence, competence, industry and determination were developed as a necessity for survival. The thrifty and sturdy ones made it; the "weak" ones did not. These values were further reinforced by the Protestant Ethic which viewed hard work not only as a virtue but as a way of life. Nearly all of the early Americans were Protestants, coming from cultures in which the Judeo-Christian tradition was dominant (Cowgill, 1972).

"Rugged individualism," "standing on your own two feet," "reaping what you sow"—do these phrases sound familiar? They all grew out of

In the United States a high value is placed on individualism, resulting in "a particular definition of personal identity predicated on independence and self-reliance." (Bob Harvey, photographer)

the early American experiences just described. An examination of modern America shows a continuation of these values as a common thread in American life. How do these values affect the experience of the aged in American society?

In our work-oriented society, the value of the individual is often equated with productivity. When the elderly are no longer in the work force, their status declines. A reduction in income and power usually accompanies this lowered status.

Also, according to Clark (1972), the high value placed on individualism in the United States results in "a particular definition of personal identity predicated on independence and self-reliance. Only by being independent can an American be truly a person, self-respecting and worthy of concern and the esteem of others" (p. 263). Because of this strong emphasis placed on independence and autonomy, one of the most persistent fears among Americans relates to dependency (see Box 9–1). Dependency is interpreted as being a burden on others.

Box 9–1

Dependence: An American Interpretation

The following statements made by elderly persons in a study conducted in San Francisco show the importance of independence in their lives:

"The important thing in my life today is I don't want to get sick again. I want to be well, take care of myself. I don't want to be dependent on my children."

"Well, my parents taught me to stand on my own feet. I'm not living up to it since I'm on an old age pension. I wouldn't be doing it if I were not so weak."

"It's very important that I do not become a burden on somebody. That's the most important thing in my life today."

"The most important thing my parents did for me was that they taught me how to be independent and self-reliant."

"I wouldn't want to get on welfare. I just wouldn't go to see them. I wouldn't want to do that—no matter what."

Source: M. Clark and B. J. Anderson, *Culture and Aging* (Springfield, Ill.: Charles C. Thomas, 1967).

Aging as a Cultural Experience

These views have in some cases interfered with the delivery of services to the elderly. Government programs are considered by some older persons to be "a hand out" or "charity" and an affront to their integrity. These individuals sometimes sacrifice needed resources to maintain their self-respect (Palmore, 1980). This insistence on their ability to provide for themselves can also make older persons unwilling to accept aid from their children.

Aging in the Eastern Tradition

The values of the east, in contrast to those of the west, serve to enhance the status of the old. Historically, reverence toward the aged has been prevalent in both China and Japan. In both of these cultures, Confucianism enhanced the position of older people by associating advanced age with the accumulation of wisdom. It was believed that as one progressed in years, moral learning as well as knowledge increased (Piovesana, 1979).

In addition, the Chinese classics of Confucianism taught the virtue of filial piety: showing loyalty, devotion and reverence to your parents. In Confucianism, the term reverence means great awe and respect. Filial piety was legislated in Japan. Individuals who failed to support their parents in old age or displayed improper mourning behavior were punished. Recognition was given to those performing their familial roles with merit (Piovesana, 1979).

Ancestor worship was also part of Chinese and Japanese customs. Practiced in Confucianism, Buddhism, and Taoism in the form of rituals, it served to link individuals to the past and preserve family traditions. In addition, it elevated the status of older family members since they were on the threshold of becoming ancestors (Piovesana, 1979).

Japanese elderly: The modern scene. *Otoshiyori*, the most common Japanese word for the aged, literally means "honorable elders." Although Japan has become one of the most industrialized countries in the world, the Japanese elderly have not lost their position of status. In fact, old age is still recognized by most Japanese as a source of prestige and honor, symbolized by the establishment of a Respect for Elder's Day as a national holiday (Palmore, 1975a, 1975c).

The continued belief in the virtue of filial piety has helped maintain the high status of the Japanese elderly. Maeda (1980) has reported that younger generations in Japan have a strong sense of filial duty to care for their aging parents, and that government programs for the elderly have been slow to develop because of the assumption that their families will provide adequately for their needs. Four out of five older Japanese live with their families (Ministry of Health and Welfare, 1973). In 1976 only 1.4 percent of older Japanese were living in old-age institutions. This rate is very low when compared with that of other industrialized nations shown in Table 9–1 and is largely due to the characteristic intergenerational living arrangements of the Japanese (Maeda, 1980).

Not only are the old cared for by their families, they also have an important role within the family unit (Palmore, 1975b). A study of Japanese aged 65 and over found that 33 percent of both sexes took full responsibility for housekeeping in their extended living arrangements, and that the majority of older women assisted with child care. Also, the elderly frequently assisted with the work of adult children especially when they were self-employed in occupations such as farming and business. The percentage of elderly in this study having no specific role within the family was only 20 percent (Tokyo Metropolitan Institute of Gerontology, 1974).

Also responsible for the high status of Japanese elderly, according to Palmore (1975a), is the "vertical" structure of the society. Most relationships in the Japanese culture tend to be hierarchical and stress deference to superiors rather than equality and independence (Nakane, 1970).

There are signs, however, that the traditional cultural values of Japan are changing. While most Japanese believe that it is natural to support aging parents, only 20 percent expect to depend on their own adult

Table 9–1. Comparison of Living Arrangements of Elderly in Japan with Other Industrialized Nations.

	Denmark (1965)	United States (1965)	Great Britain (1965)	Japan (1969)
Old people living with a child	18%	25%	33%	79.2%
Old people living with other relatives	3	7	8	0.5
Old couples living alone	45	43	33	13.1
Old individuals living alone	28	22	22	5.2
Other	6	3	4	2.0

Sources: E. Shanas et al., *Old People in Three Industrial Societies* (New York: Atherton, 1968); *Survey on the Opinion about Life after Retirement* (Tokyo: Office of the Prime Minister, 1969).

Note: The statistics for Japan are for those 60 and over; for the other countries, they are for those 65 and over.

children when they reach old age (Plath, 1973). Cultural changes may also be related to the extremely high suicide rate among the Japanese elderly which has continued to increase since World War II (Wen, 1974). Because of the rapidity with which industrialization occurred in Japan, a lag may have existed in social changes resulting from modernization. Between 1900 and 1970, Japan's manufacturing industry expanded 150 times with much of the development occurring since 1955. This growth appears especially impressive when compared to the United States whose expansion of the manufacturing industry was only approximately 9 percent of Japan's during this same time period (Oouchi, Arisawa, Wakimura, Minobe & Naito, 1971). The consequences for the elderly of this dramatic shift from an agricultural way of life to a highly modern, urbanized nation are not yet fully realized and will become more apparent for the next generation of aged individuals.

The changing demography of Japan may also affect the future position of its elderly. Currently, persons over 65 comprise 7.9 percent of the total Japanese population. The country's age structure was fairly stable for the first half of the century; a high birth rate offset increases in the older population occurring as a result of improvements in medicine, public health and the standard of living. However, the population of older people in Japanese society began increasing after 1950 as a result of the sharp decrease in the birth rate at that time and this trend continues today. Japan now has one of the lowest birth rates in the world; not surprisingly, it is predicted that Japan will also have one of the highest percentages of older people in the world by the beginning of the twenty-first century (Maeda, 1980).

In addition, Japan has dramatically increased the life expectancy of its population. In fact, it now exceeds that of the United States (Plath, 1973). Not only will older Japanese citizens of the future form a larger percentage of the population, but they will also live longer. As the correlates of modernization take their toll at the same time the elderly population is swelling in size, one cannot refrain from wondering if the Respect for Elder's Day in Japan will be more in remembrance of the past than a reflection of present reality.

China today: current perspectives. While sharing Japan's heritage of respect for the elderly, China's economic and political developments in the last century have varied dramatically from those of Japan. In China most of the population is still rural, with only a small percentage involved in modern industry.

In 1949 the Chinese Communist Party came to power with its emphasis on equitable distribution of wealth. Under Communist leadership, the economic status of the country improved and considerable gains were made in social services for all age groups. Davis-Friedmann

(1980) maintains, however, that the government of the People's Republic of China has had a minimal role in providing for its elderly population and most of the aid provided is for the childless elderly. While the government has criticized Confucian ideals and the practice of ancestor worship, it has sanctioned the role of the family in the care of older relatives.

Part of the explanation for the lack of programs designed specifically for the elderly may be that the Chinese population has not aged, as has been true in Western Europe, North America and Japan. While the elderly population has doubled in less than two generations, bringing the number of those over sixty-five to 40 million in 1980, the percentage of the old has remained fairly stable. In 1952, 3 percent of the population was 65 or older; this figure only increased one percentage point (up to 4 percent) by 1980 (The Chinese Economy Post Mao, 1978).

Because of the extremely high birth rate, the size of the population under age thirty is enormous. These demographic characteristics strongly

The Chinese have a strong heritage of respect for the elderly. (Courtesy of Colorado State University Office of Instructional Services, The Griswald China Collection)

influence government priorities regarding services and programs and tend to favor the young.

Although not receiving much assistance from the government, elderly Chinese have benefited from gains made by younger family members. Law requires Chinese children to support their aged parents. If the adult child does not do so, recourse is available for the elderly family member. In urban areas, the parent can appeal to the child's employer whereupon a portion of the child's pay will be withheld and sent directly to the parent. Because agricultural workers usually do not receive a cash salary, the abandoned parent in rural areas can petition for a part of the child's portion of the monthly grain harvest (Davis-Friedmann, 1980). Also, in rural areas only the male children are held responsible for their parents' support. Among rural families, married sons continue to live with or near their parents and share the inheritance upon their parents' deaths. By contrast, married daughters leave their parents' home and become part of the household of their husband's parents (Parish & Whyte, 1978). In fact, elderly Chinese who have daughters but no sons are viewed similarly to the childless elderly. Both groups are eligible for local welfare funds (Davis-Friedmann, 1979).

Davis-Friedmann (1980, p. 16) has observed that "those who raise several, successful, loyal children have the most comfortable old age." With the stringent measures adopted by the Chinese to control population growth, one can only speculate about the future position of the Chinese elderly as birth rates drop and the present population grows old. Reliance on adult children may be increasingly replaced by social service programs.

Box 9–2

Changes in family planning policies can alter the position of the Chinese elderly in the future. A drastic reduction in births through family-planning efforts may result in more services for the elderly as their proportion in the population increases. The following newspaper article provides a glimpse at the current views in The People's Republic of China regarding population growth.

China, in Big Effort to Slow Population Growth, is Likely to Impose Harsh Economic Punishment

Poor Xu Zhenxiang. The deputy director of the Huanren County Brick & Tile Works in China's Liaoning Province, a faithful Community Party member, made one mistake. Or, we should say, he made nine of them.

The local radio station recently announced that Comrade Xu "was dismissed from all posts within and outside the party for resisting family-planning policies, having nine children and, moreover, asking for subsidies for his family."

Comrade Xu was the victim of what is shaping up as a major effort by China to put some brakes on its burgeoning population. Chinese officialdom is referring to its birth-control efforts as "mobilization for family planning," but it is clear that the world's most populous nation intends to take strong economic measures, if necessary, to reduce its birthrate.

. . .

Economic Penalties

. . . The government is said to be formulating a family-planning law that is expected to inflict harsh economic punishment on couples who violate strict limits on family size. In the meantime, various provinces and cities have issued their own get-tough measures.

In Yunnan Province, "trial regulations" were introduced in July to encourage families to have only one child. Among other things, the plan promises that physicians, nurseries, schools and eventually employers will give preference to children who don't have any siblings. Couples who marry late and those who produce only one child will get priority in housing and assignments, and parents with only one child will get a 5% increase in their pensions when they retire.

At the same time, the plan says that unspecified "economic sanctions" are to be levied against "couples of childbearing age who refuse to practice planned parenthood despite patient propaganda and education."

In Peking, China's capital, and in the port city of Tianjin (Tientsin), the economic sanctions are spelled out. Couples who produce a third child will be fined 10% of their pay or, if they are commune workers, of their work points. The docking of pay will last for 14 years, the age at which the government concludes that most children become a member of the productive work force and aren't totally dependent upon schools, clinics, and other state-financed social services.

Source: B. Kramer, *The Wall Street Journal* (Wednesday, Oct. 3, 1979, p, 40).

A Comparison of East and West

A man in traditional China with no self-reliance as an ideal may not have been successful in his life. But suppose in his old age his sons are able to provide for him generously. Such a person not only will be happy and content about it, but is likely also to beat the drums before all and sundry to let the world know that he has good children who are supporting him in a style to which he has never been accustomed. On the other hand, an American parent who has not been successful in life may derive some benefit from the prosperity of his children, but he certainly will not want anybody to know about it. In fact, he will resent any reference to it . . . (Hsu, 1961).

Individuals are shaped by political, religious, economic and social forces within a culture. These forces affect cultural norms which in turn determine how someone in the later stages of life will be perceived. In our examination of aging in the United States, Japan and China, we have observed variations in "national characters" as dichotomies such as rural-urban, communist-democratic, and Protestant-Confucianist have been presented. Despite wide differences that exist among countries in both the east and the west, several generalizations can be made about ways in which eastern and western cultures differ. These differences are outlined in Table 9–2.

As noted in the discussion of aging in Japan and China, reliance on the group is very important in eastern cultures. Generally the person seeks support from the larger group of the family. In contrast, western nations emphasize being able to take care of oneself, to the point of fearing dependence on others. The example provided earlier by Hsu (1961) demonstrates the divergent views of the east and west regarding the issue of dependence. For Americans it *is* an issue. For older Asians, it is only natural and expected that they will rely on others in old age.

Another aspect of the family versus individual orientation is the responsibility one shows toward family members, a second factor on which eastern and western cultures tend to differ. Providing for family members, including the aged, is a high priority among members of Asian

Table 9–2. A Summary of Contrasts in Eastern and Western Traditions.

Eastern Traditions	Western Traditions
1. Reliance on the group (family)	1. Individualism
2. Obligation and responsibility to family	2. Obligation and responsibility to self
3. Emphasis on ascribed status	3. Emphasis on achieved status

Cultural Variations in Aging

cultures even though it often means sacrificing personal gain as well as privacy. While individuals in Western societies wish to please their families and fulfill their wishes, the commitment generally appears less strong than in eastern cultures. When put to the test, individual goals and needs are frequently placed above those of the family. While an Asian may ask, "What is my duty as a family member?", a westerner will more likely be asking "What is my right as an individual?"

A third major difference between eastern and western cultures pertains to the basis for admiration and respect. In the east, older persons have traditionally been revered simply because they were old. In other words, their placement in this particular age group—their ascribed status of "elderly"—has earned them respect. In the United States, respect is not attained simply through group membership. In our achievement-oriented society, one must prove oneself in order to command respect. "Proving oneself" usually takes the form of demonstrating mastery, competence, or productivity.

The Universals of Aging

In studying the wide differences that exist among populations in the pace, patterns, and styles of aging, one should not lose sight of the similarities among the old. An understanding of the common elements of the aging experience across cultures provides more of an appreciation for the existing differences.

It is difficult to identify universal patterns of any sort. It becomes even more of a task when adequate cross-cultural data is lacking in a particular area, such as aging. In spite of these problems, Cowgill and Holmes (1972) have attempted to define universal principles of the aging process. Following an analysis of the aging experience in a variety of countries, they arrived at the following eight principles:

1. *The aged always constitute a minority of the total population.* While the size and proportion of the elderly will vary among countries, this group will always be a relatively small percentage of the population of which it is a part.
2. *Older populations have more females than males* (except in societies with such practices as female infanticide).
3. *Widows comprise a high proportion of an older population* (except in cultures with the custom of automatic remarriage of widows).
4. *In all societies, some people are classified as old and are treated differently because of this classification.* In every culture, individuals at the end of their life cycle have a different status than

those in other age groups. The criteria used to determine when one has reached this status will vary from culture to culture. For example, in the United States chronological age (that is, 65) is typically used to determine when someone is old and eligible for retirement status. Measures in other cultures include stage of life cycle (for example, grandparenthood) and qualities associated with age (such as gray hair).

5. *A widespread tendency exists for people defined as old to shift to more sedentary, advisory or supervisory roles which involve less physical exertion and are more concerned with group maintenance than economic production.* This principle appears to hold true despite the wide variation in specific roles ascribed to older people. In modern societies, this shift is viewed as retirement, and the cessation of formal occupational activity is expected. In cultures lacking a formal retirement system, older persons still shift into new, less physically strenuous roles; the status associated with these roles, however, will vary from being honorific to unimportant.

6. *In all societies some older persons (usually men) continue to act as political, judicial and civic leaders.* In preliterate societies, the older village chief demonstrates this principle. In modern societies older persons often participate in legislative and parliamentary proceedings. The traditionally important role of older persons in government is suggested by the common use of the word "elder" to mean leader (Simmons, 1945). In some cultures the aged predominate in this activity, but in more modern societies they occupy only a small number of government positions.

7. *In all societies, mores prescribe some mutual responsibility between the elderly and their adult children.* This finding has been documented in western industrialized nations as well as less economically developed countries; in general though, these obligations appear to be less clear and binding in modern societies.

8. *All societies value life and seek to prolong it even in old age.* While this appears to be a common value, the strength and intensity of the effort to preserve life will vary considerably among cultures.

An International Approach to Aging

Just as countries view aging differently, the social response to the care of the aged will also vary. It is easy to think of the customs and systems

Although coming from different cultural traditions, nations must learn to work together in order to arrive at creative solutions to problems of aging. (Alicia Cook, photographer)

of one's own culture as the only ones deserving consideration. We are all culture bound to some extent, and we therefore reflect the biases inherent in our socialization experiences. Unfortunately, these ethnocentric tendencies limit one's capacity to create new models of functioning, an ability that may become critical for survival in our rapidly changing world.

Different approaches have been used by countries to meet the needs of the elderly in the past. The social programs developed reflect to a large extent the political climate and philosophy as well as the resources of a country. Although coming from different traditions, nations must learn to work together in order to arrive at creative solutions to problems of aging. As professionals in gerontology, we now have a mechanism for doing this. Established in 1950, the International Association of Gerontology serves to promote cross-cultural cooperation and the exchange of research findings (Hall & Viidik, 1980). As ideas are shared in this and other international forums, new visions can spring forth as our views of possibilities for the elderly are expanded. Hopefully, some of our workable traditions can be maintained and combined with innovative approaches as nations respond to the needs of the elderly in modern life. Exciting possibilities may emerge as we rise to meet the challenges of aging in the twenty-first century.

Suggested Activities and Exercises

1. What are your predictions for change of status among older people in the United States? What factors could lead to increased status? What factors could work against rising status among this segment of the population?
2. To what extent do you think concepts of aging can be "borrowed" from other cultures?
3. Discuss old age with foreign students on your campus. What are their views on growing old? What programs for the elderly are available in their countries? How did these discussions broaden or alter your perspective?
4. If you are planning to travel in a foreign country, arrange to visit programs for the elderly. Note the differences between these programs and the ones that you are familiar with in your own country.

References

Clark, M. Cultural values and dependency in later life. In D. O. Cowgill & L. D. Holmes (Eds.), *Aging and modernization.* New York: Appleton-Century-Crofts, 1972.

Clark, M., & Anderson, B. J. *Culture and aging.* Springfield, Ill.: Charles C. Thomas, 1967.

Cooley, C. H. *Human nature and social order.* New York: Free Press, 1956.

Cowgill, D. O. Aging in American society. In D. O. Cowgill and L. D. Holmes (Eds.), *Aging and modernization.* New York: Appleton-Century-Crofts, 1972.

Cowgill, D. O. Aging and modernization: A revision of the theory. In J. F. Gubrium (Ed.), *Late life: Communities and environmental policy.* Springfield, Ill.: Charles C. Thomas, 1974.

Cowgill, D. O., & Holmes, L. D. (Eds.). *Aging and modernization.* New York: Appleton-Century-Crofts, 1972.

Davis-Friedmann, D. *Old people and their families in the People's Republic of China*. Unpublished doctoral dissertation, Boston University, 1979.

Davis-Friedmann, D. *Retirement and social welfare programs for Chinese elderly: A minimal role for the state*. A paper presented at the annual meeting of the Gerontological Society, San Diego, California, 1980.

Hall, D. A., & Viidik, A. International and regional organizations on aging. In E. Palmore (Ed.), *International handbook on aging*. Westport, Ct.: Greenwood Press, 1980.

Hsu, F. L. K. *Psychological anthropology: Approaches to culture and personality*. Homewood, Ill.: Dorsey Press, 1961.

Maeda, D. Japan. In E. Palmore (Ed.), *International handbook on aging*. Westport, Ct.: Greenwood Press, 1980.

Ministry of Health and Welfare. *Survey of the actual living conditions of the elderly*. Tokyo: Ministry of Health and Welfare, 1973.

Nakane, C. *Japanese Society*. Berkeley: University of California Press, 1972.

Office of the Prime Minister. *Survey on the opinion about life after retirement*. Tokyo: Office of the Prime Minister, 1969.

Oouchi, H., Arisawa, H., Wakimura, G., Minobe, R., & Naito, M. *Illustrated Japanese economy* (5th ed.). Tokyo: Iwanami Publishing, 1971.

Palmore, E. *The honorable elders*. Durham, N.C.: Duke University Press, 1975. (a)

Palmore, E. The status and integration of the aged in Japanese society. *Journal of Gerontology*, 1975, *30*, 199–208. (b)

Palmore, E. United States of America. In E. Palmore (Ed.), *International handbook on aging*. Westport, Ct.: Greenwood Press, 1980.

Palmore, E. What can the U.S. learn from Japan about aging? *Gerontologist*, 1975, *15*, 64–67. (c)

Palmore E., & Manton, K. Modernization and status of the aged: International correlations. *Journal of Gerontology*, 1974, *29*, 205 – 10.

Parish, W., & Whyte, M. K. *Village and family in contemporary China*. Chicago: University of Chicago Press, 1978.

Philibert, M. Philosophical approach to gerontology. In J. Hendricks and C. D. Hendricks (Eds.), *Dimensions of aging: Readings*. Cambridge, Mass.: Winthrop, 1979.

Piovesana, G. K. The aged in Chinese and Japanese cultures. In J. Hendricks & C. D. Hendricks (Eds.), *Dimensions of aging: Readings*. Cambridge, Mass.: Winthrop, 1979.

Plath, D., Ecstasy years—Old age in Japan. *Pacific Years*, 1973, *46*, 421–28.

Shanas, E., Townsend, P., Wedderburn, D., Friis, H., Milhøj, P., & Stehovwer, J. *Older people in three industrial societies*. New York: Atherton, 1968.

Simmons, L. W. *The role of the aged in primitive societies*. London: Oxford University Press, 1945.

The Chinese Economy Post Mao. Washington, D.C.: Government Printing Office, 1978.

Tokyo Metropolitan Institute of Gerontology, Sociology Department. *Research on the object and functions of the community welfare centers for the aged (II)—A comparative study of users and nonusers*, Tokyo: Tokyo Metropolitan Institute of Gerontology, 1974

Van Arsdale, P. W. Disintegration of the ritual support network among aged Asmat hunter-gatherers of New Guinea. In C. L. Fry (Ed.), *Dimensions of an anthropology of aging*. New York: Praeger, 1980.

Wen, C. Secular suicidal trend in postwar Japan and Taiwan: An examination of hypotheses. *International Journal of Social Psychiatry*, 1974, *20*, 8–17.

Chapter 10

Ethnicity and Aging

One does not have to travel to the other side of the world to observe cultural differences. Because of past migration patterns, a rich diversity of cultural and ethnic groups exists within the United States. Most textbooks on aging, however, have focused on the dominant culture and ignored these ethnic variations. Perhaps this omission has resulted from the paucity of research conducted on ethnic groups in the past.

Professionals working with specific ethnic populations and persons engaged in policy planning have raised important questions about the applicability of data obtained on white, middle-class populations. In the 1970s and 80s, an increased interest in studying minorities arose. This interest grew partially from the increased availability of federal funds for this purpose, but also from the increased recognition of ethnicity as an important variable in the study of aging. While more information on this topic is available today than several years ago, much research is still needed. Jackson (1980) has pointed out that few minorities have been included in longitudinal studies of aging.

While common elements can be found among the elderly in all ethnic groups, socio-cultural differences that have important implications for adequate policy planning and service delivery also exist. According to Gelfand and Kutzik (1979), "the response of many service providers has been bewilderment at the different cultural norms, ranging from dietary requirements to family relationships, to which their program had to attend."

Kalish and Moriwaki (1973) have asserted that one cannot effectively theorize about, understand or provide services to older Asian Americans without knowledge of their cultural origin and socialization as well as their history as a cultural group in the United States. Certainly this statement applies to other groups as well. Each specific ethnic group has had a unique experience in this country which continues to influence behaviors and attitudes. In order to give the reader a flavor for the diversity existing among ethnic groups in the United States, a brief historical and cultural perspective will be given on four major ethnic groups in this country: Japanese Americans, Native Americans, Mexican Americans and Blacks.

The Japanese-American Elderly

Clustered geographically into only a few areas of the United States and representing a small percentage of the elderly in the nation, older Japanese Americans are not visible to the majority of Americans. Almost all of today's elderly Japanese Americans arrived in the United States and Canada during the early part of this century, primarily between 1901 and 1908. As immigrants, they usually left Japan for economic reasons and were mostly from rural farming areas of southern Japan (Endo, 1974). The majority of these sojourners were younger sons of Japanese families who could not inherit land under Japan's system of primogeniture (Connor, 1977). Upon establishing themselves in their new countries, the married men in the group sent for their spouses to join them. The single men, eager to have the support of a family yet unable to afford to return to Japan to select a bride, arranged marriages through letters and photographs. This practice became quite common and the wives obtained in this manner were called "picture brides" (Gee, 1976). In most cases, a substantial age difference existed between the two partners, with the male being older. Because of this age difference and trends in longevity, a large majority of these Japanese immigrants surviving today are women (Kalish & Moriwaki, 1973).

The main thrust of the Japanese immigration movement ended with the Exclusion Act of 1924, which prevented further immigration from Japan until 1952 when acts were passed allowing for limited quotas of Asian immigrants. The Exclusion Act of 1924 unintentionally had the effect of defining a relatively age-homogeneous ethnic cohort. Because of this, Japanese Americans can be divided into three distinct generations. The group that came with the large but brief influx of immigrants in the early 1900s are known as the *Issei*. Their American-born children are called the *Nisei*, and *Sansei* is the term used for the children of the Nisei and grandchildren of the Issei (Montero, 1979). These names are associated with the differing values, behaviors and past experiences of the three generations (Endo, 1974).

Large numbers of the Issei located primarily in Hawaii, California and other states throughout the west. Employed initially as unskilled workers, they later moved into a variety of occupations among which agriculture and small businesses predominated. Many became self-employed in these areas within a few years (Endo, 1974; Kitano, 1976).

Unfortunately, the Issei met with a great deal of prejudice and discrimination. Discriminatory practices prevented them from owning land and even becoming citizens until 1952. They were therefore unable to vote and remained in jeopardy of being deported. During World War II, they faced further insult when placed in relocation camps. In addition to loss of possessions, the internment experiences of the Issei were responsible for loss of status among the elders of the Japanese families. Their limited English skills, naiveté regarding American bureacracy, and noncitizen status prevented them from holding official positions within the camps. However their children, the Nisei, who were then in their teens and twenties, were appointed to these offices and thus dealt with the governmental authorities. This inversion of power within the Japanese families had a definite effect on the older Issei and diminished their status. Following the war, many Issei, being too old to start over, remained dependent on their children (Kalish & Moriwaki, 1973; Montero, 1979). Kalish and Yuen (1973) have hypothesized, however, that the wartime relocation merely accelerated a change that would have occurred with time through acculturation.

Issei: Growing Old in America

Most Issei came to the United States and Canada with the expectation of accumulating assets and then returning to Japan, but for most of these early immigrants their fate has been to "grow old in a foreign land, with a different value system, and odd rules of behavior" (Kalish & Moriwaki, 1973). As you can infer from information presented in the previous chapter, these first generation Japanese Americans are "growing old and facing death in a milieu much at variance with their beginnings" (Kalish & Moriwaki, 1973). Coming from a cultural heritage that stressed veneration of the aged, they now find themselves in a society that values youth.

Fortunately, the Japanese family has survived much of the trauma it has experienced in the western world. Several studies have reported that close intergenerational relations have been maintained among Japanese Americans in the United States (Kitano, 1976; Kiefer, 1974; Osako, 1979; Yanagisako, 1976). Osako (1979) found that the majority of his Issei sample lived close to their children, and 35 percent shared the same

First generation Japanese Americans are "growing old and facing death in a milieu much at variance with their beginnings." (The Coloradoan/ Bob Gunter, photographer)

household. Reflecting residence patterns, the elderly respondents reported regular and positive interactions with their kin group.

Sue and Kitano (1973) have cautioned against the stereotypical view of Japanese Americans as the "model minority." Because of the relative socioeconomic success achieved by this ethnic group and their emphasis on family ties, it is often assumed that older Issei do not need public assistance. Certainly some of them *do* need available government services, especially Issei men who never married. This group appears to have had some of the greatest adjustment problems (Kitano, 1976).

Human Services: Delivery and Utilization

Even when needing services, many aged Asians are reluctant to become involved with the bureaucratic systems of this country. This reluctance is due in part to mistrust of government stemming from incarceration experiences. Therefore, many do not receive available medical care, legal advice and financial assistance (City of Chicago, 1976).

Low utilization of available services among Asian Americans has also been attributed to language barriers and differing cultural traditions (Fujii, 1976; Kim & Condon, 1975; Holmes, Holmes, Steinbach, Hausner & Rocheleau, 1979). Montero (1979) reported that among the 1,002 Issei whom he studied, the English language was identified by one-third as the greatest difficulty they face. In fact, a large number of Issei speak little or no English. Unfortunately, few human service workers speak Japanese.

Beliefs and values regarding health and healing are deeply entrenched in ethnic traditions. However, the costs of most ethnic practices and medicines are not reimbursable through Medicare, Medicaid or insurance programs. For example, Medicare does not pay for services of a naturopath or the cost of herbal remedies often used by Asian Americans. Therefore if preferred health care is to be received, the individual must pay for it.

Many frail ethnic elderly have refused to go to institutional settings in which they would be forced to accept the cultural and dietary programs of the dominant culture and be isolated from former friends. Instead, many have chosen to remain in a familiar setting and have failed to receive adequate health care in many cases (Lurie, Kalish, Wexler & Ansak, 1976). The significance of cultural barriers in institutional settings was emphasized in a study by Lister (1977) in which Japanese staff perceived Japanese patients as depressed while Caucasian staff members saw them as simply being quiet. Some work toward caring for elderly Asian Americans within their own communities has begun, but the demand is much greater than the services available.

The Elderly Japanese Americans of the Future

Our discussion thus far has focused on the aging Issei, but what about the Nisei and Sansei? Will the services we design today be appropriate for second and third generation Japanese Americans when they reach their later years? The Nisei were all born in the United States and have attended American schools. In fact, the Nisei are a highly educated group with a large number employed in professional and technical occupations (Kitano, 1976; Schmid & Nobbe, 1965). Also, interracial marriage and suburbanization have increased among later born Japanese Americans (Bureau of the Census, 1973; Sue, Sue, Sue, 1975). While it is difficult to speculate how ethnicity will influence the Nisei and Sansei as they age, Osako (1979) predicts that the relevance of traditional values

Table 10–1. Generation Analysis of Honolulu Japanese-Americans on the Ethnic Identity Questionnaire Total and Individual Item Scores.

	Issei	Nisei	Sansei	Probability Levels of Pair Comparisons		
				Issei vs Nisei	Issei vs Sansei	Nisei vs Sansei
Mean Total EIQ Scores	159.76	142.81	139.22	.001	.001	N.S.
Mean Item Scores Item						
1 Good child is obedient	4.23	3.36	3.37	.001	.001	
5 J background prevents delinquency	3.90	3.18	2.40	.01	.001	.001
8 I show my affection	2.20	2.52	2.62		.01*	
10 Expectation of discrimination in new places	2.70	3.36	3.02	.001*	.001	.01
11 J-A's should retain part of J culture	4.44	4.06	3.85	.001	.001	
13 J-A's are deprived of opportunities	2.98	2.40	2.03	.01	.001	.01
14 Children may question parents	1.93	1.91	1.77			.01
15 Warmer relationships in J community	3.93	2.89	2.50	.001	.001	
16 No tendency to agree with Japan	2.54	2.06	2.18	.01	.01	
17 J-A's should feel 100% American	1.82	3.06	3.15	.001*	.001*	
18 Apt to hide feelings	2.77	3.12	3.45	.001*	.001*	
19 Shame that J-A's not know Japanese	3.72	3.00	3.27	.001		
20 J's have deep feeling for nature	4.13	3.06	3.08	.001	.001	
21 Disturbed if C's did not accept as equal	3.56	3.29	3.86			.001*

Item						
22 J-A's not allowed to be leaders	2.62	2.41	2.03		.001	.001
23 No strong attachment to Japan	3.56	2.29	2.17		.001	
27 Less at ease with C's	3.89	2.97	2.89	.001	.001	
28 J's no better or worse	2.61	2.07	1.74	.01	.001	.01
30 J schools later appreciated	4.13	3.43	3.48	.001	.001	
31 U.S. life ideal for J-A's	4.11	4.02	3.66	.001	.001	.001
32 Rely on relatives for help	3.55	2.57	2.87		.001	
33 Better J-A's date only J-A's	3.38	2.11	1.80	.001	.001	.001
34 Companionable parents can have respect	1.97	1.76	1.60	.001	.001	
35 Once a J, always a J	3.92	2.62	2.74		.001	
41 Noble to repay debt of gratitude	4.33	3.49	3.34	.001	.001	
42 Avoid places of discrimination	3.76	3.42	2.85	.001	.001	.001
43 Participation in group discussions	3.13	2.30	2.27	.001	.001	
46 Natural to wise-off at authority	2.63	3.32	3.14	.01*		
47 Questions interfere with group progress	3.58	2.70	2.18	.001	.001	.001
48 Prefer all-J church	3.47	1.98	2.02	.001	.001	
49 Family is let down when one lets down	3.87	3.46	3.21	.001	.01	
50 J-A and C marriages to be discouraged	2.50	1.98	1.72	.001	.001	.01

* Scores not in hypothesized direction.

J = Japanese; J-A = Japanese-American; C = Caucasian.

Source: G. M. Matsumoto, G. M. Meredith, and M. Masuda, "Ethnic Identity: Honolulu and Seattle Japanese-Americans," *Journal of Cross-Cultural Psychology,* 1970, *1,* 63–76.

is likely to be reduced as a result of acculturation and assimilation into the American culture. Results of an investigation of ethnic identity among Issei, Nisei and Sansei suggest a trend away from traditional Japanese values with each successive generation (Matsumoto, Meredith & Masuda, 1970; see Table 10–1). From the available evidence, it is certain that the Japanese American elderly of the future will be a more diversified and varied group than in the past.

The Older Native American

Nathaniel Wagner (1973) has charged that racism in America began with the arrival of Columbus in what is now North America. As Wagner puts it:

> If Columbus 'discovered' America, what was the relation of the natives inhabiting these shores to their own land? The obvious ethnocentrism of 'discovering' America is matched only by the misnaming of the inhabitants of the Western Hemisphere as 'Indians.' Columbus thought he had found the short route to India, and this inaccurate name is only now beginning to disappear as the indigenous people of this continent prefer 'native American' to 'Indians' . . . (p. 45).

Little information has been published on the Native American elderly, due in part to the fact that they constitute the smallest number of elderly among all minority groups in the United States. Approximately 45,000 native Americans are age 65 and over, accounting for about 6 percent of this group's total population. It should be pointed out, however, that the percentage of elderly among this group can be misleading. Block (1979) has suggested that the use of age 65 may be inappropriate for determining "elderly status" among Native Americans since their average life expectancy is only 44 years.

Discussions of aging regarding the Indian culture are difficult because of the great diversity that exists. According to Block (1979): "Generalizations about 266 Indian tribes, bands, villages, pueblos, and groups . . . are no more reliable than are generalizations about Europeans which fail to distinguish among Norwegians, Germans, Dutch, and French." Each tribe has its own customs, social structures and familial organization. In addition to tribal differences, the United States today has four distinct Indian populations—reservation Indians, rural Indians, migrant Indians, and urban Indians—with each group maintaining a different lifestyle (Jeffries, 1972).

With the movement of European settlers across North America, the lands of Indians were invaded and their lives disrupted. In the years

Table 10–2. Residence of Native Americans Age 60 and Over by Region.

Region	%
West	41.6
South	31.8
North Central	18.2
Northeast	8.4
United States	100.0

Source: B. S. Williams, Older American Indians, 1970. *Facts and Figures, No. 9* (Washington, D.C.: Administration on Aging, 1977).

that followed, many formal treaties were made between the Indians and the U.S. and Canadian governments, usually to the disadvantage of the Indians. In the 1830s Congress began moving Indians to allocated lands called reservations. Today, although many Native Americans are moving off reservations, the majority of the old continue to live on or near reservations. According to statistics provided by Jackson (1980), it appears that very few elderly Indians are urban residents. Most of the older Native Americans are located in the western part of the United States, as are most of the reservations, but they are represented in all areas of the country (Williams, 1977; see Table 10–2).

The Current Status of Older Native Americans

The traditional reverence given to the aged within Native American cultures has declined with modern trends such as the shift to wage work and the increase in younger tribal members who leave the reservations. These trends have undermined the role of the old in educational and advising functions and have led to the erosion of the extended family ties that have been so important in the lives of Native Americans in the past (Advisory Council, 1971; Levy, 1967). Even when wishing to support older family members, the extremely low wages received by most young Indians usually prevents them from assuming this responsibility (Block, 1979).

The data concerning the lives of Native Americans in the United States are startling. Benedict (1971) has stated that old age for Native Americans is the continuation of a state of near or actual destitution which most have experienced all of their lives. In their study of older

The majority of older Native Americans continue to live on or near reservations.
(H. Kubota, Magnum Photos)

Sioux, Murdock and Schwartz (1978) found that 60 percent of their sample had annual incomes of less than $3,000. The rate of unemployment for older Indians and the Indian population in general is extremely high. On some reservations, approximately 80 percent of the adults are without jobs (Developments in Aging, 1975). Public income maintenance programs such as unemployment insurance, workmen's compensation, and social security programs offer little assistance because they exclude the seasonal and unskilled occupations most Native Indians have had due to their limited vocational and educational skills (Farris, 1976).

Statistics from the Bureau of Indian Affairs show strong evidence of substandard housing in need of renovation and repair. It was reported that 55 percent of these homes have less than 600 square feet of living space, with inadequate heating in over half of them, and 21 percent having no electric power (Developments in Aging, 1975). Murdock and Schwartz (1978) found that approximately one-fourth of the households of the Indian elderly they studied had no running water, flush toilet, bathtub or shower. In addition, 84 percent did not have a telephone.

Native Americans have also been victims of inferior health due to factors such as the lack of basic sanitary facilities, inadequate nutrition, and limited availability of health care. They are eight times as likely as whites to die of tuberculosis, and twice as likely to die of gastritis, cirrhosis of the liver, influenza and pneumonia. In addition, the incidence of diabetes is higher among this group than in the general population (Benedict, 1971). As a consequence of these prevailing health conditions, only one out of every three Native Americans and Alaskan natives can be expected to reach age 65 (Harbert & Ginsberg, 1979).

Ogden and his colleagues (1970) have concluded that the high rates of suicide, alcoholism and homicide found among Native Americans are symptoms of underlying problems this minority group is experiencing—or, as they have expressed it, "poverty, unemployment, geographic isolation, cultural conflicts, and the resultant breakdown of old value systems leads to difficulties in adjusting to life."

Problems in Service Delivery and Utilization

The Department of the Interior, through the Bureau of Indian Affairs, has the official responsibility for the welfare of American Indians. Non-reservation Indians, however, are usually ineligible for the services offered through this agency. Table 10–3 shows service utilization rates among elderly Sioux in North and South Dakota. An examination of the table shows generally low levels of service usage.

Attempts at service delivery on reservations have met with several obstacles. As Farris (1976) points out, Native American cultures have experienced centuries of isolation, poverty, exploitation and paternalism. This unfortunate history of interactions with the dominant culture has resulted in feelings of alienation, vulnerability and suspicion. Therefore outsiders, including representatives from agencies providing mandated services, do not readily gain entrance into Native American communities. Studies have shown a clear preference among American Indians for services to be delivered by people of their own culture (De Geyndt, 1973; Red Horse & Feit, 1976). Many of the elder members of the various tribes are unable to speak English, their primary language being that of their native tribe. In suggesting techniques in working with culturally-different families, Carpenter and Bollman (1980) recommend the use of indigenous workers as paraprofessionals. They also stress the importance of establishing rapport with leaders in the ethnic community. Too often delivery systems have been based on white middle-class biases and the group being targeted for the service has had no voice in the program. As a consequence many programs have not been relevant to the real needs of the community and, therefore, have been ineffective in providing needed assistance (Farris, 1976).

With the case of nursing homes, an additional problem is apparent. Nursing homes must be licensed by states, and some states have refused to license nursing homes on reservations because of questions of jurisdiction (National Tribal Chairmen's Association, 1976). Therefore, elderly Indians in need of long-term care are forced to leave the reservation and go to the nearest health care facility, which is usually a consid-

Table 10–3. Use of Available Agency Services by Elderly Sioux Indians.

% *Using Service Agency*

Agency	Total Sample (N = 160)
Medical Services	
Community health representative	33.2
Public health—dental	40.0
Public health—medical	30.0
Medicare	10.0
Medicaid	0.6
Average medical services (mean)	22.8
Social Services	
Indian Action Team	2.5
Public health—counseling	1.9
Average social services (mean)	2.2
Home Maintenance	
Bathroom installation	10.6
Hip-log house	3.7
Scattered sites	3.7
Average home maintenance (mean)	6.0
Personal Maintenance	
Job Corps	1.3
Nursing home placement	0.6
Social Security	18.1
Expanded nutrition program	1.2
Green-thumb program	0.6
General assistance	32.5
Aid for dependent children	14.4
Food stamps	2.5
Supplemental Social Security income program	20.0
Surplus foods	37.5
Tribal work experience program	7.5
Average personal maintenance (mean)	12.4

Source: S. H. Murdock and D. F. Schwartz, "Family Structure and the Use of Agency Services: An Examination of Patterns Among Elderly Native Americans," *The Gerontologist,* 1978, *18,* 475—81.

erable distance away. Block (1979) has stressed the need for adequate and varied health services on reservations. As she points out, many services providing in-home care within the family setting have been available to the general elderly population but have not been given a high priority for the aged on Indian reservations. In their historic Declaration of Indian Purpose (1961), Native Americans made the following plea: "What we ask of America is not charity, not paternalism, even when benevolent. We ask only that the nature of our situation be recognized and made the basis of policy and action."

Aging in the Mexican-American Culture

There are currently over 517,000 Mexican Americans over age 65 residing in the United States (Jackson, 1980), and the number of elderly within this ethnic group is increasing rapidly. Between 1970 and 1975, the number of elderly of Mexican origin increased by 47.6 percent (Estrada, 1977). If these current population trends continue, Mexican Americans may eventually become the largest ethnic minority in the United States.

Large numbers of Chicano elderly (*los viejitos*) were born in this country and are descendents of the original residents of the territories annexed after the Mexican-American war. However, the majority of them have migrated to the United States from Mexico, usually in search of jobs and a better way of life. Legal immigration statistics for the United States show a significant increase among Mexican Americans since the 1950s. Accurate statistics for rates of illegal immigration are difficult to obtain, but the number of adults crossing the border illegally each year is known to be substantial (Maldonado, 1979).

The Mexican-American Family: Tradition and Change

A common thread running through the literature on Mexican Americans is the emphasis on familism. The Chicano family has repeatedly been described as a source of enduring emotional support in times of stress and crisis (Kalish and Reynolds, 1976; Madsen, 1964). Those in need of guidance, food or money are expected to turn first to the family. Seeking help from an outsider is often considered a disgrace (Murillo, 1976).

The Chicano culture is also characterized by male leadership and an age hierarchy (Alvarez & Bean, 1976). *Machismo* is the term commonly used to refer to the dominance of the male in the Chicano family. However, sex appears to become less important in determining status as a Chicano ages. The elder family member, regardless of sex, serves as head of the household and is respected and obeyed (Sotomayor, 1971).

Gilbert (1978) has emphasized the wide variation that exists among Mexican-American families and cautions against viewing *all* members of this ethnic group as having an immediate source of emotional and material help in a well-integrated family system. Variables such as geographical location, income and education have been found to influence the extent of family orientation.

The extended Mexican-American family described in the literature grew out of an agrarian existence. As a result of rapid social change since World War II, most Chicanos have moved to the cities, and this urban migration seems to have had an effect on Chicano families (Maldonado, 1975). Mirande (1977) has observed that more emphasis is being placed on the nuclear family structure rather than on extended kin relations, and the socioeconomic gap between generations is widening (Maldonado, 1979). These changes make it increasingly difficult to maintain the traditional position of the old within the family. While still respected, the elderly Chicanos have less authority today than in the past. Maldonado (1975) has summarized their situation as follows:

> Most aged Mexican Americans grew up in a rural community or on a farm. They had a function to perform then, and knew that when they reached old age they would still have a role, because they had seen their grandparents carry important roles in the extended family on the farm. Today the aged Chicanos find themselves in a city, surrounded by a system that does not need their knowledge and skills. Or they find themselves in a small town far from their children. They have prepared themselves for and looked forward to roles in old age that have never materialized (p. 215).

Most of the Chicano population resides in Texas, Colorado, Arizona, New Mexico and California. In California, the highest concentration of Mexican Americans is in Los Angeles, which contains many Chicano *barrios*. Cuellar (1978) gives the following graphic description of the effect that the rapid development of Los Angeles has had on Mexican-American communities in that city:

> Freeways have ripped through the heart of East Los Angeles, displacing members of extended families, separating friends and acquaintances, and physically dividing the community. Complete neighborhoods have been destroyed to make way for such manifestations of "progress" as the building of freeways, parking lots, and the Los Angeles Dodgers' baseball stadium (p. 209).

Such realities of modern, urban life can have devastating effects on a culture that has traditionally placed a premium on close family relationships and a reliance on kin.

Today many aged Chicanos find themselves living in a city and surrounded by a system that does not value their knowledge or skills. (Sibyl Stork, photographer)

Implications for Service Provision

The history of persons of Mexican descent in the United States is a history marked by racism. The elderly Chicanos, having been treated in large part as inferiors by the dominant culture, have survived many struggles (Maldonado, 1979). What supports are available for them in their final years of life?

Ethnicity and Aging

As we have seen, the family is viewed as a haven for the old less frequently than in the past. However, traditional notions of Chicanos "being taken care of by their own" have interfered with the delivery of needed services. In this regard, Maldonado (1975) states:

> Governmental social agencies, in "respecting the culture," may be avoiding their responsibility to provide services since they place responsibility on the Chicano family. At the same time, the agencies are not providing the family with the resources for making needed services available to the aged (p. 213).

Additionally, Kalish and Reynolds (1976) have interpreted the underutilization of services by Mexican Americans to be the result of transportation problems, awkward scheduling requirements, lack of bilingual staff members, and a history of dealing with persons in formal agencies who understand little of their culture and needs. Some older Chicanos also do not seek available services because they entered the United States illegally and are therefore still considered aliens and do not want to place themselves in jeopardy of being deported. Bell and Zellman (1976) have urged that legal residence be granted to elderly persons of foreign origin who have spent most of their adult lives in the United States. While contributing for years to the American labor force, they are too often unable to receive the public benefits to which they are entitled.

The Aged Black American

The history of blacks in the United States is perhaps better known than the experiences of other ethnic groups. Brought over from several African nations as part of the slave trade in the seventeenth and eighteenth centuries, the early blacks in this country served in bondage to wealthy slave owners. Even today most aged black persons, having been born only a few decades after the abolition of slavery, have experienced a lifetime of oppression by the dominant white culture.

Only recently has decisive action been taken to improve the opportunities for blacks in American society. As a result of the civil rights movement of the 1960s, strides have been made through federal legislation and legal action, thus increasing broader participation of blacks in the occupational and educational structures of our country. These changes, however, appear to have had more impact on the young than the old.

Blacks presently constitute the largest ethnic minority among the elderly of our nation. At the beginning of this century almost 90 percent

332

of all blacks were living in the southern region of the United States. While the majority still remain in the South, their migration to northern, urban areas has increased, particularly among the young (Jackson, 1980).

Income and Employment

Elderly blacks surveyed in 1974 identified income as their number one problem. In 1977 more than a third of the black aged were living below the poverty level (U.S. Department of Health and Human Services, 1980). While a disparity between the incomes of whites and nonwhites exists at all age levels, Dowd and Bengston (1978) found that this gap widens after age 65.

Most older blacks of today have generally accrued little, if any, re-

Black aged, when compared with whites, are less well educated, have less income, suffer more illnesses, die sooner, have poorer quality housing and less choice as to where they live and where they work. (Priscilla Solomons Davis, photographer)

Ethnicity and Aging

tirement benefits. Unfortunately, early social security programs did not include domestic housework and farm labor—the occupations in which most elderly blacks were employed during their lifetimes (Bixby & Irelan, 1969). Even with the expanded Social Security coverage, the shorter life expectancy of blacks as compared to whites prevents many elderly blacks from living long enough to collect these benefits (Morgan, 1968).

Private pension coverage has grown considerably in the United States over the past several decades, and more blacks are now qualifying for this coverage as they move from employment in agricultural and personal services to jobs in manufacturing, transportation and professional services. While these gains will lead toward a narrowing income gap between black and white retirees in the future, blacks who are now over 65 are relatively unaffected by these trends (Snyder, 1979).

Health

Statistics show that blacks tend to use medical services less than whites. For example, Lindsay (1971) has reported less frequent visits to physicians by blacks than by whites. There are several plausible explanations for these findings. First of all, individuals with few economic resources often are unable to afford the amount required before services are provided at no charge. Other inhibitory factors are related to the location and staffing patterns of health care facilities. Several investigators have identified neighborhood-based facilities as a major determinant of service use by older minority persons (Bell, Kasschau & Zellman, 1976; Dorsett-Robinson, 1974). Transportation is often a problem for older persons of ethnic descent, and they therefore tend to stay within the geographical boundaries of their neighborhood (Davis, 1975; Lawton & Krassen, 1973). With regard to staffing, underutilization appears to be associated with lack of minority representation. When evaluating mobile medical care to elderly blacks, Bell (1975) found low utilization rates to be a function of the white, middle-class orientation and staffing of the program. This infrequent use of available services can be extremely detrimental to the health of older blacks, especially when they resort to self-care practices that pose additional threats to their physical well-being. Folk practices related to healing are common among older persons in most ethnic groups. In Box 10–1, Dr. Robert Pieroni describes his encounter with the folk medicine used by blacks in the rural south.

As mentioned in our discussion of institutionalization in Chapter Seven, few minority persons reside in long-term care facilities. Among the black population, rates of institutionalization are extremely low. Examining longevity trends for black and whites from U.S. Census data, Ehrlich (1975) found that the death rates for these races are reversed at age 75 and over. While blacks have higher mortality rates up to this age,

Box 10–1

A Physician's Encounter with Folk Medicine

Dr. Loudell F. Snow (1974), in her classic review "Folk Medical Beliefs and Their Implications for Care of Patients: A Review Based on Studies Among Black Americans," describes the black folk medical belief system as 'a composite of rare elements of African origin, survivals from the folk and formal medicine of a century ago, and selected beliefs from modern scientific medicine.' She aptly described how folk medicine beliefs are frequently at odds with scientific medicine in many respects and emphasized the need for health workers to be cognizant of these differences and their influences on patient behavior.

Seven years ago, after finishing my internal medicine residency in Boston, I began practicing and teaching in Alabama. Previously, I had been familiar with some of the common medical folk practices among both Northern Whites and Blacks, as well as other groups such as the Amish with whom I had some contact as a medical student in Pennsylvania. I soon found I had much to learn!

It should be emphasized at the outset that many folk practices and beliefs are ubiquitous and occur among many regions, cultures and races. Some beliefs and practices, for numerous reasons, however, are found predominantly among Blacks, especially in the Southern states. Many of these practices are neutral in that they have no untoward effects on health; a few practices are actually beneficial. During my medical practice in Alabama, I have had much contact with the many folk medicine practices that are actually harmful to patients' health and well-being. Many of these practices are used or, at least, promulgated by the older segment of the Black population where folk beliefs are given more credence.

As I write this, I have before me a vial of "sour dirt" acquired from an elderly Black female who was hospitalized last year with weakness and fainting due to severe anemia. She obtained this "sour dirt" from a creek bank, the location of which is a carefully guarded secret. Previously she had eaten copious amounts of Argo's laundry starch. . . . The manufacturer was compelled to put "not for internal use" on the box, but even this has not halted its frequent internal consumption. Hematologists have noted that many of those who practice pica are actually deficient in iron because of nutritional inadequacies or blood loss. Consumption of clay, dirt or starch binds iron in the gut resulting in a vicious cycle until the patient is so anemic hospitalization may be required. The extent of morbidity and possible mortality resulting from pica can only be estimated. . . . Although there may be a physiological basis for pica, folk tradition, especially among older Blacks, has perpetuated this harmful practice.

In many respects, the medical profession and society itself have contributed to and bear responsibility for some of the harmful folk practices. Inaccessibility to medical care by Blacks because of poverty, lack of education and prejudice has certainly contributed to alternative health care systems and beliefs including folk practices. Fear of a hostile world in general and distrust of organized medicine in particular is a frequently recurring and often justified theme found by those who have analyzed Black medical beliefs. Until society can correct these inequities, it is imperative that we at least be aware of potentially dangerous "health" practices and lend our support through educational and other efforts to help eradicate them.

Source: R. E. Pieroni, "Folk Medicine of the Black Elderly," *Quarterly Contact,* 1981, 4, 7. (A publication of the National Caucus and Center on Black Aged, Inc.)

white death rates are double those for blacks for the over 75 age group. Ehrlich concluded that those individuals who survive the hardships to live to an advanced age comprise a special "hardy" group that is physically less vulnerable.

How Do They Cope?

Dancy (1977) has concluded from his analysis of the black aged that, when compared to whites in the same age group, they are less well educated, have less income, suffer more illnesses, die sooner, have poorer quality housing and less choice as to where they live and where they work. How do they cope with these conditions? What factors help them deal with the stresses and strains of their daily lives?

Religion appears to play a very important role in the lives of older blacks (Jackson & Wood, 1976). In one study of Southern blacks, 90 percent of the older individuals in the sample said that they regularly engaged in prayer (Swanson & Harter, 1971). Spiritualism has provided strength and reassurance to many blacks faced with adversity and has contributed to their ability to effectively cope. The interview presented in Box 10–2 illustrates the prominence of religious beliefs among aged blacks. It is interesting to note that for blacks in America, their church is the one institution not controlled by whites.

Box 10–2

Elderly Blacks in New Orleans

Ninety-four black adults living in New Orleans were randomly selected and interviewed by Swanson and Harter (1971). The following interview with an elderly man reflects the strong religious orientation the investigators found to be common among their sample.

Q. What is your biggest problem today?

A. None at all, I got no problems, thank you, Jesus. I work two days a week and been working all my life.

Q. Is it hard work?

A. It ain't hard work. I been there twenty-five years.

Q. Is there anything you don't like about it?

A. There ain't nothing hard. I just like it here.

Q. Do you have any other problems?

A. Not that I know of. I don't worry nobody and nobody worry me, just that I get to heaven when I die.

Q. Were you ever upset about your job?

A. I don't get upset. I stayed twenty-five years. I must like it.

Q. Are you ever upset with your friends?

A. No. I don't get upset with nobody. It ain't no friend if you get upset with him.

Q. Do you ever get upset with your wife?

A. I don't. If she got me upset I would have left her. We been together fourteen years so you know nothing upsets my mind.

Q. Are you ever upset about world affairs?

A. Nothing worries me.

Q. Are you ever upset about finances?

A. I don't have that.

Q. Are you ever upset about your health?

A. I don't been sick.

Q. Often people have ups and downs, feeling fine one day and blue the next. Have you had these different moods yourself?

A. No not indeed. I told you I don't have no problems.

Q. Well then what is the most serious problem you have ever had?

A. I had none. I never had no serious problem. I been a man since I was 21. I never been in trouble. I work.

Q. Have you always had a job?

A. I been working since I was 8. I was born in the country. I got no problems, no children, just me and my wife. Just Jesus is all I got to worry about.

Q. Have you ever felt that life was not worth living?

A. No I never felt that way.

Q. What would you do if you discovered that you had a serious problem, a problem that maybe you couldn't handle by yourself?

A. This is up to the Lord.

Source: W. C. Swanson and C. L. Harter, "How Do Elderly Blacks Cope in New Orleans?" *Aging and Human Development*, 1971, 2, 210–16.

Ethnicity and Aging

Contrary to persistent stereotypes, most aged blacks do not live in large or extended families (Jackson, 1980). Family ties are nonetheless very important to black communities and serve as a source of strength. Aged family members are valued because, as Jackson (1973) points out, they often have important social roles in black families and serve as important resources for younger family members. For example, grandmothers often take considerable responsibility for raising grandchildren (Jackson & Wood, 1976). Jackson (1973) views this aspect of black families as a strength and advocates that interventions designed to improve the life of the black elderly build on this role rather than interfere with it.

Characteristics of black families in general have been discussed, but it must be remembered that there is considerable heterogeneity among black families. Certainly not all black elderly are poor, uneducated, and in failing health. While general descriptions of ethnic groups can be useful, stereotyping is an easy pitfall (Jackson, 1974). More must be learned about the various subgroups within the black culture, for example the ways in which urban blacks differ from rural blacks and the characteristics of middle-class blacks. As we gain more accurate information, more appropriate public policies can be developed (Ehrlich, 1975).

Implications of Ethnicity

As the impact of policies and programs becomes a central concern of our federal government, it becomes increasingly important to understand variations in American families as any program would not have the same effect or be utilized in the same way by all families. Coming from many different cultural backgrounds, American people have passed on to their children different expectations, family interaction patterns, and ways of participating in the wider society. An awareness of ethnic variations is particularly important in serving older Americans for their life experiences have been deeply influenced by their cultures of origin (Woehrer, 1978, p. 329).

Four major ethnic groups have been discussed in this chapter—Japanese Americans, Native Americans, Mexican Americans and Blacks. These groups represent only a small sample of the rich diversity of cultural groups that exist in the United States. In addition to a large number of Asian-American and Hispanic groups, a variety of white ethnic populations are now growing old in America. In fact, approximately nine million European immigrants have entered the United States since 1940 (Fandetti & Gelfand, 1976).

Gelfand (1979) advocates that courses on ethnicity be required in all gerontology and mental health programs, and Kastenbaum (1979) believes that "the education of health care professionals is not complete if ethnicity is excluded." These statements can apply to professionals in other areas of human services as well. As professionals, we often underestimate the influence of ethnicity on individuals. Other times we fail to accept it. With regard to American Indians, Farris (1976) has charged that "cultural pluralism is usually only acceptable as long as the Indian confines his 'Indianness' to nonthreatening areas such as dances, tribal lore, native crafts, and so forth." If we are serious about wanting to improve the status of ethnic minorities in this country, an increased effort will be needed to become informed and sensitive to culturally-relevant variables.

Organized interest in the minority elderly began in the late 1960s and is still in its formative stages (Butler, 1975). In order for significant changes to occur, it is essential that the involvement of local minority leaders be sought for program planning and development. Also, more encouragement should be given to minority youth to enter human service professions.

While being old and a minority can be a "double-jeopardy" position, as many have contended, there can be many strengths inherent in ethnic traditions. Bengston (1979) believes that while minority status may bring problems to the aged, the shared symbols, rituals and meanings of a culture can also be an important resource when coping with the changes that occur with age. Perhaps the best approach to serving the minority aged is to formulate policies that will take ethnic variations into consideration and also strengthen the existing helping systems which have traditionally functioned in these cultures.

Suggested Activities and Exercises

1. Interview the director of a local human service agency and inquire about efforts that have been made to more effectively serve ethnic minorities. Are the program's brochures printed in a language other than English? Are any members of the staff bilingual? Does the agency employ paraprofessionals from ethnic communities? Are statistics available on utilization rates by ethnic group?
2. Specialized services can be very expensive. What responsibility do you think the government has to provide for the unique needs of elderly ethnic minorities? To what extent should existing programs be altered?
3. If you were asked to respond to the above question for *specific* ethnic groups, how important would the following variables be in determining your response: recency in U.S., percentage in population, reasons

for being in this country, the role of government versus the role of families, and cost to the government?

References

Advisory Council on the Elderly American Indian. Working paper prepared for the Special Committee on Aging, U.S. Senate, November, 1971.

Alvarez, D., & Bean, F. The Mexican-American family. In C. H. Mindel & R. W. Habenstein (Eds.), *Ethnic families in America*. New York: Elsevier, 1976.

Bell, B. D. Mobile medical care to the elderly: An evaluation. *The Gerontologist*, 1975, *15*, 100–3.

Bell, D., Kasschau, P., & Zellman, G. *Delivering services to elderly members of minority groups: A critical review of the literature*. Santa Monica, Ca.: Rand Corp., 1976.

Bell, D., & Zellman, G. *Issues in services delivery to ethnic elderly*. Paper presented at the annual meeting of the Western Gerontological Association, San Diego, Ca., 1976.

Benedict, R. A. A profile of Indian aged. In *Minority aged in America*. Ann Arbor: Institute of Gerontology, University of Michigan—Wayne State University, 1971.

Bengtson, V. L. Ethnicity and aging: Problems and issues in current social science inquiry. In D. E. Gelfand & A. J. Kutzik (Eds.), *Ethnicity and aging*. New York: Springer, 1979.

Bixby, L. E., & Irelan, L. M. The Social Security administration program of retirement research. *The Gerontologist*, 1969, *9*, 143–7.

Block, M. R. Exiled Americans: The plight of Indian aged in the United States. In D. E. Gelfand & A. J. Kutzik (Eds.), *Ethnicity and aging*. New York: Springer, 1979.

Bureau of the Census. *Japanese, Chinese and Filipinos in United States*. Washington, D.C.: U.S. Government Printing Office, 1973.

Butler, R. N. *Why survive? Being old in America*. New York: Harper & Row, 1975.

Carpenter, K., & Bollman, S. R. The family life educator and culturally different families. *Family Perspective*, 1980, *14*, 119–24.

City of Chicago, Mayor's Office for Senior Citizens, Research Division. *A summary of the status of elderly Asians in Chicago*. Chicago, Ill.: City of Chicago, 1976.

Connor, J. W. *Tradition and change in three generations of Japanese Americans*. Chicago: Nelson-Hall, 1977.

Cuellar, J. El senior citizens club: The older Mexican American in the voluntary association. In B. J. Myerhoff & A. Simic (Eds.), *Life's career—Aging*. Beverly Hills, Ca.: Sage, 1978.

Dancy, J., Jr. *The Black elderly: A guide for practitioners*. Ann Arbor: University of Michigan. 1977.

Davis, K. Equal treatment and unequal benefits: The Medicare program. *Milbank Memorial Fund Quarterly*, 1975, *53*, 449–88.

Declaration of Indian Purpose. Presented at the American Indian Chicago Conference, Chicago, Illinois, June 13–20, 1961.

DeGeyndt, W. Health behavior and health needs in urban Indians in Minneapolis. *Health Service Reports*, 1971, *88*, 360–66.

Developments in aging: 1974 & January-April, 1975. *Report of the Special Committee on Aging* (United States Senate). Washington, D.C.: U.S. Government Printing Office, 1975.

Dorosett-Robinson, J. (ed.) *The black elders: Workshop and conference proceedings*. Carbondale, Ill.: College of Human Resources, Southern Illinois University, 1974.

Dowd, J. J., & Bengston, V. L. Aging in minority populations: An examination of the double jeopardy hypothesis. *Journal of Gerontology*, 1978, *33*, 427–36.

Ehrlich, I. F. The aged black in America—The forgotten person. *The Journal of Negro Education*, 1975, *44*, 12–23.

Endo, R. Japanese Americans: The "model minority" in perspective. In R. Gomez et al. (Eds.), *The social reality of ethnic America*. Lexington, Mass.: D.C. Heath, 1974.

Estrada, L. F. The Spanish origin elderly: A demographic survey, 1970–1975. *Aging Research Utilization Report*, 1977, *1*, 13–14.

Fandetti, D. V., & Gelfand, D. E. Care of the aged: Attitudes of white ethnic families. *The Gerontologist*, 1976, *16*, 544–49.

Farris, C. E. American Indian social work advocates. *Social Casework*, 1976, *57*, 494–503.

Fujii, S. M. Elderly Asian Americans and use of public services. *Social Casework*, 1976, *57*, 202–7.

Gee, E. Issei women. In E. Gee (Ed.), *Counterpoint: Perspectives on Asian America*. Los Angeles: Asian American Studies Center, University of California, 1976.

Gelfand, D. E. Ethnicity, aging and mental health. *International Journal of Aging and Human Development*, 1979, *10*, 289 – 97.

Gelfand, D. E., & Kutzik, A. J. (Eds.) *Ethnicity and aging*. New York: Springer, 1979.

Gilbert, J. *Extended family integration among second generation Mexican Americans*. Santa Barbara: Social Process Research Institute, University of California, 1978.

Harbert, A. S., & Ginsberg, L. H. *Human services for older adults: Concepts and skills*. Belmont, Ca.: Wadsworth, 1979.

Holmes, D., Holmes, M., Steinbach, L., Hausner, S., & Rocheleau, B. The use of community-based services in long-term care by older minority persons. *The Gerontologist,* 1979, *19,* 389–97.

Jackson, J. J. *Minorities and aging.* Belmont, Ca.: Wadsworth, 1980.

Jackson, J. J. National Caucus on the Black Aged: Black aged and politics. *Annals of the American Academy of Political and Social Sciences,* 1974, *415,* 140–59.

Jackson, J. J. *Proceedings of Black aged in the future.* Durham, N.C.: Center for the Study of Aging and Human Development, Duke University, 1973.

Jackson, M., & Wood, J. L. *Aging in America, No. 5: Implications for the black aged.* Washington, D.C.: National Council on the Aging, 1976.

Jeffries, W. R. Our aged Indians. In *Triple jeopardy . . . myth or reality?* Washington, D.C.: National Council on the Aging, 1972.

Kalish, R. A., & Moriwaki, S. The world of the elderly Asian American. *Journal of Social Issues,* 1973, *29,* 187—209.

Kalish, R. A., & Reynolds, D. K. *Death and ethnicity: A psycho-cultural study.* Los Angeles: University of California Press, 1976.

Kalish, R. A., & Yuen, S. Y. Americans of east Asian ancestry: Aging and the aged. In S. Sue & N. N. Wagner (Eds.), *Asian Americans: Psychological perspectives.* Ben Lomond, Ca.: Science and Behavior Books, 1973.

Kastenbaum, R. Reflections on old age, ethnicity, and death. In D. E. Gelfand & A. J. Kutzik (Eds.), *Ethnicity and aging.* New York: Springer, 1979.

Kiefer, C. *Changing cultures, changing lives: An ethnographic study of three generations of Japanese Americans.* San Francisco: Josey-Bass, 1974.

Kim, B. C., & Condon, M. E. *A study of Asian Americans in Chicago: Their socioeconomic characteristics, problems, and service needs.* Washington, D.C.: National Institute of Mental Health, DHEW, 1975.

Kitano, H. H. L. *Japanese Americans: The evolution of a subculture.* (2nd ed.) Englewood Cliffs, N.J.: Prentice-Hall, 1976.

Lawton, P. M., & Krassen, E. Federally subsidized housing for the elderly Black. *Journal of Social Sciences,* Summer-Fall, 1973.

Levy, J. E. The older American Indian. In E. G. Youmans (Ed.), *Older rural Americans: A sociological perspective.* Lexington: University of Kentucky Press, 1967.

Lindsay, I. B. *The multiple hazards of age and race: The situation of aged blacks in the United States.* Washington, D.C.: U.S. Government Printing Office, 1971.

Lister, L. Cultural perspectives on death as viewed from within a skilled nursing facility. In E. R. Prichard et al., *Social work with the dying patient and family.* New York: Columbia University Press, 1977.

Lurie, E., Kalish, R. A., Wexler, R., & Ansak, M. On Lok Senior Day Health Center. *The Gerontologist,* 1976, *16,* 39–46.

Madsen, W. *The Mexican Americans of South Texas.* New York: Holt, 1964.

Maldonado, D., Jr. Aging in the Chicano context. In D. E. Gelfand & A. J. Kutzik (Eds.), *Ethnicity and aging.* New York: Springer, 1979.

Maldonado, D., Jr. *The Chicano aged.* Social Work, 1975, *20,* 213–16.

Matsumoto, J. M., Meredith, G. M., & Masuda, M. Ethnic identity: Honolulu and Seattle Japanese-Americans. *Journal of Cross-Cultural Psychology,* 1970, *1,* 63–76.

Mirande, A. The Chicano family: A reanalysis of conflicting views. *Journal of Marriage and the Family,* 1977, *39,* 747–56.

Montero, D. Disengagement and aging among the Issei. In D. E. Gelfand & A. J. Kutzik (Eds.), *Ethnicity and aging.* New York: Springer, 1979.

Morgan, R. F. The adult growth examination: Preliminary comparisons of physical aging in adults by sex and race. *Perceptual and Motor Skills,* 1968, *27,* 595–99.

Murdock, S. H., & Schwartz, D., F. Family structure and the use of agency services: An examination of patterns among elderly Native Americans. *The Gerontologist,* 1978, *18,* 475–81.

Murillo, N. *Chicanos, social and psychological perspectives.* St. Louis: Mosby, 1976.

National Tribal Chairmen's Association. *Summary report: National Indian Conference on aging.* Phoenix: National Tribal Chairmen's Association, 1976.

Ogden, M., Spector, M. I., & Hill, C. A., Jr. Suicides and homicides among Indians. *Public Health Reports,* 1970, *85,* 75–80.

Osako, M. M. Aging and family among Japanese Americans: The role of ethnic tradition in the adjustment to old age. *The Gerontologist,* 1979, *19,* 448–54.

Pieroni, R. E. Folk medicine of the black elderly. *Quarterly Contact,* 1981, *4,* 7.

Red Horse, J. J., & Feit, M. *Urban Native American preventive health care.* Paper presented at the American Public Health Association Meeting, Miami Beach, Florida, 1976.

Schmid, C. F., & Nobbe, C. F. Socio-economic differentials among nonwhite races. *American Sociological Review,* 1965, *30,* 909–22.

Snow, L. F. Folk medical beliefs and their implications for care of patients: A review based on studies among black Americans. *Annals of Internal Medicine,* 1974, *81,* 82–96.

Sotomayor, M. Mexican-American interaction with social systems. *Social Casework,* 1971, *5,* 316–22.

Sue, S., & Kitano, H. (Eds.) Asian Americans: A success story? *Journal of Social Issues,* 1973, *29,* 1–209.

Sue, S., Sue, D. W., & Sue, D. W. Asian Americans as a minority group. *American Psychologist,* 1975, *30,* 896–10.

Swanson, W. C., & Harter, C. L. How do elderly blacks cope in New Orleans? *Aging and Human Development,* 1971, *2,* 210–16.

Synder, D. C. Future pension status of the black elderly. In D. E. Gelfand & A. J. Kutzik (Eds.), *Ethnicity and aging.* New York: Springer, 1979.

U.S. Department of Health and Human Services. *Characteristics of the Black elderly: 1980.* Washington, D.C.: U.S. Government Printing Office, 1980.

U.S. Senate Special Committee on Aging. *The multiple hazards of age and race: The situation of the aged blacks in the U.S.* Washington, D.C.: U.S. Government Printing Office, 1971.

Wagner, N. N. A white view of American racism. In S. Sue & N. N. Wagner (Eds.), *Asian Americans: Psychological perspectives.* Ben Lomond, Ca.: Science and Behavior Books, 1973.

Williams, B. S. Older American Indians, 1970. *Facts and figures, No. 9.* Washington, D.C.: Administration on Aging, 1977.

Woehrer, C. E. Cultural pluralism in American families: The influence of ethnicity on social aspects of aging. *The Family Coordinator,* 1978, *27,* 329–39.

Yanagisako, J. The process of change in Japanese-American kinship. *Journal of Anthropological Research,* 1976, *31,* 196–224.

Part V

Epilogue

Chapter 11

Enhancing
the Adult Years

In studying developmental processes in this text, the need for adequate preparation has been an recurring theme. Mondale (1976) has suggested that "we must shape education in its broadest sense to help us meet these needs." In order to enhance development, we must shift from a remedial to a preventative focus. Prevention can be attempted at the individual, societal and governmental levels. In this concluding chapter, we will discuss ways of effectively preparing individuals for transitions of adult life, modifying societal attitudes, and formulating appropriate public policies.

Preparation for Life Transitions

We encounter transitions throughout our lives which present us with new demands and challenges. Figure 11–1 shows the relationship among the major cycles of adult life. An examination of each cycle shows transition points discussed throughout this text. Although individual and social-class differences exist, many of the major life events of adulthood are predictable and correspond to certain life stages and approximate chronological ages. The transitions can be smoother through appropriate socialization experiences. According to Albrecht and Gift (1975), anticipatory socialization for adult roles occurs through "preparatory

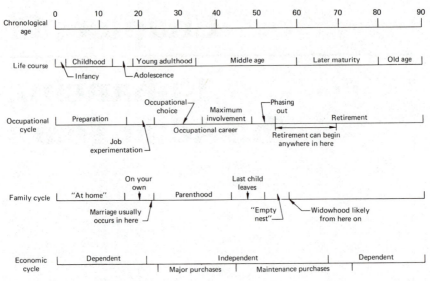

Figure 11–1. The relationships among the major cycles of life. (Source: R.C. Atchley. "The life course, age grading, and age-linked demands for decision-making," in N. Datan and L.H. Ginsberg (eds.), *Life-Span Developmental Psychology: Normative Life Crises.* New York: Academic Press, 1975, p. 264.)

education, planning, observation, and attempting some of the role requirements in situations where competent performance is not critical" (p. 240). For example, anticipatory socialization for the parenting role can involve enrollment in preparenting classes, optimal planning of spacing and number of children, observation of positive parental role models, and perhaps experience gained through such activities as babysitting. At the other end of the life span, anticipatory socialization for retirement can include engaging in preretirement lifestyle planning, participating in estate-planning workshops, interacting with persons who have made a positive adjustment to retirement, and attempting to live on a reduced income before it becomes a necessity.

Through adequate preparation and role rehearsal, competence can be fostered and resources developed. When transitional events and their contingencies are approached in this way, adjustment is usually easier and developmental transitions are prevented from becoming crises. Albrecht and Gift (1975) have further elaborated on this concept as follows:

> The competent performance of a role assumes that an individual clearly perceives and defines role expectations and has the resources and experience to accomplish his tasks. In adult life, an individual may have resources and experiences but lack a clear definition or perception of what is expected of him, if his anticipatory socialization

348

has been inadequate. The result is that the individual is confused about how to mobilize his resources for action. He is not prepared for his problems; he does not know how to define the situation and respond. Ambiguity frequently arises as a result of unclear and/or conflicting expectations surrounding the social situations and events. Situations and events are defined as crises when they are not anticipated. Present problems are crises when they are not easily solved. If the expectations associated with an event are clear and the individual possesses sufficient resources to meet the expectations, there usually is no adult life crisis (p. 239).

In the past, professionals in both marriage counseling and family life education have generally been preoccupied with problems. Identifying strengths instead of problems and utilizing these strengths as a foundation for further growth have been fairly recent developments in the mental health field (Miller, Corrales & Wackman, 1975). In the past decade, we have witnessed a proliferation of programs aimed toward preparation and enrichment. Gradually parent education programs, preretirement seminars, and human growth centers have become an established part of our society. Such programs facilitate increased use of our potential as we act out our roles in life.

Combating Ageism

At the beginning of this text, the concept of ageism was presented. As you have learned, many of the characteristics and attributes that we

Box 11–1

Quiz: Facts on Aging

Respond to each item and then check your responses with the key provided at the bottom of the next page. What misconceptions do you continue to have about aging?

T F   1. The majority of old people (past age 65) are senile (i.e., defective memory, disoriented, or demented).

T F   2. All five senses tend to decline in old age.

T F   3. Most old people have no interest in, or capacity for, sexual relations.

T F   4. Lung capacity tends to decline in old age.

T F   5. The majority of old people feel miserable most of the time.

T F   6. Physical strength tends to decline in old age.

T F   7. At least one-tenth of the aged are living in long-stay institutions (i.e., nursing homes, mental hospitals, homes for the aged, etc.).

T F 8. Aged drivers have fewer accidents per person than drivers under age 65.

T F 9. Most older workers cannot work as effectively as younger workers.

T F 10. About 80% of the aged are healthy enough to carry out their normal activities.

T F 11. Most old people are set in their ways and unable to change.

T F 12. Old people usually take longer to learn something new.

T F 13. It is almost impossible for most old people to learn new things.

T F 14. The reaction time of most old people tends to be slower than reaction time of younger people.

T F 15. In general, most old people are pretty much alike.

T F 16. The majority of old people are seldom bored.

T F 17. The majority of old people are socially isolated and lonely.

T F 18. Older workers have fewer accidents than younger workers.

T F 19. Over 15% of the U.S. population are now age 65 or over.

T F 20. Most medical practitioners tend to give low priority to the aged.

T F 21. The majority of older people have incomes below the poverty level (as defined by the federal government).

T F 22. The majority of old people are working or would like to have some kind of work to do (including housework and volunteer work).

T F 23. Older people tend to become more religious as they age.

T F 24. The majority of old people are seldom irritated or angry.

T F 25. The health and socioeconomic status of older people (compared to younger people) in the year 2000 will probably be about the same as now.

KEY: True—Items 2,4,6,8,10,12,14,16,18,20,22,24
False—Items 1,3,5,7,9,11,13,15,17,19,21,23,25

Source: E. Palmore, "Facts on Aging: A Short Quiz," *The Gerontologist*, 1977,. 17, 315–20.

generally ascribe to older persons are simply not true. Even when presented with empirical evidence contradicting many of our previous notions about aging, we tend to hold onto these false assumptions because they have been so deeply engrained and reinforced by our society.

Ageism will continue as long as individuals grow up with inaccurate perceptions of what it means to be old. Studies show that attitudes and stereotypes are developed early in life and tend to be stable and enduring (Klausmeier & Ripple, 1971). Stereotypes of the aged can be especially problematic because they not only affect interactions with older persons but they also influence people's own self-concepts as they themselves advance in years. After reviewing the findings on children's attitudes toward the elderly, McTavish (1971) concluded that rejection and prejudice toward older persons by the young is widespread. More recent studies have also confirmed the tendency of young children to attribute negative attributes to the old (Chitwood & Bigner, 1980; Seefeldt, Jantz, Galper & Serock, 1977).

How can ageism be combated? Seefeldt et al. (1977) believe that the process should begin early and urge schools to provide children with curriculum experiences designed to prevent the formation of negative attitudes toward the elderly. By presenting children with realistic portrayals of older persons, many of the negative stereotypes and associations can be avoided. Box 11–2 shows an illustration from a book entitled *A Treasure Hunt* (Wilson & Wilson, 1980) which attempts to overcome the stereotyped view of the elderly as passive and dependent. Funded by the National Institute on Aging, the project of writing and illustrating the book was undertaken by Christopher and Dagmar Wilson, both in their sixties, to make children more aware of the active daily lives of the elderly.

Actual experiences with healthy older persons can be important as well (Bennett, 1976), yet studies reveal that children today have limited contact with the older generation. In one study of 180 children between the ages of three and eleven, investigators found that only 39 of the children were able to identify an older person they knew outside of their family unit (Serock, Seefeldt, Jantz & Galper, 1977). In addition, Chitwood and Bigner (1980) reported that less than a quarter of their sample of preschool children had contact with an older person as frequently as once or twice a week. While most of the children had grandparents over 65, 90 percent of them lived a considerable distance from their older relatives.

Seefeldt and her associates (1977) suggest using active, healthy older persons as volunteers in the classroom to increase contact between the old and the young. This approach can also be used in college classrooms in which students are studying developmental processes of

The hunters said goodbye to Mr. Chips and went to the house of old Mrs. Snips.

Mrs. Snips had white hair and wore glasses. She smiled when the hunters told her why they had come to visit her. She was making a white wedding dress. Janet watched the old lady's quick fingers stitching and snipping, and wished that she could learn to sew.

"Come one day after school," said Mrs. Snips, answering Janet's wish. "I will help anyone who wants to make a dress or mend a sail. You can help me by threading needles."

In a corner of the room was a dressmaker's dummy, and tied to the dummy by a piece of red ribbon was a rolling pin.

"A rolling pin makes me think of the bakery," said Jan. "Let's visit Mr. Bun, the baker."

Source: C. Wilson and D. Wilson, *A Treasure Hunt* (Washington, D.C.: U.S. Government Printing Office, 1980, pp. 18–19).

adulthood. Also on the college level, field work experiences involving contact with the elderly can enrich classroom learning and expand students' awareness of what it means to be old in American society. Box 11–3 contains an account of the meaningfulness of such an experience for an 18-year-old student enrolled in an adult development and aging course.

Box 11–3

A Field Work Summary

It is Wednesday afternoon, about 3:00. I'm finished with classes for the day. Inside, in the pit of my stomach, a sensation of "I'd rather be doing something else" makes itself known as I make the drive to your house. Then with a knock on the door, your dog's familiar bark, and a friendly hello, all the previous tensions and feelings escape me, and are replaced with a contentness that being with you brings.

The times are good. From sitting here and talking in your three-room home to doing little errands and paying your late bills. Walking around City Park or testing to see "how young at heart" you really are by going to "Avogadros" for ice-cream—your treat, you insist. Shopping and hugging "my adopted grandmother" good-bye as we part for another week. I even laugh to myself when I get home and remember when you told the store clerk I was your granddaughter and could fix anything (based on one time when I put on your new watchband for you).

All these memories flood my mind. I know that in the future when the Mountain Bell commercial comes on and I'm sitting in front of a fire feeling sentimental, I will think of you. You have taught me so much. Oh, Mrs. Case, you have taught me so very much.

From Maslow I learned that humans must have certain needs met: physiological, safety and security, love and belongingness, self-esteem, and self-actualization.

From you I saw the tiny house with cracked linoleum and walls to match, heard about "Meals on Wheels," and your friends. I saw the growth—the laughter, the playfulness, the young soul in an old body.

From my textbook I read that general intellectual decline in the old is largely a myth.

From you I saw the crossword puzzles and dictionary and observed your alertness and knowledge of current events.

From class I learned that one's sexuality doesn't leave with old age.

From you I listened to talk of your male friends and your matchmaking ideas for me.

From my textbook I read that there are two important features of the family in later life: 1) the personal relationships, and 2) the way it can organize itself as a help-giving unit.

From you I found that although you have no family now, those that you meet become as your family.

From class I heard that widowhood is a crisis with which women must learn to cope.

From you I saw a lady whose husband had died after only 10 years of marriage leaving you a widow at 29. A strong lady who makes the best of all circumstances, who takes life and lives it.

Lastly, from myself, I had thoughts of "this will be a good experience for me. It will be good to help an elderly person in the community."

From you, I was helped. I learned how important mutual dependence is for a relationship. For your needs to be met, I must let you meet mine.

I sit back and sigh and think about what my objectives were when I began this "project":

To learn through exposure to a new situation.
To develop a friendship with an elderly person.
To not have my frame of reference be that of "a project" but as a structured opportunity.
To let someone who hasn't had much chance to get out really see some things.

And now, I've realized that just being together doesn't make the case for a sharing of hearts. I could not enter in your life and expect to start you doing "new and wonderful" things. Instead I needed to come in with a gentle and approachable spirit, waiting for the invitation into your life and letting you share that with me. For me to become a part of your life, not for us to start anew and share neither of our present lives, for that would be like building a house with no foundation.

Source: Written by Laura Evans for *HD 322 Adult Development and Aging* at Colorado State University.

Public Policy: The Government's Role in Improving the Quality of Life

What responsibility does the government have to contribute to the quality of the later years of life? While there is controversy over what the government's role should be, it is true that since the early 1960s the United States government has greatly expanded its services targeted toward older citizens. Part of the greater responsiveness of governmental structures is due to the increased size of the aged population. Also, the needs and rights of older individuals have been brought to the attention of legislative officials by such groups as the American Association of Retired Persons, the National Caucus of the Black Aged, and the Gray Panthers.

Through a country's public policies, national goals are established which are then implemented through a variety of programs. Clearly articulated policies are essential for the effective development and delivery of services. Gold and his associates have asserted that "if aging policy means an intentional, coherent, overall plan about what the U.S. should do about aged citizens, then the United States does not have a social policy on old age." They go on to say that programs for the elderly have tended to be developed unsystematically without adequate integration of services (Gold, Kutza & Marmor, 1977).

Cohen (1976) has disagreed with this position. From his point of view, a clear statement of policy objectives was provided in Title I of the Older Americans Act of 1965. The problem has been that the policy has not been effective in serving as a basis for gerontological activities. The objectives to which Cohen was referring are as follows:

1. An adequate retirement income.
2. The best possible physical and mental health.
3. Suitable housing available at affordable costs.

4. Full restorative services for older persons requiring institutional care.
5. Opportunity for employment without discriminatory practices based on age.
6. Retirement in health, honor and dignity.
7. Pursuit of meaningful activity within the widest range of opportunities.
8. Efficient community services provided in a coordinated manner and readily available when needed.
9. Immediate gain from proven research knowledge.
10. Freedom, independence and the free exercise of individual initiative in planning and managing their own lives (U.S. Department of Health, Education and Welfare, 1974).

The fourth White House Conference on Aging, advertised in this poster, provided a forum for older Americans to voice their concerns to policymakers. (Courtesy of Population Reference Bureau, Inc.)

Setting the Stage For the Years Ahead

Ruth Gordon

The 1981 White House Conference On Aging

Some of the current criticism of America's policy for the aged surrounds the issue of using age as the sole criterion by which one is eligible for services. All of the programs funded under the Older Americans Act merely stipulate that a person must be 60 years of age or older in order to be a recipient of services. In addition, special old age exemptions are given for federal and state taxes, and discounts for public transportation and entertainment events are frequently offered to senior citizens. The debate over this issue may become more heated in the 1980s as we face the high cost to society of programs for the elderly and the demonstrated failure of these programs to address the elderly with the greatest needs (Klemmack & Roff, 1980; Kutza, 1981).

Box 11–4

The Elderly and Politics

And what input do the elderly have in the political process? Attempts have been made to identify the perceived needs of the elderly through such tools as needs assessment surveys. Also some older persons like Maggie Kuhn, leader of the Gray Panthers, have had a strong voice in activist groups while others have testified at public hearings or served in a decision-making capacity as elected officials. However, efforts to unite the majority of the elderly into an effective voting bloc have been largely unsuccessful. "Senior power" appears to be more of an idealized concept than an actuality. The reason for this appears to lie in the heterogeneity of the older population. While high voting rates can be found among the old when compared to younger age groups (Jones, 1977), older Americans appear to have few common interests (Carter, 1969). The position of elderly persons on political issues can be predicted more by their early socialization experiences and their present social and economic circumstances than by age. This heterogeneity, combined with the tendency to have strong party alliances, usually frustrates attempts to unite older people to fight for a common cause (Campbell, 1971).

Despite debates over policy matters, federal initiatives have resulted in a wide array of existing programs that currently serve the elderly. It is generally agreed that a wide range of services is required to meet the needs of the heterogeneous over-65 population. The focus of some programs is primarily preventative and supportive while others offer rehabilitative services.

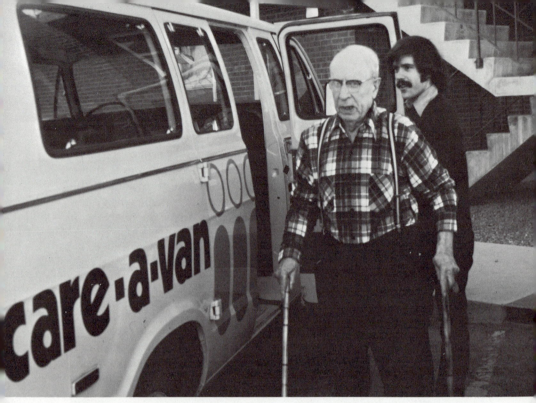

Transportation services for the disabled elderly help them to maintain their independence and allow them to be contributing members of society. (Courtesy of Colorado State University Office of Instructional Services)

As public policies for the aged are further refined, it will be essential to maintain flexibility. It is difficult to accurately predict all the changes that will take place during the next several decades. An effective public policy will be one that can be readily adapted to changing needs as they arise.

Aging in the Future

Maggie Kuhn has said of the present aging population (Hessel, 1977):

> We are a new breed of old people. There are more of us alive today than at any other time in history. We are better educated, healthier, with more at stake in this society. We are redefining goals, taking stock of our skills and experiences, looking to the future (p. 14).

As we seek to eliminate the elements of our cultural milieu that interfere with optimal functioning and begin to provide more choices and opportunities in the later years of life, the future for the aged appears to hold great promise. Yet we are part of a changing and complex world that will hold many unforeseen challenges. As we begin to fill in the gaps of our knowledge about adulthood and aging through continued research efforts, we will be better able to meet these challenges. However, highly trained gerontologists from a wide range of disciplines will be needed for this purpose. Colleges and universities are preparing for these future demands by increasing their course offerings and degree programs on the biological, social, psychological and developmental aspects of aging. The future is ours to build—it is our responsibility to engage in thoughtful planning and bring our fullest creative energies to bear on this task.

Suggested Activities and Exercises

1. What major life transitions do you expect to encounter in the next ten years? What anticipatory socialization experiences will help prepare you for these transitions?
2. What do you foresee in your own future? Visualize yourself at age 70. What will your life be like in terms of family, friends and lifestyle? How will your life be different from the way it is now?
3. Find out what courses are offered at your college or university that will allow you to continue your study of adult development and aging. What research projects related to aging are being conducted on your campus? Are interdisciplinary gerontology degree programs available in your geographical area?

References

Albrecht, G. L., & Gift, H. C. Adult socialization: Ambiguity and adult life crises. In N. Datan & L. H. Ginsberg (Eds.), *Life-span developmental psychology: Normative life crises.* New York: Academic, 1975.

Atchley, R. C. The life course, age grading, and age-linked demands for decision making. In N. Datan & L. H. Ginsberg (Eds.), *Life-span developmental psychology: Normative life crises.* New York: Academic, 1975.

Bennett, R. Attitudes of the young toward the old: A review of research. *Personnel and Guidance Journal,* 1976, *44,* 136–39.

Campbell, A. Politics through the life cycle. *The Gerontologist,* 1971, *2,* 112–17.

Carter, M. K. Politics of age: Interest group or social movement. *The Gerontologist,* 1969, *9,* 259–63.

Chitwood, D. G., & Bigner, J. J. Young children's perceptions of old people. *Home Economics Research Journal,* 1980, *8,* 369–74.

Cohen, E. S. Editor's comment on Aging in America: Toward the year 2000. *The Gerontologist,* 1976, *16,* 270–75.

Gold, B., Kutza, E., & Marmor, T. R. United States social policy on old age: Present patterns and predictions. In B. Neugarten & R. Havighurst (Eds.), *Social policy, social ethics, and the aging society.* Washington, D.C.: National Science Foundation, 1977.

Hessel, D. T. *Maggie Kuhn on aging.* Philadelphia: Westminister Press, 1977.

Jones, R. *The other generation: The new power of older people.* Englewood Cliffs, N.J.: Prentice-Hall, 1977.

Klausmeier, J. J., & Ripple, R. *Learning and human abilities.* New York: Harper & Row, 1971.

Klemmack, D. L., & Roff, L. L. Public support for age as an eligibility criterion for programs for older persons. *The Gerontologist,* 1980, *20,* 148–53.

Kutza, E. A. Toward an aging policy. *Social Policy,* 1981, *12,* 39–43.

McTavish, D. G. Perceptions of old people: A review of research methodologies and findings. *The Gerontologist,* 1971, *11,* 90–101.

Miller, S., Corrales, R., & Wackman, D. B. Recent progress in understanding and facilitating marital communication. *The Family Coordinator,* 1975, *24,* 143–52.

Mondale, W. S. The lifetime learning act: Proposed legislation. *The Counseling Psychologist,* 1976, *6,* 67–68.

Palmore, E. Facts on aging: A short quiz. *The Gerontologist,* 1977, *17,* 315–20.

Seefeldt, C., Jantz, R. K., Galper, A., & Serock, K. Using pictures to explore children's attitudes toward the elderly. *The Gerontologist,* 1977, *17,* 506–12.

Serock, K., Seefeldt, C., Jantz, R. K., & Galper, A. As children see old folks. *Today's Education,* 1977, March–April, 70–73.

U.S. Department of Health, Education and Welfare. *Older American Act of 1965, as amended, and related acts.* Washington, D.C.: U.S. Printing Office, 1974.

Wilson, C., & Wilson, D. *A treasure hunt.* Washington, D.C.: U.S. Government Printing Office, 1980.

Author Index

A

Abrahams, J. R., 140
Ackerman, S., 142
Adams, B., 62, 64, 65, 67
Adams, J. A., 144
Adams, N., 43
Adelson, J., 67
Advisory Council of the Elderly American
  Indian, 325
Aisenberg, R., 267, 268
Aker, G. F., 150
Albert, W. C., 222
Albrecht, G. L., 347–349
Alder, W., 241
Allen, L. R., 118–119
Alvarez, D., 329
Anderson, B., 64
Anderson, B. J., 301, 303
Anderson, C., 175
Annon, J. S., 175
Ansak, M., 321
Archambault, F. X., 174
Ard, B. N., Jr., 92
Arisawa, H., 306
Aristotle, 66–67

Arlin, P. K., 142–143
Ashton, P. T., 142
Astin, H. S., 86–87
Atchley, R. C., 28, 111, 112, 113, 114, 115,
  348
Atlee, E., 5

B

Babic, A., 112
Backman, E., 38
Bacon, E., 66
Baley, N., 14
Ballmer, H., 86
Baltes, P. B., 14, 132–134, 135
Bank, S., 65–66
Barat, C., 104
Barber, C. E., 236
Barnett, L. D., 46–47
Barrnett, R. C., 98
Barrett, E., 93
Baum, W., 147–148
Bean, F., 329
Beattie, W., 236
Bedell, J. W., 287

Cook, J. T., 235
Cooley, C. H., 301
Cooper, P. E., 52
Cormack, M. L., 26, 27
Cormier, R. H., 286
Corrales, R., 349
Cottrell, F., 113
Cowgill, D. O., 298–299, 300, 302, 311
Cox, M., 35
Cox, R., 35
Coxby, P. C., 22, 86
Craik, F. I. M., 145, 147
Crate, M. A., 208
Cuber, J. F., 28, 30, 31, 32
Cuellar, J. B., 254, 330
Cumber, B., 52
Cumming, E., 65, 192
Cunningham, S. M. M., 85–86
Curtis, H. J., 240
Cutler, S. J., 197
Cutts, N. E., 51

D

Dalderup, L. M., 218
Dalton, G. W., 92
Dancy, J., Jr., 336
Darling, J., 41
Darrow, C. M., 4
Datan, N., 188
Davis, G. C., 163, 165
Davis, G. E., 150–151
Davis, K., 334
Davis, K. E., 37
Davis-Friedmann, D., 306–307
Day, D. A., 67, 118
de Beavoir, S., 93
de Frain, J., 101, 102
de Geyndt, W., 327
De Jong, J. F., 52
Denker, E. R., 85
Dennis, W., 155
Derlega, V. J., 22, 23
de Ropp, R. S., 237
De Vries, H. A., 221
di Bona, P., 38
Dickinson, E. E., 277
Domey, R. J., 218
Donaldson, G., 132
Dorsett-Robinson, J., 334
Douvan, E., 67

Dowd, J. J., 333
Driscoll, R. F., 104
Dyer, E. D., 51
Dyer, D., 54–55

E

Eaton, D., 100, 101
Edelwich, J., 94–95, 96
Edwards, J. N., 196
Ehrlich, I. F., 334, 338
Eichorn, R. L., 212, 213
Elder, G. H., 81
Elliott, N., 24
Elwell, F., 194, 196
Endo, R., 318–319
Entine, A. D., 105
Epley, R. J., 268
Epstein, C. F., 93
Erbes, C., 220–221
Erickson, R. C., 267
Erikson, E. H., 6–8, 180
Estrada, L. F., 329
Etten, M. J., 216, 234
Evans, L., 272, 277
Evans, L., 353–555
Ezell, S., 95–96

F

Fandetti, D. V., 338
Farberow, N. L., 201
Farrel, W., 44
Farris, C. E., 327, 339
Favero, R. V., 200
Feifel, H., 251, 267
Feit, M., 327
Feld, S., 196
Feldman, H., 51
Fellini, F., 93
Ferber, M. A., 100
Fields, S., 188–189
Finkle, A. L., 175
Fitts, W. J., 267
Fitzgerald, J., 142
Fletcher, J., 258
Foner, A., 68
Ford, M. E. N., 46
Fox, E. M., 59
Fozard, J. L., 146–147
Frank, E., 175
Frederick, J. F., 278

Fredericks, M. L. C., 218
Freedman, J. L., 67
Freudenberger, H. J., 96
Friedlander, W. A., 115
Friedman, R., 22
Friis, H., 68
Fujii, S. M., 321
Fulton, R., 252, 283

G

Gadlin, H., 233
Gagnon, J. H., 165
Galper, A., 351
Garney, M. J., 192–193
Gary, A., 22
Gee, E., 318
Gelfand, D. E., 317, 338–339
George, L. K., 150
Gianturco, D. T., 289
Gifford, R., 63
Gift, H. C., 347–349
Gilbert, J., 329–330
Gilligan, C. F., 142
Ginault, M., 104
Ginsberg, L. H., 10, 198, 326–327
Glaser, B. J., 266, 268
Glick, I. O., 281–281
Glick, P. C., 44, 50
Godow, A., 163
Gold, B., 355
Goldsen, R. K., 46
Goodman, J., 98
Goodrow, B. A., 151
Gorer, G., 279, 282
Gotard, E., 52
Gottesman, L. E., 232
Gould, G., 55
Gould, R., 83, 185, 187
Gove, W. R., 44, 100
Graney, M. J., 151
Greenberg, J. S., 174
Greene, G., 52
Greenspoon, S., 267
Greer, J. M., 283
Griffith, J., 52
Grindstaff, C. F., 53–54
Gruber, H. W., 222
Gubrium, J. F., 43
Guilford, J. P., 132
Guilford, R. B., 51

Gupta, J. R., 25
Gurin, G., 196
Gurthrie, J. P., 253
Gutmann, D. L., 188, 189, 203
Guttmacher Institute, 163

H

Haan, H., 118
Haan, N., 67
Haeberle, E. J., 162
Halamandaris, V. J., 222, 224, 226
Halikes, J. A., 281, 282
Hall, D. A., 314
Hall, D. T., 100
Hall, E., 258
Hall, E. S., 100
Hamberg, M. V., 162
Hamner, T. J., 47
Handschu, S. S., 233
Harbert, A. S., 10, 236, 327–328
Harel, Z., 226-227
Harker, J. O., 147, 149
Harrill, I., 220, 221
Harris, L., 58, 100, 101, 102, 102–103, 149, 151
Harroff, P. B., 28, 30, 32
Harter, C. L., 336–337
Hartley, J. T., 147, 149
Hartner, R., 52
Hausner, S., 321
Haven, C., 68, 198
Havens, E. M., 100
Havighurst, R. J., 8–9, 64, 91–92, 190, 191–192, 193, 194, 195
Hawke, S., 51
Hayes, M. P., 28
Hayflick, L., 238
Hays, W. C., 151
Heddscheimer, J. C., 83—84
Heifetz, M. D., 258
Hendricks, C. D., 235–236
Hendricks, J., 235—236
Henning, M., 93
Henry, W., 192
Henze, F. L., 46
Hessel, D. T., 358
Hetherington, E. M., 35
Hettlinger, R., 162
Hey, R. N., 52–53
Heyman, D. K., 112

Hill, R., 46
Hime, V. H., 270–271
Hinton, J., 267
Hobbs, D. F., Jr., 55
Hochschild, A. R., 100
Hoffman, E., 62–63
Hoffman, L. W., 47–48, 49, 50
Hoffman, M. L., 47–48, 49, 50
Hokusai, 155–156
Holland, J. L., 82
Holmes, D., 321
Holmes, D. D., 311–312
Holmes, M., 321
Holmes, T. H., 198, 200
Holstrom, L., 100
Homer, 66
Hooper, F. H., 142
Hooper, J. D., 88—89
Hooper, J. O., 87, 88
Horn, J. L., 132, 135
Houseknecht, S. H., 52—53
Howard, A., 254
Howell, S., 220
Hsu, F. L. K., 310
Hudson, J. W., 46
Hughton, G. A., 142
Hutchinson, E., 232
Hyams, D. E., 234–235
Hyerstay, B. J., 267

I

Irelan, L. M., 334

J

Jackson, D. A., 272
Jackson, J. J., 232, 317, 325, 329, 332–333, 338
Jackson, M., 336, 338
Jacobs, F., 93
Jacobson, M. M., 212–213
Jacoby, S., 39
Jantz, R. K., 351
Jardim, A., 93
Jeffries, W. R., 324
Johnson, A. I., 253
Johnson, V. E., 165, 168, 169, 171–172
Joncich, G., 190
Jones, H. E., 14
Jones, R., 357
Jourard, S., 22, 23
Jung, C. T., 189

Jury, D., 259
Jury, M., 259

K

Kahana, E., 61, 62
Kahana, E., 61, 62
Kahn, J., 22
Kahn, M. D., 65
Kalish, R. A., 254, 267, 318, 319, 321, 329, 332
Kaplan, H. S., 174
Kaplan, M., 117, 119
Kart, C. S., 207, 214, 215, 216, 217, 218, 219, 226
Kass, M. J., 167, 168, 175
Kasschau, P. L., 116–117, 334
Kastenbaum, R., 223, 251, 267–268, 269, 271–272, 278
Kasworm, C. E., 85
Katchadourian, H. A., 168–169, 170–171, 172, 173–174
Kaufman, A., 236
Kaufman, D., 267
Kay, E., 105
Kelleher, C. H., 106
Kelly, J. R., 35–36
Kendig, W. L., 105–106
Kiefer, C., 319
Kim, B. C., 321
Kimmel, D. C., 45, 63–64
King, K., 162
Kinsey Institute for Sex Research, 174
Kitano, H. H. L., 319, 320, 321
Kivett, V. R., 58
Klatzky, R. L., 145, 146
Klausmeier, J. J., 351
Klein, E. B., 4
Klemmack, D. L., 196, 357
Knott, J. E., 253
Knowles, M. S., 85, 150
Knox, D., 51
Knupfer, G., 44
Kobasky, M., 150
Koch, J., 34, 35
Koch, J., 34, 35
Kohlberg, L., 142
Kramer, B., 309
Krassen, E., 334
Kreps, J., 117
Kubler-Ross, E., 252–253, 265, 267, 268, 269, 277, 278, 279–280, 283
Kuhn, M., 357, 358

Mayo, C., 86
Mead, M., 93, 100, 149
Mendelsohn, G. A., 208
Mendes, H. A., 59
Meredith, G. M., 323, 324
Metress, E. S., 207, 214
Metress, J. F., 207, 214
Michelangelo, 155
Mihoj, P., 63
Miller, D. B., 222
Miller, H., 108, 111
Miller, S., 349
Mills, E. W., 83
Minnigerode, F. A., 45
Minobe, R., 306
Mirande, A., 330
Mitford, J., 275
Moberg, D. O., 197
Molchanov, E., 174
Mondale, W. S., 347
Monk, A., 112
Montagu, A., 21, 168
Montero, D., 318, 319, 321
Montgomery, J. E., 28
Montgomery, J. P., 38
Moore, J. W., 10
Moos, G. E., 200–201
Moos, R. H., 208–209
Morgenthaler, E., 57
Morison, R. S., 259
Moriwaki, S. Y., 201, 318, 319
Mosley, N., 51
Moss, R. E., 222, 224, 226
Mousseau, J., 32
Moustakas, C. C., 281
Mueller, E., 50
Munley, A., 272, 277
Murdock, S. H., 325–326, 328
Murillo, N., 329
Murstein, B., 24

N

Naito, M., 306
Nakane, C., 305
Nass, G. D., 24
Nehrke, M. F., 142
Nesselroade, J. R., 14
Neugarten, B. L., 5, 10, 60–61, 62, 164, 172, 187–188, 191–195
Nobbe, C. F., 321
Noelker, L., 226, 227

Norman, D. A., 146
Novis, F., 210
Nowak, C., 11

O

O'Brien, S., 117
O'Connor, M., 255
O'Connor, S. D., 97
Oden, M., 14
Ogden, M., 327
Oken, D., 267
Okun, M. A., 150, 151, 154
O'Leary, S., 56
O'Meara, J., 116
Oouchi, H., 306
Orth, C. D., 93
Orthner, D. K., 118
Ory, M. J., 52
Osako, M. M., 319–320, 321, 324

P

Palmore, E., 12, 110–111, 237, 286, 300–301, 304, 305, 349–350
Pancoast, D. L., 197–198
Papalia, D. L., 197–198
Parish, W., 308
Parke, R., 56
Parkes, C. M., 198, 277–278, 281
Parsons, J., 210–211
Parsons, T., 251–252
Patterson, C., 212
Patterson, J. E., 50
Patterson, S. B., 55
Pattison, E. M., 251, 252, 264–265, 266
Paul, L., 269–270
Payne, B. R., 112
Penn, R., 82–83
Peterson, P., 189
Pfeiffer, E., 163, 165
Philibert, M., 297
Phillips, D., 272
Piaget, J., 141, 142, 143
Picasso, P., 155
Piedmont, E., 104
Pieroni, R. E., 334, 36
Pine, V. R., 272, 275
Pines, A., 95, 96
Piovesana, G. K., 304
Plath, D., 305–306
Pleck, J. H., 44, 67

Veiga, J. F., 93
Veil, C., 104
Vernadakis, 218
Veroff, J., 196
Verwoerdt, A., 163–165
Vetter, B. M., 98
Viidik, A., 314
Vinokur, A., 200
Vogel, I., 99
Vogelsang, J., 81

W

Wackman, D. B., 349
Wagner, N. N., 324
Wainwright, W. H., 54–55
Wakimura, G., 306
Walker, K. E., 100
Wall, M., 117
Walsh, D. A., 147, 149
Walsh, R. P., 272
Walters, J., 35
Walz, T., 52–53
Wang, H. S., 165
Ward, D. E., 218
Warren, A. B., 218
Wason, P. C., 142
Wasserman, S., 163
Watson, J. A., 58
Waugh, N. C., 146
Wechsler, D., 134–135, 155
Wedderburn, D., 63
Weg, R. B., 220–221
Weinrich, R. C., 80
Weinstein, K. K., 60–61, 62
Weisman, A. D., 267–269
Weiss, R. M., 281
Weitzman, L. J., 32–33, 98
Welsh, R., 163
Wen, C., 306
Wertmüller, L., 93

West, J. B., 47
Westoff, C. F., 50
Wexler, R., 321
Whelpton, P. K., 50
Whitbourne, S. K., 142, 150
Whyte, M. K., 308
Whyte, W. H., Jr., 67
Wilkinson, M. L., 24
Williams, B. S., 325
Williams, J. M. B., 277
Williams, J. H., 99, 172
Williams, R. M., Jr., 46
Williamson, J. B., 272
Williamson, N. E., 23–24, 33, 47
Wilson, C., 351, 352–353
Wilson, D., 238
Wilson, D. A., 351, 352–353
Wilson, K., 51
Woehrer, C. E., 338
Wolstenholme, J. E. W., 255
Wood, J. L., 336, 338
Woodruff, D. S., 4, 89–90, 179–180
Worchester, D. A., 51
Worthy, M., 22
Wright, B., 209–210
Wright, F. L., 155
Wrigley, A. P., 50
Wurthmann, H. R., 23–24, 33, 47

Y

Yangisako, J., 319
Yankelovich, D., 94
York, J. L., 226, 232–233
Youmans, E. G., 194

Z

Zarit, S. H., 222
Zellman, G., 332, 334

Subject Index

effects on family, 210–213
employment, 210, 212
excess, 233–234
grief reactions, 208
societal attitudes, 209–210
Disease, 207–213, 215–220, 222–223, 241, 245 (*see also* Chronic illness; Dying; Health
Disengagement theory, 192–193
Discrimination
age, 105–106, 108, 139, 356
physical disability, 209–210
race, 139, 232, 319, 324, 331, 332, 336
sex, 98–99
Divorce, 28, 34–35, 40, 84, 199, 285, 286
Double-jeopardy position, 339
Dual-career marriages, 100–103
Dying, (*see also* Death)
disclosure of diagnosis, 266–268
fear of, 253–254
stages of, 265
trajectories, 265–266
treatment of, 266–271

E

Eastern societies, 188–189, 304–311
Ecological validity, 149
Education, 80, 84–90, 150–155, 194, 298–299, 330, 336, 338, 339, 347, 348, 351–353, 358 (*see also* Andragogy; Death, education; Sex education)
EEG, 255–256
Ejaculation, 169–171, 174–175
Elderly persons, *see* Aged persons
Employment, *see* Work
Empty nest, 56, 117, 199, 348
Endocrine system, 217–218, 240 (*see also* Sex hormones
England, *see* Britain
Erikson's stages, 6–8, 180
Error-accumulation theory of aging, 240
Estrogen, *see* Endocrine system; Sex hormones
Ethnicity and aging, 104–105, 111, 114, 194, 201–202, 232, 317–340
Blacks, 105, 114, 332–338, 355
Japanese Americans, 318–324
Mexican Americans, 329–332
Native Americans, 324–329
Euthanasia, 257–262

Exercise, 216, 221–222
Extramarital relationships, 25, 35, 163–164

F

Face lifts, 214
Family (*see also* Cross-cultural comparisons)
and ethnicity, 325, 329–330, 338
and industrialization, 224–225, 298
and work, 57, 95, 100–103
interaction, 57–59, 197, 232–233, 305, 308 (*see also* Parent-child relations)
life cycle, 15, 348
planning, 308–309 (*see also* Fertility)
system, 15–16, 224–225, 254, 277
Facts on Aging Quiz, 349–350
Fathering, 56–57
Fatigue, 140, 151, 202
Feedback, and educational intervention, 154
Fertility, 5, 50, 54, 306, 307–309 (*see also* Childlessness; Children, value of)
Filial piety, 304
Fluid intelligence, 132–135
Formal operations, *see* Cognitive development
Formal support systems, *see* Support networks
France, 102, 104, 242
Friendship, 44, 66–69
Funerals, 272–277, 284 (*see also* Death; Dying; Grief)

G

Gay relationships, *see* Homosexuality
Gender characteristics, changes with age, 189–190 (*see also* Sex differences)
Generations, 57–59, 197, 318–319, 321–324 (*see also* Cross-sectional research)
Genetic factors, 238–240, 243
Geriatrics, 222
Germany, West, 102, 242
Gerontology,
definition of, 6
training in, 12, 339, 359
Glaucoma, 218
Governmental policies, *see* Policy

Kidneys, 217
Kübler-Ross, and stages of dying, 265
Kuhn, Maggie, 356

L

Labor-force participation, 332
  of older persons, 105–106, 109
  of women, 96–100, 225–226
Learning, 144, 149–155, 350 (see also Education; Life-long learning; Memory)
Legislation, 36–37, 59, 105, 108, 210, 224, 226, 236, 260, 271, 332
Leisure, 80, 117–119
Lesbian relationships, see Homosexuality
Levels of cognitive processing, see Information processing
Levinson's stages of adult development, 183–187
Life-change units, 198–200
Life events, 198–199
Life expectancy, 165, 221, 226, 227, 241–245, 285, 306, 324, 327, 334, 336 (see also Longevity)
Life, length of, see Longevity
Life-long learning, 89–90, 150
Life review, 182
Life structures, 183–187
Life transitions, see Transitions
Life satisfaction, 68, 179, 194–198, 226, 289, 334, 335, 350
Lipofuscin, 240
Living arrangements, 57–58, 236–237, 304–305 (see also Housing; Long-term care)
Living will, 260–262
Loneliness, 68, 285, 350
Longevity, 5, 202–203, 240, 241, 245, 298–299, 334 (see also Life expectancy)
Longitudinal research, 12–14, 28, 132–134, 223, 241, 317
Long-term care, 222–237, 252, 321, 349–350
  alternatives to placement, 227, 235–237, 356
  facilities, 223–224, 226–232
  families and, 224–227, 232–233
  history, 223–226
  residents, 223, 227, 232, 237
Long-term memory, see Memory
Looking-glass theory, 301
Love, 21, 24–25, 166
Lungs, changes with age, 216, 349 (see also Respiratory diseases)

M

Mate selection, 25–27, 46
Marital roles, 32–33, 56, 100–101
Marital satisfaction, 28
Marital status, of the aged, 286
Marriage, 199, 287, 289, 348
  and work, see Dual-career marriages
  arranged, 25–27
  renewable trial, 36–37
  stages, 33–34
  termination of, 28, 34–35 (see also Divorce)
  types of, 28–32
Marriage contract, 35–37
Matrimonial advertisements, 27
Maturity, 182–183
Medicaid, 222, 224, 321, 328
Medicare, 115, 222, 224, 321, 328
Medication, 175, 234, 268–269, 279, 280, 281–282
Memory, 136–139, 145–147 (see also Intelligence; Learning)
Menopause, 164, 172–173
Mental abilities, see Cognitive development; Intelligence
Mental health, 44, 94–96, 179, 189, 198–203, 233, 327, 339, 348–349, 350, 355
Mentor, 91–93
Mexican Americans,
  family, 329–330
  number of, 329
  residence patterns, 330
  service utilization, 331–332
Midlife career change, 83–85, 199
Midlife transition, 83–84, 164, 172–174, 186
Migration, see Mobility, geographical
Minority aging, see Ethnicity and aging
Mobility, geographical, 113, 289, 298, 318–319, 329, 332–333
Mobility, social, 298–299
Mneumonic, 146, 153 (see also Memory)
Modernization, and aging, 294–301, 306
Mourning, see Grief
Multiple sclerosis, 210, 211–212, 217
Muscles, 215, 216, 217, 221, 239

N

National Caucus of the Black Aged, 355
Nations,
  developing, 15–16, 50, 115, 216, 272 (see also Modernization, and aging)

Nations (*continued*)
industrialized, 15–16, 50, 115, 216, 272, 304–305, 306 (*see also* Industrialization)
Native Americans, 324–329
employment, 325–326
health, 326–327
housing, 326
life expectancy, 324, 327
residence patterns, 325
service utilization, 327–328
Sioux, 325, 327–328
Never-married, *see* Single persons
Nigeria, 50
Nursing homes, *see* Long-term care
Nutrition, 216–217, 219–222, 234, 236, 241, 326, 328 (*see also* Diet)

O

Obesity, 220–221
Occupational cycle, 348
Occupations, *see* Jobs; Work
"Old-old," 15
Older Americans Act, 355–357
Older persons, *see* Aged persons
One-child families, 50–51
Oral histories, 147–149
Organic brain syndrome, 233, 234–235, 349
Organ replacement, 238, 255–256
Osteoarthritis, 215
Osteoporosis, 215

P

Parent-child relations, in later life, 57–59, 304–305, 308, 312, 319–320
Parenting, 54–60, 348
Paternity leave, 57
Pensions, 115
People's Republic of China, 242, 310–311
aged in, 307–308
birth rates, 308–309
political developments, 306–307
Personality, 82, 150, 179, 183, 187–191, 194–195, 202–203, 278
Physical health, *see* Health
Piagetian theory, 141–143
Pneumonia, *see* Respiratory diseases
Policy, 57, 101–103, 111, 115–116, 236, 256, 308–309, 317, 329, 338–339, 355–358

Politics, *see* Legislation; Policy, Voting
Population profiles, *see* Demography
Poverty, *see* Income
Practice effects, 13, 139
Premarital sex, 162–163
Preretirement planning, 116–117
Presbycusis, 219
Presbyopia, 218
Primary memory, *see* Memory
Procreation, 51–52
Progeria, 240
Progesterone, *see* Endocrine System; Sex hormones
Programmed-aging theory, 238–240
Prostate gland, 175, 217
Psychometric approach to intelligence, 134–140
Public policy, *see* Policy

R

Racial differences, *see* Ethnicity and aging
Reaction time, 139, 350
Refilled nest, 56
Religion, *see* Spiritual concerns
Remarriage, 35, 287, 289, 311
Reminiscence, 181–182
Response time, 139
Research methods, 12–14
Residence patterns, *see* Housing; Living arrangements
Respiratory diseases, 216, 263, 326
Retention, *see* Memory
Retirement, 80, 108–114, 199, 245, 298–299, 312, 333–334, 348, 355–356
adjustment to, 111–114
early, 116
flexible, 111
mandatory, 108–111
preparation for, 116–117, 348–349
Retrieval processes, *see* Memory
Rites of passage, 272
Roles, 15, 16, 54, 100, 112, 195, 210–213, 269, 277, 284, 285, 286, 288, 289, 298, 305, 312, 338, 347–349 (*see also* Marital roles; Sex roles)
Role loss, 10, 194, 196
Role models, 92–93, 289, 348
Role theory, 210, 211
Rural, 50, 194, 197–197, 224, 236, 297, 306, 308, 310, 324, 325, 338

S

SAGE, 188–189
Scandanavia, 24 (see also Sweden)
Secondary memory, see Memory
Self, 14–15, 179–183, 187, 188, 208, 254, 269, 287
Self-actualization, 188
Self-disclosure, 22–23
Self esteem, of the aged, 167, 233, 301, 351
Senility, see Organic brain syndrome
Senses, 140, 145, 151, 216, 218–219, 233, 349 (see also Hearing; Vision)
Sex differences, 32–33, 44, 67, 162, 189–190, 201–202, 212, 219, 311
Sex discrimination, see Discrimination, sex
Sex education, 162–163, 168, 175
Sex hormones, 172–173 (see also Endocrine System)
Sex roles, 32–33, 46–47, 98–99, 190, 225–226
Sexual behavior, 162–163, 165, 245, 349, 354
Sex concerns, 164, 174–175, 199
Sexual response,
  cycle, 168–171
  change with age, 171–172
Short-term memory, see Memory
Siblings, 64–66
Single persons, 39–44, 286
Single-parent families, 59–60, 225
Skin, 214–215
Smell, see Senses
Social-class differences, 15, 111–112, 338, 347
Social clock, 11
Social participation, 67–68
Social policy, see Policy
Social Readjustment Scale, 198–200
Social Security, 108, 111, 114–116, 222, 224, 225, 276, 326, 328, 334
Social system, 15–16
Sociogenic aging, 11
Spiritual concerns, 188–189, 197, 236–237, 336–337, 350
Status of older persons, 201, 298–301, 303, 304, 310–311, 312, 329–330
Storage process, see Memory
Stress, 198–201 (see also Mental health)
Stroke, 216
Suicide, 201–202 (see also Death, by suicide; Grief)
Support networks, 44, 194, 197–198, 232, 274–275, 277, 279, 289, 329–330, 338

Sweden, 38, 57, 111, 242 (see also Scandanavia)
Switzerland, 102

T

T'ai Chi, 189, 221
Taste, see Senses
Teeth, loss of, 216–217, 220
Tertiary memory, see Memory
Terminal drop hypothesis, 140–141
Terminal illness, see Dying
Testosterone, see Endocrine system; Sex hormones
Time perspective, 191
Touch, see Senses
Transitions, 4–5, 112–113, 161, 172–173, 179, 183–187, 198, 201, 232, 289, 347–349 (see also Midlife transition)
Transportation, 68, 151, 198, 298, 332, 334, 357, 358

U

Unemployment, 103–105, 199, 326, 327
Universals of aging, 311–312
University students, 46–47, 85–86, 90, 162–163, 174
Unmarried persons, see Single persons

V

Values, 47–50, 161–162
Vision, 218, 222 (see also Senses)
Visual-motor skills, 134, 137, 139–140
Vocational development, theories of, 90–93
Volunteerism, 112–113, 271, 351, 353–355
Voting, 356

W

Wear and tear theory of aging, 238
Weight, see Obesity
Wechsler Adult Intelligence Scale-Revised, 134–140
Werner's syndrome, 240
White House Conference on Aging, 50, 356
Widowhood, 40, 84, 164, 165, 284–289, 311, 348, 354
  adjustment to, 287–289
  incidence of, 285–286, 311
  remarriage, 287, 289